Praise for *The Life of Geor*

"Nancy Henry's new biography of George Eliot is trul
Eliot. Henry writes with all thirty-seven of her predece̲s̲.̲.̲.̲ ̲.̲.̲ ̲.̲.̲.̲.̲.̲ɑ as she carefully selects the material that needs repeating, discarding, or modifying. Her massive bibliography results from her thorough research, something difficult to achieve with a figure like George Eliot about whom so much is written, but for which Henry has gained a reputation as a most conscientious – I would say *the* most conscientious – of George Eliot scholars."

Kathleen McCormack, *Florida International University*

"…this learned, adventurous new biographer has changed the landscape of George Eliot studies."

The George Eliot Review, *November 2012*

"Driven neither by hero-worship or spite, Henry's 'critical biography' demonstrates what treasure there is still to be found in even the most worked-over subjects. The trick is to ask the questions that everyone else assumed had been answered years ago."

The Guardian, *2 June 2012*

"Henry provides a useful reminder that that old-fashioned pejorative, adulteress, might have been applied to Eliot as well as to Agnes, and she provides a sensitive analysis of the novels in the light of that insight."

The New Yorker, *6 August 2012*

BLACKWELL CRITICAL BIOGRAPHIES

General Editor: Claude Rawson

This acclaimed series offers informative and durable biographies of important authors, British, European and North American, which will include substantial critical discussion of their works. An underlying objective is to re-establish the notion that books are written by people who lived in particular times and places. This objective is pursued not by programmatic assertions or strenuous point-making, but through the practical persuasion of volumes which offer intelligent criticism within a well-researched biographical context.

Also in this series

The Life of George Eliot

A Critical Biography

Nancy Henry

WILEY Blackwell

Library of Congress Cataloging-in-Publication Data

Henry, Nancy, 1965–
The life of George Eliot: a critical biography / Nancy Henry.
    pages   cm
  Includes bibliographical references and index.
  ISBN 978-1-4051-3705-8 (hardcover: alk. paper)
  ISBN 978-1-118-91767-1 (paperback: alk. paper)
1. Eliot, George, 1819–1880.   2. Novelists, English–19th century–Biography. I. Title.
  PR4681.H46 2012
  8230.8–dc23
  [B]

                                                                                2011047212

A catalogue record for this book is available from the British Library.

For Graham Handley

Contents

Contents

List of Illustrations

Every effort has been made to trace copyright holders and to obtain their permission for the use of copyright material. The publisher apologizes for any errors or omissions in the above list and would be grateful if notified of any corrections that should be incorporated in future reprints or editions of this book.

Acknowledgments

This book has taken shape over several years and I wish to thank those who have supported it and me along the way. I thank Claude Rawson for inviting me to contribute to the Blackwell Critical Biography Series. At the press, Emma Bennett, Ben Thatcher, and Louise Spencely have patiently seen it through to completion.

At the University of Tennessee, the English Department's John C. Hodges Better English Fund, the College of Arts and Sciences, and the University's Office of Research have provided financial support for this project. I want especially to thank Chuck Maland and Stan Garner. As Heads of the English Department, they guided me toward all the available resources offered by the department and university and also provided their personal support and encouragement. Also at the University of Tennessee, I wish to thank my colleagues in the Nineteenth Century Division, Amy Billone and Gerard Cohen-Vrignaud, as well as the members of the Nineteenth-Century British Research Seminar (funded by the Humanities Initiative).

I owe a particular debt to my research assistants. Andrew Lallier offered his expertise in German philosophy and literature and provided insightful readings of individual chapters. Katie Burnett set the highest standards for meticulous research and careful editing and was a model reader of the entire manuscript. Claudia Martin also offered her expert knowledge and research skills on nineteenth-century legal matters.

I am grateful to my colleagues in the profession at large for their work on George Eliot and for our ongoing conversations about Victorian literature and culture. I wish to thank George Levine, Kathleen McCormack, Andrew Brown, Tonny van den Broek, Dermot Coleman, Peter Brier, and Bill Baker. For their various forms of support, I also wish to thank Carolyn Williams, Rebecca Stern, Jen Hill, Michael Rectenwald, Mary Poovey, Chris Looby, Linda Bree, Katherine Bright-Holmes, Jenn Fishman, Sanghee Lee, Michael Conlon, Gayle Whittier, and Melissa Zinkin.

For friendship and support that cannot be measured, and without which I could not have completed this book, I wish to thank Tom Cooper, Jean Levenson, Jeannie Van Vleck, Pat Dickinson, Barbara Handley, Cori McIntyre, and Angel O'Dell.

A version of material contained in Chapter Five was previously published in *Victorian Literature and Culture* 39.2 (2011). I thank the editors for their permission to reprint that material here.

My greatest debt is to Graham Handley. The idea of my writing a biography of George Eliot emerged from our conversations throughout the 1990s. Once the idea became a reality, he supported me in every step of the process. It is a pleasure to dedicate the book to him.

List of Abbreviations

AB	*Adam Bede*
Ashton, *GE*	Rosemary Ashton, *George Eliot: A Life*
Ashton, *GHL*	Rosemary Ashton, *G. H. Lewes: A Life*
Bodenheimer, *Real Life*	Rosemarie Bodenheimer, *The Real Life of Mary Ann Evans*
Collins, *Interviews*	K. K. Collins, *George Eliot: Interviews and Recollections*
Cross, *Life*	John Walter Cross, *George Eliot's Life*, 3 vols.
DD	*Daniel Deronda*
FH	*Felix Holt*
GEL	*The George Eliot Letters*, vols. 1–9, ed. Gordon S. Haight
GEJ	*The Journals of George Eliot*, eds. Margaret Harris and Judith Johnston
GHLJ	George Henry Lewes Journals
GHLL	*Letters of George Henry Lewes*
Haight, *Biography*	Gordon S. Haight, *George Eliot: A Biography*
Impressions	*Impressions of Theophrastus Such*
The Mill	*The Mill on the Floss*
Poetry	*The Complete Shorter Poetry of George Eliot*, 2 vols., eds. A. G. van den Broek and William Baker.
Scenes	*Scenes of Clerical Life*
SM	*Silas Marner*

1

The History of a Writer

George Eliot and Biographies

She believed that her husband was one of those men whose memoirs should be written when they died.

(*Middlemarch* 326; ch. 36)

Toward the end of her life, George Eliot wrote: "The best history of a writer is contained in his writings – these are his chief actions." In the same 1879 letter to Mrs Thomas Adolphus Trollope, she further and more emphatically declared that biographies "generally are a disease of English literature" (*GEL* 7:230). These assertions were prompted by the death in 1878 of her companion of twenty-four years, George Henry Lewes, himself a writer of biographies including *The Life and Works of Goethe* (1855). She declined to write her autobiography, or to cooperate with would-be biographers of herself or Lewes. She did not want details of her personal life to affect evaluations of her writing or to overshadow her own and Lewes's posthumous reputations. The care of those reputations was centrally important to her in a way that is consistent with questions about history and individual lives that her novels raise. All of her novels implicitly ask how the past influences the present, and how the present, as she put it in the Finale to *Middlemarch* (1871–2), "prepares" the future: "we insignificant people with our daily words and acts are preparing the lives of many Dorotheas . . ." (785; Finale). But George Eliot was not an insignificant person. She was someone whose memoirs would be written. As far as she could, she wanted to prepare the conditions of how she would be remembered after her death.

Eliot's preoccupation with the writings that survive the writer is evident from her first published fiction, "Poetry and Prose from the Notebook of an Eccentric" (1846–7).

The Life of George Eliot: A Critical Biography, First Edition. Nancy Henry.
© 2012 Nancy Henry. Published 2012 by John Wiley & Sons, Ltd.

Borrowing a convention used by Sir Walter Scott and others, she introduces a narrator who has decided to publish the notebooks of his recently deceased friend Macarthy. In her last book, *Impressions of Theophrastus Such* (1879), her narrator Theophrastus introduces his character sketches by imagining that he will leave his manuscripts to a friend, whom he asks "to use his judgment in insuring me against posthumous mistake" (13; ch. 1). She had originally thought of titling that work "Characters and Characteristics by Theophrastus Such, edited by George Eliot" (*GEL* 7:119). In between Macarthy and Theophrastus, Latimer in her short story, "The Lifted Veil" (1859), writes the story of his life as he approaches what he preternaturally knows will be the moment of his death. Edward Casaubon in *Middlemarch* asks his wife Dorothea to labor on with his "Key to All Mythologies," and Eliot herself completed and published the last two volumes of Lewes's *Problems of Life and Mind* (1879) after his death. With the combination of hindsight and foresight characteristic of her fictional narrators, she was deeply interested in the "history of a writer" – whether looking back to the origins of the writing, as in her journal entry, "How I Came to Write Fiction" (1857) – or looking forward to the inevitability of posterity's judgment in an age when biographies were popular enough to merit being called a disease of literature. Her condemnation of biographies seems to have been a reflex of her anxiety about the representation of her own history as it would be written and live on – along with her published writings – after her death. As it happened (or as she designed), her widower John Walter Cross was the first to "edit" her papers, including her letters and journals, to produce his *George Eliot's Life as Related in her Letters and Journals* (1885).

I will be drawing on Eliot's own views about telling life stories because her novels, essays, poetry, and letters provide insights into the possibilities for constructing such narratives with a self-consciousness associated with later, post-modernist assumptions about the fluid boundaries between fact and fiction. Her insights are particularly relevant for a biography that seeks to explore connections between the author's life and writings. In a section on "Story-Telling" in her posthumously published "Leaves from a Notebook" (1884) she writes:

> The only stories life presents to us in an orderly way are those of our autobiography, or the career of our companions from our childhood upwards, or perhaps of our own children. But it is a great art to make a connected strictly relevant narrative of such careers as we can recount from the beginning. (*Poetry* 2:203)

She made this statement about the art of ordering narratives in the 1870s when she was experimenting with narrative structure – first in *Middlemarch* and then more radically in *Daniel Deronda* (1876) – and it has implications for the biographer as well as the novelist. She chose to narrate the "careers" of her characters in *Daniel Deronda* out of sequence, questioning the notion that beginnings are inevitable, and intentionally altering the established bildungsroman formula epitomized in the first chapter of *David Copperfield* (1849–50), "I am Born." In contrast, the first chapter of *Daniel Deronda* begins with an epigraph (written by Eliot): "Men can do nothing without the make-believe of a beginning." The story proceeds *in medias res* before flashing back to illustrative anecdotes from the childhoods of its major characters, Daniel Deronda and Gwendolen Harleth. The form of story-telling in her last novel initiated a transformation in a narrative that would be adopted and developed by Henry James, Joseph Conrad, James Joyce, Virginia Woolf and others.

A biography may seem to have a natural beginning – the birth of its subject – but how we choose to select and relate the sequence of events that follows, especially with the benefit of hindsight and an abundance of factual material pre-ordered by past biographies, must be determined by narrative interest. In her novel of Renaissance Florence, *Romola* (1862–3), the narrator observes, "as in the tree that bears a myriad of blossoms, each single bud with its fruit is dependent on the primary circulation of the sap, so the fortunes of Tito and Romola were dependent on certain grand political and social conditions which made an epoch in the history of Italy" (21; ch. 2). The goal of biography is to provide the most accurate account possible of the author's history, including not only a chronology of what she wrote but the circumstances and events that are contexts for those writings.

Biographical facts about the author may not be discoverable in fiction, but the author's "character" is there to be read. Eliot was intensely aware of the sense in which "the history of a writer is contained in his writings." In committing his words to paper and publishing them, the writer reveals himself and his life in intimate if not always ordered ways. This is why her most self-conscious reflections on the relationship between life and writing in *Impressions of Theophrastus Such* take the form of chapters entitled "Looking Inward," and more temporally, "Looking Backward." Theophrastus takes the example of Jean-Jacques Rousseau (1712–78) when observing that "half our impressions of his character come not from what he means to convey, but from what he unconsciously enables us to discern" (5; ch. 1), and applying this observation to himself. The biographer of a writer must look backward to the historical record and inward to the character or persona of the author that is "contained," as Eliot said, in her writings. Through such a reconstruction of the author using the historical record and the writings, we have at least as good a chance of knowing Mary Anne Evans/Marian Lewes/George Eliot/Mary Ann Cross today as those who knew her only in childhood, or those who knew her only as admiring visitors at her Sunday afternoons at the Priory.[1]

It is tempting to take Eliot's criticism of biographies as a "disease" of English literature – made after she had become one of England's most famous novelists and therefore the object of biographical speculation and invasive inquiries – as her definitive opinion on the subject. Her views about biographies, however, were not always so negative. In 1839, after reading J. G. Lockhart's *Memoirs of the Life of*

Sir Walter Scott (1837–8), she commented to her friend Maria Lewis: "All biography is interesting and instructive" (*GEL* 1:24). Her first major publication was the translation of a work that is an interrogation of biographical sources, David Strauss's *Life of Jesus, Critically Examined* (1846). She was devoted to the truth exposed in the biblical scholar's account, but she lamented the harsh light of historical inquiry that seemed to spoil the poetry in the life of Jesus. The story of a life (miracles and all) is more satisfying than the dissection of that story. At the beginning of her authorial career, Eliot defended Elizabeth Gaskell's *Life of Charlotte Brontë* (1857) against the objections of her publisher, John Blackwood, who referred to it disdainfully as "this bookmaking out of the remains of the dead. . ." (*GEL* 2:323). She told Blackwood that while some might find what she called "the life of Currer Bell" in bad taste and "making money out of the dead," she and Lewes found it "admirable – cried over it – and felt the better for it" (*GEL* 2:330).

Some Victorians viewed biography as "making money out of the dead" because biographies were so prevalent and popular, read even by those who did not wish to become the subject of biographies themselves. Eliot specified that it was "the system of *contemporary* biography" that she disliked and that had "perverted" the form. As far as she was concerned, "my works and the order in which they appeared is what the part of the public which cares about me may most usefully know" (*GEL* 6:67–8). In his *Eminent Victorians* (1918), credited with initiating modern biography, Lytton Strachey referred disparagingly to the Victorian form: "Those two fat volumes, with which it is our custom to commemorate the dead – who does not know them, with their ill-digested masses of material, their slip-shod style, their tone of tedious panegyric, their lamentable lack of selection, of detachment, of design" (6).[2] But if the two-volume memorial seemed a static, moribund object by the time Strachey was writing, it is important to remember that debates about the nature of biography, and (in the case of authors' biographies) its relationship to literary criticism, were very much alive in the Victorian period.[3] In 1841, when Lewes was contemplating a biography of Percy Bysshe Shelley and had published an article on the poet in the *Westminster Review*, J. S. Mill wrote to him with criticism of the piece that is prescient of future debates up to the present:

> I think you should have begun by determining whether you were writing for those who required a *vindication* of Shelley or for those who wanted a *criticism* of his poems or for those who wanted a biographic Carlylian analysis of him as a *man*. I doubt if it is possible to combine all these things but I am sure at all events that the unity necessary in an essay of any kind as a work of art requires at least that one of these should be the predominant purpose & the others only incidental to it. (qtd. in Kitchel 28)

Mill expresses the now-familiar view that the work of the critic and the biographer are separate and cannot be successfully combined. Thomas Carlyle's biographies defined the great man theory of history rather than the kind of literary criticism that

Lewes wanted to put into his biographies. It was a view that Lewes, who never wrote the biography of Shelley, nonetheless ignored in his *Life and Works of Goethe*.

A critical biography of George Eliot in the twenty-first century has the opportunity to reflect on the contradictory attitudes toward biography from the nineteenth century to the present, using them to ask broad historical and critical questions. In particular, what is the relationship between an author's lived experience and the imaginative literature that she produced? This question has been asked and answered in many ways over the past two centuries as literary biography emerged simultaneously with realist novels, which often took their form from the shape of fictional characters' lives, so that the two genres seem to influence and inform each other. The problem of which, if any, historical context is helpful – even essential – to interpreting works of literature has divided later critics and authors, who seem as conflicted as their Victorian predecessors about the importance of biography in relation to literary criticism.[4]

Twentieth-century trends in literary criticism tended to deny the relevance of the author's life to the understanding of literary texts. New Criticism was a dominant interpretive methodology, separating and privileging the Arnoldian Victorian strain of criticism of "the thing itself" from the more popular strain of Victorian biography. It further derived from Modernist assumptions articulated by T. S. Eliot in "Tradition and the Individual Talent" (1919) and honed by professional critics within the academy into the 1960s. William K. Wimsatt and Monroe C. Beardsley in *The Verbal Icon: Studies in the Meaning of Poetry* (1954) and Cleanth Brooks in *The Well-Wrought Urn: Studies in the Structure of Poetry* (1947) explicitly disavowed connections between the author's life and his writing while seeking to judge the quality of a work according to a set of formal criteria.[5]

This impulse to appreciation was challenged and virtually eliminated by various forms of politicized literary studies in the 1970s to 1980s.[6] In its various manifestations in the 1970s and 1980s, post-structuralist theory also reacted against New Criticism's elevation of the work of art to argue that all writing constituted a "discourse," which must be read as part of a broader "intertext" – a nightmare scenario for the New Critics. Yet, post-structuralism shared with New Criticism the isolation of the text from its biographical contexts. The polemical positions of Roland Barthes and Michel Foucault perpetuated the anti-biographical bias that had been ingrained by New Criticism.[7] Biographies of authors or literary lives continued to be popular, but biographical criticism did not have a place in the theoretical approaches to literary texts that dominated the 1980s and 1990s. The exclusion of biography, first from formalism and then from densely theoretical discourse analysis, perpetuated an opposition that Eliot identified when she wrote to the American historian George Bancroft in 1874 about her objection to the "system of *contemporary* biography," complaining that "the mass of the public will read any quantity of trivial details about a writer with whose works they are very imperfectly, if at all, acquainted" (*GEL* 6:67).

Eliot's association and denigration of biography and "the public" looks forward to the elitism that characterized later dismissals of biographical criticism. New Critics continued a Modernist agenda of elevating art above more popular forms of writing. The early signs of what became a concerted effort to separate the popular from the good are evident in Eliot's writing beginning with her disregard for popular tastes when writing *Romola*. Her experiences with readers who insisted on finding "originals" for her characters, as well as those who attributed her anonymous fictions to someone else, disillusioned her. The belief that most readers misunderstood her work led her to write primarily for the few who would understand, so that her later work became more complex, challenging, and allusive. Just as Ezra Pound and T. S. Eliot had made poetry more difficult for ordinary readers to understand, so New Critics helped to distinguish great art from popular writing. Eliot's observations in the 1870s, firstly that the mass of readers care more about the trivial details of the author's life than about her writings, and secondly that the history of the writer is to be found in his writings, are consistent with two trends that would develop in the twentieth century: the insistence that what is popular is low and the separation of the author from his or her work. In other words, George Eliot's attitudes late in her career anticipate the exclusion of biography from literary criticism.[8]

Even in the 1990s when New Historicism made the "turn" back to history, its advocates did so with a post-structuralist lack of interest in the author. Critics pursued historical connections between literary and non-literary historical discourses, but continued to discount the relevance of the author.[9] While the "death of the author" hypothesis has been counter-productive to thinking about the importance of the author's life to his or her writing, the concept of the "intertext" is useful in "deconstructing" the boundaries, for example, between the literary artifacts canonized as art and other forms of writing. Critical biography may benefit from the fundamental insights of post-structuralism to offer fresh approaches to the relationship between the historical material (letters, journals, legal documents, etc.) – by which we know and reconstruct history – and the imaginative works produced by the writers of the past. It is time to rethink how the experiences of the author factor into larger questions about whether and how historical contexts explain the production and aid the interpretation of literary works. Mary Ann Evans/Marian Lewes/George Eliot, the person of many names, voices, and performances, was something more than a site of ideology. We may appreciate her writing more fully by recognizing its author as a person whose history can be told, in her words, "in a strictly relevant narrative." We may learn from the Modernist Strachey, who argued that "Human beings are too important to be treated as mere symptoms of the past" (5), and from the young Mary Ann Evans who wrote: "All biography is interesting and instructive" (*GEL* 1:24).

Within George Eliot studies, Rosemarie Bodenheimer's *The Real Life of Mary Ann Evans* (1994) broke new ground through its close, attentive reading of Eliot's letters and the astute connections that it makes between the language of her letters, fiction, and poetry. Bodenheimer recognizes that Eliot's letters should count among the writings that are the best history of her life.[10] Though Bodenheimer does not adopt any single theoretical approach, she deconstructs fundamental oppositions, including fact and fiction, author and character, literature and history. She also establishes that the author must inevitably be reconstructed from her fictional and non-fictional textual "performances." Letters, like novels, assume an audience. The author who published under the name George Eliot signed her letters in many ways over the course of her life, and she was always highly conscious of both the person she was addressing and her own identity as the writer of letters. Without denying or forgetting the real person, Bodenheimer nonetheless recognizes "the impossibility of knowing anything that is not somebody's fiction of the self in the guise of a story about another" (*Real Life* xiv). The writer, in short, is inevitably a character in the biographer's narrative of her life.

I will reconsider existing narratives about Eliot's life, focusing on some unresolved problems in those narratives, such as why she was silent about her mother, why she and Lewes could not marry, and the importance of Agnes Lewes as the "other woman" in her married life. In addition, I will draw on George Eliot's own thinking about the shape of individual lives – articulated by the narrator of her "political" novel, *Felix Holt* (1866) who contends that "there is no private life which has not been determined by a wider public life" (43; ch. 3). I will also engage literary critical traditions of interpreting her work within the broader context of theoretical approaches to studying literary texts generally. By questioning some unsupported claims that have been repeated in previous biographies, I hope to offer a new way to think about how the narrative of Eliot's life as reconstructed from the available evidence – itself a fascinating story often inflected or even conflated with aspects of her fiction – may profitably be read along with the literary works that continue to entertain, engage, and enlighten us. Her writings were in fact her "chief actions," and it is their enduring power that makes her a worthy subject of critical biography.

George Eliot and Biography

When Eliot read biographies of authors she admired, or incorporated biography into her criticism of literary works, she was particularly mindful of the moral judgments on personal actions that might cloud the appreciation of the literary texts. She therefore protested against a notion that is still being debated today – that immoral acts (or even opinions) on the part of the author somehow invalidate the importance of his writing. In a letter to her friend Sara Hennell in 1849, she argued:

> it would signify nothing to me if a very wise person were to stun me with proofs that Rousseau's views of life, religion, and government are mistakenly erroneous – that he

was guilty of some of the worst bas[ne]sses that have degraded civilized man. I might admit all this – and it would be not the less true that Rousseau's genius has sent that electric thrill through my intellectual and moral frame which has awakened me to new perceptions, which has made man and nature a fresh world of thought and feeling to me – and this not by teaching me any new belief. (*GEL* 1:277)

The genius of Rousseau, whose autobiographical *Confessions* (1782–9) so moved her, transcended anything additional she might (with skepticism) learn about his personal beliefs or actions. To her, his beliefs are less relevant than his perceptions and ability to convey them in ways that thrilled his readers.

Eliot's strong views about the superiority of genius and art to petty considerations of personal (especially sexual) behavior ironically foreshadowed controversies about her own conduct in relation to the moral and aesthetic value of her fiction. A high-minded few thought her relations with Lewes compromised her artistic achievements, as when Elizabeth Gaskell refused to believe such a noble book as *Adam Bede* (1859) could have been written by one whose life did so "jar against it" (qtd. in Haight, *Biography* 312). Lewes had declared in his *Life and Works of Goethe* that as a biographer, he would "neither deny, nor attempt to slur over, points which tell against him": "The man is too great and too good to forfeit our love, because on some points he may incur our blame" (xi). Eliot and Lewes display an intriguingly proto-Modernist willingness to separate the author's artistic achievements from his conduct, his actions from his writing, even while admitting that biographies of great authors are important and that drawing out the author's character from his writing is a crucially, historically valuable endeavor.

In essays published before she began writing fiction, Eliot includes biographical sketches of her subjects. In "German Wit: Heinrich Heine" (1856), for example, she provides an account of the poet's life. Her willingness to judge (or not judge) Heine's beliefs and acts reflects her conviction about separating art from the artist, while still finding the artist's life relevant enough to discuss in a consideration of his writing. Of Heine's sick-room conversion to Theism, she writes: "It is not for us to condemn, who have never had the same burthen laid on us; it is not for pygmies at their ease to criticize the writings of the Titan chained to the rock" ("German Wit" 224). In reviewing editions of Edward Young's poetry, as well as treatments of his life in "Worldliness and Other-Worldliness: The Poet Young" (1857), however, her role is to "recall the incidents of his biography with as much particularity as we may, without trenching on the space we shall need for our main purpose – the reconsideration of his character as a moral and religious poet" ("Worldliness" 166). She suggests that Young's character is "distinctly traceable in the well-attested facts of his life, and yet more in the self-betrayal that runs through all his works" ("Worldliness" 184). Her ultimately devastating critique of a poet she once loved associates the moral qualities of the man and his writing. She argues that "the religious and moral spirit of Young's poetry is low and false" and "*Night Thoughts* are the reflex of a mind in which the higher human sympathies were inactive" ("Worldliness" 185). Despite resisting moral judgments of the authors she admires, she is nonetheless prone to criticize the character of a poet to whose art she objects. Young's poetry is deficient because his mind was deficient, and this is a greater aesthetic, intellectual, even moral sin than any physical "baseness" Rousseau might have committed or any "erroneous" opinion he might have held.

Here we begin to see how morality and artistic representation become associated. If the author's writings are his chief actions, his behavior and beliefs are irrelevant to the value of his writing. Good writing is good character. Truth in writing is a form of moral truth, as she argued in her essay, "The Natural History of German Life" (1856):

> Art is the nearest thing to life; it is a mode of amplifying experience and extending our contact with our fellow-men beyond the bounds of our personal lot. All the more sacred is the task of the artist when he undertakes to paint the life of the People. Falsification here is more pernicious than in the more artificial aspects of life. ("Natural History" 264)

Eliot included versions of this aesthetic credo in her early works when establishing the moral imperative of realism, and she remained consistent in her basic beliefs – perhaps influenced by her own sensitivity to criticism about her relationship with Lewes – though her emphasis and terms of expressing them altered as she grew more disdainful of the mass reading public. Her early works are committed to truthful, realistic representations of ordinary people. By the time she wrote *Impressions of Theophrastus Such*, she was dedicated to exploring the morality of writing, broadly conceived as the literary archive that reflects and preserves national character. Her work shows this transformation from a belief in writing as a means of amplifying experience for immediate sympathy to writing as a means of passing on truth to posterity in the form of superior literature.

In her essays, such as those on Young, Dr Cumming, and Heine, Eliot invokes biographical details to enhance her analyses of literature. When reviewing biographies, she is self-conscious about the genre. For example, she writes of Thomas Carlyle's *Life of John Sterling* (1851): "We have often wished that genius would incline itself more frequently to the task of the biographer... a real 'Life', setting forth briefly and vividly the man's inward and outward struggles, aims, and achievements, so as to make clear the meaning which his experience has for his fellows" ("Thomas Carlyle" 299). Before she became a famous novelist worthy of a biography, and before her disavowals of biography, she felt great enthusiasm about the meaning that a man's "experience has for his fellows" and she learned from the art of biography, applying it to future novels in which she set forth the "inward and outward struggles" of her fictional men and women. She also believed that the author's writing was a "reflex of the mind" ("Worldliness" 185), concluding that the art and the life might profitably be studied together, the one illuminating the other. These critical reviews show that biography was central to her thinking as she was preparing to write fiction. Some of her opinions remained consistent, while others were transformed by her experiences as a novelist.

Eliot's authorial career began with a biography, her translation of Strauss's *Life of Jesus*, which, as the scrutiny of a life narrative pieced together from the testimonials of the Gospels, differed from other works of the German Higher Criticism such as Ludwig Feuerbach's *Essence of Christianity* (1841). Ideas about biography were heavily influenced in the first half of the nineteenth century by Carlyle's biographical writing from *Sartor Resartus* (1831) and *Heroes and Hero-Worship* (1841) to his biographies of John Sterling and Frederick II of Prussia (1858). The distinctive role assigned to men and women of genius was foremost in Eliot's thinking about biography, even as she focused on ordinary lives in her fiction. How does the life of the genius differ from that of the ordinary man? *Middlemarch* encapsulates this opposition, which is central to its structure and our understanding of Dorothea's fate. Without the Prelude about St Theresa and latter-day St Theresas, our reading of Dorothea's failures and our experience of the novel would be completely altered. Eliot was able to read the autobiographies of the sixteenth-century saint (1515–82), *Life, The Way of Perfection* (both before 1567) and *The Interior Castle* (1577), only because St Theresa was a heroine of history whose writings survived and were passed on to the future. In contrast, Dorothea's unhistoric life is summed up in a manner frightening to anyone contemplating his or her place in posterity: "a fine girl who married a sickly clergyman, old enough to be her father, and in a little more than a year after his death gave up her estate to marry his cousin – young enough to have been his son, with no property, and not well-born" (*Middlemarch* 784; Finale). The narrator further summarizes the painful, reductive opinion of the ignorant and provincial judges of Dorothea's life: "Those who had not seen anything of Dorothea usually observed that she could not have been 'a nice woman,' else she would not have married either the one or the other" (784; Finale). In telling her story, the narrator rectifies history and mitigates the harsh struggle for existence in which only the lives of the great are written and remembered. But the optimism and idealism of telling ordinary lives that shone through even the darker moments in her earlier novels is subdued. She tells the story of the ordinary in contrast to the great with a melancholy image of unvisited tombs. Milly Barton's grave is visited, as is Maggie Tulliver's at the end of *The Mill on the Floss* (1860); but in *Middlemarch*, Dorothea's tomb may be among the unvisited.[11]

Eliot's assumptions and statements about the importance of biography in the 1850s may have been influenced by her deepening relationship with Lewes and her participation in the research and writing of his *Life and Works of Goethe*. Lewes's multi-faceted career began with biographical work. He never wrote his biography of Shelley, but he wrote *A Biographical History of Philosophy* (first pub. 1845–6), a work that assumes the lives of the philosophers are relevant to an understanding of their ideas. It constructed a narrative of the history of philosophy through a series of discrete narratives about the lives of the philosophers, all in the service of making the history of philosophy interesting and accessible. It was one of Lewes's many publications in which he sought to popularize difficult and specialized forms of knowledge such as philosophy and science. He was very successful in these efforts, so it is interesting to see how this volume changed as it was repeatedly revised through the 1850s and 1860s. Eventually, he dropped the title of "biographical," thereby suggesting that he, along with Eliot, grew increasingly skeptical about the bio-graphical mode of explaining an author's writings. Lewes, like Eliot, eventually became disillusioned with the tastes of the general reading public, and his late scientific work was aimed at an elite, educated audience. At least in the years prior to her writing fiction, however, Eliot and Lewes shared a belief in the intimate relationship between art and the life of the artist – the reason why Lewes devoted much of his biography of Goethe to literary analyses, making the analogy: "In the life of a great Captain, much space is necessarily occupied by his campaigns" (xi). In this respect, the practice and art of biography were essential to Eliot's career and intellectual life. Biography is one of the literary genres that influenced how she thought about fiction and chose to trace the lives of her fictional characters, whether or not those characters were also writers.

Eliot's later rejection of biography as a disease of English literature and her reluctance to cooperate with biographers followed from her notoriety as an adulterous woman and her fame as a novelist. She was scarred by readers of *Scenes of Clerical Life* (1858) and *Adam Bede* – initially licensed by the anonymity of the author and later by the phenomenal success of the works – who attempted to find "originals" for her fictional characters. She reacted defensively, seeing such reductions of her work as an insult to her creative powers as an artist. It is here that we see the beginning of an idea, developed as a result of her personal experience, that life and writings should be kept separate from each other. This view about separating the author's life from his or her writings also influenced her fiction. After *The Mill on the Floss*, there are few one-to-one correspondences between her characters and people she knew, though people she knew claimed to be originals, and critics continue to identify them.

The very notion of "originals" – from the "keys" to *Scenes of Clerical Life* and *Adam Bede* circulated after the publications of these works, to Gordon Haight's essays on "George Eliot's Originals" (1958) – raises a set of aesthetic and conceptual problems. If a real person, in Eliot's words, "suggested the groundwork" (*GEL* 3:85–6) for a fictional character, in what sense can they be an "original" unless their life story is told in the fiction? The simplistic notion of an "original" from which a fiction is copied ignores the distinction between character and plot. From Amos Barton to Tom Tulliver, the Dodson sisters and Mr Casaubon: even if a real person (Reverend Gwyther of Nuneaton, Isaac Evans, the Pearson sisters, Mark Pattison) inspired the characters, imagination takes over in placing those characters in a set of fictional circumstances and playing out the events of their lives in ways that depart

11

completely from the histories of the real people. Biography is not the identification of originals, although the critic is justified in exploring those notions of historical and literary "originals" with which Eliot played in her late work: Isaac Casaubon and Edward Casaubon; later St Theresas; Greek Theophrastus and English Theophrastus.

As the mid-Victorian period's most intellectual and philosophical novelist, Eliot was more self-conscious about the aesthetic and moral dimensions of fiction generally – and her own realism in particular – than any of her contemporaries. The principles she articulated in her literary criticism and worked into her early fiction in the form of the narrator's comments contributed to her well-deserved reputation as an innovator. She advocated a brand of realism that was to influence the novel at the height of its popularity and artistic achievement in the mid-nineteenth century, but she also tested the limits of that realism. Her work became more dense and allusive, less popular, and less autobiographical all at the same time as it moved in the direction of aestheticism and Modernism. Her insights into life, art, and the relationship between the two can be useful in understanding how her experiences – including her extensive reading – are in her writing and how that writing became the chief action of her life.

The Mill on the Floss is often called Eliot's most autobiographical novel. This idea was encouraged by Cross, perhaps on Eliot's own authority, since she wrote about the experience of writing the novel as mining the layers of her past (*GEL* 3:129). Her "Brother and Sister" sonnets (1869) treat some of the same events from her childhood. "Looking Inward" and "Looking Backward" in *Impressions* are auto-biographical meditations on the notion of autobiography, but are written in the voice of a character/author unlike any other in her fiction. Outside of the letters and journals, we have few directly autobiographical writings by Eliot. "How I came to write Fiction," an essay within her journal (November 30, 1858), is an exception. But other works do offer revelations about "originals" in relation to fiction, including especially *Romola*, in which the lives of the real historical figures become part of her art. What is the basis for recreating an historical figure like Savonarola and probing his psychology? The answer is his own extensive writings and generations of biographies about him, on which she drew heavily in writing her historical novel. As her only novel that inserts fictional characters into an historical tableau of characters who actually lived, *Romola* is a unique case, as will be discussed in the following chapters. Eliot's letters reveal how mining her own past in *The Mill*, mining the historical record in *Romola*, and writing those recollections and researches into fiction also transformed her.

Like W. M. Thackeray's *Pendennis* (1848–50) and Charles Dickens's *David Copperfield*, Eliot's novels may count as fictional biographies – the record and detailed analyses of individual lives. These bildungsroman novels are actually also the portraits of the artist/author, as is E. B. Browning's *Aurora Leigh* (1856). Eliot resisted this particular sub-genre and her protagonists are never primarily authors. That she never modeled a female author/character on herself is consistent with the belief, which grew as her career as a novelist progressed, that the author's experiences should not be confused with his writing and that her fiction should tell the stories of unexceptional, ordinary people.

From her first short fiction, "The Sad Fortunes of the Reverend Amos Barton" (1857), Eliot used the shape of human lives to give form to her narratives. In *Middlemarch* the narrator invokes the eighteenth-century novelist Henry Fielding, a "great historian, as he insisted on calling himself, who had the happiness to be dead a hundred and twenty years ago" (132; ch. 15). In contrast, she identifies herself among the "belated historians" telling a tale of modern life at a modern pace. As an historian/ novelist, like Fielding in *Tom Jones* (1749), she was also an implicit if fictional biographer. In *Daniel Deronda*, she wrote of perhaps her most villainous character:

> Grandcourt's importance as a subject of this realm was of the grandly passive kind which consists in the inheritance of land. Political and social movements touched him only through the wire of his rental, and his most careful biographer need not have read up on Schleswig-Holstein, the policy of Bismarck, trade-unions, household suffrage, or even the last commercial panic. (499; ch. 48)

In imagining the biographer of the character whose story she is telling, she comments on what kind of information such a biographer would need. In this case, it is not knowledge of broad social movements, references to which she ingeniously slips into her novel to provide the reader with context of the time about which she was writing (ten years prior to the novel's composition).

The French Revolutionary Wars are a backdrop to *Adam Bede*'s 1799 setting, but they touch the characters' lives only when Adam spends his savings to keep his brother from becoming a soldier. In the late fifteenth-century Florence of *Romola*, everyone is affected by political events. While some lives, like that of Felix Holt, are touched by political movements, such as the Reform Act of 1832, other people (especially women) live remote from the national or international political scene. In *Daniel Deronda*, Gwendolen does not understand the "last commercial panic" that impoverishes her family, and in marrying Grandcourt, as the narrator explicitly tells us, she marries a man thoroughly removed from the social upheavals of his age unless they affect the rents he collects from his tenants. This is the case with most of her characters, and she prefers to tell their life stories through details that reveal a psychological perspective on character formation that was ahead of its time.

Her narrators' selection of details (chosen as though from innumerable possibilities) contributes to the realism of Eliot's novels. The narrators give a selective history of domestic events in the characters' lives with the intention of shedding light on their moral development. Adam Bede leaves home but returns from a sense of duty; Maggie is misunderstood by her family; Silas is betrayed by his closest friends; Mrs Transome is unhappy in her marriage; Lydgate has a predilection for beautiful, dangerous women; Daniel believes himself to be illegitimate; and Gwendolen

13

strangles a canary. What we know, and therefore how we judge, is tightly controlled by the narrator, and what she chooses not to tell may be as significant as what she does. What kind of childhood did Hetty have? Who were Tito's biological parents? What really happened between Gwendolen and her stepfather?

None of these characters is based on someone Eliot knew; none is wholly autobiographical; none is an author. Consistent with her earliest statements about realism, she wrote in an unpublished fragment: "The fundamental power, the basis of the best preeminence, is that of seeing and observing things as they are in the ordinary experience of our kind" (*Impressions* 168; Appendix). The point of view is Wordsworthian. Ordinary life makes great art, ironically, since ordinary people are not equipped to appreciate that art. Ordinary people would rather read vulgar biographies. Eliot did not write the story of St Theresa but rather wrote the story of Dorothea, a later St Theresa whose potential was never realized. In the anecdote from St Theresa's childhood, the "national ideal" is specifically contrasted to "domestic reality." A chapter epigraph in *Daniel Deronda* conjures the shadow of life not lived: "Men, like planets, have both a visible and an invisible history" (139; ch. 16). On the one hand, this alludes to the invisible, internal life of a person, and on the other hand, it seems to invoke a parallel, counter-factual, experience. For Dorothea, this was the life of a modern saint, which eluded her. In the chapter introduced by this epigraph, Daniel first considers the life he might have led as Sir Hugo's acknowledged son. But that is a false shadow because the real alternative life he might have led is that of a Jew. Eventually, Daniel realizes and recovers his unlived Jewish life. In resuming that parallel life *in medias res*, he becomes part of a cultural identity larger than himself, giving his individual life a greater, corporate purpose. Eliot signals political events of the 1860s, as when Daniel awaits his mother in Italy, "the very air of Italy seemed to carry the consciousness that war had been declared against Austria, and every day was a hurrying march of crowded Time towards the world-changing battle of Sadowa" (533; ch. 50). And yet the Austro-Prussian War does not change Daniel's life; what does change it is the meeting with his mother and the knowledge that he is Jewish.

Daniel Deronda ends before revealing whether Daniel will become part of a larger social movement, but he and Fedalma in the long poem, *The Spanish Gypsy* (1868), are the only characters that Eliot presents with such an opportunity. Eliot could also be ironic about history, as when the narrator contextualizes the insignificant Anna Gascoigne in *Daniel Deronda*:

> I like to mark the time, and connect the course of individual lives with the historic stream, for all classes of thinkers. This was the period when the broadening of gauge in crinolines seemed to demand an agitation for the general enlargement of churches, ball rooms, and vehicles. (74; ch. 8)

In simultaneously providing a knowledge of broader historical contexts but choosing in most of her works to focus on the private, internal, emotional history of her characters, Eliot offers clues to her own ideas about biography and about what matters when we seek to understand an individual human life. Toward the end of her career, she seems conflicted. Felix Holt is reluctantly swept up in local politics and effects that have rippled out from national reform legislation, and in the end he consciously returns to a modest domestic life. Fedalma inherits the responsibility to lead the Gypsy people to a new nation. After these are the stories of Dorothea and Lydgate, which are tragic in their failures. Finally, Deronda allies himself with the greater good of the Jews, and the moral value of that choice is affirmed in the chapter of *Impressions*, "The Modern Hep! Hep! Hep!" But which is more important – our national ideal or our domestic realities? Daniel's story suggests that national ideals are more important than doing good at home. Rather than just representing the humble domestic realities of insignificant people, Eliot's later work self-consciously thematizes the opposition between the great and the ordinary. The vision of Jewish nationalism in *Daniel Deronda* is contrasted to the insignificant "speck" that Gwendolen imagines herself to be at the end of the novel.

Eliot's writing and the questions it asks about how individual lives determine, and are determined by, a broader social context, lead to questions about how we should understand her life. Which contexts are relevant? Her remarks in letters on political events from Reform Bill riots in Nuneaton to the Zulu War? Her involvement in British colonialism through her investments and her influence in leading Lewes's sons to emigrate to South Africa? Or, the quiet, private struggles with religious doubt, her sometimes immobilizing insecurity about her morality and abilities, her sexual desires and frustrations? Should we consider the Divorce Act, the Married Women's Property Act, the founding of Girton College? Theories of evolution or "the development hypothesis" in the writings of Herbert Spencer, Charles Darwin, and Lewes influenced her intellectual life and fiction, but the extension of railways affected her more practically than the Reform Bills or scientific theories. The notion of social context can be overwhelming to the biographer (or the novelist). Eliot's own fictional situating of human lives in social and cultural contexts suggests that we need to keep as much of this complexity in mind as possible. Unlike novels, however, lives are not unified by themes. The art of biography may lie in identifying the themes that make the story of a life more like a novel than an objective recording of facts and events.

As a book of character types, *Impressions of Theophrastus Such* repeatedly questions the very notion of originality in life and art. Theophrastus is the only one of her fictional creations that merges author, narrator, and character and does so through biographical fragments that do not contribute to an overall narrative but rather amount to a self-conscious meditation on the relationship between the three personae. To complicate matters, he also has an historical "original," the ancient Greek philosopher. At the same time in the 1870s that she was dismissing a genre (biography) to which she had once been so attached, in her last work she played out the notion that an author's writings are his chief acts, and in doing so, she deconstructed the author/character binary in uniquely self-conscious fashion. The reticent narrator knows that he can only be known by what he writes: "It is my habit to give an account to myself of the characters I meet with: can I give any true account of my own?" (*Impressions* 3; ch. 1). Already here, we see the self-reflexiveness of this work. Theophrastus is an author but as a fictional character the people he meets are, inevitably, also characters (as highlighted by their unrealistic names). The pun is on character: can he give an account of himself as a character and also of his moral character? Did George Eliot view the people she met as characters? Did she think of her authorial/narrative voice as that of a character, leaving clues to his/identity in his dissection of other characters? The pun is also on "impressions": "Impressions of Theophrastus Such" are his impressions of others and also our impressions of him via these written impressions of others. It is an impressionistic work during the early era of what would come in fact to be called impressionism. It differs from ancient Theophrastus's *Characters* precisely because we are supposed to take the moods and crotchets of the modern London bachelor into account when reading his sketches. It is a playful, instructional challenge to see both the fictional author Theophrastus and the "real" author George Eliot "contained" in the writing.

Although criticized from the time of its publication to the present, Cross's *George Eliot's Life* is a text more aware of its own subjectivity than is usually recognized. Cross modestly calls his effort "*an autobiography* (if the term may be permitted)" and states his view that, "'All interpretations depend on the interpreter,' and I have judged it best to let George Eliot be her own interpreter, as far as possible" (qtd. in *GEL* 1:xiii). Writing in the 1880s under the influence of Eliot's late life and writing – and in the context of an emerging aestheticism and proto-Modernism – Cross deserves more credit for creating a work that was continuous with Eliot's own writing and thinking about biography. He was, after all, writing a life of "George Eliot," not Marian Evans Lewes or Mary Ann Cross.

Similarly, I would like this *Life of George Eliot* to take its cue from Eliot's insights into the stories of lives. Her life is the more remarkable when we think of her own invisible, counter-factual life – lived out as a housewife and mother in Nuneaton, never having reached London and the intellectual and professional opportunities it provided. Might she have been a nineteenth-century version of Shakespeare's sister in Virginia Woolf's *A Room of One's Own* (1929)? This leads us back again to Eliot's own views about how lives are lived and their potential realized. What were the unique historical opportunities that made George Eliot possible? They were not only (as Gordon Haight's version of her life might suggest) her meeting with Lewes (though this was a crucial, personal event), but a seizing of nineteenth-century advantages never before possible for a woman writer, combined with the distinctive character traits that led her to struggle against an "imperfect social state" (*Middlemarch* 784; Finale).

16

George Eliot in Biography

One might argue that Eliot had good reason to worry about her future biographies, and that she rightly withheld facts about her life. We assume that Cross had access to his wife's thoughts about what her first biography should be and that he offered facts and anecdotes as selectively as her narrators dole out information about characters. Any biography of Eliot today must rely on past biographies. It must also be critical and resist the power of a biographical narrative that has taken on a self-referential life of its own. I will give an overview of how the standard narrative of Eliot's life has been constructed, indicating the ways in which I hope to revise it.

For years after her death on December 22, 1880, biographical studies of Eliot relied on Cross's *Life*. Mathilde Blind published her *George Eliot* (1883) first, but Cross was able to select and edit letters and journals available only to him. In doing so he created an image of the author while omitting anything he thought would undermine that image, thereby respecting her wishes as he understood them. From the publication of Gordon Haight's *George Eliot and John Chapman* (1940) through the 1970s, accounts of Eliot's life were dominated by the revisionist investigations of Haight, who in his nine-volume edition of the *Letters* and in his own *George Eliot: A Biography* (1968) sought to replace Cross's image with one of his own making. Critics have depended on Cross, and then on Haight, using them to interpret fictional characters, or using fictional characters to fill in what the biographies lack. While some of Eliot's fictional characters and situations can offer biographical insight, much more can be learned through close attention to language and textual allusion.[12] Allusion and intertextuality are not usually considered relevant to biography, but to the extent that they reflect Eliot's reading – so essential to her life – they are biographical. The characters she met in fiction are as likely to provide clues to her fictional characters as the real life people she met. George Eliot started out taking figures from the past, such as her aunt Elizabeth Evans (Dinah Morris) and transforming them into fiction. In part because this method was exposed and implicitly impugned her abilities as an artist, she developed a complex interplay of real life models whether historical, like the fifteenth-century monk Savonarola in *Romola*, or people she actually knew, like her brother Isaac.[13]

The publication of the letters marked a turning point, and Haight's biography was the first to take advantage of this material, establishing him as "the founder of George Eliot studies" (Haight, *Originals* vii). His biography narrates the seven volumes of letters that he had by that time collected and draws on Lewes's journals and other materials collected from the descendants of Charles Lewes. Important works appeared between Cross's *Life* and Haight's *Biography* (1885–1968). Haight mentions Leslie Stephen's *George Eliot* (1902) and credits *George Eliot's Family Life and Letters*, edited by Arthur Paterson (1928), for introducing the Lewes family (on whose cooperation he relied for letters and remembrances), but he is less interested in biographical research conducted by women in the 1930s, including works by Anne Fremantle (1932), Blanche Colton Williams (1936), and Anna Kitchel (1933).

Following Haight, Eliot's life has been approached from numerous revisionist standpoints, incorporating new information (Ashton) as well as the perspectives of feminism (Redinger; Rose, *Parallel Lives*; Uglow), psychoanalysis (Johnstone), and post-structuralism (Bodenheimer). Some have aimed to be popular retellings (Hughes; Karl; Taylor; Maddox). Numerous short works have also retold the story of Eliot's life with distinctive critical insights (Brady; Hardy). Other work has contributed to our knowledge of focused aspects of Eliot's life (Collins, *Interviews*; McCormack, *English Travels*). And while the letters may establish a certain shape to the story of Eliot's life, it is useful to read all biographies with a critical eye, especially to repeated but unsubstantiated statements.

There has been much archival research published since Haight's biography: George Eliot's journals have been edited by Margaret Harris and Judith Johnston (1998). William Baker has produced an edition of Lewes's letters (3 vols; 1995, 1999), and the complete *Autobiography of a Shirtmaker* by Edith Simcox has also been published (1998). All of this material allows us to correct details, add information, and expand the foundational archival research published by Haight. Even more importantly, we have the opportunity to review and reinterpret the narrative that previous biographies have provided and to do so not only with the benefit of new facts and documents, but also with the benefit of massive numbers of critical interpretations of the fiction. Textual sources, including the notebooks for *Daniel Deronda* (Irwin) and *Romola* (Thompson), as well as numerous books and essays, place Eliot's work in the historical contexts of Victorian science, politics, religion, philosophy, and literature. Avrom Fleishman has updated a list of Eliot's reading (2010). The following chapters will integrate critical with biographical revelations and insights, reconsider assumptions about the relationship of history to literature as encouraged by various theoretical models, question biographies that have come before, and engage the fiction in fresh relation to the most pressing concerns of critics and readers.

Haight's biography, while still the standard source, has inevitably been criticized. Ira Bruce Nadel published an evaluation of "George Eliot and Her Biographers" (1982), which is useful for its recognition and summary of neglected Eliot biographies as well as for its historical perspective on biography generally.[14] Nadel calls Haight's biography "the apotheosis of the scholarly, academic biography," reflecting "a stage in the writing of literary lives by academics" ("George Eliot and Her Biographers" 114). Noting Haight's "suppressed hostility to psychologising" (116), as well as his dedication to accumulating facts without interpreting them, Nadel particularly criticizes Haight's biographical theme. Drawn from a comment by the phrenologist George Combe (1788–1858) based on an examination of a cast of Mary Ann Evans's head and quoted with approval in Charles Bray's autobiography, *Phases of Opinions* (1884), the theme is: George Eliot needed "some one to lean upon" (Nadel 116; Haight, *Biography* 51). That Haight takes up a phrenological observation uncritically seems surprising today, and while it does not discredit the basic narrative he established based on his collection of the letters, his anti-feminist assumptions have understandably disturbed subsequent biographers. So while Kathleen Adams could still publish a book about the men Eliot "leaned on" as late as 1980 (*Those of Us*), Redinger and Rose (1983; 1985) take aim at the idea and phrase, as do Brady (1992) and others. It is true that Eliot wanted a partner in life and someone to love. This makes her typical within Victorian society. Those figures in her life who remained single (Maria Lewis, Sara Hennell, Herbert Spencer, Edith Simcox) are the exceptions, as are such figures in her fiction, some of whom have been disappointed in an initial love (Seth Bede, Priscilla Lammeter, Silas Marner, Mr Brooke).

While more recent biographers reject Haight's theme of Eliot's not being "fitted to stand alone" (another phrase of Combe/Bray qtd. in Haight, *Biography* 51) and needing "someone to lean upon," they fail to realize how the bias that informed this sexist view also informs other aspects of his narrative of Eliot's life. There is a Victorian prudishness in Haight's work. He follows earlier biographers in emphasizing that Eliot and Lewes acted on principle and embraced Feuerbach's notion of love (rather than law) as being the only true basis of marriage. There is truth in this, and we need not reproach the couple's brave actions in defying "the World's wife" in order to see that, marriage being a legal category, they were not married. Adultery (of Chapman, Hunt, Lewes) is what gives the spice to Eliot's biographies as to so many Victorian stories, and when examining its various forms, we need not rely solely on other Victorian terms. Aspects of Haight's work reveal his bias toward marriage and a reticence about sexual matters, and especially non-normative sexual matters, reflective of his time.

Haight deciphered Chapman's sexual activity as recorded in his diaries, but there may be more to say about how Eliot encoded sexuality in her fiction (which as a Victorian novelist she was obliged to do), as well as about her knowledge of alternative sexualities. Haight's prudishness is evident in essays, including "Male Chastity" (1971) and "George Eliot's Bastards" (1981). His use of the term "bastards" in the biography, along with his repeated references, for example, to Agnes Lewes's "brood" of "bastards" (*Biography* 132, 135) betrays a disgust with children, real or fictional, born out of wedlock. One has to wonder whether it was this kind of moral judgment (even if directed at others connected to Eliot rather than to her) that she feared when contemplating her own biography. For the most part, Haight keeps to that tradition Nadel describes as the non-analytic accumulator of information. We should remember that he was a biographer writing from the 1940s through the 1980s who quoted F. R. Leavis with approval and wrote about his contemporary New Critic W. K. Wimsatt (1976). While influenced by New Criticism, he left in-depth literary analysis to others who were also beginning to apply their skills to Eliot's novels quite apart from the biographical research that helped to revive her reputation.[15]

Among the specific prejudices of Haight's account that persist in later biographies and therefore need to be redressed are his assumptions that Eliot's mother was neglectful and irrelevant to her daughter's life and writing; that Eliot was morbidly insecure and needed Lewes's protection; that Agnes Lewes was a promiscuous breeder and also unimportant to Eliot's life and writing; his related unsubstantiated assertion that Lewes was unable to divorce because of his generosity (rather than his own adultery); his lack of interest in Eliot's knowledge of complex sexualities; his impression that her letters were "not planned and composed with care" (xli); and his belief that she married Cross out of a conservative desire to be married, rather than for his financial management and biographical skills (xliv). I plan to reexamine these aspects of Haight's master narrative as taken up by later biographers and critics.

In *Middlemarch*, Mrs Bulstrode mistakenly believes that "her husband was one of those men whose memoirs should be written when he died" (326; ch. 36). The narrator uses this touchstone of greatness ironically to show her quiet heroine's illusory opinion of her husband, who is no better than an ordinary sinner. The tragedy of Harriet Vincy Bulstrode's life is her disillusionment with her husband and the shame she is bound by marriage and honor to share with him. George Eliot's memoirs were written when she died, and her story has been rewritten almost countless times. In the chapters that follow, I will attempt to say some new things about the history of the writer whose life Basil Willey called a "graph" of the changes that marked the Victorian era (*GEL* 1:xlii). I will attempt to situate that life in relation to the historical changes that transformed the realist novel and "prepared" the future of English literature.

Notes

1. In fact, in *Identifying the Remains*, Collins argues that her contemporary readers knew very little about her life and certainly much less than we now know. Her Victorian readers experienced "a persistent uncertainty over who she was and what she believed" (4).
2. On the development of the genre in the nineteenth century, see Benton, *Literary Biography*.
3. On the forms of Victorian biographies, as well as the literature about them, see Atkinson, *Victorian Biography Reconsidered*.
4. See Epstein, *Contesting the Subject*. On the emergence of the novel and biography, see McKeon in that volume. Nadel notes that the heyday of psychoanalytic biographies was 1920–35. On biographic form, see also Nadel, *Biography*, and Rose, "Fact and Fiction in Biography."
5. During this period, important biographies continued to be written. See Benton, *Literary Biography*, as well as Ellmann, *Golden Codgers* and Edel, "The Poetics of Biography."
6. Feminist literary criticism, while doing away with evaluative criticism, actually revived biography as part of its recovery of neglected women writers (Booth; O'Brian).
7. Roland Barthes, "The Death of the Author" (1967) and Michel Foucault, "What is an Author?" (1969).

8. In *The Return of the Author* (1981; trans. 1996), Eugen Simion traces Barthes's hostility to biography back to Proust's objections to Sainte-Beuve (an author whose work Eliot knew well). I am suggesting that we find the origins of this anti-biographical impulse in Eliot's own comments.

9. See Epstein, *Contesting the Subject* and Backsheider, *Reflections on Biography*. As post-structuralism informed the discipline of history, historians also took new, discursive approaches to biography. For an example of such a biography relevant to the context of Eliot's life, see Kali Israel, *Names and Stories*.

10. See Bodenheimer, *Knowing Dickens* and Nadel, *Biography*.

11. On Eliot's novels in relation to contemporary Victorian biographies, see Atkinson 41–3.

12. The introduction to the New Riverside edition of *The Mill on the Floss* (2004) attempts to complicate the idea of the novel as autobiographical and of Maggie as a young Mary Ann Evans.

13. See Knoepflemacher, "Fusing Fact and Myth"; McCormack, *English Travels*; Newton, *Modernising George Eliot*; and Henry, "The Romola Code." Such studies identify a proto-modernist self-consciousness and playfulness in Eliot's fictionalizing of history and real life. In *George Eliot's Intellectual Life*, Fleishman argues against readings that see modernist or even postmodernist elements in Eliot's writing.

14. For other helpful summaries of past biographies, see Handley, *Guide* and Margaret Harris's entry on Biographies in the *Oxford Reader's Companion to George Eliot*.

15. An example is the work of Barbara Hardy (1959). It is interesting to note that in the twenty-first century, Hardy turned to a biography of George Eliot, calling it "A Critic's Biography."

2

Early Years
1819–50

Altogether, my father's England seemed to me lovable, laudable, full of good men, and having good rulers, from Mr. Pitt on to the Duke of Wellington, until he was for emancipating the Catholics; and it was so far from prosaic to me that I looked into it for a more exciting romance than such as I could find in my own adventures...

(*Impressions* 23–4; ch. 2)

In *Impressions of Theophrastus Such*, the narrator's Midlands childhood bears many resemblances to that of his creator. Though he is an adult recalling how he idealized his father's England when he was a boy, his claim that he looked into this English past "for more exciting romance than such as I could find in my own adventures," might well describe George Eliot's creative practice for much of her career. With exceptions, including *Impressions*, *Daniel Deronda*, *Romola*, and most of her poetry, Eliot's major works are set in an historical period that would have been better remembered by her parents than by her.

Eliot certainly did not idealize the early decades of the nineteenth century in her novels, or necessarily share the Tory views ironically characterized by Theophrastus as belonging to his father, but in *Scenes of Clerical Life*, *Adam Bede*, *The Mill on the Floss*, *Silas Marner*, *Felix Holt*, and *Middlemarch*, she "looked into" the previous generation for "exciting romance" just as the Egyptian sorcerer in the first paragraph of *Adam Bede* looks into his drop of ink. Through her own memories and those of others, as well as through research and imagination, she recreated provincial England at the time of Prime Ministers William Pitt the Younger (1759–1806) and the Duke of Wellington (1769–1852), when the leading authors were William Wordsworth

The Life of George Eliot: A Critical Biography, First Edition. Nancy Henry.
© 2012 Nancy Henry. Published 2012 by John Wiley & Sons, Ltd.

Figure 1 Robert Evans, 1842 (John Walter Cross, *George Eliot's Life*, William Blackwood and Sons, 1885)

(1770–1850) and Sir Walter Scott (1771–1832). In this way, she represented to her contemporary Victorian readers their own national childhood, their social, political, and cultural inheritance. The child is father of the man, the woman and the generation.

In his *George Eliot's Life*, Cross offers an interesting, personalized perspective on the importance of this historical context for Eliot's life and fiction. His unique intimacy with the subject of his biography and his position as a late Victorian demand that we consider his perspective seriously. While we cannot know exactly what his wife told him, as opposed to what he learned in subsequent research into her life through interviews with friends and family, or what he deduced from reading her fiction (which he had read before he met her in 1869), his observations are still valuable. Born in 1840, Cross was 44 years old when he introduced his *Life* by trying to explain what the French Revolution would have meant to George Eliot's father:

> The date of her birth was removed from the beginning of the French Revolution by just the same period of time as separates a child, born this year, 1884, from the beginning of the Crimean War. To a man of forty-six to-day, the latter event seems but of yesterday. It took place at a very impressionable period of his life, and the remembrance of every detail is perfectly vivid. Mr Evans was forty-six when his

23

youngest child was born. He was a youth of sixteen when the Revolution began, and that mighty event, with all its consequences, had left an indelible impression on him, and the convictions and conclusions it had fostered in his mind permeated through to his children, and entered as an indestructible element into the susceptible soul of his youngest daughter. (*Life* 1:4)

Cross also quotes passages from *Impressions* to show how Eliot's childhood was influenced by her father's fear of revolution, disorder, and chaos and to explain her own conservative nature, which opposed violent or too rapid change.[1] And yet she had in her also the spirit of a rebel against tyranny and injustice, as well as an enthusiastic openness to new discoveries and intellectual exploration. It was after reading Cross's biography that a friend from her time as editor at the *Westminster Review*, William Hale White, lamented that he could not recognize the Marian Evans he knew:

> I do hope that in some future edition, or in some future work, the salt and spice will be restored to the records of George Eliot's entirely unconventional life. As the matter now stands she has not had full justice done to her, and she has been removed from the class – the great and noble church, if I may so call it – of the Insurgents, to one more genteel, but certainly not so interesting. (Collins, *Interviews* 36)

If Cross over-simplified her conservatism, Hale White romanticized her radicalism. But Cross had a sense of how that awareness of past and present informed her character and her writing, how she looked into the past for Romance but embraced and contributed to the transformations that were occurring at every level of Victorian society during her life. He explained to his late Victorian audience that she was born in the last year of George III's reign: "Byron had four years, and Goethe had thirteen years, still to live. The last of Miss Austen's novels had been published only eighteen months, and the first of the Waverley series only six years before" (*Life* 1:6).

He does not mention Shelley's characterization of George III in "England in 1819" as "An old, mad, blind, despised, and dying King" (Shelley 446, l. 1) in response to the "Peterloo Massacre" in Manchester (August 16, 1819). And while Cross, unlike later biographers, saw harmony rather than tension between the conservative and progressive (if not insurgent) aspects of her character, he is nonetheless right to emphasize the undeniable way in which her Romantic pre-Victorian inheritance combined with her distinctly Victorian experiences to generate the power of her imagined worlds:

> Her roots were down in the pre-railroad, pre-telegraphic period – the days of fine old leisure – but the fruit was formed during an era of extraordinary activity in scientific and mechanical discovery. Her genius was the outcome of these conditions. It could not have existed in the same form deprived of either influence. (*Life* 1:10)

24

Neither the "days of fine old leisure" nor the days of "scientific and mechanical discovery" were as harmonious as Cross describes. England in 1819 was a time of post-war economic depression, mass migrations to urban centers, and worker unrest attendant upon the pains of industrialization. It was a time of agitation for reform, fear of revolution, and reactionary backlash.[2] Throughout her fiction, Eliot rejected the simple nostalgia of preferring past to present, or a naïve view of progress preferring everything new to a benighted past. Her narrator in *Felix Holt* observes:

> Posterity may be shot, like a bullet, through a tube, by atmospheric pressure from Winchester to Newcastle: that is a fine result to have among our hopes; but the slow old-fashioned way of getting from one end of our country to the other is the better thing to have in memory. (5; Introduction)

Memory and hope coexist and coincide. Theophrastus sums up the view: "Many ancient beautiful things are lost, many ugly modern things have arisen; but invert the proposition and it is equally true" (18; ch. 2).

Everyone is influenced by the historical circumstances into which they are born. Mary Ann Evans was not only formed by that mingled consciousness of past, present, and future, but George Eliot developed a theory of history and a mode of narration in her fiction that emerges from the narrator's omniscient awareness of the characters' pasts, presents, and futures. By setting her novels in England's past, she could narrate in the present tense but with a knowledge of the nation's future.

In her poem, "A Minor Prophet," written in 1865 and published in 1874, she distilled the relationship between backward and forward looking, which is so complexly developed in her fiction. She used a variation on these lines as the epigraph for the final chapter of *Felix Holt*, suggesting their significance to her: "Our finest hope is finest memory;/And those who love in age think youth is happy,/Because it has a life to fill with love" (*Felix Holt* 397; Epilogue).[3] George Eliot, who found secure and lasting love at a mature age and only subsequently began writing fiction, was able to explore the relationship between our finest hope and finest memory in part because she had already lived such a full life and experienced the joys and pains of various "loves" by the time she began to write. As the final love of her mature life, Cross found these lines so central to her identity and her writing that he used them as the epigraph to his biography: "Our finest hope is finest memory."

A Life to Fill with Love

Mary Anne Evans was born on November 22, 1819, at South Farm on the estate of Arbury Hall near Nuneaton, Warwickshire in the West Midlands of England, an area George Eliot would refer to in *Silas Marner* as our "rich central plain."[4] Her mother,

Christiana Pearson Evans (1788–1836) was the second wife of Robert Evans (1773–1849).[5] Robert was born in the village of Roston Common, Derbyshire. Like his father, he became a carpenter. While practicing his trade in the neighboring village, Ellastone in Staffordshire, he was employed by a local landowner, Francis Parker, Jr. Through this connection, around 1799 Robert began to manage the estate owned by Francis Parker Sr. at Kirk Hallam in Derbyshire. In 1801 Robert married Harriet Poynton, a lady's maid to the wife of the elder Francis Parker. The marriage was a convenient and happy one for the couple and their employers. It allowed the Evanses and their two children to move to Warwickshire with the Parkers in 1806 when Francis Parker, Sr. inherited Arbury Hall and its magnificent estates from his cousin (the childless Roger Newdigate).

Upon inheriting the property, Francis Parker, Sr. assumed the family name of Newdigate. He soon became involved in legal suits contesting his cousin's will, which gave him the estate for his life only, leaving it away from Francis Parker, Jr. after his father's death and giving it to another relative. The intricacies of the will and lawsuits, which inevitably plagued Robert Evans as the employee of the disputing families, made an impression on Mary Ann. Memories of these legal disputes may have inspired the complex Transome inheritance plot of *Felix Holt*, for which Eliot sought detailed legal advice. This background may also have influenced her interests in lawsuits and wills generally. The plot of *The Mill on the Floss* turns on Mr Tulliver's ruinous determination to "go to law"; Mr Featherstone's multiple wills are central to *Middlemarch*; and Sir Hugo's inability to leave his property to his daughters creates the context for the multiple plots of *Daniel Deronda*.

As estate manager for the Newdigate family, Robert had responsibility for overseeing the tenants, as well as for various forms of land usage including farming, timber-cutting, and coal mining. The coal seam beneath the Arbury property was particularly rich and had been exploited by the previous generation of Newdigates, remaining their primary source of income. Canals on the property were connected to a canal system that shipped coal throughout the north of England, where industrial expansion in the urban centers in turn enriched the landed aristocracy by creating new markets for coal. The image of coal-laden ships floating into port that opens *The Mill on the Floss* seems to be informed by a memory of coal barges on the canal from Mary Ann's childhood and transferred to her fictional River Floss, the "black ships – laden with fresh-scented fir-planks, with rounded sacks of oil-bearing seed, or with the dark glitter of coal" (23; bk. 1, ch. 1). The narrator observes how "the great river flows for ever onward, and links the small pulse of the old English town with the beatings of the world's mighty heart" (256; bk. 4, ch. 1). Commerce and the transportation networks that arose to serve it, including canals and eventually trains, connected isolated rural villages with the rest of the world and gave a young, imaginative girl a visible link with life beyond the confines of her home. Shortly after Mary Ann's birth, her family moved to Griff House, a large brick farm-house on a coach road, so that stepping out to watch the coaches became part of her early

Figure 2   Griff House, "The farm offices" (John Walter Cross, *George Eliot's Life*, William Blackwood and Sons, 1885)

memories – a thrilling glimpse of the present that she would turn into a figure of nostalgia for the past once these coaches had been supplanted by railroads.

Robert's position of authority meant that he was effectively the most important connection between the working men on the estate and their aristocratic employers, a fact that may shed some light on the origins of Eliot's own social and political perspectives. In *Impressions*, her narrator reminisces about a father who "knew very well what could be wisely expected from the miners, the weavers, the field-labourers, and farmers of his own time – yes, and from the aristocracy" (19; ch. 2). It is clear that Eliot, like Theophrastus, believes that those who have experienced the "mixed commonality" of our "national lot" have a superior perspective on life generally (19; ch. 2). In later life, Eliot lamented losing contact with the common people whose experiences she had sought to represent in her early fiction. In this way, Robert Evans remained an influence on George Eliot.

These details are important for understanding the extent to which the Evans family's fate was entwined with that of an aristocratic family, a fact of which Mary Ann was conscious from childhood and which influenced representations of the aristocracy in "Mr. Gilfil's Love Story," *Adam Bede, Felix Holt, Middlemarch,* and *Daniel Deronda*. Her father's position allowed the young Mary Ann a glimpse of the life enjoyed by the aristocracy combined with the knowledge that such luxury and privilege were not her lot. She stored her observations from this period, incorporating them into her fiction, especially "Mr. Gilfil," with its detailed description of the architecture and interior design of Arbury Hall (Cheverel Manor in "Mr. Gilfil") and the earlier generation of Newdigates who had "Gothicized" the Tudor manor according to the late eighteenth-century fashion. The influence of this inside perspective on her social superiors is evident in the depiction (with varying degrees of sympathy) of characters with an inherited sense of superiority, such as the Cheverels in "Mr. Gilfil," the Donnithornes in *Adam Bede*, the Debarrys in *Felix Holt*, the Chettams in *Middlemarch*, and the Mallinger-Grandcourt family in *Daniel Deronda*.

The economic, emotional, and at times sexual interactions among classes (the aristocracy, middle classes, peasants, servants, adopted children of ambiguous class) represented in her fiction seem to draw on elements of her family's experiences. In "Mr. Gilfil," the heir to a childless couple's estate flirts dangerously with their adopted ward. In *Adam Bede*, the heir to his grandfather's estate seduces a local dairy maid, the orphaned niece of a tenant farmer. In *Silas Marner* the adopted daughter of a weaver refuses to leave her father and take up an inherited place as the natural daughter of the local squire. In *Felix Holt*, the adopted daughter of a Dissenting preacher learns that she is the inheritor of an estate, her parentage having been obscured in part due to her natural father exchanging identities with a man who subsequently becomes a servant to the local nobility. In *Daniel Deronda*, the heir to a baronetcy marries a penniless middle-class girl and makes his illegitimate son by another woman his heir. Theophrastus mysteriously observes that his father had been "companion to a young nobleman who was deaf and dumb" (19; ch. 2). Such intertwining of the lives of the privileged and the lowly was part of Eliot's realist aesthetic, with its initial moral, democratic imperative to represent all classes, and has the effect of questioning the ideologies and the mechanisms of transmission behind the land-based system of inheritance.

Our knowledge of Robert Evans is not confined to Adam Bede, Mr Tulliver, or Caleb Garth, fictional characters with whom he has been associated. Responding to a published reference to her as a "self-educated farmer's daughter," Eliot gave a rare, explicit account of her father to Charles Bray – whom she might have expected to know these facts already:

> Now my Father did not raise himself from being an artizan to be a farmer: he raised himself from being an artizan to be a man whose extensive knowledge in very varied practical departments made his services valued through several counties. He had large knowledge of building, of mines, of plantation, of various branches of valuation and measurement – of all that is essential to the management of large estates. (*GEL* 3:168)

Resenting those who hunted down originals for fictional characters, as well as any public speculations about her life, she wrote further, "if my Father is to be mentioned at all – if he is to be identified with an imaginary character, my piety towards his memory calls on me to point out to those who are supposed to speak with information what he really achieved in life" (*GEL* 3:169).

As her fame grew (and her infamy faded but did not disappear), Eliot decided not to respond to public surmises about her childhood and the family from which she was estranged. Her reference to her "piety" toward her father's memory predicts the thoughts about autobiography she would articulate much later in *Impressions* and may give us a clue to her reticence about her own family background, including its secrets:

> In all autobiography there is, nay, ought to be, an incompleteness which may have the effect of falsity. We are each of us bound to reticence by the piety we owe to those who have been nearest to us and have had a mingled influence over our lives; by the fellow-feeling which should restrain us from turning our volunteered and picked confessions into an act of accusation against others, who have no chance of vindicating themselves; and most of all by that reverence for the higher efforts of our common nature, which commands us to bury its lowest fatalities, its invincible remnants of the brute, its most agonizing struggles with temptation, in unbroken silence. (5; ch. 1)

Certainly this is an explanation of reticence and silence, but it is interestingly ambiguous whether the reticence that comes from the piety we owe to others involves their "lowest fatalities" and "agonizing struggles with temptation," or our own. The question arises: who might Eliot subject to "an act of accusation" in telling the story of her life? Why was she so reticent about her early life, pushing biographical speculators (successfully as it turned out) away from her relationship with her mother and toward her relationship with her brother?

In 1809, Robert's wife, Harriet Poynton Evans, was still attending Mrs Parker Newdigate and was pregnant with her third child. Apparently, Mrs Newdigate became ill, and Harriet contracted the illness, which proved fatal to both women. Harriet died after giving birth to a child, who also died a few days later (Hughes, *Last Victorian* 11; Taylor 7). Robert was left a widower with two young children. He was expanding his business activities beyond Arbury into the Nuneaton community generally and establishing a solid professional and social reputation that his family would subsequently seek to uphold. His status and his children required that he make a good second marriage. In 1813, he married Christiana Pearson, the youngest daughter of Isaac Pearson and Ann Pearson, whose roots were in the nearby areas of Arley, Fillongley, and Astley (all in Warwickshire). Because Isaac Pearson farmed his own land and was a "leading inhabitant of the parish of Astley" (Evans and Wood 410) and his wife (née Baxter) came from a family of well-to-do farmers, the marriage may have been perceived by Christiana's family as elevating Robert's social position, a notion advanced by Cross and repeated by subsequent biographers (*Life* 1:12). Christiana's brother Isaac Pearson and her three sisters were all respectably married and living within proximity to her new home. Her sister Elizabeth and her husband

Richard Johnson were witnesses at her wedding (Dodds, *George Eliot Country* 28). After her marriage, this extended family continued to be a presence in her life, as Robert's diaries attest.[6] Biographers from Cross on have identified the three sisters as the Dodson sisters in *The Mill on the Floss*.[7] Christiana's mother, Ann Pearson, died in 1795, long before the marriage of her youngest daughter. Her father Isaac Pearson died in 1829, and at the time was living at Astley Hall Farm (Evans and Wood 410). It seems probable that Mary Ann knew her maternal grandfather, though he does not feature as a character and the Dodson sisters frequently refer to their "poor" departed father.

Upon marrying Robert, Christiana assumed the role of stepmother to his children (Robert and Fanny Evans, aged 11 and 8 when she married). She soon bore a daughter, Christiana (Chrissey) (b. 1814), a son Isaac Pearson, named for her father and brother (b. 1816), and Mary Ann (named for her grandmother and aunts). As biographers have noted, the very names of the children suggest the primacy of Christiana's family within her marriage (Haight, *Biography* 3). So Mary Ann came into the world as the third child of a second marriage with two half-siblings and two siblings. There is nothing in itself extraordinary about being the child of a second marriage at this time, but her family situation helps us to recognize patterns in her fictional families. In her works, we find second marriages (*Silas Marner, Middlemarch, Daniel Deronda*), widows and widowers (*Adam Bede, Silas Marner, The Mill, Felix Holt, Middlemarch, Daniel Deronda*), half-siblings (*Daniel Deronda*), adopted children (*Silas Marner, Felix Holt, Daniel Deronda*), and nieces and nephews living under the care of uncles and aunts (*Adam Bede, Middlemarch, Daniel Deronda*). With the exception of *The Mill*, her fiction represents few simple nuclear families without involved and extenuating circumstances complicating the lives of the parents and children, and even in *The Mill*, the extended families exert an important influence on the Tullivers.[8]

On March 16, 1821, less than two years after Mary Ann was born, Christiana gave birth to twin boys who lived only ten days (Haight, *Biography* 3). They had been christened Thomas and William after two of Robert's brothers. Thereafter (if not before), she suffered from poor health (Haight, *Biography* 4). The physical strain of a twin pregnancy so soon after her previous pregnancy, plus the emotional toll of losing both children, must have been great. It is not clear whether her subsequent invalid state was primarily physical in nature or whether she also suffered from depression following the death of the boys, or both, but it is certain that for as long as Mary Ann could remember, her mother was a semi-invalid whose health was a central concern within the family, dictating decisions about the children.[9]

It was after this sad event that the family of five children was broken up. The teenage Robert was sent back to Derbyshire to become sub-manager for the Parker estate at Kirk Hallam, and his younger sister Fanny went with him to keep house. Chrissey was sent to a boarding school run by Miss Lathom in Attleborough (where one of her aunts lived). Mary Ann and her brother Isaac were sent across the road from Griff to a Dame school for part of each day. It was at this time that the youngest brother and sister were left to play together, and Mary Ann conceived the deep love for (and vulnerability to) her older brother, the memories of which she would draw on in *The Mill* and her "Brother and Sister" sonnets. At age eight, Isaac was sent to a boarding school in Foleshill near Coventry and Mary Ann went to join her sister at Miss Lathom's. The removal of all the children from the home by 1824 suggests that Christiana may have been unable physically or psychologically to care for her own three children on a daily basis and that the elder stepdaughter either did not want or was not wanted to help. The five-year-old Mary Ann, now separated from her parents and beloved brother, began at this time to suffer from the "night terrors" that she told Cross recurred throughout her life (*Life* 1:14). She never wrote about these in letters, however, and did not treat them in fiction until she gave similar night terrors to Gwendolen in *Daniel Deronda*.[10]

In 1828 Chrissey and Mary Ann were sent to Mrs Wallington's boarding school in Nuneaton. Isaac went to a private tutor in Birmingham (Haight, *Biography* 19). The young Mary Ann was an excellent pupil and seems always to have had an intense imaginative and intellectual life stimulated by widely various reading and the study of languages. Beginning with French, she taught herself (with the help of tutors) Italian, German, Latin, and Greek; later she would take up Spanish and Hebrew. She was also accomplished in music and in composition. She read her first Scott novel, *Waverley* (1814) in 1827 (Haight, *Biography* 7). Scott would remain a favorite author and important influence throughout her life. At this time, she emerges from the scant records we have as being exceptionally bright, socially awkward, linguistically and musically talented, but also highly strung, anxious, and prone to tears and hysterical outbreaks.

Like many bright children, she was attracted by, and attractive to, her teachers. While at Mrs Wallington's from 1828–2, she became a favored pupil of her devoutly evangelical, Irish-born teacher, Maria Lewis. Lewis became a mentor to her as well as friend. It was from this time that Mary Ann's own evangelical turn of mind can be detected. When she removed to the Misses Franklins' school in Coventry in 1832, she continued to correspond with Miss Lewis, who was a confidante about her religious feelings and also a visitor to her home. The Franklin sisters were Baptists, so that between her teachers and her uncle Samuel Evans (her father's youngest brother) and his wife Elizabeth Evans (both Methodist preachers), she came into contact with a variety of unorthodox religious views. Her aunt provided a model of how religion could empower women and give them a public voice (albeit a controversial one). As her formal education progressed, she was exposed to new people with different points of view in the larger town of Coventry. Through a world of books and ideas that was opening up to her, she nonetheless also withdrew into a religiosity that narrowed her own views but focused her reading, steeping her in the Bible and other religious texts as well as the history of Christianity.

Her need for a supportive, intellectual, and maternal friend while she was away at various schools is highlighted by the recollections of a schoolmate from Mrs Wallington's. In 1881, following Eliot's death but prior to any full-length biographies, this unidentified fellow pupil published her recollections in the *Women's Journal*. She describes the young Mary Ann in terms generally consistent with other accounts. But one observation stands out: "She was ever at the head of her class, and certainly loved learning for learning's sake; so devoted, indeed, was she to it that, to the astonishment and perhaps disgust of her schoolfellows, she always cried when the holidays came" (Collins, *Interviews* 4). This schoolfellow's distant memories of Mary Ann's love of learning are no doubt correct, but the revelation that she cried at holidays may also suggest, that for some reason, Mary Ann did not look forward to returning home.

Duteous Reticence and Unbroken Silence

Christiana Evans's apparent distance from her children has been handled variously by biographers. Cross insisted that she was a "shrewd, practical person with a considerable dash of the Mrs. Poyser vein in her" and that her children were "thoroughly attached to her" (*Life* 1:13). The Mrs Poyser connection has persisted in subsequent biographies, which have been forced to rely on Cross's comments as being the closest to the source as possible because George Eliot's own perceived silence on the subject of her mother is impenetrable. Cross and Edith Simcox (whom Cross acknowledges) interviewed Fanny Evans Houghton, Isaac Evans, Maria Lewis, Cara Bray, and Sara Hennell, and yet turned up no new information (Simcox 141–5, 220–5). Despite Cross's warnings about not drawing too heavily from fiction, lack of information has inevitably driven biographers to speculate based on supposed fictional clues.

Haight gives little space to Mrs Evans. Although he asserts that Mrs Tulliver's sisters, the Dodsons, match the Pearson sisters exactly, and that Maggie and Tom are based on Mary Ann and Isaac, he nonetheless also insists that Mrs Evans did not resemble the "scatter-brained Mrs. Tulliver" and that "there was nothing of Mr. Tulliver in Robert Evans" (*Biography* 2–3). Speaking of Mary Ann being sent to boarding school, Haight also claims: "Whatever traumatic effect the early separation from her mother may have had on Mary Ann, the separation from Isaac hurt her more keenly" (*Biography* 6). He assumes that because she wrote more about her love for her brother (in literature and letters) than she wrote about her mother, that the relationship was therefore more important.

This seems unlikely, and subsequent biographers with a feminist sensibility, unwilling to dismiss Mrs Evans in a few lines – and latterly more aware of the connotations of "trauma" – have recognized that it is precisely the silence that is most revealing, though inevitably frustrating when attempting to ascertain facts. Redinger is insightful on the relationship. She portrays Christiana as "withdrawing in a

Figure 3   Watercolor of Mary Ann Evans by Caroline Bray, 1842 (© National Portrait Gallery, London)

way common to women who do not really desire the families they produce" and effecting an "exodus of the children" (29). Her interpretation of the mother–daughter relationship has influenced others. Hughes compares Christiana to Mrs Tulliver, "a kind of Mrs. Poyser minus the energy and wit, but with a similar strain of angry complaints issuing from her lips" (*Last Victorian* 15). Later, discussing *Adam Bede*, Hughes nonetheless falls back on Mrs Poyser's supposed similarities with Mrs Evans. Karl's assertion that she was a "strict disciplinarian in the home, a person who was efficient with her children and husband and brooked no opposition in her domestic role" (7) seems to be pure fiction. Because Bodenheimer's focus is on the letters, which tell us nothing about Christiana, she is largely silent on the subject of Eliot's relationship to her mother.[11]

In the nine volumes of her letters collected by Haight, Eliot makes very few references to her mother. The first letter in the first volume refers to her mother's illness (January 6, 1836). In this letter to Maria Lewis, tellingly – since the mother had been a semi-invalid since at least 1821 – her illness is not as distressing to the family as the sudden unexpected illness of Robert Evans. Mary Ann wrote that her "dear Mother has suffered a great increase of pain, and though she has for the last few days been much relieved, we dare not hope that there will be a permanent improvement." Christiana had been diagnosed with a fatal illness – possibly inoperable breast cancer – as early as April 1835. Given that Christiana had been ailing for years prior to the diagnosis, we have to wonder what a "permanent improvement" would mean. The letter continues: "Our anxieties on her account though so great have been since Thursday almost lost sight of in the more sudden and consequently more severe trial which we have been called to endure in the alarming illness of my dear Father" (*GEL* 1:3). She goes on to say that "bleeding and very powerful medicines" have put her father out of danger. She does not mention powerful medicines being given to her mother, but that possibility, given the constant attendance of the doctors, seems likely. The trial of the family is "more sudden and consequently more severe," suggesting that the mother's invalid state was so familiar that it was "lost sight of" – even as it worsened – in alarm over Robert's illness, which was the first of subsequent attacks of kidney stones.[12]

Christiana died a month after this letter was written on February 3, 1836. Mary Ann was sixteen years old. We have no further letters from Mary Ann until one dated May 26, 1838, again to Maria Lewis. Cross mentions that he could find no letters from January 1836–8, and no letters have surfaced. In 1846 or 1847, Mary Ann recalled her letters from Maria Lewis and entrusted them to Sara Hennell (Simcox 145; Hands 18–19). But there is a break in the surviving letters to Maria Lewis during the period of Mary Ann's mourning over her mother. Redinger thinks that Edith Simcox saw the recalled letters to Lewis from 1836–8 when she interviewed Sara Hennell, but that they subsequently disappeared: "Obviously, someone withdrew these letters from the chance of publication. Who, and why? And why did George Eliot want the letters back?" (38).

If we look for patterns rather than for one-to-one correspondences, then the mothers in Eliot's fiction may offer clues to Christiana's character, as she may offer clues to theirs. Yet these figures are contradictory: Milly Barton, Mrs Poyser, Lisbeth Bede, and Mrs Tulliver in the early fiction, when Eliot was drawing most heavily on her previous experience, offer various models of mothering. They are all, however, represented as undergoing different kinds of stress directly related to their roles as mothers. Milly is loving and serene, but she suffers silently because her husband's economic means do not meet the needs of their large family, and she dies giving birth to a child she was not strong enough to bear. Mrs Poyser struggles to balance the care of her children with the management of her household, dairy, and brewery. She is irritable, dotes overly on her youngest child, and eventually takes to her bed with an undefined illness. Lisbeth Bede is neurotic, fretful, overly doting on her eldest, favorite son Adam; she is at times dismissive and even unkind to her younger son Seth. Mrs Tulliver is high-strung and dissatisfied with her husband, whose financial troubles disorient her simple world defined largely by her rigidly conventional, domineering sisters; she favors her son Tom and is critical of her wayward daughter, Maggie. We sympathize with her because she is bullied by her sisters and because, late in the novel, she softens and gives Maggie the affection she had earlier withheld. Gritty Moss, Maggie's aunt, is a minor character who is also overburdened with childbearing and economic difficulties. While these fictional examples can tell us nothing definitive about Eliot's experience of her mother, it is at least safe to conclude that, as an adult, she associated child-rearing with stress and ill health, and she continued to represent motherhood as a state of anxiety throughout her fiction. Mrs Transome, Mrs Holt, and Mrs Davilow are also anxious mothers. Mrs Transome's defining characteristic is disappointment in her sons.[13]

There is a theory that Christiana may have been an alcoholic, which would account for many of the mysteries relating to decisions about her children as well as to the silence surrounding her life. Kathleen McCormack suggests this possibility in *George Eliot and Intoxication*, a book that surveys the extensive range of metaphoric and literal forms of intoxication in Eliot's work within the context of drinking and drug use (mostly opium) in the nineteenth century. McCormack investigates the historical record of Eliot's life in conjunction with the pattern of alcoholism and alcoholic parents in her fiction. Tracing Robert Evans's substantial alcohol purchases as recorded in his diary, she establishes that Christiana had plenty of access to alcohol at home in the 1830s, as well as to the opium/alcohol mixtures prescribed by doctors for illnesses of all sorts. The portrait of a female alcoholic in "Janet's Repentance" has been recognized as both original in fiction and accurate.[14] Drinking parents who cause misery to their family include Thias Bede (a chronic drinker) and Mr Tulliver (an occasional drinker). As McCormack shows, drinking and drug use pervade Eliot's fiction with perhaps the most extreme alcoholic after Janet's husband Dempster being Raffles in *Middlemarch*. Both men suffer from the accurately described symptoms of *delirium tremens*. McCormack follows the tradition of those seeing significance in the absence of information about Christiana, observing that "the nearly complete silence abut her mother in over forty years of diaries, journals, and letters conforms to the usual responses of children of alcoholics" (*George Eliot and Intoxication* 205).

This is an example of a mystery that may never be solved by biographers, but it is also a case in which both general patterns and specific representations within the fiction might provide psychological insight – if not factual proof – into the life of the author. Gay Sibley, who does not cite McCormack's earlier argument, nonetheless puts forward an intriguing case for Christiana's alcoholism through a close reading of Mrs Poyser's behavior and through an application of contemporary medical studies of female alcoholics to diagnose both Christiana Evans and Mrs Poyser. This is a methodology that has been profitably used by critics to diagnose Gwendolen in *Daniel Deronda* as a victim of sexual abuse (though without positing any "original" for the character).

One reason that McCormack's and Sibley's speculations should be taken seriously follows from Sibley's notion that Eliot hid or coded Mrs Poyser's alcoholism in a way that makes it invisible to any but the most careful reader looking to discover it. Sibley writes that in *Adam Bede*, Eliot "deliberately disguises her own mother as a fictional alcoholic, while artfully closeting that character in her narrative much as her own mother, Christiana Evans, had been closeted in life" (184).

Disguise was a technique Eliot would develop in her fiction, especially later through cryptic literary allusions and coded communications with Lewes and others. This practice adds another layer of meaning to her fiction. It may also be seen as part of her secretive tendencies, which seemed to respond to the necessity of concealment both in her life and writing.

Having been criticized by John Blackwood for the explicit portrait of a female alcoholic in "Janet's Repentance" – and exposed as basing the portrait on a real person (Nancy Buchanan, who may or may not have been an alcoholic) – Eliot might well have returned to the topic of female alcoholism in a more veiled manner. Certainly she would not have wanted to invite speculation about any connection between carefully hidden secrets in her family life and characters in her fiction, even though at the time she wrote "Janet's Repentance" and *Adam Bede*, she herself was veiled in the anonymity of a pseudonym that had not yet been connected to her true identity. Intentional veiling and coding were means by which Eliot represented other taboo subjects in her later fiction, including homosexuality in *Romola* and incest/sexual abuse in *Daniel Deronda*. The perhaps less intentional drawing on personal experience to create characters is also evident in her fictional triangles, which recreate and replay the sexual triangle in which she was involved as the mistress of a man whose wife was still living (Agnes Lewes).[15] Even if the fictional character of Mrs Poyser is a closet alcoholic, it does not follow that Mrs Evans was like her. Janet is one kind of alcoholic (one who repents). Mrs Poyser has a different profile (though Sibley thinks she reforms as well). Christiana may have been like the pill-popping Mrs Pullet or the opium addict Molly. Snake oil tonics and prescribing doctors are also at the center of *Felix Holt* and *Middlemarch*.

Whether or not Mrs Poyser should be seen as a portrait of Mrs Evans, Sibley mounts a convincing case that Mrs Poyser is an alcoholic, closeted both within the fictional world of Hayslope and within the narrative of *Adam Bede*. The strong presence of family memories throughout the novel would tend to support the appearance of a character based on Christiana. The carpenter Adam, who works his way up to estate manager through a close connection with a young squire, has undeniable parallels to Robert Evans, while Adam's Methodist brother Seth and the young Methodist preacher, Dinah Morris, have their inspirations in Robert's Methodist brother Samuel and his wife Elizabeth.

In a journal entry later published as the "History of Adam Bede" (November 30, 1858), Eliot addressed the contemporary desire to find "originals" for her fictional characters, insisting that "there is not a single *portrait* in 'Adam Bede'; only the suggestions of experiences wrought up into new combinations" ("History of Adam Bede" 542). Like *Scenes*, *Adam Bede* is full of remembered details. The name of Adam's teacher, Bartle Massey, was the actual name of her father's teacher in Derbyshire (Kathleen Adams 5). The pub where Thias Bede drinks, "The Waggon Overthrown," is mentioned by Robert Evans in a letter as the site of a protest meeting of colliers in 1842: "the meeting was at the Waggon Overthrown that is about a mile from Bedworth" (qtd. in Kathleen Adams 17). Such colorful names seemed too good for Eliot to resist, and may give us some warrant to tease out the "combinations" of fact turned into fiction in these early works. And yet, to insist on equating a person with a character would result in the rather strange fantasy that Robert Evans (as Adam) stole his brother's girl and married her as perhaps a better match than the real Mrs Poyser-like Christiana Evans. Eliot's practice of drawing on reality but also mixing it with fiction in a strong, original narrative offers us the opportunity to experience both the value and the dangers of biographical speculations concerning the author's works.[16]

It has not often been suggested in biographies that Adam's mother Lisbeth Bede shares characteristics with Christiana Evans, probably because Adam is so often associated with Robert, and this would weirdly associate Adam's mother with Robert's wife. But, again, there are no one-to-one correspondences between Eliot's life and art, and a variety of combinations are at work. If Christiana, like Robert, is present in *Adam Bede*, her characteristics are dispersed among various characters. Eliot's identification with Adam is clear. He is the talented, successful son who wants to leave his village but turns back out of duty, a negative, counterfactual fantasy of what might have happened to Mary Ann had she never left home.

Then again, there is something of Mary Ann in Seth, unfavored but dutiful to his mother. Lisbeth Bede is a character whose querulous mothering grates on everyone. We have sympathy for her as the wife of an alcoholic, but her complaints might be seen as driving her spouse to his drinking. It is in reference to her that the narrator makes the famous observation about the pain of seeing our family likeness in our relations: "Nature, that great tragic dramatist, knits us together by bone and muscle, and divides by the subtler web of our brains; blends yearning and repulsion; and ties us by our heartstrings to the beings that jar us at every movement" (*AB* 40; ch. 4). It is also an odd twist of *Adam Bede*'s ending that Dinah Morris (usually thought to be based on Eliot's Aunt Elizabeth Evans) bonds with Mrs Bede and then seems to replace her. Dinah and Adam's children are named Adam after their father and Lisbeth after their grandmother.

The Evangelical Phase

Certainly the religious and moral ideas of the Dodsons and Tullivers were of too specific a kind to be arrived at deductively, from the statement that they were part of the Protestant population of Great Britain. (*Mill* 257; bk. 4, ch. 1)

Eliot's memories of her life at Griff House, Nuneaton, and Coventry are most vividly recalled in her early fiction. For example, the town of Milby in "Janet's Repentance" is based on Nuneaton, where she lived while attending Mrs Wallington's (1828–32). These were the years leading up to the passing of the First Reform Bill, which subsequently became a watermark of historical change in her fiction, especially *Felix Holt* and *Middlemarch*. In 1832, a riot broke out in Nuneaton during a local election, and it made an impression on the young school girl, who later represented an extended mob scene in *Felix Holt*, inserting her title character into its midst. The scene suggests a fear of mob violence and the novel as a whole is ideologically skeptical about democracy in general and voting reform in particular. She also represented a less threatening crowd in pre-Reform Middlemarch, one that detects and mocks the insincerity of Mr Brooke's commitment to reform.

These were also years of reforming religious movements. It was during her time at Mrs Wallington's that, under the influence of Maria Lewis, she first began to sympathize and identify with Evangelicalism. By the nineteenth century, those whose beliefs and practices were closest to their Catholic origins were known as High Church Anglicans, while those who deviated furthest from the rituals and ceremonies of Catholicism but remained within the Anglican fold were known as Low Church. The Evangelical revival established Methodism in the 1730s and continued to have influence in a variety of forms throughout the early nineteenth century including a fundamentalist, reforming movement within the church itself. The Reverend Tryan in "Janet's Repentance" was inspired by the Evangelical curate in Nuneaton, John Edmund Jones (Haight, *Biography* 9). Tryan's Sunday night sermons attract the poor, leading to the suspicion that he is a Dissenter and making him the object of distrust and hatred among more conventional townspeople, particularly Janet's husband, the lawyer Dempster.

The brand of evangelicalism with which Mary Ann associated was a more personalized form of Anglicanism that sought to reform the Church of England from within, rather than break away from it, as did multiple dissenting sects. In various ways and to varying degrees, Dissenters and Evangelicals offered a democratic extension of spiritual power to individuals. These movements and denominations were therefore appealing to the disenfranchised and impoverished working classes in the rapidly industrializing cities and were associated with radical political reform, or even revolution, and were often viewed with suspicion. Conservative prejudice against Baptists, Presbyterians, Independents, Unitarians, and various unnamed fringe groups persisted in the nineteenth century, and the wave of Evangelicalism within the church also came under suspicion for its closeness to dissent.[17]

In her youthful phases of sometimes extreme pietism, Mary Ann remained within the Church of England, but she came into contact with a variety of Dissenting sects and maintained a personal tolerance for different religions, hating bigotry of all sorts, even though in her youth she showed less tolerance than she later would in her fiction. Her comments on the subject in one letter to Maria Lewis show both her toleration and her ironic wit, even in the midst of piety, when recommending a religious book, John Williams's *A Narrative of Missionary Enterprises in the South Sea*

Islands (1838): "It is deeply interesting; truly the 'isles are submitting to the Lord' and literally 'wailing for His law'..." (*GEL* 1:12). Though the recommendation is serious, the tone is subtly mocking. Missionary work as a form of coercion would become increasingly distasteful to her.[18] She continues, again ironically: "Mr. W. is a dissenter but the B[isho]p of Chester highly recommended his work ... and it has since been purchased by all denominations. If you have any bigots near you there could not be a better book for them" (*GEL* 1:12). The passage intermingles skepticism about Williams's missionary work and the authority of the Bishop of Chester with ironic criticism of "bigots" who might be got to read the work of a Dissenter because it was authorized by a bishop. It reflects the fundamental belief in tolerance evident from her critical treatment of Dempster's persecution of Tryan in "Janet's Repentance" through to her defense of the Jews in *Impressions of Theophrastus Such*. Furthermore, the comment suggests that as early as 1838, her doubts about the supremacy of the very religion her epistolary rhetoric otherwise professed had already taken hold of her nineteen-year-old mind.

In the 1830s, there was also a counter-movement to Evangelicalism, which advocated a return of the Church of England to its Catholic roots (excepting acknowledgment of the Pope's authority). Known as the Tractarians for their series of publications, *Tracts for our Times* (1833–41), members of the Oxford Movement, as it was also called, instigated an influential, rather elitist push toward conservative reform within Anglicanism that stirred debate and controversy. Typically, Mary Ann was aware of this movement, and her reading (which temporarily excluded novels) included the *Tracts*. In May 1839, she wrote to Maria Lewis that the Oxford Tracts,

> evince by their compliments to Rome, as a dear though erring Sister, and their attempts to give a romish colour to our ordinances, with a very confused and unscriptural statement of the great doctrine of justification, a disposition rather to fraternize with the members of the church ... than with pious non-conformists. (*GEL* 1:26)

Expressing simultaneous disdain and respect for the *Tracts*, she refers to the "extensive learning, the laborious zeal, and the deep devotion of those who propagate them" (*GEL* 1:26). She criticized the social and intellectual elitism of the Tractarians, whose teachings trickled down from Oxford to the provinces, as she wrote in "Amos Barton," "the effect of the Tractarian agitation was beginning to be felt in backward provincial regions" (*Scenes* 2; ch. 1). It is significant that she was reading the work of both Dissenters and Tractarians at this time, passionate as ever in her pursuit of the truth and not as certain of it as she sometimes seems when writing to Miss Lewis.

Robert Evans was a respectable Church of England member, probably best characterized as Broad Church, falling in between the High Church Anglicans and the Low Church Evangelicals. He was not so intolerant, however, as to reject his younger brother Samuel and sister-in-law Elizabeth, and as Haight notes, in

Coventry he was somewhat "touched by the evangelical spirit" (*Biography* 34). His conservative nature determined that he was not likely to deviate far from the religious beliefs and practices of his aristocratic employers or of the traditions in which he was raised. Like many of his contemporaries with aspirations to raise themselves socially and establish respectability, he was prone to associate dissent with a dangerous radicalism.

Too little of Mrs Evans is known to speculate on her religion, but there is no reason to think that she held any other than orthodox views. The indictment of unthinking Protestant conformity that the narrator of *The Mill* applies to the Dodson sisters, may reflect on Mrs Evans: "Their religion was of a simple, semi-pagan kind, but there was no heresy in it, – if heresy properly means choice, – for they didn't know there was any other religion, except that of chapel-goers, which appeared to run in families, like asthma" (257; bk. 4, ch. 1). The narrator's satiric account of the "emmet-like" Dodsons and Tullivers in a chapter entitled "A Variation of Protestantism Unknown to Bossuet," is often cited, but the discourse on the middle-class provincial mindset actually ends on a note of approbation, observing that the pride of the Dodson race "identified honour with perfect integrity, thoroughness of work, and faithfulness of admitted rules; and society owes some worthy qualities in many of her members to mothers of the Dodson class" (258; bk. 4, ch. 1). The reference to mothers is interesting if we remember that the Dodsons were inspired by the Pearsons. Rather than a particular mother, it is mothers of this class that should be appreciated, even when their habits grate on their children. Conventionality is unthinking, but it is constant and decent, so at least George Eliot believed in 1860. The teenage Mary Ann Evans was anything but unthinking, and her letters suggest that in the late 1830s what she thought about most was religion in relation, not so much to her eternal soul, as to her egoistic self.

In the clergymen who populate her fiction, Eliot surveyed the range of Christian beliefs within the Church of England. Her early works show the Low Church newcomers to the provinces (Barton and Tryan), as well as the outlying movements of Methodism (*Adam Bede*) and the unnamed sect to which Silas Marner belongs. Rufus Lyon in *Felix Holt* is "minister of the Independent Chapel usually spoken of as 'Malthouse Yard'" (44; ch. 3), and is ineffectually bent on debating with the high church Rector, Mr Debarry, or at least his curate, the Reverend Theodore Sherlock, BA. Mr Bulstrode in *Middlemarch* was once "an eminent though young member of a Calvinistic dissenting church at Highbury" in London who thought of "the ministry as a possible vocation, and inclined towards missionary labor" (578; ch. 61), but his professional and social ambitions led him to wealth and a very different kind of future. His history is recalled in the character Mixtus in *Impressions*, who once ministered and proselytized in industrial cities but later felt far removed from that past (ch. 9). On the whole, Eliot's fiction concentrates on orthodox clergymen and their varying degrees of conformity on a spectrum from harmless laxity to hypocrisy, from Maynard Gilfil, Mr Irwine (*Adam Bede*), Mr Stelling, Dr Kenn (*The Mill*),

Mr Cadwallader, Mr Farebrother, Mr Casaubon (*Middlemarch*), the Reverend Gascoigne (*Daniel Deronda*), and the narrator's father in *Impressions of Theophrastus Such*.[19]

Throughout her life and work, Eliot was aware of the religious changes and conflicts that characterized the pre-Victorian era into which she was born and whose controversies she had followed in her youth as an avid reader and ardent Christian. In *Middlemarch*, Mrs Farebrother speaks for the generation of Robert and Christiana Evans. Her son says that she is "like old George the Third" and "objects to metaphysics" (159; ch. 17). His mother responds that when she was young: "We knew our catechism, and that was enough; we learned our creed and our duty. Every respectable Church person had the same opinions. But now, if you speak out of the Prayer-book itself, you are liable to be contradicted" (159). In conversation with Lydgate, who represents a progressive, reforming mentality that attracts her son, Mrs Farebrother asserts that she would never disrespect her parents by giving up what they taught her, concluding vaguely: "Any one may see what comes of turning. If you change once, why not twenty times?" (159). This caricature of religious conventionality is as sympathetically drawn as the conservative politics of the narrator's father in *Impressions*, but Mrs Farebrother's comments remind us that George Eliot "turned" several (if not twenty) times before arriving at her final stance in relation to Christianity.

Before her mother's death, Mary Ann was pious in a way acceptable to her family because they could recognize her beliefs as an evangelical aspect of Anglicanism. Maria Lewis, for example, was a welcome guest in their home. In the 1836 letter in which she tells her friend about her parents' respective illnesses, she writes: "My mother and sister unite with me in love to you, and my Brother begs me to present his kind regards" (*GEL* 1:3). The year after her mother's death and her recall home from school, Mary Ann served as bridesmaid in her sister Chrissey's marriage to a local doctor. This is usually the date from which biographers notice that Mary Anne, as she was christened, began spelling her name Mary Ann. Chrissey's departure with her husband for their new home in the village of Meriden five miles north of Coventry left her younger sister as the sole woman at Griff and therefore obliged to keep house for her father and brother. This is the time when she entered into an intense religious phase, bordering at times on fanaticism. Her extreme piety lasted approximately from Chrissey's marriage in 1837 through to 1841, as documented in her letters during this time. Critical thinking and skepticism leading to doubt is evident earlier in her letters so that in all, the archly Calvinistic part of her life was a short, reactionary response to unhappy domestic conditions.[20]

A variety of factors may have contributed to Mary Ann's brief turn to a self-denying, Christian asceticism that exceeded the bounds of her previous evangelicalism as well as the bounds of respectability, so important to her father and brother. These include grief at her mother's death and anger at being removed from the school where she had thrived, thus ending her formal education. She may also have resented having her role in life reduced to housework, or have been depressed at finding so little sympathy for her own aspirations within a male-dominated home. It is clear that she saw no promising prospects for her future at this time. And so without denying the seriousness of her religious faith, it is safe to say that the expression of faith itself was a form of rebellion. She knew that she was regarded as a problem by her family. Though her services as a maiden aunt and spinster daughter were valuable, the ultimate goal was for her to marry. The young woman occupied with keeping a household, churning butter, and making pies and jams, had an intense imaginative, intellectual life with few outlets other than the religious letters she wrote to receptive religious friends. Turned inward, her passion took the form of a self-searching and self-scourging conscience. Her anger was partially directed at Isaac who, as a man, enjoyed certain pleasures that, she later wrote, she would have denied him at the time when she went about "like an owl," neglecting her appearance and eschewing other vanities (Cross, *Life* 1:157; Haight, *Biography* 19).[21] She doesn't specify the nature of Isaac's pleasures, but they may have included hunting and drinking.[22]

While she made a detailed moral argument against reading novels, her reading in religious literature of all sorts was vast. Her letters are tissues of biblical quotations from both Old and New Testaments. This knowledge of the Bible would enable her to compose the sermons preached by Dinah Morris in *Adam Bede* and Savonarola in *Romola*. Furthermore, the practice of punctuating her own prose with quotations was a formal characteristic of her writing that would become more pronounced as her career progressed, both in the addition of chapter epigraphs beginning with *Felix Holt* and in the uncited quotations that are naturalized allusions to other works in her own voice. By the time she began writing fiction, she would also be an expert in German biblical criticism.

The religious ardor of young women trapped in their circumstances appears with a sympathetic irony and distance in Maggie Tulliver in *The Mill* and Dorothea Brooke in *Middlemarch*. After the rebellious Maggie is subdued through the near bankruptcy of her father and the impoverishment of the family, she briefly finds an outlet in religious belief. Upon arbitrarily reading *The Imitation of Christ* (1418–27) by Thomas à Kempis, she hears a voice from the past that speaks to her painful life, and she embraces submission, a move sympathetically recounted by the narrator. With all the enthusiasm of a convert, she "sat in the deepening twilight forming plans of self-humiliation and entire devotedness; and, in the ardour of first discovery, renunciation seemed to her the entrance into that satisfaction which she had so long been craving in vain" (273; bk. 4, ch. 3). The narrator wisely observes: "She knew nothing of doctrines and systems – of mysticism or quietism, but this voice out of the far-off middle ages was the direct communication of a human soul's belief and experience, and came to Maggie as an unquestioned message" (273).

Maggie's religious phase does not last for long. While she searches for solutions, consolations, and enthusiasm, she turns to religion, but the emphasis of her encounter with Thomas à Kempis is on her connection with another human reader from the past, whose markings in the book draw her to certain passages, making them seem the more relevant to her life. She is led away from her pious isolation by Philip Wakem, who brings her works of literature by Scott and Madame de Staël that introduce her to an intellectual, imaginative world and take her out of her domestic misery. Philip entreats Maggie to escape her "narrow self-delusive fanaticism": "it is stupefaction to remain in ignorance – to shut up all the avenues by which the life of your fellow-men might become known to you" (305; bk. 4, ch. 3). The physically deformed, artistic Philip voices opinions about the importance of wide reading as a way of knowing fellow men that are consistent with Eliot's. Like Mary Ann, Maggie turned to religious consolation when she felt isolated and alone, but through Philip's encouragement, Maggie's imagination – and by implication her moral sense – is awakened. Eliot clearly infused aspects of herself into both characters, replaying her emergence from fanaticism but denying to Maggie the happy outcome that she experienced herself.

In *Middlemarch*, Dorothea Brooke's religious experience is also contrasted to the Catholic Middle Ages, specifically that of the Spanish St Theresa. The "not yet twenty" (8; ch. 1) Dorothea was "enamoured of intensity and greatness, and rash in embracing whatever seemed to her to have those aspects; likely to seek martyrdom, to make retractions, and then to incur martyrdom after all in a quarter where she had not sought it" (8; ch. 1). Her friends view her as a problem because she is a beautiful heiress, who puts off prospective suitors with her "strange whims of fasting like a Papist, and of sitting up at night to read old theological books!" (9; ch. 1). There can be no doubt that in Maggie and Dorothea, George Eliot looked back at her youthful religious phase with the knowledge that such ardor cannot last and must be channeled in other directions or burn itself out. Foreshadowing the analysis of modern Dorotheas in *Middlemarch*, the narrator of *The Mill* observes of the early nineteenth century: "The days were gone when people could be greatly wrought upon by their faith, still less change it" (124; ch. 12). Though *The Mill* and *Middlemarch* suggest that early nineteenth-century society offered no outlet for the energies of ardent young women like Maggie and Dorothea, Eliot was able to write their stories only because she found a way out of the restrictions imposed on women and those growing up in provincial society generally.

Critics and biographers have taken different views of Eliot's religious belief. Most biographers tend to emphasize the extremes of her renunciations (especially her refusal to read novels or attend the theatre, and her disapproval of oratorio, etc.). This emphasis makes her later rejection of religion and her passionate embrace and pursuit of the pleasures she renounced all the more dramatic as a narrative. Intellectual historians, not surprisingly, represent a spectrum of views. In *Theology in the Fiction of George Eliot* (2001), Peter Hodgson argues that the Christian beliefs of her youth never completely left her and continued to inform the moral perspective of her fiction. In this he affirms what Nietzsche later condemned in *Twilight of the Idols* (1889) speaking of English morality and citing

Eliot as an example: "They are rid of the Christian God and now believe all the more firmly that they must cling to Christian morality" (Nietzsche 515). At the other extreme, Avrom Fleishman in *George Eliot's Intellectual Life* (2010) downplays the relevance of evangelicalism to her later thought and writing (23). Valerie Dodd places Eliot's immersion in contemporary religious debates within the philosophical context of her search for truth, while Barry Qualls and Mary Wilson Carpenter have emphasized the consistency of biblical typology in her work. Mary Ann ultimately lost her zeal as a convert away from Christianity and became tolerant of those who found consolation in religion, but first, having sought and found what she believed to be the truth, she took a principled stand that brought her into conflict with her father and ultimately became a lesson in compromise.

It may seem surprising that Eliot had such an intense religious phase; on the other hand, it may seem strange that she lost her religion so completely once she made up her mind about what she believed to be the truth. Rather than considering the question from a theological point of view, it is worth thinking about what religion could do for Mary Ann Evans from approximately the time she met Maria Lewis in 1828 through her mother's death in 1836 – after which her religiosity intensified – up until her meeting with the Brays in 1841. Clearly her Methodist aunt, although married, provided a model of what a woman might do other than, or in addition to, being a wife and mother. It was a very different model from that provided by her ailing mother, who was often too ill on Sunday mornings even to attend church (McCormack, *Intoxication* 204). If Mrs Evans was as "sharp-tongued" as Mrs Poyser, she might have been a highly intelligent woman, perhaps finding housework and child-rearing an unsatisfying channel for her intelligence.

Many unhappy housewives in life and literature resorted to drug therapies or relapsed into invalidism. The figure of the invalid wife was common in Jane Austen's works in characters such as Lady Bertram in *Mansfield Park* (1814) and Mary Musgrove in *Persuasion* (1818). Aunt Pullet in *The Mill* is the best example in Eliot's fiction. Wealthy through marriage and childless, she has no work to occupy her and cultivates her hypochondria with an enabling spouse who keeps track of her medicines:

> "There's the 'pills as before' every other night, and the new drops at eleven and four, and the 'fervescing mixture 'when agreeable'". (101; bk. 1, ch. 9)

Such an empty, medicated fate must have horrified Mary Ann, who combined her intelligence with a relentless work ethic and puritanical distaste for opiates of all kinds. There was no reason for Mary Ann to think that she could fashion a career outside of marriage or that she could become a scholar. There was no Cassandra Fedele – "the most learned woman in the world" whom Romola intends to seek out in Venice – to emulate. Her models of contemporary women writers were limited and included the popular moralist Hannah Moore, against whom she would later strike out in the intensity of backlash against Christian moralizing. Writing in 1848 to her neighbor John Sibree, with whom she exchanged an intense and flirtatious series of letters discussing politics and religion, she said of Moore,

> She was that most disagreeable of all monsters, a blue-stocking – a monster that can only exist in a miserably false state of society, in which a woman with but a smattering of learning or philosophy is classed along with singing mice and card playing pigs. (*GEL* 1:245)

The most educated, intellectual women she met in her early life were religious, and it makes sense that she should have channeled her energies into religious reading, thinking, and practices.

The premise of *Middlemarch* is that an ardor like Dorothea's has no channel in the early decades of the nineteenth century and the dispersing of her talents among hindrances is the alternate life Mary Ann Evans might have lived. Dorothea's project of drawing plans for workers' cottages seems an ironic glance at Mary Ann Evans's search for a meaningful contribution to society (in addition to her theological quest for truth). Her own project, conceived in 1839 but never completed, was a Chart of Ecclesiastical History, which seems a desperate attempt to press her intellectual inclinations into the service of Christianity (Haight, *Biography* 24). Bodenheimer observes of her ongoing correspondence with Maria Lewis during this period that while it "served as an intellectual and expressive lifeline that reached out of the family, it was necessarily confined by a continuing deference to Lewis and by the discourse of evangelical piety within which Mary Ann had to contrive to speak her mind" (*Real Life* 32). In 1841, Mary Ann was on the verge of breaking the confines of religion and the discourse of evangelical piety, and at the age of twenty two, was about to learn how to speak her mind.

Holy War

– I fear nothing but voluntarily leaving you. I can cheerfully do it if you desire it and shall go with deep gratitude for all the tenderness and rich kindness you have never tired of shewing me. (Mary Ann Evans to Robert Evans; *GEL* 1:129)

In June 1841, Isaac married Sarah Rawlins, who came from a prosperous middle-class family that lived in the neighborhood of Edgbaston in Birmingham. Sarah was ten years older than Isaac, and her father was a friend of Robert Evans's. Mary Ann attended the wedding in Birmingham with her sister Chrissey and served as a bridesmaid. After a series of stressful family negotiations detailed in her letters, Mary Ann moved with her father to Foleshill, a suburb of Coventry about five miles from

Griff. Isaac and his wife moved into Griff House, where the Evans family had lived since 1820 and where Isaac would live until his death in 1890.

Isaac now assumed his father's position as manager of the Newdigate estate. Mary Ann was now managing a smaller household, and Isaac's independent behavior was no longer a gall to her Puritanism, which was beginning to relax as she had more time for reading and contemplation. Her first months were lonely and she wrote to Maria, "I have no one who enters into my pleasures or my griefs, no one with whom I can pour out my soul, no one with the same yearnings the same temptations the same delights as myself" (*GEL* 1:102). She missed her old home at Griff, and she had not yet made new friends. She accepted her duty to take care of her retired father, and she was reading deeply in works of religion and theology.

At least part of the intention of moving to a less isolated locale was to provide Mary Ann with opportunities for meeting a husband, but the move had an effect quite unintended by her father. In the neighborhood of Coventry she found new friendships that opened up a world of free intellectual exchange and inquiry, as well as social fellowship. In 1841, she purchased the second edition of Charles Christian Hennell's *An Inquiry Concerning the Origin of Christianity* (1838; 1841). The Hennells were Unitarians who lived in Hackney in London. Charles followed his father into the mercantile business and the family worshipped at the Unitarian Gravel Pitt Chapel. Hennell's book is consistent with her readings in religious history and theology at the time, but it may have had added interest to Mary Ann because of local connections: the author's uncle, Samuel Hennell, was a ribbon manufacturer in Coventry. In 1836, Charles Hennell's sister Caroline (called Cara) married another Coventry ribbon manufacturer, Charles Bray. Charles Bray's sister Elizabeth Bray Pears was Mary Ann's next-door neighbor at Foleshill and her first new friend there. Mary Ann would soon meet the members of this extended family whose influence on her future personal, intellectual, and professional life would be profound.

Coventry's economy was closely tied to the silk weaving and ribbon manufacturing business. With its strong liberal traditions, it did not experience as much labor unrest as other manufacturing towns during the "Hungry Forties" and era of Chartist agitation. Many of the wealthy manufacturers were also philanthropists who experimented with institutions for helping the working classes, and Bray was particularly involved in providing equal education for children, including those of Dissenters.[23] Mary Ann had attended school in Coventry at the Misses Franklins until 1835 and, in 1841, she resumed her acquaintance with her Baptist teachers. More important, however, was the acquaintance with her neighbor, Mrs Pears, with whom she became involved in some charitable work aimed specifically at helping the miners during difficult economic times. Mrs Pears, whose husband was a wealthy ribbon manufacturer (and would become mayor of Coventry), introduced Mary Ann to her brother, Charles. Influenced in early life by Methodism and Unitarianism, Charles had on the one hand come to a progressive, rationalist perspective on life through the free intellectual inquiry to which he was devoted by the time he met Mary Ann. On the other hand, he pursued the more traditional path of training for a business career by working in a London warehouse for three years before returning to Coventry to work for his father. Upon his father's death in 1835, he inherited the family ribbon manufacturing business.

More has been made of Bray's Owenite socialism and conversion to phrenology than of his activities as a capitalist manufacturer. His embrace of social reforming ideologies and enthusiasm for current theories may have created a conflict with his business pursuits and affected his ability to maintain a successful business. He was active in promoting anti-Corn Law legislation and in 1842 met Richard Cobden and John Bright, leading radical, free-trade advocates and politicians. Writing in 1881, Bray reflects: "I was not a Free Trader only" (*Phases of Opinion* 68). Describing free trade in social Darwinian terms, he observes that though wealth within the nation generally increased, at the time he was writing, economic downturns causing poverty and distress recurred "about every ten years": "Supply and demand," he laments, are now left to "chance and selfish instincts only" (69). In an interesting contrast, the Tory Robert Evans reported to his employer in 1842 that he was sorry to say that there were anti-Corn Law petitions circulating in Coventry. Politically and religiously speaking, he was not predisposed to like Mary Ann's new friends.

Figure 4 Charles Bray (Coventry History Centre)

During Mary Ann's time in Coventry (1841–50), Charles Bray was at the height of his prosperity. He had purchased a home, Rosehill, in 1840 just before her arrival. In 1841 he had published his second book, *The Philosophy of Necessity*. Later, in 1857, just three years before the general decline of the industry due to a Free Trade treaty with France in 1860, he gave up the business and was forced to sell Rosehill. By the time George Eliot was a wealthy novelist, Charles and Cara's financial situation had become so precarious that Eliot wrote Cara in 1861 delicately offering to help (Haight, *Biography* 459). But throughout the 1840s, they enjoyed economic prosperity and a lively intellectual and social life. During the difficult final years of her life in the Midlands, Mary Ann considered Rosehill her second home.[24]

In 1859, Eliot reflected on "the strong hold Evangelical Christianity had on me from the age of fifteen to two and twenty and of the abundant intercourse I had with earnest people of various religious sects" (*GEL* 3:230). Whereas she had already been intimate with Methodists, Baptists, and Evangelicals, during her new life at Foleshill, she would meet Independents (the Sibree family), and perhaps most importantly Unitarians, a sect associated with progressive social and political views. After Cara Hennell married Charles Bray at age 21, according to his autobiography, he challenged her religious faith, hoping to convert her to his own rationalist views (*Phases of Opinion* 48). Shaken in her beliefs, she turned to her brother, Charles Christian Hennell, inspiring him to undertake research for the work that became *An Inquiry Concerning the Origin of Christianity*, which Mary Ann had probably already read by the time she met the Brays in November of 1841.

Hennell's book, which was influential on Eliot's thinking about Christianity at this time, and to which she returned in 1847 and again when it was reissued in 1870, demystified without rejecting the events recorded in the New Testament, offering an historically grounded, humanistic perspective on the moral teachings of Jesus, which was consistent with his Unitarian beliefs. Hennell's critical method is concerned specifically with discrediting the miracles in the Gospels by exposing their inconsistency, improbability, and derivation from other textual sources. His approach was remarkably similar to work being done by German biblical scholars of the time, though he came to know this only after he had written the book. Again, reconciling his findings that the miracles in the Bible cannot stand up to rational scrutiny, he nonetheless searches for a naturalistic basis for the morality of Jesus's teachings. Summarizing his conclusions in his Preface, he writes:

> Most of the doctrines of Christianity are admitted to be so much in accordance with the purest dictates of natural reason, that, on recognizing the latter as the supreme guide, no violent disruption of the habits and associations of the religious world is necessary . . . The contemplation of the Creator may still be indulged, and lessons of morality and wisdom still sought, according to the forms which Christianity has consecrated. (vi–vii)

Without ever explicitly endorsing the Unitarian religion that stood behind Hennell's conclusions, Mary Ann found his rational, naturalizing perspective on Christian morality to be in accord with her own views, and his humanism would provide a foundation for her own future humanist philosophy as expressed in her fiction. It is no wonder that she was also drawn to Hennell himself and the members of his family.

Mary Ann met Cara's sister Sara Hennell in July 1842. She met Charles Christian and his fiancée Rufa Brabant in October of 1842. The sisters Cara Bray and Sara Hennell, like their brother Charles, remained Unitarians, though the Brays did not attend church in Coventry. While Mary Ann never became a Unitarian herself, as her father feared, Unitarianism was the denomination of Protestantism with which she could most closely identify in later years, when she occasionally attended Unitarian services, and it remained the branch of Christianity with which she felt the most affinity, at least until her Anglican marriage to John Cross in 1880.[25]

Just as she had been extreme in her evangelical piety, so Mary Ann was extreme in her rejection of religion. It was a difficult, awkward situation for the conservative, conventional men of her family, who above all in their own respectable lives sought to avoid extremes. As the narrator ironically observes of the town of Middlemarch and the surrounding neighborhoods: "Sane people did what their neighbors did, so

Figure 5   Caroline (Cara) Bray, 1850 (Coventry History Centre)

that if any lunatics were at large, one might know and avoid them" (9; ch. 1). On January 2, 1842, Mary Ann made the now famous gesture of refusing to attend church with her father and visiting friend Maria Lewis, thereby starting what she referred to as a "Holy War." She had met the Brays only two months before and had not yet met Sara and Charles Hennell, but biographers and critics often assume that these new friends influenced her change of beliefs. Yet the acquaintance was too short at this time to have done anything more than embolden her to say what she had come to believe based on her readings and to act according to her conscience.

Bodenheimer, who has given close attention to the letters during this period, writes of her friendship with the Brays: "The combination of freethinking and emotional receptivity which Mary Ann Evans found in the Brays was the necessary condition for the sudden eruption of her Holy War" (*Real Life* 61). The act of refusing to go to church, Bodenheimer argues, was a test put to both Mr Evans and Maria Lewis to find out whether their love and friendship could stand the difference of opinion with which they were confronted: "She could now risk such a test because there was, at last, an alternative conduit for her intellectual and affectional life in her new friendship with the Brays" (*Real Life* 62). Neither her father nor Maria Lewis responded well to this test, though by ultimately relenting Mary Ann was able to repair the damage she had caused to her relationship with her father and her friend. She later regretted what she had done by not compromising her principles for the sake of others, repenting for the pain and dissension she had caused during this period (Cross, *Life* 1:113). And yet, her intense desire to pursue truth and knowledge, as well as her need for personal fulfillment, would lead to further rifts with her family.

Mary Ann had already suffered from the instability and domestic conflict surrounding the decision to move to Foleshill, which she was made to understand was for the benefit of introducing her into society where she might find a husband. So it was further unsettling during the months of the Holy War when Robert Evans threatened to leave their Foleshill house, Bird Grove, and move to a cottage in Packington on the estate of one of his employers. Mary Ann was forced to contemplate an independent life as a teacher or perhaps governess, an inevitable option for unmarried women and one taken by her friend Maria Lewis as well as by her half-sister Fanny.

Eventually, after spending several weeks with Isaac and his wife at Griff and participating in negotiations which included the possibility of moving in with Chrissey and her growing family in Meriden, the Holy War was settled by a compromise. Mary Ann moved back to Bird Grove with her father, who, despite his threats, was dependent on his devoted youngest daughter to care for him. Bodenheimer summarizes what Mary Ann accomplished by the momentous act of temporarily refusing to attend church and then later agreeing to attend without believing: "She agreed to misrepresent herself in the eyes of the world in order to maintain both the household and the private integrity of her mind... This shift, the submission to worldly opinion from which she is internally independent, was at the center of Mary Ann Evans's experience in the Holy War" (*Real Life* 73–4). This solidification of internal independence as more important than worldly opinion prepared her for future confrontations with what her narrator calls in *The Mill* "the World's Wife." Specifically, it prepared her for her future relationship with the married George Henry Lewes.

This conflict also offered an opportunity for Mary Ann to break away if she had dared, and her letters suggest that it was less doubt about her ability to support herself than a powerful sense that she would be abdicating a duty to her father that kept her from leaving home. For the next several years, she performed the duties of an unmarried daughter, keeping house, visiting family, and attending church. Yet during this time of devoting herself to her father, her mind was expanding through her reading and her contact with the Brays and their circle of family and friends. She would not leave the Midlands until after her father's death.

This temptation to leave family and responsibilities behind is replayed again and again in her fiction. Adam Bede leaves home but returns immediately, thinking of his brother and mother left to manage his alcoholic father. Maggie is compelled to leave home and teach school for a time, but she returns to her family in St Oggs, feeling that her first ties are the most important in her life. She leaves again with Stephen but returns again to face social ostracism for the sake of what she feels for her family. Romola is turned back by Savonarola when she seeks to leave her husband, and though she eventually does leave Tito, after his death she returns to take care of his mistress and children. Felix Holt, who had left home despising his father's snake oil business, returns to take care of his widowed mother. Camden Farebrother, though intellectually yearning to pursue his scientific interests, remains in Middlemarch to provide for his widowed mother and sisters. Ezra Cohen returns from his European studies after his father takes his sister Mirah and leaves his mother alone in London.

With this recurring pattern, Eliot confirms the choice Mary Ann made to remain with her father at this potential turning point in her life, but in none of her fiction does she allow a character to play out a story comparable to her own, one in which the hero or heroine manages to both meet compelling duties to family and also to escape completely from the limitations imposed by those duties. Duty to family is different from duty in marriage, and leaving because of injury is different from leaving because of ambition. Those who leave families to pursue ambition (the Princess in *Daniel Deronda*) or those who are injured and misunderstood (Will's mother in *Middlemarch*) are either minor or merely background characters. Mary Ann had both motivations at this point in her life, and yet she willingly stayed. Perhaps the greatest significance of the Holy War episode is that it marks the moment when Duty replaced God as the abstraction for which she would willingly suffer injury and subdue ambition.

Duty within marriage based on a contract or promise, rather than birth, was something she had yet to experience or fully formulate her opinions about. A series of experiences with married men prior to her irregular "marriage" to Lewes implicated her in sexual infidelities. In November 1843, Charles Hennell married Rufa Brabant in London with Mary Ann serving as a bridesmaid (her third time). Rufa's father, Dr Brabant, invited Mary Ann to visit him and his wife at their home in Devizes in Wiltshire to compensate for their daughter's departure. At first she enjoyed her time with Dr Brabant, whose intellectual liveliness and focused attention on her must have been seductive. Although not usually read in this way, the accounts she wrote to Cara may have an edge of irony in them: "I am in a little heaven here, Dr. Brabant being its archangel" (*GEL* 1:165). Looking back, she later told Sara that she had been "laughing in her sleeve" while burning incense to the doctor, who happened to be the only deity at hand (*GEL* 1:225). Her trip was brought to an early end when Mrs Brabant's sister alerted the blind Mrs Brabant to the flirtation between the doctor and the young woman he called his "Deutera." The Latin pun, which Mary Ann claimed to find clever (but may have found pretentious), suggests the doctor's pedantry. His own daughter also went by a Latin nickname.[26] Mrs Brabant asked the young visitor to leave, and Dr Brabant apparently did not intervene or defend her. It was an embarrassing episode from which Mary Ann emerges as susceptible to intellectual and sexual attentions from men and Dr Brabant appears foolish.

He would not disappear entirely from her life, but George Eliot would have her revenge. The doctor apparently talked about a great philosophical work he intended to write but never did (Linton, *My Literary Life* 43–4). This project must have been a germ of Mr Casaubon's unwritten "Key to All Mythologies," and Brabant's behavior (which was a pattern) may be reflected in that of Casaubon, an older man too egotistical to see the inappropriateness of his attentions to a young woman. The mysterious (to her friends) and ridiculous way in which Dorothea is temporarily enamored of Mr Casaubon and his learning suggests personal experience viewed with the same ironic distance as Dorothea's religious enthusiasm. Despite her negative experience with Brabant, he was a link between her and the German biblical scholar David Strauss, whose work she was about to translate, and later in the 1850s in Germany, Brabant would bring about a meeting between Strauss and his English translator.

Mary Ann's first step toward authorship and first opportunity to put her learning to professional use came when Charles Hennell asked her to take over the translation of David Strauss's *Das Leben Jesu* (1835–6) as *The Life of Jesus, Critically Examined* (1846). Knowledge of the German Higher Criticism at this time was limited to an intellectual avant-garde (Dodd 88–9). Hennell had not read Strauss when he wrote *An Inquiry*, but by the time his second edition came out in 1841 (the one Mary Ann owned), he had read *Das Leben Jesu* and could comment on its importance. But there was still no English translation. Dr Brabant knew Strauss and wanted to promote his work in England. A leading Unitarian radical MP, Joseph Parkes (whose daughter Bessie would later become a friend of George Eliot's), offered to fund the project of translating and publishing the book. He thought that the dissemination of German biblical critiques would aid in his primary concern – political reform. Rufa Brabant began the translation before her marriage, but apparently the task was too difficult for her. In 1844, Mary Ann agreed to take it on and would spend two years (1844–6) completing the task.

Strauss's book applies a rational, scientific method to its comparative study of the life of Jesus as told in the four Gospels.[27] The controversial study had already run through several German editions, which Strauss had revised in various ways. The fourth edition was chosen for the English translation. The style is dry and dispassionate, weighted with detail and scholarly apparatus. Characteristically, Mary Ann fretted over every detail. She corresponded extensively with Sara Hennell about the meaning of the German words and the problem of selecting English equivalents. She also needed to call on her knowledge of Greek and Latin and occasionally Hebrew, a language she would not study seriously until much later:

> There is one word I must mention, – *Azazel* is the word put in the original of the O.T. for the scape-goat. Now I imagine there is some dubiousness about the meaning and that Strauss would not think it right to translate *scape-goat*, because from the tenor of his sentence he appears to include Azazel with the evil demons. (*GEL* 1:195)

The exchange with Sara brought the two women closer together and was an outlet for the frustrations and doubts about authorship that George Eliot would experience throughout her career. Sara, another unmarried former governess but more intellectual, sophisticated, and progressive in her thinking, had replaced Maria Lewis as Mary Ann's primary audience. Before their close relationship faded with Mary Ann's move to London, this bond would become even more intense with Mary Ann taking the role of "husband" in their intimate and at times passionate correspondence.

By the time she began translating Strauss, as she wrote to her father in 1842, she already viewed the Scriptures as "mingled truth and fiction" (*GEL* 1:128), but she also saw and felt the poetry in the story and language of the Gospels. These texts had great personal meaning for her, despite her inability to believe in their revealed truth. Strauss's lack of sensitivity to the beauty and poetry of the biblical narratives, as well as the difficulty of the translating itself, left Mary Ann depressed. Near the end, when her father was also ailing, she complained to Cara Bray, who repeated it to Sara, that she was "Strauss-sick – it made her ill dissecting the beautiful story of the crucifixion, and only the sight of her Christ-image and picture [of Christ] made her endure it" (*GEL* 1:206). This is understandable in a former Evangelical Christian for whom the story of Christ had once been so personally and spiritually significant. Strauss does indeed dissect the story: Were Christ's feet nailed to the cross or only his hands? Was he given vinegar or wine? What was said by his mockers? By him? Was Mary there? Where can we see the influence of ideologies and mythmaking in the supposed factual testaments? In a typical passage, he writes: "if the historical evidence go to

Figure 6   Sara Hennell, 1850 (Coventry History Centre)

prove that the feet also of Jesus were nailed, it must be concluded that the resuscitation and the power of walking shortly after, either happened supernaturally or not at all" (3:256). Where Strauss sought only to be rational, Mary Ann often agreed with him, but it was dispiriting and disillusioning to be forced into such intimacy with his analytic language. Emotionally trying as it was, in completing this demanding labor, she brought one of the foremost examples of German Higher criticism to English audiences, and though she was paid only twenty pounds and her name did not appear on the title page, she was soon known in progressive circles as the translator of Strauss.

Expanding Worldview

Throughout the 1840s, the Brays' house, Rosehill, situated a mile outside of Coventry and a mile from her home at Foleshill, provided a space for intellectual exchange and socializing, much as 142 Strand and much later Eliot's London home, the Priory, would do. There, she met a diverse, educated, politically progressive string of visitors. In 1848, she met and impressed Ralph Waldo Emerson. In his 1881 autobiography, finished just weeks before his death, Charles Bray recollected that the spot under the acacia tree on the lawn at Rosehill,

> is still associated with the flow of talk unrestrained, and the interchange of ideas, varied and peculiar according to the character and mood of the talkers and thinkers assembled there; for every one who came to Coventry with a queer mission, or a crochet, or was supposed to be a "little cracked" was sent up to Rosehill.
>
> It is a sad pleasure now to call to mind how some of those who have left their mark on the world and are gone, entered for a time within our small circle at Coventry in those by-gone days. (*Phases of Opinion* 70)

In addition to the part these gatherings at Rosehill played in her intellectual development, and the respite they provided from a sometimes contentious and dreary home life, they perhaps most importantly led to connections that would launch Mary Ann's literary career. When Charles Bray purchased the *Coventry Herald* in 1846, she began to contribute essays and reviews, including a review of J. A. Froude's controversial *The Nemesis of Faith* (1849), a novel recounting the religious doubts of its clergyman hero. She later met Froude at Rosehill. The *Life of Jesus* also came from her Rosehill connections. She met its London publisher, John Chapman, on a visit to Sara Hennell in London in 1846, a connection that would lead directly to her moving to London and lodging at Chapman's house in 1850.

Even while working on the translation of Strauss, the possibility of supporting herself by writing seemed less realistic than making a good marriage. In 1845, she entertained and declined a proposal of marriage from a picture-restorer whose identity remains a mystery. She had been hopefully introduced to the young man by her sister and brother-in-law, Fanny and Henry Houghton in Baginton, where they lived just two miles from Griff. After her initial enthusiasm, she became disenchanted with the young man and quickly put an end to the brief affair. The fact that he had been so ardent as to write to her father asking to marry her occasioned considerable guilt on her part, though she could not feel that she had made a mistake.[28]

Because her friendship with the Brays was so strong and intimate, it is worth commenting on their marriage and the way it may have worked into her fiction. The Bray's marriage was an equal one socially and typical of the way leading business families intermarried in Coventry. The Hennells' uncle in Coventry was in the ribbon trade and Charles's sister had also married another manufacturer (Taylor 53). Mary Ann felt an affinity with Charles from the start. When interviewed late in life, Maria Lewis said that the two walked together like lovers (Simcox 224–5). Bray later recalled the compatibility and admiration he felt; he was amazed at her knowledge, and though they sometimes quarreled, they quickly made up (*Phases of Opinion* 73–4). Some biographers speculate that Charles Bray and Mary Ann were lovers

Figure 7 Rosehill (John Walter Cross, *George Eliot's Life*, William Blackwood and Sons, 1885)

(Hughes; Maddox), but there is no evidence for this. There is, however, some evidence of Charles's interesting psycho-sexual profile from childhood and of his unorthodox behavior within his marriage.

Charles told his mentor, the phrenologist George Combe, that at the age of twelve he was seduced by the family's cook and thereafter was sexually active. Combe recorded this in a diary entry, decoded by Gordon Haight and quoted by later biographers.[29] Combe advised Bray to moderate his amative inclinations. It seems that Cara could not have children. During Eliot's time in Coventry, the Brays adopted a baby, generally assumed to be Charles's. They raised Nelly as their own child until she died in 1865 (*GEL* 4:180). But it has also been claimed that Bray fathered other children – seven in all – with the same mother as Nelly. Biographies vary in their handling of this, but since 1980 when Kathleen Adams argued that the mistress, Hannah Steane, was kept by Bray in Coventry and that all the children had the fictional name of "Gray" and their parents listed on birth certificates as Hannah and Charles Gray (54), other biographers have followed suit by adopting this story (Taylor; Hughes, *Last Victorian*; Ashton, *GE*).

Complicating this scenario, Rufa Hennell told John Chapman that Cara was in love with another man, Edward Noel. A literary, cosmopolitan widower with three children and a relation of Byron's, he made frequent visits to Rosehill; Cara and Mary Ann visited him in 1851 (Haight, *Biography* 92). Chapman says Bray encouraged the affair, but given Chapman's own incessant self-justifications, this could be projection. None of it can be substantiated, but it is clear that Bray was not satisfied by his wife alone. Whether he fathered only Nelly or six others as well, there were secrets in the Bray family, and Mary Ann's intimacy with both Charles and Cara suggests that she knew and kept their secrets.

This may have relevance for Eliot's fiction, particularly the domestic situation of the Cass family in *Silas Marner*. As in all her fiction, there is no one-to-one correspondence between fictional and real-life character, but Nancy Lammeter Cass bears some resemblance to Cara Bray. Nancy loses a child and thereafter is unable to have more (153; ch. 17). When her husband raises the idea of adoption, she rejects it:

> To adopt a child, because children of your own had been denied you, was to try and choose your lot in spite of Providence: the adopted child, she was convinced, would never turn out well, and would be a curse to those who had wilfully and rebelliously sought what it was clear that, for some high reason, they were better without. (154; ch. 17)

Nancy does not know about Godfrey's daughter Eppie, and when she learns about her, she changes her mind about adoption but is frustrated when Eppie remains loyal to her adopted father Silas. Godfrey's marriage to Molly before the action of the novel begins shows an "amativeness" expressed, as in the case of Charles Bray, through a relationship with a lower-class woman. Although Cara did adopt Nelly, there was a mysterious episode with a previous baby, which Mary Ann visited and reported on while its parents were away, but that baby was returned, suggesting that perhaps initially Cara also had doubts about adoption.

These irregularities in the Brays' marriage broadened Mary Ann's experience beyond her own family and may well have led her to think unconventionally about marriage. Chrissey's marriage at this time was a sad model, as she was perpetually pregnant and her husband was on the verge of bankruptcy. He would in fact become bankrupt and borrow heavily from Mr Evans – money that came out of Chrissey's inheritance. The scenario of the Clarke family suggests that of Lydgate (minus the children) whose medical practice also fails, and the combination of excessive childbirth and poverty appears in the "Sad Fortunes of Amos Barton," as well as in the sympathetic portrait of the Moss family in *The Mill*, which seems to represent the economic wages of marrying for love in a similar manner to that of the Price family in Jane Austen's *Mansfield Park*. Certainly the political as well as the personal conversation at Rosehill was cultivating Mary Ann's tolerance for ambiguity in contrast to her evangelical intolerance just a few years before. In the domestic arrangements of John Chapman and G. H. Lewes in London, she would encounter comparable liaisons and advanced thinking about love, sex, and marriage, justified by progressive philosophical and political ideas.

Following her move to London and her first encounter with Chapman and his household in 1850, she returned to the safe haven of her friends in Coventry and continued to meet visitors there. Among these was Katherine Gliddon Hunt and Thornton Hunt, who arrived on a visit with John Chapman in 1851. Marian wrote: "Good Mrs. Hunt has left behind a very pleasant impression. I think she is the most thoroughly unaffected being I ever saw" (*GEL* 1:352). In the same letter she mentions the dissolution of the partnership that had initially formed the *Leader*. She could never have predicted that the Hunts, as we will see in the next chapter, would be a significant, if indirect, part of the sexual triangles in which she found herself involved in London. Whatever direct or indirect role the Brays and Hennells played in her rejection of Christianity, their society and connections helped her to transcend the limitations of her country upbringing and conceive of a very different future life beyond her Midlands home.

In addition to expanding her thinking, the Brays expanded her experience of the world outside of the Midlands. In October of 1845, taking a break from the Strauss translation, the friends took a trip to Scotland, allowing Mary Ann a literary pilgrimage to spots familiar to her from Scott's novels, including a visit to Scott's home, Abbotsford. Although this particular journey was cut short by the news that

Figure 8   Earliest known photograph of Mary Ann Evans, 1840s (Coventry History Centre)

her father had broken his leg and required her attention at home, in general Mary Ann learned that she loved to travel. She would spend much of her future life traveling in England and abroad.

Inevitably, Robert Evans's health declined and Mary Ann was able to act on her conviction about duty by attending him to the end. She nursed him from September 1848 through May 1849 and found a spiritual lesson in the renunciation of these months, writing to Charles Bray: "Strange to say I feel that these will ever be the happiest days of life to me. The one deep strong love I have ever known has now its highest exercise and fullest reward – the worship of sorrow is *the* worship of mortals" (*GEL* 1:283–4). She also had an ominous, exaggerated fear of what she would be like without the moral influence her father had exerted throughout her life: "I had a horrid vision of myself last night becoming earthly sensual and devilish for want of that purifying restraining influence" (*GEL* 1:284). With a return of puritanical language in what must have been her exhausted state on the eve of her father's death, she imagines herself "earthly sensual and devilish" in unspecified ways. Writing to the non-religious, non-moralizing, adulterous Bray, the confession is particularly intimate. It is possible that the freedom she would soon have to be earthly sensual may have been exciting as well as frightening.

Following Robert Evans's death on May 30, 1849, and funeral on June 6, she set off with the Brays to enjoy the foreign travel that would eventually become central to her intellectual and creative life. Just as she needed this escape after the exhausting efforts of caring for her father, so in the future she would take extended trips following the draining efforts of composing her books. On this trip, she and her friends traveled to France, Italy, and Switzerland. She was mourning her father and possibly depressed about her future. Her father had not been particularly generous to her in his will compared to her other siblings. He left her £2,000 in trust and £100 in cash. She would be dependent on the income from this trust (and on Isaac to distribute it) until she could find a means of supporting herself (or found a husband).

In Geneva, she parted with her friends, electing to stay and live on her own for the first time and for an indefinite period, in the end lasting from July 1849 through March 1850. At first she stayed in a boarding house. She wrote to the Brays that she was surprised to find that people thought her traveling alone was odd (*GEL* 1:301). But even though she was in a transitional period, recovering from the ordeal of her father's death and thinking about the future, she maintained the strong sense of herself that allowed her to disregard the critical judgments of society.

Drawing on her small inheritance, she passed the time reading, people watching, and writing sketches of the cosmopolitan mix of characters she met that seem preparations for her later fiction writing. As winter set in, she found it more comfortable to leave the boarding house and lodge in the home of François D'Albert Durade. D'Albert Durade was a painter with a cultivated middle-class family into which Mary Ann fit easily. According to her letters she felt pampered by the maternal Mme D'Albert, whom she called Maman, and she seemed particularly close to

M. D'Albert, who painted one of the few portraits of her. She did not get close enough to incite jealousy, though biographers have speculated about the nature of the relationship because she used the familiar "Tu" address to M. D'Albert in letters she wrote to him in French and which he later destroyed (Haight, *Biography* 79). Furthermore, the painter Philip Wakem in *The Mill*, hopelessly in love with Maggie, is short in stature with a deformed spine, as was D'Albert Durade. The family remained life-long friends, and the surviving letters suggest a relatively formal relationship in which Eliot emphasized family relations – both hers and theirs.

In 1859, she wrote to D'Albert, who became the French translator of several of her novels, in response to his queries about her religious stance:

> When I was at Geneva, I had not yet lost the attitude of antagonism which belongs to the renunciation of *any* belief – also, I was very unhappy, and in a state of discord and rebellion towards my own lot. Ten years of experience have wrought great changes in that inward self: I have no longer any antagonism towards any faith in which human sorrow and human longing for purity have expressed themselves; on the contrary, I have a sympathy with it that predominates over all argumentative tendencies. (*GEL* 3:230–1)

Figure 9 Oil painting of Mary Ann Evans by D'Albert Durade, 1849 (© National Portrait Gallery, London)

Thus she retrospectively sums up her condition as she approached the age of 30. She felt no more obligations to family. She had liberated herself from the restrictions of Christian dogma, and she had just enough income to leave home and begin looking for a way to support herself – to pursue her ambition and find her vocation.

When Theophrastus recalls the Midlands of his youth, he reflects not just on Eliot's childhood but on the fiction she had written. When he describes "our quiet little rivers here and there fit to turn a mill-wheel, our villages along the old coach-roads" (25; ch. 2), he recalls not just the reality of rural England but the mill in *The Mill on the Floss* and the stagecoach in *Felix Holt*. And in saying that these signs of civilization on the face of the landscape "are all easily alterable lineaments that seem to make the face of our Motherland sympathetic with the laborious lives of her children," he invokes a metaphor of national genealogy that helps explain the larger themes in Eliot's fiction, particularly the belief in national identity as a modern substitution for the forms of Christianity that Eliot and many of her contemporaries were in the process of relegating to England's past. This was the position she had come to 30 years after the most significant turning point in her life – the decision to move to London and never return to live in the Midlands. Here, also, looking back at her novels, she invokes a metaphor of motherhood – the people of England are the children of the Motherland. In 1850, Mary Ann Evans, the daughter from the country whose own mother remains such a mystery, was poised to leave her home. Eight years later she would take the pseudonym George Eliot and would write compellingly about mothers, as well as the laborious and various lives of their children.

Notes

1. Cross cautions: "But we must be careful not to found too much on such *suggestions* of character in George Eliot's books; and this must particularly be borne in mind in the 'Mill on the Floss'" (1:31).
2. Karl in particular stresses the oppressions and injustices of the era into which Mary Ann was born.
3. "A Minor Prophet" reads "Our finest hope is finest memory, / As those who love in age think youth is blest / Because it has a life to fill with love" (*Poetry* 1:177–8; ll. 292–4).
4. She was christened "Mary Anne Evans," but her father always wrote her name as Mary Ann, and after her mother's death, she too began signing her name "Mary Ann."
5. Haight's edition of the letters gives both 1788 (1:lxv) and 1785 (1:3) as the date of Christiana's birth. An internet search of genealogical databases suggests 1788 is the correct date. On Eliot's relationship to the Midlands, see Handley, *George Eliot's Midlands*.
6. I am grateful to the Nuneaton Public Library and Museum for providing me with a transcription of the diaries (October 1830–February 1832) and to Kathleen McCormack for sharing her notes on the 1835 diary.

7. Mary Evarard of Attleborough (Aunt Glegg); Ann Garner of Astley (Aunt Deane); Elizabeth Johnson of Marston Jabbett (Aunt Pullet). For more information on the Pearsons, see Kathryn Hughes, "Enter the Aunts."

8. Recent revisionist scholarship on the complexities of Victorian families include works by Corbett, Cleare, and Marcus.

9. Cross and other early biographers do not mention the birth and death of twins, though Haight does. It is odd that Redinger, having the benefit of Haight's biography, overlooks this traumatic experience in Christiana's life and writes that it was the birth of Mary Ann (rather than the births and deaths of the twins) that seemed to push her over an edge of maternal suffering: "she never recovered from the debilitating effects of giving birth to Mary Ann" (29). The frequency of Christiana's illnesses emerges in Robert Evans's Diaries (Nuneaton Public Library).

10. In 1874, the poet James Thomson sent Eliot his poem, "City of Dreadful Night," explaining that he saw, "through all the manifold beauty and delightfulness of your works, a character and an intellectual destiny akin to those of that grand and awful Melancholy of Albrecht Dürer which dominates the City of my poem" (*GEL* 6:61). Two days later he wrote again to qualify that the poem was written in "sleepless hypochondria" and that he was aware that the "truth of midnight does not exclude the truth of noonday" (*GEL* 6:61). He saw a darkness in Eliot's work that was often overlooked by contemporary readers.

11. Taking a psychoanalytic approach, Johnstone argues that "Eliot's notable silence on the subject of her mother is the silence of painful affect in response to the loss of her mother – a loss which she associated with the deaths of siblings" (78). She attributes Eliot's silence, then, to a dual withdrawal process on her mother's part: the first at the time of her infancy, when the twins died in 1821; the second at the occasion of her mother's death in her adolescence (78–9).

12. Cross says she died after a long illness. Haight says her death was "probably cancer" (*Biography* 21). Taylor seems to be the first to declare that she died of "breast cancer" based on a letter from Robert Evans to Colonel Francis Newdigate on April 12, 1835, almost ten months before Christiana died. This diagnosis is probably right, though the actual letter is difficult to decipher. In it Robert writes that "Mr Hodgson has a bad opinion of Mrs Evans's [Brest], he believes it to be a cancer and advises her not to have it taken out as he believes it would grow again and much quicker than it has done" (Evans to Newdigate, Newdigate Family Collection, Warwickshire County Record Office). "Brest" is a good guess, but the letters of this particular word are unclear and other interpretations such as "Back" should be considered, even if the word were not misspelled and if it were not so unlikely that Robert would write to his employer about his wife's breast.

13. After her marriage in 1837 to Edward Clarke, Chrissey bore nine children, five of whom died, and her husband became bankrupt, leaving her an over-burdened and impoverished widow dependent upon her brother Isaac for financial support. Chrissey's situation led to much anxiety on Marian's part after she had moved to London, and she even considered helping Chrissey and her family emigrate to Australia.

14. The story portrays an abusive alcoholic husband and his wife's quiet, humiliating refuge in drink. Eliot had recently read Gaskell's *Life of Charlotte Brontë* and was moved by the account of Branwell's alcoholism. The Dempsters are based on the Buchanans.

Mrs Buchanan had been Nancy Wallington, the daughter of Mrs Wallington whose school Mary Ann attended and was a fellow teacher and friend of Maria Lewis, hence the connection with abused and alcoholic women was quite close. In a rare admission of originals for her characters, Eliot told her publisher John Blackwood (who objected to the portrayal of Janet's vice), that the real Dempster was more disgusting than her character and the real Janet's fate much worse (*GEL* 2:347).

15. It is ironic that later in her life it was rumored that Agnes Lewes was "insane, or a hopeless drunkard," which Haight asserts without any citations (*Biography* 490).

16. For an extreme example of taking real life people as originals see Mottram.

17. The Test and Corporation Acts of 1672/3 stipulated that only practicing members of the Church of England could hold public office, thereby excluding Dissenters (or Nonconformists), Catholics, and non-Christians. The Acts were repealed in 1828. Subsequently, English Catholics received the franchise in 1829, Jews in 1858.

18. In *Impressions*, Theophrastus refers disdainfully to the English as "possessors of the most truth and the most tonnage to carry our purer religion over the world and convert mankind to our way of thinking" (150; ch. 18).

19. See Lovesey, *Clerical Character*. Following Haight, McCormack notes in *English Travels* that Isaac's son Frederick, who entered the church, may have been a model for Fred Vincy, who just avoids entering the church.

20. Mary Ann's letters show that she initially took pleasure in her role as aunt to Chrissey's first born son and later to the daughter named for her, but sadly Chrissey's future life would be one of multiple childbirths (and deaths), as well as poverty, widowhood, illness, and an eventual early death in 1859.

21. The only letters we have prior to her rejection of religion in 1841 are to Miss Lewis, Martha Jackson, and her Methodist aunt and uncle, Elizabeth and Samuel Evans. Presumably she wrote other letters that do not survive.

22. For example, Robert Evans mentions Isaac organizing a party for shooting rooks at Arbury to celebrate his twenty-third birthday (Haight, *Biography* 28).

23. On the industrialization, poverty and social responses to them in mid-century Foleshill, see Stephens, ed., "The City of Coventry."

24. On Bray's business and philosophy in the context of mid-Victorian political economy, see Coleman, "Being Good," ch. 2.

25. The same Unitarian minister performed the burial service at Highgate Cemetery for George Lewes and George Eliot. In Eliot's case he read selectively from the Anglican service (see Haight, *Biography*; Collins, *Identifying the Remains*).

26. "Rufus" means red haired and is from the Latin for red. Rufa would be the feminine form. Esther's father in *Felix Holt* is the sympathetic but somewhat ridiculous Rufus Lyon.

27. On the controversy it stirred in Germany, see Richard S. Cromwell's *David Friedrich Strauss and His Place in Modern Thought* (1974).

28. For speculation about the identity of the young man, see Kathleen Adams, ch. 5.

29. See Haight, "George Eliot's Bastards." Of course none of this is mentioned in Bray's autobiography.

3

London and Lewes
1850–4

Few women, I fear have had such reason as I have to think the long sad years of youth were worth living for the sake of middle age.

(December 31, 1857; *GEJ* 72)

As we have seen, Mary Ann's family had long seen her as a problem. Their attempts to marry her respectably failed. They disapproved of her progressive friends. After living abroad, she had traveled literally and figuratively further than ever from their experiences. When she returned to London from Geneva on March 18, 1850, accompanied by D'Albert Durade, she stayed first with Isaac's family at Griff and then with Chrissey's family. However, after the liberating discovery in Geneva that she could live on her own, she felt stifled by provincial English society as well as bored and uncomfortable in her role as maiden aunt, remarking in letters that "old associations are rather painful than otherwise to me" (*GEL* 1:332) and wondering why she had returned to see "people who don't want me" (*GEL* 1:335). Soon, however, she moved into a more comfortable living situation with the Brays at Rosehill (where D'Albert Durade, who had stayed on in England, visited from May 7–10) and resolved to move to London and live on her modest inheritance supplemented by her writing.

Her new life would be even more unconventional than her family could imagine. She had evolved considerably from the young woman who was too pious to attend the London theater in 1838. Strife and compromise with her father had made her more tolerant and conciliatory. Her first major publication, the translation of Strauss, had given her confidence as had the time living abroad. And yet her immediate future

The Life of George Eliot: A Critical Biography, First Edition. Nancy Henry.
© 2012 Nancy Henry. Published 2012 by John Wiley & Sons, Ltd.

would be characterized by a series of emotional relationships and symbolic acts, particularly the dramatic "running off" with Lewes in 1854, which would eventually lead to a complete break with those she had loved in the past, but would also create the conditions for her new identity as an author.

With the prospect of a life beyond Coventry, she now longed for the cultural vitality of London and the opportunities it offered for putting to use talents that were belatedly developing. The Brays helped to find her lodging at 142 The Strand, the office and home of their friend John Chapman, with whom she already had a professional relationship as the publisher of *The Life of Jesus*. She made a trial visit to Chapman's house for two weeks in November 1850, returned home for Christmas, and moved back to Chapman's on January 8, 1851, eager to begin her new life.

A single woman living in lodgings, writing professionally and mixing with the (predominantly male) journalistic and intellectual circles was unusual but not unheard of in London in the 1850s. She thought the change required a new name; from the time she moved to London she began to call herself Marian rather than Mary Ann, perhaps believing that it sounded more sophisticated. Whatever the reasons for her choice, it signified a new, independent identity. In pursuing a career as a writer, she had been encouraged by the example of Eliza Lynn (later Linton), a young woman who had boarded with the Chapmans in their previous residence in Hackney and was making her way as an author.[1] Yet Marian's bravery in moving to London should not be underestimated. To appreciate the symbolic as well as practical significance for her, we should again recall those fictional characters who try but fail to escape a confining domestic environment, including Adam, Maggie, Romola, Felix, and Mordecai.

In her fiction, she imagined what life was like for those who did not migrate from country to city and who, unlike her, could not escape their past and change their lives. Her ambitions were much greater than finding a man to support her. She knew that London was where she should be. These early years in London were crucial to the development of her critical thinking and the formulation of her aesthetic beliefs and practice. They provided her with a perspective from which to view the first 30 years of her life, which she would recall and reshape in her fiction, featuring characters who did not achieve what she had. These were emotionally charged years, which established another experiential basis for fiction after she eventually gained some distance from them and was able to recollect them in relative tranquility. Though most of her novels are set geographically and temporally in a world that invokes her parents' generation and her own childhood, their plots and character-izations are inflected with aspects of her experience as an adult.

Not surprisingly, the intellectual and affective dimensions of her life overlapped and were at times indistinguishable. Her letters to Maria Lewis had demonstrated the passion with which she could speak and write to someone whom she wanted to stimulate her mind. At that time, her intellectual needs took a religious form, but once she rejected that religion Marian quickly outgrew the role of student to a mentor whose mind could not match hers. She then transferred her intellectual passions to Sara Hennell. She also demonstrated a pattern of attraction to men, including Charles Bray, Dr Brabant, and Chapman, from whom she could learn and who seemed to take her ideas seriously. Because of her passion for thinking and learning, the exchange of ideas had always been sexually charged. That a desire for knowledge on the part of a naïve young woman might become one with sexual desire and result in illusions about the men who offered the promise of intellectual compatibility is suggested by situations in her novels. The insight that men could manipulate the intellectual yearnings of women is a distinctive feature of her narratives about women's lives.

In *The Mill on the Floss*, Philip adores Maggie. Lacking sexual physicality to attract her, he seduces her mind by providing books and literary conversation, thereby creating a bond that inhibits her sexual desire for Stephen. Though Philip is on the whole a sympathetic character, he is also calculating in his selfish desire to command declarations of affection from Maggie, knowing that she cannot love him completely and that her promises to him place her in conflict with her brother. In *Middlemarch*, Dorothea is mortified to learn from her sister Celia that Sir James has been humoring her plans to improve workers' cottages because he hopes to marry her. Most famously and powerfully, Dorothea is deluded in her admiration of Casaubon by her Quixotic ideal of marrying an older man who can educate her while she serves the greater end of his important scholarly investigations. These fictional scenarios reflect George Eliot's recollection and representation of her earlier experiences and are an example of how she transformed personal insights into complex psychological situations in her fiction. Not only was she drawn to intellectual men, but intellectual men were drawn to her, even when they could not admire her physically.

In May 1851, the charismatic and visionary but somewhat disorganized Chapman began the process of purchasing the *Westminster Review*, a periodical that had a long history of advancing liberal, even radical, thought. He wanted to revitalize the journal as a forum for intellectual debate, but he was over-committed professionally, financially, and personally, and he lacked the intellectual discipline to achieve this without help. Recognizing Marian's extraordinary talents and intellectual superiority, Chapman invited her to become his editorial assistant. As it turned out, Marian Evans acted as the editor of the *Westminster Review* – anonymously by her own request – from 1851–4, an intellectually exciting and emotionally turbulent period in her life.

Like his professional pursuits, Chapman's domestic situation was chaotic. He lived with his wife Susanna, 14 years his senior and manager of the boarding house. The household also consisted of their children and the children's governess Elizabeth Tilley – Chapman's mistress. Marian had perhaps unknowingly walked into a dangerous and compromising situation. Her presence as a lodger in the household was a temptation to Chapman, whose diary for 1851 shows that he selfishly sought to confuse the intellectual and romantic aspects of their relationship.[2] His attentions to her drew suspicion and eventually jealousy on the part of both his wife and mistress. Emotions ran so high at 142 Strand in March 1851 that Marian returned to Coventry, her attempt to live alone in London an apparent failure. She would remain there until Chapman visited in May 1851 and persuaded her to resume her position as lodger and her new role as editor. She returned to London in September 1851 after his purchase of the *Westminster* was complete. Once divested of its sexual charge, her relationship with Chapman was symbiotic. From her, he gained a remarkably competent editor, and by editing the journal she made professional contacts that advanced her reputation and career.

Despite this entangled romantic episode, she kept her focus on work, revising Chapman's Prospectus for the journal, which helped draw investors and contributors. She was ultimately responsible for putting the *Westminster* at the forefront of mid-Victorian intellectual debate. In her capacity as editor she met, worked, and socialized with the male and female authors who were or would become leading intellectual and literary figures in the mid-Victorian world, including Charles Dickens, Wilkie Collins, Richard Owen, Harriet Martineau, and Bessie Rayner Parkes. The artist and champion of women's causes, Barbara Leigh Smith, would become one of her closest friends.[3]

After her liaison with Chapman cooled into a professional relationship, she began spending time with the scientific and sociological theorist Herbert Spencer, whom she met in August 1851. Spencer was at the time a sub-editor at the *Economist* magazine. The two attended concerts and theater performances together. Her strong desire for intellectual companionship led her to a brief, intense emotional involvement with him, which came to a crisis in July 1852 with his rejection of her expressions of love. He retrospectively wrote that, despite admiring her intellectually, "The lack of physical attraction was fatal" (*GEL* 8:43). Spencer never married. Mindful of his own image, he gave an account of his friendship with Marian Evans before she became George Eliot in his *Autobiography* (1904):

> Of course, as we were frequently seen together, people drew their inferences. Very slight evidence usually suffices the world for positive conclusions; and here the evidence seemed strong. Naturally, therefore, quite definite statements became current. There were reports that I was in love with her, and that we were about to be married. But neither of these reports was true. (1:399)

Spencer's attempts to control information about their relationship during his lifetime were largely successful. He intervened in Cross's representation of his relationship with Eliot, resulting in the details of that relationship being obscured until much later.[4]

Reviewing the contents of the letters written in July 1852 when Marian was vacationing alone at the seaside town of Broadstairs in Kent (where Spencer briefly

Figure 10 Herbert Spencer, photograph by John Watkins, 1860s (© National Portrait Gallery, London)

joined her), we can see the reason for such caution. Knowing that he could not love her, she asked:

> I want to know if you can assure me that you will not forsake me, and that you will always be with me as much as you can and share your thoughts and feelings with me. If you become attached to some one else, then I must die, but until then I could gather courage to work and make life valuable, if only I had you near me. (*GEL* 8:56–7)

Despite the emotional letters, Spencer's biographer Mark Francis believes that Marian was the love of Spencer's life and that his denial of this was a "betrayal of his affections and of his much vaunted truthfulness" (59). Francis points out the differences between the original manuscript and the published version of Spencer's *Autobiography*. In the unpublished portions of the manuscript, Spencer emphasizes Marian's feminine qualities, whereas the published version leaves an impression of her as distinctly masculine, in accord with his story that it was her physical unattractiveness (rather than his own fear of intimacy) that prevented him from loving her fully. Going against the grain of most George Eliot biographies, Francis believes that Spencer declared his love first, but was incapable of reciprocating the intensity of her response. Francis thinks Spencer never escaped from "the bondage of his love" for her (62) and that his thoughts in later life about his only love affair "were the tormented effusions of an unfulfilled personal loss" (64).

Francis's view that the relationship was more important to Spencer than to Marian is supported by the fact that the desperation of her self-abasing letter passed quickly, and by the end of July she wrote to Spencer that she was "not unhappy" and suggests that they "forget the past," offering him "such companionship as there is in me" (*GEL* 8:61). Back in London, she was coming to admire another *Westminster* contributor and friend of Spencer's, George Henry Lewes, to whom Chapman first introduced her during a chance encounter in a bookstore on October 6, 1851 (*GEL* 2:97–8). But Lewes did not take a prominent place in her life until the following year when Spencer reintroduced them. Lewes was an accomplished journalist and drama critic, as well as a playwright, actor, and novelist. A progressive thinker, he foresaw the importance and authority of scientific inquiry and was already contributing to the popularization of natural science in articles he wrote in addition to his literary and theater reviews. His interest in science would intensify and become more serious and specialized. As we will see, an aspect of Eliot and Lewes's mutual influence on each other was their abandonment of popular writing, which had characterized the early years of their relationship, and their decision instead to concentrate on writing for an elite, educated audience that was more suited to their respective, astonishing self-taught knowledge.

Marian's letters to the Brays at this time reveal her deepening respect for Lewes, whom she had initially described as a "miniature Mirabeau" (*GEL* 1:367) in reference to the Frenchman's face, which was, like Lewes's, pitted from small pox. Given the rejection she had experienced from men whose minds she had once admired (Chapman and Spencer), but who felt compelled to point out her lack of physical attractions, perhaps the lack of conventional beauty attracted her the more to the man the Carlyles referred to privately as "the ape." Lewes's "ugliness" has been overstated by biographers based on comments by gossipers like the Carlyles (Charles Duffy 222–3; Crompton 90). Ugliness, however, like beauty, is relative. The most intriguing observation of Lewes's appearance came from Charlotte Brontë, who wrote after meeting him that "the aspect of Lewes' face almost moves me to tears – it is so wonderfully like Emily – her eyes, her features – the very nose, the somewhat prominent mouth, the forehead – even at moments the expression" (qtd. in Ashton, *GHL* 104). The strange comment is quoted in Gaskell's *Life of Charlotte Brontë*, but we do not know what Lewes or Marian thought of it.

Whatever she felt about her own attractiveness or that of Lewes, Marian was charmed by his sparkling conversation and humor, which would in the future constitute a healthy counter-balance to her tendencies toward solemnity in

Figure 11 George Henry Lewes, pencil drawing by Anne Gliddon, 1840 (© National Portrait Gallery, London)

conversation as well as to the sometimes debilitating self-doubt and depression she suffered. From her first novel to her last book, she would make what might seem like the obvious observations that "there is no direct correlation between eyelashes and morals" (*AB* 154; ch. 15) and that "wit cannot be seated in the upper lip, and that the balance of the haunches in walking has nothing to do with the subtle discrimination of ideas" (*Impressions* 7; ch. 1). Furthermore, some of her most physically beautiful characters are the least moral (Hetty in *Adam Bede*, Tito in *Romola,* and Rosamond in *Middlemarch*), though this should be qualified by noting the combination of beauty and goodness in Dorothea in *Middlemarch* and Mirah and Daniel in *Daniel Deronda.* Her interest in the relationship between inner and outer beauty seems to be a response both to her own experience, to the theories of Spencer (who insisted on a correlation between physical and mental beauty), and to the ideas of phrenology, which neither she nor Lewes could accept.[5]

Marian was right to detect what she referred to as Lewes's "mask of flippancy" (*GEL* 2:98). His cheerfulness and energy disguised the fact that he was passing through a period of depression, even despair, at the time they began to know each

Figure 12   George Henry Lewes and Agnes Lewes with Thornton Hunt. Pencil drawing by William Makepeace Thackeray, 1848 (© National Portrait Gallery, London)

other, as he later wrote in his diary (*GHLĴ* January 28, 1859; qtd. in Haight, *Biography* 133). His domestic life was, like that of Bray, Chapman, Thornton Hunt, Wilkie Collins, Dickens, and many other Victorians, irregular. When he met Marian on October 6, 1851, he was living with his wife, Agnes, and four sons: Charles (b. 1842), Thornton (b. 1844), Herbert (b. 1846), and Edmund (b. 1850). A daughter would be born on October 21, 1851. At some unknown date, Agnes Lewes had become involved with her husband's closest friend, Thornton Hunt, who had his own wife, Katherine Gliddon Hunt, and a family that would eventually grow to include ten children. These were the same Hunts that Marian had met at Rosehill in May 1851 when Chapman visited and urged her to return to London. Katherine was pregnant at the time, and Marian had liked her particularly.

The *Leader* and the Legacy of Shelley

Lewes and Thornton Hunt had met when Lewes was an acolyte of Thornton's father Leigh Hunt (1784–1859). Lewes contacted the elder Hunt – a living representative of the Romantic era in poetry – in 1834 when he was planning to write a biography of Shelley. After meeting Leigh Hunt, Lewes became one of the young admirers who gathered around the iconic political radical, friend to the second-generation Romantics including Shelley, and founder of the "Cockney School" of poetry. Lewes soon became friends with Thornton, who as a child had known Shelley. Thornton and Lewes later became professional collaborators as well as intimate friends.[6] Their mutual admiration for Shelley has led biographers to claim that they took inspiration from the Romantic poet's radical views not only about politics and religion but also about sex and marriage.[7] However, there is no evidence apart from his association with Hunt that Lewes advocated "free love," "wife swapping," or even a form of socialism that would do away with marriage. And there is surprisingly little direct evidence of Hunt's views. Biographies uniformly make claims about Lewes's belief in free love but without citing evidence of it.

Figure 13 Leigh Hunt's circle, including George Henry Lewes, Vincent Hunt, and William Bell Scott. Etching by William Bell Scott, 1830s (William Bell Scott, *Autobiographical Notes of the Life of William Bell Scott*, Harper and Brothers, 1892)

In 1850, Lewes and Hunt co-founded the radical periodical, the *Leader*. The journal was divided into two parts: Thornton was the political editor, writing much of the content of the journal's first half devoted to politics; and Lewes was the literary editor, soliciting book reviews and acting as the regular theater critic in the journal's second half devoted to culture. Established in the wake of the Chartist reform movement of the 1840s, the journal advocated a variety of political reforms and freedoms. It also upheld a realist literary aesthetic, suggesting a connection between political reform and literary realism.[8] Lewes would move away from this connection between art and politics in his later critical writings about realism, just as for George Eliot realistic representation eventually became more of an aesthetic value for its own sake rather than a practice associated with a democratizing politics.

Lewes worked diligently to launch the journal, traveling to the north of England to generate subscriptions and contributions from backers with industrial ties while Hunt remained in London. In Lewes's surviving letters to Hunt from 1849, he usually addressed his friend "Dear Thornton" (less frequently "Brother Thornton"), and he almost always signed them with "God bless you" and "brother Lewes," or simply "Brother."[9] Existing letters show no evidence that Lewes thought Hunt and Agnes were having an affair, much less that he encouraged such relations.

Lewes never published his biography of Shelley, primarily because he could not get sanction from the poet's widow, Mary Shelley (Ashton, *GHL* 20), but his review article of various editions of Shelley's work in the April 1841 issue of the *Westminster* gives us an indication of his perspective on Shelley's life and poetry. He argues that Shelley should not be measured by any "moral yard of our own" ("Percy Bysshe Shelley" 305) and recommends "stepping down from our judgment seats and examining the man and his actions, not from *our* central point of view, but rather from *his*, which is the only just method" (305). The article makes clear that Lewes had definite views about the value of biographical criticism, which he would apply to his later biography of Goethe. He says nothing specific about Shelley's sexual behavior or opinions beyond the fact that his first marriage was unhappy and that he has been unfairly accused of sexual misconduct. Shelley felt justified in leaving a wife he did not love for a woman he did. Even though his writing advocated the type of "free love" for which he became notorious to his own and later generations, he married Mary Shelley, who, along with his parents, became the executor and protector of his literary estate.[10]

Shelley's belief in "free love" has been used to fabricate a version of Lewes's young married life. Echoing previous biographers, but citing no sources, Ashton writes of Hunt and Lewes: "Worshippers of Shelley, they adopted the poet's advocacy of free love inside marriage" (*GHL* 5). Ashton also claims that Lewes "embraced the Shelleyan principles of free thinking in religion and free living in sexual matters, condoning, and even encouraging, his wife Agnes's adultery with his friend

Thornton Hunt" (*142 Strand* 109). Without documentation, it is difficult to make this leap from Shelley's views to Lewes's conduct, and subsequent biographers of George Eliot, such as Hughes, and biographers of her friends and acquaintances, such as Mark Francis, cite Ashton as a source for these claims, though they also appear earlier in Haight's *Biography*.

It is true that the *Leader* published articles exploring various forms of socialism from Owen to Fourier. Hunt, for example, contributed an article on "Social Reform" (October 19, 1850) in which he wrote that communism "is directly antagonistic to any idea of personal property, either in things, in privileges, or in the actions of others; and among the theoretical consequences it follows that perfect Communism would destroy the institution of marriage" (710). Hunt's piece, however, intends to explain rather than advocate such extreme views, as is evident when he writes: "This is the alarming and opprobrious consequence which is generally alleged against Communism" (710).

This generally positive interpretation of communism in the year that the English translation of Marx's *Communist Manifesto* (1850) was published is interesting for what it tells us about Hunt's, Lewes's, and Eliot's exposure to such radical political philosophies in 1850.[11] But it tells us nothing about their ideas on the subject of sexual freedom, any more than the article Haight cites as evidence of Hunt's belief in "free love" (*Biography* 131). That article, "The Discipline of Art" (*Leader* July 3, 1852, 639–40), refers to the impossibility of disciplining human passions, but does so in the context of artistic representation. Haight uses this quotation to support his claim: "Agnes had merely followed her feelings; it was a principle they all accepted" (*Biography* 131). Hughes uses the same quotation to support even more sensational claims (*The Last Victorian* 142).

There is at least one surviving, unpublished letter from Thornton Hunt to the radical activist George Jacob Holyoake that suggests the nature of his views. The impetus for the letter is Hunt's concern that Holyoake is being too rash in excluding from his Secularist movement those whose morals he disapproves. Hunt complains, "in insisting upon 'moral' conduct on the part of persons aiding movements, you may do a gross injustice" (Hunt to Holyoake, National Co-operative Archive, Manchester). He is particularly interested in refuting a position called "moral" but which is actually economic: "the one argument which remains to contravene systematic anarchy in the intercourse of the sexes; that is, the necessity of monogamy for progeny." Arguing implicitly for "perfect freedom" in sexual relations, he contends: "The seducer is mean and false; no candid man can be a seducer, but you will find some difficulty, without the help of Bible or Koran, to establish an act of *malum in se* against the man who holds that there ought to be no restraint on personal affection except conventions for the benefit of offspring." Written on September 13, 1852, this letter comes closer than any evidence provided in previous biographies of Eliot and Lewes to explaining a philosophy behind Hunt's relationship with Agnes. The two were about to embark (or had already embarked) on an otherwise inexplicable course of producing illegitimate offspring, even while both remained within the conventions of their respective marriages, as this letter suggests, only for the benefit of the children.[12]

Certainly, Hunt's letter to Holyoake (not cited by any biographers) supports the notion that he believed in freedom of sexual relations within the social conventions beneficial to offspring. But the conclusion that Agnes and Lewes shared his beliefs must remain, in the absence of evidence, mere conjecture. I will return to the dubiousness of the frequently made claim that Lewes encouraged Hunt's affair with Agnes because they "all accepted" a philosophy of "free love," but first, it will be useful to review the evidence of Lewes's relationship to Shelley's ideas. His writings show a self-consciousness about Shelley's influence on his own generation, and while he touches on politics and personal morality, Lewes is always primarily interested in the aesthetic value of Shelley's art.

In 1841, Lewes admired Shelley's freedom of spirit, but he wrote about Shelley in Victorian terms, perhaps because he was writing in the respectable if liberal *Westminster*, or out of respect for Mary Shelley, who was still living. What seems to attract Lewes to Shelley is the poet's "unyielding worship of truth" ("Percy Bysshe Shelley," *Westminster Review,* 307), and the consistency of his conduct with his views. He contrasts Shelley's admirable behavior with that of the morally depraved, licentious Byron, whose conduct he does not shrink from judging and condemning and whose poetry he prudishly vows not to read. He describes Shelley as a man for whom women are "neither slaves nor angels – but women" (331): "if a wife be meant to be a *partner* of your life – a sharer in your spiritual hopes and successes as well as in your material ledger successes, then it is in Shelley you will find the true ideal of woman" (331). In defense of Shelley, he invokes Mary Shelley's mother, Mary Wollstonecraft, who strongly advocated female education in her *Vindication of the Rights of Women* (1792). These same views were ones Marian Evans would approve when she wrote her own article "Margaret Fuller and Mary Wollstonecraft" (*Leader* Oct. 13, 1855, 988–9).

Lewes's reading of Shelley the man and poet is important for our understanding of both the personal beliefs he would bring to his relationship with Marian Evans and the literary climate that the two would help to create in their capacity as literary critics in the 1850s. If he embraced Shelley's writings about "free love" in 1841, he gives no indication of it in his review; instead he shows respect for women and advocates equal partnership rather than sexual freedom as the ideal in marriage. Later writings by Lewes demonstrate a consistent desire for equality between spouses, leading us to wonder about his relationship with Agnes and also uncannily predicting his future meeting with Marian Evans.

Another example of this foreshadowing is *The Apprenticeship of Life* (March 30–June 8 1850), a novel Lewes began in the *Leader* but unaccountably never finished. The novel is a quasi-bildungsroman of Amand, who marries Hortense when he is very young. After ten years of marriage, he falls in love with Adrienne, the daughter of General Laboissière, a powerful politician. The narrator resumes the life of Amand ten years after his marriage, thereby suggesting an autobiographical connection since in 1850 Lewes, too, had been married for ten years. He describes Amand's feelings when questioning whether he could be in love with another woman who is "not handsome":

> Perhaps, however, the peculiarity of her face is even more powerful than beauty; for it is full of character, it is strange, unlike what you have seen before. . . . That is the verdict on first inspection. Learn to know Adrienne, and you will understand how, if a man did love her, he would love her with the devotion of his life. (*Leader* May 25, 1850, 211)

Lewes had not quite mastered the technique of what we now call "free indirect discourse," so the thoughts of Amand seem confused with those of the narrator. He later apologizes for his style when he pauses his story to discourse on the morality of Amand's dilemma and the realism of his subject matter: "I am trying to give expression to the *truth*, recording . . . life as I actually observe it" (*Leader* June 1, 1850, 236). Noting that readers may be shocked at Amand's love for another woman and his viewing his wife as an obstacle to that love, Lewes continues, "but I ask my fair antagonist whether she thinks consonant with *truth* that Amand should outlive his passion for Hortense, and whether having outlived it, he was not, by the laws of his own passionate nature, forced to love again? Do we not see similar cases every day of our lives?" (236).

This unfinished novel is significant for several reasons. Firstly, its questioning of marriage and its implicit argument for divorce are consistent with debates carried on in the pages of the *Leader* at the time.[13] Secondly, it gives some insight, albeit obscure, into Lewes's own situation. Was he the man who had fallen out of love with his wife and found greater fulfillment with another? Or could he be describing the experience of Thornton Hunt, still his closest friend, who had fallen in love with another man's wife? Although Lewes had not even met Marian Evans at this time, he would later describe her in language that echoes his narrator's, "learn to know Adrienne." He wrote of Marian in his journal for January 1859, "to know her was to love her" (Ashton, *GHL* 194).

Finally, his narrative technique of defending the *truth* of his subject matter against an imagined skeptical lady reader is uncannily like that George Eliot would use in her early novels, albeit more effectively and artfully. Lewes had previously published two novels, *Ranthorpe* (1847) and *Rose, Blanche and Violet* (1848). Presumably, he recognized his own limitations as a novelist and never aspired to greatness in this genre. His literary criticism, on the other hand, is some of the best of its time, and it mirrored Eliot's statements about realism in her review essays. The Prospectus for the *Leader*, expressing its philosophy and intentions as a radical journal and used to solicit financial support, shows that Lewes and his collaborators saw a relationship between art and politics:

> The ARTS will be treated in a congenial spirit. . . . Original composition, in prose or verse, will complete the round. ESSAYS on literary or social topics, VERSES animated by the living interests of the day, FICTION expressing what of life eludes mere newspaper intelligence, political or literary discussion – these will lend their help to our main purpose – to the free utterance of opinion, and the restoration of heart-feeling to the business of life. (March 30, 1850, 22)

In its general statement about the objectives of the journal, the Prospectus appeals to a Romantic spirit whereby "immortal influences" are inherited from the past and transmitted to the future. The *Leader* will represent life as it is, disseminating information globally and nationally and promoting above all freedom of speech:

> We intend it for a direct reflex of Life, as it exists – in its triumphs and in its trials, in its errors and in its achieved truths, in its relics of the past, its enduring influences, and its eternal hopes. We shall strive to animate those hopes and the endeavour which they inspire. For the struggling nationalities abroad, we will offer a voice from among the English people; in the English people we will strive to reawaken a frank and wise nationality; so that the Present, which discerns the wasted efforts of the Past, may learn to know its own opportunities and expedite the achievements of the Future. The boldness of our out-speaking we justify by a reverential spirit, and by a hopeful faith that trusts less to the contrivances of man, than to the immortal influences whose freest action we shall seek to promote. (22)

Hunt and Lewes felt themselves to be inheritors of a particular Romantic-era spirit – that of revolution and freedom. And yet for Lewes more than Hunt, that spirit would have to find an historical shape that was right for the mid-nineteenth-century context. Hunt seemed to keep alive rather than adapt earlier Romantic, revolutionary ideals. In this respect Lewes already had much in common with Mary Ann Evans, who also wrote about Truth as Lewes wrote about Freedom – in abstract terms that seemed in need of a modern application or embodiment.

As a young woman, Mary Ann Evans had imbibed the atmosphere of her father Robert Evans's Toryism, the other legacy of those early decades of the nineteenth century, which was fundamentally opposed to the radicalism of Shelley and Leigh Hunt. Neither Eliot nor Lewes was political in the same sense as Thornton Hunt. Their strongest beliefs concerned the pursuit of truth and particularly truth in art. And so, remarkably, in 1849–50, just before they met, they were in their separate lives and in their separate ways working toward a theory of realistic representation that would crystallize when they came together. Soon, together they would develop and disseminate a theory of realistic representation that Eliot put into practice and which would become the Victorian period's distinctive contribution to the genre of the novel.

Lewes's review article on Shelley helps write the genealogy and create the mythology of a coherent group of writers we now call the Romantics. Lewes had direct connections to this previous generation of poets (through Leigh Hunt and Mary Shelley). During the same period, Mary Ann Evans, at home in Coventry, was emerging from her intense religiosity and rediscovering Byron, Shelley, Coleridge, Southey, and her favorite, Wordsworth (Haight, *Biography* 29). Like Lewes, she had only one degree of separation from some of the Romantic poets in 1843 when she stayed with Dr Brabant, who had been a physician to both Samuel Taylor Coleridge (1772–1834) and Thomas Moore (1779–1852). The legacy of Romanticism was very real to young writers in the 1840s, who were simultaneously influenced by this inheritance and searching for their own voice in reaction to it. Lewes's ability to define the distinctive qualities of the past generation was characteristic of the insight that enabled him to recognize the value of Eliot's fiction, which established new standards of realistic representation through plots that are mostly set during the previous generation and explore in fiction the same relations of past, present, and future as invoked in the *Leader* Manifesto.[14]

Lewes's focus on Shelley as the poet whose life and writing embodied the pursuit of "truth" shows us how the Victorians were interpreting the past and preparing a future for English literature in which the realist novel would predominate. In the years after the "Hungry Forties" and the European revolutions of 1848, the spirit of which the *Leader* encouraged, that realist novel form would help replace radicalism and revolution with middle-class morality and liberal reform. In his article on Shelley, Lewes observes that after the French Revolution "there arose a band of poets to utter the new doctrines" ("Percy Bysshe Shelley" 319). Scott took refuge in a dead past, Wordsworth in an impossible state of Nature, and Moore in Orientalism (320). Only Shelley was a poet standing for the pursuit of truth as truth presented itself to him, for "all truths are *truths of periods*, and not truths for eternity" (317).

While Lewes's idealism reflects his position as a young inheritor of Romantic ideas, he was less political and more conservative than his enthusiastic friend Thornton Hunt. We can imagine them both being carried away with the prospect of invigorating Shelleyan principles, but Lewes changed with his times (and helped direct them), while Hunt, as far as we know, seemed to cling to a youthful radicalism, which Lewes would come to regard as simply an excuse to escape responsibility. Thornton showed characteristics for which his father Leigh Hunt was well known and which were famously caricatured by Dickens in his portrait of Mr Skimpole in *Bleak House* (1852–3). It is clear from Thornton's letter to Holyoake that his rejection of conventional morality includes rejecting the obligations to pay his debts, as he writes to defend the morality of a man from the judgment that "if he does not adopt the ordinary truth of morality – pay his way, do all he can to rise in life, and keep 'faithful' to one woman, he must be a scamp, not reputable" (Hunt to Holyoake, Sept. 13, 1852). Thornton's irresponsibility would continue to harass Lewes for years to come in ways he could not predict when they were launching the *Leader* in 1849.

Lewes's passionate writing about truth in literature and life is similar to Marian's writing about truth in her letters at the same time. In 1839, she told Maria Lewis her opinion about the superiority of truth over fiction and her preference for histories and biographies: "When a person has exhausted the wonders of truth, there is no other resort than fiction" (*GEL* 1:23). In 1841, the year of Lewes's article on Shelley, she was experiencing religious doubt and wrote delicately to Maria that her "only desire is to know the truth, my only fear to cling to error" (*GEL* 1:120–1). In 1843, she wrote to Sara Hennell that "we turn to truth of feeling as the only universal bond of union" (*GEL* 1:162). This passionate desire for truth may be – like duty – another form of her past religious fervor. It may also be a correlative of the Shelleyan Romanticism so admired by Lewes. In some uncharacteristic letters written to her Coventry friend John Sibree in 1848, for example, she expressed her enthusiasm for foreign revolutions, but she also demonstrates the preference for gradual reform that would characterize her political position throughout her life (*GEL* 1:254). In her fiction, she would translate her dedication to truth into the language of realism, leading a literary trend in which Romantic idealism for social change coalesced with the authority of scientific inquiry and its pursuit of truth in the form of facts, developing a new aesthetic in fiction.

The views about truth in life and literature that Lewes and Marian Evans were formulating simultaneously but independently reveal how, on the one hand, both writers were products of their generation, and on the other hand, how both were seizing new ideas that they would make distinctly their own. They were equipped by their reading with an understanding of the past that enabled them to shape the future. In their respective critical reviews, they saw "truth" in literature as a moral imperative, a position that would be central to Eliot's early work and would influence the fiction of the mid-nineteenth century. Toward the end of her life, the argument for the moral value of telling the truth in fiction (realism) would seem less important to make than the argument for the moral value of writing good literature. As we will see, it was a subtle shift of emphasis that tracked the experiments of her contemporaries in aestheticism and eventually what we now call Modernism.

Comparing their ideas before they met, we can see how Lewes and Marian would be attracted to each other and how naturally they would join forces in their critical essays to articulate the value of truth in literature for their own generation. Furthermore, Lewes's article on Shelley in the *Westminster*, the journal Marian Evans would later edit, shows his emerging voice as an influential literary critic, moving beyond the British Romantic aesthetic in both poetry and fiction to advocate new and original forms of writing in ways that accorded with George Eliot's own ideas about literature and that would influence her later experiments in realism.

Triangulated Desire and the Other Woman

Although the facts about this period in each of their lives are obscure because many documents, including Lewes's diaries, are presumed to be destroyed, it is probable that Lewes and Marian became intimate at the end of 1852 or beginning of 1853.[15] In October 1853, Marian moved out of Chapman's house and into her own lodgings in Cambridge Street, not far from where Lewes was living. In December 1853, she resigned as editor of the *Westminster*. Work continued on the *Leader,* and she contributed a number of reviews, helping Lewes to meet deadlines in April 1854 when poor health prevented his working. He had in fact experienced something of a physical breakdown from overwork and perhaps psychological strain. His doctor ordered him first to the countryside for a month's rest and, when that failed, to try a then-fashionable "water cure."[16]

At the time that Marian's relationship with Lewes was deepening, Hunt and Lewes were conducting the *Leader* together and Lewes was still living at home with Agnes, though it seems certain that Agnes was also involved with Hunt. While Lewes was unhappy, he may not have given up on the marriage yet. But from the beginning, Lewes's complicated married life involved Marian in triangulated relationships in which she occupied various positions. The emotions she experienced and the conditions she observed found their way into her fiction, which from the first abounds in erotic triangles, secrecy, deception, scandal, and gossip. These experiences can help to identify and explain the patterns of such triangles in her fiction. Such patterns were available to her as narrative conventions in Victorian fiction, and indeed, in all literature. Any novelist would be interested in both the psychological dimensions and the narrative possibilities of infidelity, betrayal, guilt, and jealousy, and such features would predominate particularly in the "sensation" fiction of the 1860s. And yet George Eliot never aspired to the type of popular success that would exploit these conventions. Rather, the triangular aspects of her plots have deeper sources in her personal life and in that permanent condition of being at once the "other woman" and the second wife.

There are several social issues to consider when thinking about how George Eliot's personal experience informs her fictional representations of marriage and triangulated desire. These are: deception (inside and outside of marriage), adultery, second marriages (both legal and not legal), and divorce. We have seen that Marian had direct experience of adultery from her observations of the Brays, flirtation with Brabant, affair with Chapman, and relationship with Lewes. Her two closest male friends in 1852, Bray and Chapman, were unfaithful to their wives but remained married. Second marriages were common in the Victorian period, and bigamous relationships (often involving a man with one legal and one non-legal family) were common enough that Marian had encountered several examples among her close friends. Other irregularities were also known and to a degree tolerated. Barbara Leigh Smith Bodichon's father, for example, never married her mother, whose social

Figure 14 Barbara Bodichon, ambrotype by Holmes of New York (© National Portrait Gallery, London)

status was significantly below his. While Benjamin Leigh Smith treated Barbara and her three siblings well, providing for their education and inheritance, they were still marked with the stigma of illegitimacy. This stigma did not, however, prevent Barbara – who inherited enough money from her father to live on – from having a successful personal and professional life.

One reason why the various configurations of adultery and bigamy were so pervasive was the restrictive nature of divorce laws. Marian was much more likely to know people who were in adulterous or bigamous relationships than to know people who were divorced. There were famous cases, such as Caroline Norton's, and there was much agitation for relaxing the divorce laws in journals, including the *Leader*.[17] The very years in which Marian Evans entered into her unconventional union and assumed her role as Mrs Lewes were the years when the reform of the divorce laws – and hence the very nature of the matrimonial bond – were being debated. Dickens's highly public legal separation from his wife in 1858, for example, was much discussed in the London literary world (Nayder). It is hardly surprising that betrayal, adultery, second marriages, and the states of matrimony generally are so central to her fiction.

They were central to most Victorian fiction, but Eliot's case is distinctive because of her own ambiguous position as neither wife nor mistress, or perhaps more accurately, as both.

Agnes Jervis Lewes is a shadowy figure in biographies of Eliot and is rarely considered relevant in criticism of Eliot's novels. She is known as the woman who committed adultery with Thornton Hunt, and is said to have begun bearing Hunt's children prior to Lewes's meeting Marian in October of 1851. Her letters do not survive, and we have no way of knowing what she thought or believed. The pretty little blond woman, affectionately known as Rose, might lie behind a character like Rosamond in *Middlemarch*, the pretty blond wife who made Lydgate's life so miserable. Most importantly, all of Eliot's fiction was written with the background presence of Agnes Lewes in her life, and we must keep this in mind when considering the biographical circumstances under which she created her fictional plots and characters.

Lewes and Agnes were married in 1840. Hunt and his wife Katherine began their communal living arrangement in Bayswater in 1844. Members of the household

Figure 15 Thornton Hunt and Katherine Gliddon Hunt (as identified by Molly Tatchell in her *Keats-Shelley Memorial Bulletin* essay "Thornton Hunt"). The artist is unknown but could be Samuel Laurence, who lived with the Hunts in the 1840s

included Katherine's extended family as well as the artist Samuel Laurence and his wife. In 1849, they moved into another communal house in Hammersmith with a reconfigured group of friends and family (Tatchell 15–17). The Leweses never lived in these houses, as was asserted in some earlier biographies, though they visited frequently. Unreliable accounts of contemporary gossip, including Eliza Lynn Linton's novel *Christopher Kirkland* and memoir *My Literary Life*, have associated what may have been a practical economic arrangement or an experiment in communal living with the practice of free love amongst members of the household. But there is no evidence of this and certainly none to support the idea that because the Leweses were part of this circle of friends that they therefore believed or practiced free love.[18]

It is thought that Hunt began his affair with Agnes in 1849 because on April 16, 1850, Agnes gave birth to Edmund Lewes.[19] At that time, Lewes and Agnes were living with their three sons, Charles, Thornton, and Herbert. A fourth son, St Vincent, had died in March 1850, just before Edmund's birth and the publication of the *Leader*'s first volume. Lewes officially registered Edmund's birth, listing himself as father. In a *Leader* article from the time, he relates an interview with a practitioner of mesmerism: "As a final question I asked about my family, which consists of four boys and a human Rose in the shape of their mother" (June 15, 1850, 285).

On October 21, 1851, Lewes registered the birth of a daughter, Rose Agnes Lewes. In the summer of 1852, when Marian was in Broadstairs pondering her relationship with Spencer, Lewes moved out of his family's London home at 26 Bedford Square, Kensington and lodged in the flat of a friend (*GHLL* 1:191; Ashton, *GHL* 333). After his departure, Agnes would bear two more children: Ethel Isabella Lewes (October 9, 1853) and Mildred Jane Lewes (May 26, 1857) (Ashton, *GHL* 122). It was a family of dependents that Lewes and Eliot would support until the end of their respective lives. It certainly seems unfair that they should have to bear the financial responsibility for Thornton Hunt's disbelief in the conventional morality of paying one's debts, and yet Agnes, whose own voice has been completely silenced in the historical record, has been hardly treated by Eliot biographers, even ostensibly feminist ones. Haight, for example, refers to Agnes's "illegitimate brood" (*Biography* 132) and her "mingled brood" (145).[20]

Agnes may be represented in biographies as a pariah hidden away with her illegitimate brood, but Lewes visited her and her children regularly until the end of his life, and Marian, following her success as George Eliot, paid to support Agnes and her family. It is therefore useful to think about Marian's position with respect to Agnes throughout her entire relationship with Lewes. In particular, French critic René Girard's classic study of triangulated desire in Western literature and the nineteenth-century novel, *Deceit, Desire and the Novel* (1961), may provide a way to think about triangulations in Eliot's life and writing. Girard argues: "The great novelists reveal the imitative nature of desire" (14). Among Girard's many insights into the "mimetic desire" that structures novels from Cervantes to Virginia Woolf and including Eliot's contemporary Gustave Flaubert (1821–80), is that the object of desire is less important than the relationship between the one who desires and the "mediator" whose desire he imitates. What Girard calls the "*vaniteux*" will desire any object so long as he is convinced that it is already desired by another person whom he admires (7). Furthermore: "The mediator's prestige is imparted to the object of desire and confers upon it an illusory value" (17). The relationship between those who desire (usually two men who become rivals) is more important than either man's relationship to the desired object/woman.

In her ground-breaking study of male homosocial desire, *Between Men* (1985), Eve Kosofsky Sedgwick picks up on the male bond that Girard mentions but does not pursue, except in terms of rivalry and jealousy. She notes that later psycho-analytic, Marxist, and feminist critics offer "analytical tools for treating the erotic triangle not as an ahistorical, Platonic form. . . but as a sensitive register precisely for delineating relationships of power and meaning" (27). For her, triangulated relationships reveal social structures and power dynamics, especially of class, gender, and sexuality.

Girard does not write about Eliot, and Sedgwick writes about *Adam Bede* in a context unrelated to the sexual triangles that characterize the novel. Subsequently, critics have not tended to apply theories of triangulated desire to Eliot's work. The most seductive aspect of Girard's theory is that it leads us to find triangles everywhere. His work in the 1960s was responding to structuralist criticism, and he is careful to make the triangle a literary device. Characteristically for the period, he does not introduce biographical connections. Even Sedgwick's more historicizing project in 1985, influenced by Lacan, Marx, and feminist criticism, is similarly uninterested in any biographical dimensions of the texts.

There is an empirical basis for the erotic triangles that proliferate in Eliot's fiction. The notion that the "mediator's prestige" confers an illusory value on the object of desire might apply to lives as well as to art, especially lives as steeped in literary traditions, theatricality, fictional personae, and secrets as those of Thornton Hunt and Lewes. Thornton's love for Lewes may have conferred a value on Agnes as a potential lover that would explain the attraction more successfully than the simple notion that he believed in "free love." As Eliot would observe of people's motives generally: "sagacity, persuaded that men usually act and speak from distinct motives, with a consciously proposed end in view, is certain to waste its energies on imaginary game" (*Mill* 39; bk. 1, ch. 3). "We live from hand to mouth," she continues, "with a small family of immediate desires. . . ." Biographers, too, must resist being overly sagacious in attributing motives. Hunt was certainly a man of Romantic principles, but his personal actions may have turned on small attractions, desires and rivalries rather than an ideology of "Shelleyan" free love. We do not know if Hunt had other lovers, but we know that for a time he was fixated on Agnes to an irrational degree of self-justified irresponsibility. His conception of himself as a rival to Lewes is encapsulated in his Romantic, anachronistic act of challenging Lewes to a duel when the latter suggested that his failure to help support Agnes was dishonorable (GHLJ, December 16, 1856, qtd. in Haight, *Biography* 218).

In Eliot's fiction, mimetic desire appears in Arthur Donnithorne's attraction to Hetty, the woman Adam Bede loves, and Adam's attraction to the woman his brother loves, Dinah Morris. In "The Lifted Veil," Latimer is attracted to his brother's fiancée, Bertha; William Dane is attracted to his "brother" Silas's fiancée in *Silas Marner*; and, in a gender reversal, Maggie is attracted to her cousin Lucy's fiancé Stephen in *The Mill*. In *Middlemarch*, we also see rivalry in Will Ladislaw's attraction to his hated cousin Casaubon's wife, and Casaubon's irrational jealousy of Will, which seems to exceed consideration for the love object, Dorothea. Eliot offers interesting variations on the Girardian triangle when some of her "rival" males concede without a fight. Seth Bede, for example, passively accepts his brother Adam's marriage to his beloved Dinah, and Daniel Deronda is also passive with respect to Gwendolen's marriage to Grandcourt, a man he mistakenly believes is enjoying the inheritance he might have had if Sir Hugo had acknowledged him as a son.

Eliot's experience with adultery – her own with Chapman and Lewes as well as those of her close friends – was of an intense kind that seared itself into her consciousness and shaped her identity. As she drew heavily on her memories, dwelling on and returning to particular aspects of those youthful experiences – such as the religious yearnings of Maggie Tulliver and Dorothea Brooke – so she would continue to draw on her experiences and observations of triangular desire as viewed from various perspectives. Adam Bede feels rage at Arthur's seduction of Hetty; Silas Marner feels bitterness toward William for conniving to steal Sarah; Maggie suffers paralyzing guilt in trying to decide whether it is wrong to love Stephen; Dorothea feels bewildered and hurt when she suspects that Will Ladislaw may be romantically involved with Rosamond; Rosamond is determined to "enslave" Will, drawing him into a triangle with her husband Lydgate; and Gwendolen feels horror when she learns about her fiancé Grandcourt's past affair with the married Lydia Glasher and the four children (the same number Agnes is said to have had with Hunt) it produced.

Sexual subject matter had to be integrated carefully into Eliot's plots. Given the constraints of Victorian society and publishing, she treated sexual relations delicately, even cryptically, but nonetheless boldly. In "Amos Barton" and *Adam Bede*, her focus is on how irresponsible sex (within and outside of marriage) leads to pregnancies that pose fundamental problems of life and death for the women involved. As we will see, by the time she was ready to depart from the fiction of English rural life and take on the recreation of a completely different cultural, historical milieu in the Italian Renaissance setting of *Romola*, she used her remarkable learning and knowledge to encode alternative sexualities that we do not usually associate with her fiction.

Second Marriages and Divorce

Rosemary Ashton discovered that Lewes was the product of a second marriage that was not legal, and she notes that Lewes's own domestic situation (leaving his legal wife and living with another woman) shows an "uncanny resemblance" to that of his father (Ashton, *GHL* 9). Lewes never knew his father, who left for Bermuda before he was born, and he probably never knew that his father was not married to his mother and had another family. We really do not know what he knew, but if he did know that his father had abandoned his mother and her children, it may have made him a less enthusiastic proponent of "free love" than his "brother" Thornton Hunt. The Lewes children fathered by Hunt seem not to have known that they had a father other than Lewes, at least according to a letter that Ethel Lewes Welsh wrote to biographer Blanche Colton Williams in 1938.[21] Welsh writes: "My Mother bore nine Children to my Father, George Henry Lewes ... it was a most wicked thing to ever connect my Mother's and Mr. Thornton Hunt's names together" (qtd. in Ashton, *GHL* 180). Ashton writes: "Amazingly, the younger children seem not to have known that their father was not Lewes but Thornton Hunt" (180). But this is not so amazing: Edmund and Rose had plenty of reason to believe the man with whom their mother lived when they were born, who signed their birth certificates, whose name they bore and who visited regularly, was their father. Indeed, he was their legal father, and it seems unlikely that they ever accepted the carefully kept secret that he was not their biological father. It would be more surprising if they had accepted Hunt as their father, the convention of marriage being, as Hunt's letter admits, in his opinion, for the benefit of the children.

The adults kept up the fiction, as Lewes's mother may have done with the fiction that Lewes's father was dead. Ethel and Mildred were wrong in thinking that Agnes bore nine children to Lewes, and Ethel seems to have lived out her life in America in a state of denial concerning biographical details that had been published by 1938. But legally speaking, unless and until such paternity could be disproved by showing that Lewes had no "access" to Agnes at the time of her conception (and no one did try to prove such a thing), Lewes was her father. Such epistemological questions seem relevant to Eliot's treatment of parenthood and the relationship of identity to knowledge of parenthood. Her last novel features a young man who cannot know who he is until he knows who his parents are, and for the first half of his life is burdened by a misconception about the identity of his father.

Mary Ann Evans had no uncertainty or ambiguity about her parents, but she was the child of a second marriage. What did she know about her father's first wife? What did her mother know (and say) on the subject? When Marian entered into her relationship with Lewes, she shared with her own mother (about whom she so seldom spoke) the position of being a "second wife," who perhaps had strong feelings about the first wife and the first wife's children. Lewes's mother was also remarried (albeit never legally married for the first time). Lewes disliked his stepfather, who was apparently sometimes cruel to his mother. Eliot also watched this drama play out. Second marriages feature prominently in her fiction as plot devices and as psychological states of deceit, jealousy, and resentment on the part of spouses and children. Godfrey Cass's wife Nancy does not know about his first marriage to Molly in *Silas Marner*, and in *Romola*, Tito deceives his mistress Tessa into thinking they are married, thus managing to lie both to his wife and the "other woman." In *Daniel Deronda*, Mrs Davilow is twice widowed, and the deliberately vague nature of the misery she suffers in the second marriage nonetheless resembles what we know of the suffering Lewes's mother endured in her marriage to Captain Willim. Daniel's mother is also remarried and has multiple children with a man whom Daniel never meets but who is legally his stepfather.

Second marriages are particularly important in *Middlemarch*. Mr Featherstone's complicated wills are the result of his two marriages, which connect him to both the Garths and the Vincys. Bulstrode is the second husband of his first wife, making him a (belatedly acknowledged) step-grandfather to Will Ladislaw. His marriage to his second wife makes him an uncle to Fred and Rosamond Vincy. Illegitimacy also comes into play. Raffles marries Featherstone's mistress, becoming a stepfather to Featherstone's illegitimate son, Joshua Rigg, who inherits the old man's much-coveted property.

A codicil to Casaubon's will forbids Dorothea to marry on penalty of disinheritance. In this context, Celia and her husband Sir James, Sir James's mother, and their friend Mrs Cadwallader discuss the issue of a woman's second marriage. Mrs Cadwallader, wife to the rector of the parish in which Sir James's property lies, insists that the widowed Dorothea should marry as soon as possible to prevent her insanity on the one hand, and seduction by Ladislaw on the other. Lady Chettam objects to any marriage that preempts a respectable period of mourning, telling Mrs Cadwallader, "I am sure you would be the last woman to marry again prematurely, if our dear Rector were taken away" (516; ch. 55). Mrs Cadwallader responds: "It is lawful to marry again, I suppose; else we might as well be Hindoos instead of Christians" (516; ch. 55). This hint that remarriage is at the heart and origin of the Church of England, invoking the marriages of Henry VIII (including that to his dead brother's wife), reflects Eliot's skepticism about Christian institutions generally. It also ironically emphasizes the cultural relativity of marriage practices, since Mrs Cadwallader is probably thinking of "suttee," a Hindu ritual in which a widow throws herself on her husband's funeral pyre and burns (rather than live to remarry). Remarriage becomes a symbol of Christianity and civilization, another notion mocked in the sham Catholic wedding ceremonies performed during festivals by the charlatan conjuror in *Romola*. In the discussion of remarriage in *Middlemarch*, Dorothea, for her part, does not mind the meddling Mrs Cadwallader's comments as long as there is no law obliging her "to take any piece of blood and beauty that she or any body else recommended" (517; ch. 55). Her story represents the perils of free choice, and despite the painful consequences of her marriage, she will always resist subjection to laws obliging compliance in what should be private matters of the heart.

Furthermore, there may be a personal dimension to the representation of Mrs Bulstrode, who knows very little about those aspects of her husband's past that were gradually coming to light in Middlemarch society. She knows only that "he had married a widow who was much older than himself – a Dissenter, and in other ways probably of that disadvantageous quality usually perceptible in a first wife if inquired into with the dispassionate judgment of a second" (576; ch. 61). Clearly, Eliot sought that ironically described dispassionate judgment of the first wife by the second. In the wake of *Adam Bede*'s success, she wrote about Agnes Lewes in a letter as she would write of many of her characters – with an attempt to extend sympathy: "I am also angry with myself for having spoken of her faults. ... All such talk is futile. And I always hate myself after such attempts to vindicate one person at the expense of another" (*GEL* 3:91). It was natural that the second wife should dislike the first, but Eliot felt sympathy for Agnes, and this is reflected in some of her mistress characters, including Tessa in *Romola* and Lydia Glasher in *Daniel Deronda* who, along with their illegitimate children, are kept hidden from societal view.

This account of how George Eliot retrospectively and realistically represented the impossibly complex relationships that constituted Victorian marriage shows how such representations, whether of the more sensational erotic triangles or the mundane jealousies and resentments of second wives and stepchildren, might derive from her own observations and experiences. She never recreated a situation that directly reflected her own, but more intriguingly, she imaginatively reconfigured what she had seen and felt. Her union with Lewes was the prelude to her remarkable period of creativity and literary output. She had been inside of adulterous triangles with Chapman, but with Lewes she would fictionally assert a new identity as wife, beginning with a bold act that challenged the Victorian morality she would spend the rest of her life simultaneously defying and embracing.

Poste Restante, Weimar

In July 1854, Marian Evans and George Henry Lewes took the momentous step of traveling together to Germany in a gesture that announced their intention to live together as a couple. She had told only Charles Bray and John Chapman of her plans. She had seen Sara and Cara at Rosehill in June, never mentioning her plans, and afterwards wrote cryptically to Sara that she was "preparing to go to 'Labassecour,'" the fictional name for Belgium in Charlotte Brontë's novel *Villette* (*GEL* 2:165). Her female friends, therefore, were shocked to receive a note addressed to them and Charles:

> Dear Friends – all three
> I have only time to say good bye and God bless you. Poste Restante, Weimar for the next six weeks, and afterwards Berlin.
>> Ever your loving and grateful
>>> Marian (*GEL* 2:166)

The shock proved damaging to their friendships for some time to come.

This dramatic act began for Marian and Lewes a period of intellectual and social enlightenment that would prove worth the sacrifice of offending friends and scandalizing society. En route to Weimar, they passed through Antwerp, Brussels, Liege, Cologne (where they ran into Dr Brabant, who introduced them to David Strauss), Mainz, and Frankfurt before settling for three months in Weimar followed by four months in Berlin. Their choice of Weimar was determined by Lewes's work. Having established himself as a biographer with the *Life of Maximilien Robespierre* (1849) and his *Biographical History of Philosophy* (1845/6), he sought to put his diverse literary skills and knowledge into the effort of writing the first English biography of the German poet, novelist, and man of science, Johann Wolfgang Goethe (1749–1832), who lived for most of his career at Weimar. During this period, Lewes also wrote essays for the *Leader* to help fund their travels and to support Agnes and the children, including an essay on the German Jewish poet Heinrich Heine and some travel pieces on Weimar in the voice of his persona "Vivian." Marian wrote a review essay of Victor Cousin's biography of Madame de Sablé (and other works on famous French women who hosted salons) for the *Westminster*, which she called "Women in France" (October 1854).

In Weimar, they enjoyed social acceptance in a European community of artists and intellectuals that included the famous composer and pianist Franz Liszt, who was living openly with a married lover, Princess Sayn-Wittgenstein, in a manner that seemed to vindicate their own situation. They found people in their new social set more tolerant of their relationship than the censorious, gossiping friends and acquaintances they had left behind. They received some indication of London gossip in letters from Chapman, Bray, and Thomas Carlyle. The latter was not impressed or convinced by Lewes's eager attempts to contradict rumors that he had left Agnes for Marian (*GEL* 2:176–8; Haight, *Biography* 161). But such distressing letters, demanding that they defend their actions, did not prevent their delight in hearing Clara Schumann play the piano, their attendance at Wagner's operas, or their satisfaction in living openly as a couple.[22]

In their first experience traveling and living together, the couple established a pattern of cultural tourism, socializing, reading (both alone and aloud), and helping each other with their respective research and writing. It was a pattern they would repeat for the following 24 years of their relationship. In this case, the primary subject of research was Lewes's *Life and Works of Goethe*. Later, Marian would assist him with scientific research on excursions throughout England. When she began writing fiction, he traveled with her to scout out locations for *The Mill on the Floss*, *Romola*, *The Spanish Gypsy*, and *Daniel Deronda*.[23] And when she completed a major work, they would take extended vacations to recover from the stress and anxiety that came to attend the creative process for her.

The work they produced on the first trip reveals the issues that preoccupied them personally and intellectually. In the Madame de Sablé essay, Marian argues – ironically for a woman who was about to disguise her identity with a male pseudonym – that there was a "distinctively feminine condition" that "inevitably gives rise to distinctive forms and combinations" and makes women's literature different from that written by men ("Women" 8). On the one hand, she identifies a "physiological basis for the intellectual effectiveness of French women," namely the "small brain and vivacious temperament" of the Gallic race ("Women" 10–11). On the other hand, she sees a secondary, social cause for the importance of French women's writing in "the laxity of opinion and practice with regard to the marriage-tie" (11), concluding "unions formed in the maturity of thought and feeling, and grounded only on inherent fitness and mutual attraction, tended to bring women into more intelligent sympathy with men" (11). The sentiment seems born of her current social situation of intellectual equality in Germany. The notion that mature relationships are superior to rash, immature attractions would appear in her fiction, as when the narrator of *Adam Bede* asks: "How is it that the poets have said so many fine things about our first love, so few about our later love? Are their first poems their best? or are not those the best which come from their fuller thought, their larger experience, their deeper-rooted affections?" (*AB* 503; ch. 51).

Lewes's *Life and Works of Goethe* tells us both his thoughts on biography and his views on marriage through his discussion of some problematic facets of the German poet's life story, particularly his early infatuation with a peasant girl named Frederika, whom he thought of marrying but in the end did not, as well as Goethe's later unmarried cohabitation with Christiane Vulpius, whom he eventually married. Lewes excuses Goethe's behavior toward Frederika in ways that seem to reflect on his own marriage to Agnes and also to predict central themes in Eliot's fiction, including the mistake Adam Bede avoided by not marrying Hetty and the mistake Lydgate makes in marrying Rosamond. Lewes writes:

> The thoughtlessness of youth, and the headlong impetus of passion, frequently throw people into rash engagements; and in these cases the *formal* morality of the world, more careful of externals than of the soul, declares it to be nobler for such rash engagements to be kept, even when the rashness is felt by the engaged, than that a man's honour should

be stained by a withdrawal. The letter thus takes precedence of the spirit. To satisfy this prejudice a life is sacrificed. A miserable marriage rescues the honour; and no one throws the burden of that misery upon the prejudice. I am not forgetting the necessity of being stringent against the common thoughtlessness of youth in forming such relations; but I say that this thoughtlessness once having occurred, reprobate it as we may, the pain which a separation may bring had better be endured than evaded by an unholy marriage, which cannot come to good. (*Life and Works of Goethe* 103)

This emphasis on the impetuosity of youth and sexual passion, and the long-term consequences of following the letter of the law rather than the spirit of the soul, sounds like Shelley. Perhaps most importantly, it shows Lewes bringing his own experiences to his interpretation of Goethe's life. The married couples in Eliot's fiction suggest that Lewes's experience confirmed her belief in the dangers of rash passions that lead to marriage and in the injustice of laws that bind unhappy couples in marriages from which there is no legal escape.

On November 3, 1854, they left Weimar for Berlin, where they continued to find social acceptance in a group of artists, intellectuals, and scholars. Lewes worked on Goethe and Marian read copiously. She did so much translation of the German quotations for Lewes's book that Haight maintains the work "might be considered a composite production with George Eliot as silent collaborator" (*Biography* 173). She was also translating the seventeenth-century Dutch-Jewish philosopher Baruch Spinoza's *Ethics* (begun by Lewes) for which she thought she had a publisher (*GEL* 2:189). Earlier she had worked at translating Spinoza's *Tractatus Theologico-Politicus* (1670), and their interest in the philosopher (about whom Lewes had written in the *Westminster*) was one of the many intellectual bonds they shared (Atkins). Translating Spinoza seemed a logical course for Marian following on her translation of Strauss, but the publishing deal brokered by Lewes would ultimately fall through. As a result, her work on Spinoza (and his possible influence on her thought) went unrecognized in her lifetime.

Quite apart from the limited amount of writing she produced, the trip to Germany was significant in many ways for Marian. It marked a turning point in her domestic and intellectual life and in her public and private identity. Some saw her as a "fallen woman," but she now saw herself as a committed domestic companion. It was not her first trip to the Continent; she had traveled abroad with the Brays in 1849 and lived on her own in Geneva. But cohabiting in emotional and sexual intimacy with a man who was also her intellectual equal – and doing so with a freedom she had never found in her previous, vexed relationships with men – opened her eyes and her mind to new aesthetic worlds: visual, musical, and literary. Haight notes her "naiveté" at this beginning of her aesthetic education (*Biography* 151). But it is hardly surprising that her critical skills of art appreciation were just developing considering her origins and – apart from her voracious reading – her relative cultural deprivation prior to living in London. In the future, she pursued an astonishing course of self-education in art, music, theatre, as well as philosophy, social theory, and science.

Eliza Lynn Linton would recall that, in 1851, Marian impressed her as an awkward provincial (*My Literary Life* 94). And perhaps she was provincial in ways that she would later translate with satirical sympathy in her fictional characterizations, for example in Dorothea Casaubon's honeymoon in Rome. But she combined her extensive reading in all genres and on all subjects with an innate aesthetic sensibility, so that she could remark that when seeing Liszt play, she saw genius and real inspiration for the first time (August 10, 1854; *GEJ* 21–2). In her development over the coming years as an artist, critic, and connoisseur of high art, she would ask urgent questions about the nature of genius and the value of culture, questions pressed upon her through her own status as a genius and artist representing the best that English literature offered in her time.

On March 11, 1855, Marian and Lewes left Berlin and retraced their steps of eight months earlier through Cologne and Brussels. Happy to be "home," they faced a set of practical questions about what and where that home would be. They now confronted the scandal they had created and evaded by leaving England. Upon their return, Marian stayed alone in Dover, working on the translation of Spinoza, while Lewes went to find lodgings for them close to London and to work out the complexities of his own marital situation. In his absence, Hunt had left the *Leader* to become an editor at the *Daily Telegraph*, and Agnes had contracted significant debts for which Lewes was legally responsible. Marian apparently also wanted definitive confirmation that Agnes did not wish for a reconciliation with her husband.[24] After this stressful period of separation, as well as economic and emotional uncertainty, the couple settled south of the Thames in Richmond, taking lodgings as Mr and Mrs Lewes, fictional identities to which they would adhere for the rest of their lives together.

Today the decision of two adults to live together in a committed relationship seems unexceptional, but at the time it was a radical gesture that served to alienate and isolate the woman from social respectability much more than the man. Marian was not "received," even by her own and Lewes's acquaintances, and she clung to her belief in the moral rightness of this relationship based on love rather than legal marriage to sustain her through a difficult period when many regarded her unjustly as the woman who had wrecked the Lewes home. Though she had always been skeptical about the "noose of matrimony" (*GEL* 1:54), and Lewes was separated from his wife, they did not set out to defy the institution of marriage. They simply felt and acted on the belief that a true marriage was one of minds and of affections regardless of legal status. The reasons Lewes could not divorce his wife are more complex than biographers have led us to believe. This complexity is important for getting a clearer picture of Marian's situation and the social and psychological pressures she experienced as her creative talents flourished.

Notes

1. Linton's later hostile reminiscences about Lewes would come to play an important role in the misrepresentation of his life in subsequent biographies.
2. Haight first published Chapman's diary in *George Eliot and John Chapman* (1940).
3. For an account of those Eliot met at the *Westminster*, see Rosemary Ashton, *GE* 1. Barbara Leigh Smith had a romantic affair with Chapman in 1855 before she married Eugene Bodichon, a doctor and French resident of Algeria.
4. He kept her letters to him, depositing them in the British Library with the stipulation that they not be available until 1985, a century after Cross's *Life* appeared. They were published accurately for the first time in Vol. 8 of *GEL* in 1978.
5. Spencer published an article, "On Beauty," in the *Leader* (1854). On the relationship of Spencer's ideas to Eliot's novels, see Paxton.
6. Lewes first contacted Leigh Hunt on October 2, 1834 (Ashton, *GHL* 15). They would continue to correspond up through 1839, mainly about Lewes's proposed Shelley biography, which he dropped in December 1839 (Ashton, *GHL* 18–19). It seems that he met Leigh Hunt, and Thornton Hunt, in person in 1837 (Ashton, *GHL* 24–5, 331).
7. At the end of the eighteenth century, Mary Wollstonecraft and William Godwin were proponents and practitioners of free love (though they did legally marry). Both believed the contemporary laws for marriage treated women as property, and therefore rejected marriage as an institution. Godwin wrote explicitly on the topic in *Political Justice* (1793) (Todd, St Clair). Shelley drew from *Political Justice* and made free love a frequent topic in both his essays and poetry, most notably *Queen Mab* (1813), his essay, "On Marriage" (1817), and *Epipsychidion* (1821) (St Clair).
8. Hunt left the journal in 1855 to take on a role as editor of the *Daily Telegraph*, while Lewes left his position as editor in 1854, though he continued to contribute articles. The journal was published under the title the *Leader* until 1859, edited by various associates. In some histories of radical journalism, Hunt is credited with starting the journal. In other accounts, Lewes alone is mentioned. For a good overview of the history of radical journalism in nineteenth-century England, including the place of the *Leader* and of Hunt, see Koss; Andrews; Escott; and Brick.
9. For example, on December 23, 1849, Lewes wrote "Dear Brother Thornton," and signed, "God bless you dear Thornton, / Ever your own loving, / Brother." (*GHLL* 1:183–5).
10. Throughout his life, Shelley had extra-marital relationships with women while continuing to espouse free love and denounce marriage in his poetry. Though he had already voiced objections to marriage, Shelley eloped with and married his cousin, Harriet Westbrook, in 1811. In 1814, he began a relationship with Mary Wollstonecraft Godwin, with whom he would elope that year, taking along her half-sister, Claire Claremont (who would later become Byron's lover). When Harriet committed suicide in 1816, Shelley and Mary married, but he continued to see women outside of the marriage. *Epipsychidion* (1821) is largely autobiographical in nature and traces his relationships with individual women over the course of his lifetime (Bieri 210–15, 228–30, 275, 297).
11. Chapman met Marx while dining with his friend Andrew Johnson on July 27, 1851. Johnson was a clerk at the Bank of England and a friend of Marx's (Haight, *George Eliot and*

John Chapman 124, 195). There is no indication that Eliot ever met Marx, nor does she refer to his writings, though she mentions communism on several occasions throughout her career.

12. I am indebted to Michael Rectenwald for identifying and transcribing this letter. His work on nineteenth-century secularism helps to place the letter in a larger historical context. See "George Eliot and Secularism" in *George Eliot in Context.*

13. The novel itself drew signed letters to the paper on the subject, and its "Open Council" sections printed letters both for (Francis Worsley on June 15, 1850, 278) and against (Francis W. Newman on June 28, 1850, 325) divorce reform.

14. On Lewes's importance as a literary critic, see Orel and Kaminsky.

15. Ashton, *GE* 104. Hughes suggests that by the time she was at Broadstairs, Marian was already in love with both Spencer and Lewes (*The Last Victorian* 133–4).

16. See McCormack, "George Eliot: Poetry, Fiction and European Spas."

17. The major debate came when Hunt published an article on "ideal Communism" (October 19, 1850). His representation of communism's relationship to personal property and marriage laws sparked a series of angry letters and articles published both in the *Leader* and in other papers, including the *Edinburgh Review* and the *Morning Chronicle.* These articles insisted that Hunt's piece advocated and circulated the tenets of communism, which represented a threat to marriage, family, and individualism (Brick 130–8).

18. At the time the Hunts supposedly lived in their "commune," the works of Charles Fourier and Robert Owen were circulating. Their writings advocated a system of communal living that also included the dissolution of legal marriage. Numerous Four- ierian and Owenite communities formed in Europe and the United States where the members eschewed traditional forms of legal marriage and took up practices of free love (see Riasanovksy; Brisbane; Kern).

19. He was probably named for *Leader* patron Edmund Larken and not for the bastard son Edmund in *King Lear* as Haight insinuates ("The Carlyles and the Leweses" 99).

20. Bullett uses the term "brood" (94). Taylor refers to Agnes's "brood of bastards" (149). Karl remarks that Agnes and Hunt's "breeding season lasted over seven years" (61). Hughes refers to "the batch of children Hunt had sired on Agnes" (328).

21. The letter written on December 2, 1938, shortly before Ethel died in California at age 86, is partially quoted by Ashton (*GHL* 180) and was apparently in the possession of the now- deceased Gordon Haight rather than deposited in the Beinecke.

22. For a detailed account of this first visit to Germany, see Röder-Bolton, *George Eliot in Germany*, which examines the journals Eliot kept during the journey and detailed research into the cultures she experienced there.

23. For an account of these journeys and their relationship to the fiction, see McCormack, *English Travels.*

24. The story that Agnes wished Lewes could "marry Miss Evans" (Haight, *Biography* 179) is based on dubious evidence. Haight reports the story from Edith Simcox who claims Cara Bray told her the story, which came from a destroyed letter.

4

Marian Lewes and George Eliot
1855–60

"... perhaps posterity will believe in Liggins. And why not?"
(George Eliot to Charles Bray, *GEL* 3:171)

Before she ever met Chapman or Lewes, Mary Ann Evans had opinions about marriage and divorce. In 1838, during her intense religious phase, she complained to Maria Lewis of the "marrying and giving in marriage that is constantly being transacted" as an example of earthly ties "so brittle as to be liable to be snapped asunder at every breeze" (*GEL* 1:6). Her emphasis is on the earthly ties that she was trying so hard to transcend through her piety and also on the importance of constancy in human relations. The institution of marriage was never as sacred to her as relationships of love between people. By 1848, she was no longer religious and was inclined to criticize the legal bond of marriage once the emotional connection had been severed. When she read Charlotte Brontë's *Jane Eyre* (1847), she sympathized with the character of Rochester, referring in a letter to Charles Bray to the "diabolical law which chains a man soul and body to a putrefying carcass" (*GEL* 1:268). The emphasis is interesting for its lack of sympathy with Rochester's legal wife, Bertha, the "madwoman in the attic." When the *Leader* ran its series of articles and letters debating the various threats to marriage and ultimately advocating the reform of the

The Life of George Eliot: A Critical Biography, First Edition. Nancy Henry.
© 2012 Nancy Henry. Published 2012 by John Wiley & Sons, Ltd.

divorce laws, at one point Lewes was obliged to defend Hunt from the charge that his advocacy of communism threatened to destroy the institution:

> Let us further suppose that *marriage* will be destroyed; can any one, conversant with human nature, suppose this destruction to be possible with all that marriage has of holy, all it has of vital, all it has of social – *that* which always has been marriage and always will be? To what, then, does this terror of "destruction" amount? . . . so long as human nature remains, so long will our tendencies, convictions, and habits reign paramount over *all* schemes of legislation. ("Communism as an Ideal" 734)

And so it seems that from about 1847 to 1850, Eliot and Lewes were not only arriving at similar opinions about art but also about the nature of marriage.

Prior to leaving with Lewes for Germany, Marian had, in addition to editorial responsibilities at the *Westminster*, been translating another important German work, Ludwig Feuerbach's *Das Wesen des Christenthums* (1841) as *The Essence of Christianity* (1854). The book was on a continuum with the critiques of Christianity posed by Hennell and Strauss. Feuerbach took an anthropological approach to analyzing Christianity that would influence Karl Marx, among others. Marian was particularly sympathetic to Feuerbach's general approach so that the task of translating was not as emotionally wrenching as had been the translation of Strauss. She found many points of agreement with his notion that religion was fundamentally human rather than divine, answering human needs and projecting ideals as deities to be worshipped. Feuerbach argued that the essence of Christianity should be found in human relations, a notion that Eliot would emphasize repeatedly in her fiction. As Feuerbach summarized his argument:

> We have reduced the supermundane, supernatural, and superhuman nature of God to the elements of human nature as its fundamental elements. Our process of analysis has brought us again to the position with which we set out. The beginning, middle and end of religion is MAN. (184)

Feuerbach viewed God as a projection of "man," of the human species idealized, elevated, and then worshipped by man.

Furthermore, Marian's translation of *The Essence of Christianity*, which appeared in July 1854 just before she left for Germany with Lewes, provided philosophical support for the notion of a higher ideal in marriage: "for a marriage the bond of which is merely an external restriction, not the voluntary, contented self-restriction of love . . . is not a true marriage, and therefore not a truly moral marriage" (271). Although the trip to Germany was initially an experiment in living together, and the couple did not call their union a marriage until much later, Eliot used an argument similar to that of Feuerbach when justifying her relationship with

Lewes. In an 1855 letter to Cara Bray about the seriousness of her attitude toward marriage generally, and toward Lewes particularly, she echoed her letter of 1838 in which she complained about ties so brittle as to be "snapped asunder at every breeze": "Light and easily broken ties are what I neither desire theoretically nor could live for practically" (*GEL* 2:213–14). She makes it known that the strength of the tie has nothing to do with laws or ceremonies. What follows, as Feuerbach argued, is that people who do not feel bound to each other by love should not be bound by the law.

Her own preference for permanent ties did not prevent her from supporting the act of divorce. The sympathy she felt for Rochester in *Jane Eyre*, for example, was extended to an approval of Milton's views about divorce as expressed in a revealing 1855 review of Thomas Knightley's *An Account of the Life, Opinions, and Writings of John Milton*. Lewes was once again ill, and she was again helping him meet his responsibilities to the *Leader*. In this context, her focus on Milton's statements about divorce is particularly significant. She compares Milton's arguments to those of Caroline Norton – who was campaigning for women's marital and property rights – and refers to Norton's 1855 pamphlet *A Letter to the Queen on Lord Chancellor Cranworth's Marriage & Divorce Bill*. Quoting Milton's pathetic portrayal of a man "bound fast to an uncomplying discord of nature" who sees that "his bondage is now inevitable," she writes that it is:

> A picture, alas! too often realized since the year 1644, when it was thus powerfully drawn. For want of a more modern pendant to Mrs. Norton's plea, it is worth while to take up Milton's, and consider what such a mind as his had to urge on the husband's side of this painful subject. ("Life and Opinions" 157)[1]

Her invocation of Norton shows that she could sympathize with the injured woman in cases of unhappy marriages, but she chooses to stress the plight of the husband, seeming to wish for a modern male counterpart to Norton who would take the husband's side.

The binding nature of matrimony, the injustice of marriage laws, and the wrongs suffered by husbands were topics that Eliot had contemplated for years, and were particularly on her mind in this early period of her relationship with Lewes. So it is not surprising that such topics emerge in her literary reviews, and, eventually, in her fiction. Despite her decision to call her own partnership a marriage, and even despite the intellectual and domestic happiness she clearly enjoyed within that "marriage," her fiction can be scathing in its representation of the various ways in which the marital bond might become destructive to the material and emotional lives of both husbands and wives. This impulse to criticize marriages in which the spouses are bound to "an uncomplying discord of nature," only intensified over the course of her career as a novelist. True to her moral and aesthetic principles of sympathizing with all points of view, her fiction reflects the suffering of husbands and wives.

Before considering the individual marriages in Eliot's fiction, and through them her interrogation of marriage generally, it is important to review just how complicated Lewes's marital situation was. Why couldn't Lewes divorce? Mathilde Blind (1883) states that at the time Lewes met Marian Evans, he "found his conjugal relations irretrievably spoiled" (85) and he "could not get a divorce" (86). Cross echoes Blind when he explains that at the time of his meeting with Marian, Lewes found his "previous family life irretrievably spoiled" (*Life* 1:234).[2] Neither Blind nor Cross discusses Agnes, Hunt, or their children.

Early twentieth-century biographies offer interesting variations. Elizabeth Haldane (1927) writes: "Lewes had put himself out of court by his union with another" (92). Anne Fremantle (1933) writes that Lewes could not divorce because "his own mode of life can hardly be called moral" (60). Anna Kitchel (1933) notes that "even personal immorality . . . would not have prevented his obtaining a divorce if he had never condoned his wife's unfaithfulness" (152).[3] Blanche Colton Williams (1936) claims that the fact that Lewes as well as Agnes, "had been false to earlier marriage vows, would have prevented his being freed" (103).[4]

Haight's biography put to rest any question of Lewes's immorality or his living with Marian as reasons preventing his divorce and instead established – by sheer undocumented assertion – the notion of Lewes signing Edmund's birth certificate as an act of condonation forever precluding divorce: "Lewes, having once condoned [Agnes's] adultery, was forever precluded from appealing for divorce" (Haight, *Biography* 132).[5] Ashton (1991) asserts: "Lewes registered Edmund as his own child; when he met and fell in love with Marian Evans, he was debarred from seeking a divorce on the grounds – not changed under the partially liberating Divorce Act of 1857 – that he had thereby condoned his wife's adultery" (*GHL* 99–100). Later, Ashton (1996) qualifies: "There was no possibility of his ever getting a divorce, since he had under the law condoned Agnes's relationship with Hunt by registering Edmund and Rose as his own children" (*GE* 102).[6] No case histories, precedents, or evidence of any kind are cited to support this claim.

This may seem like a technicality, but the persistence of the story today suggests its importance. It sets a defensive tone by offering a definitive legal reason that Eliot and Lewes continued in a union unsanctioned by law. It makes the couple a victim of Lewes's generosity, a rigid divorce law, and Agnes's adultery, thereby shifting the emphasis away from Eliot and Lewes's relationship, which however highly theorized and justified, remained adulterous. It is also part of the reason for representing Agnes as a brood mare or "cheerful and impenitent" (Haight, *Biography* 491). Haight writes that as long as Agnes lived, "the archaic English law governing divorce would prevent Lewes from marrying anyone else. He paid dearly for his generosity in acknowledging Edmund" (145). But Haight does not say which law he means since adultery on the part of the wife was a primary reason for most divorces and condonation was a legal concept open to interpretation and predicated on proof.

Where did the condonation theory originate? In 1886, the Reverend Charles Gordon Ames – an American Unitarian minister – published a pamphlet entitled *George Eliot's Two Marriages* to defend Eliot's union with Lewes as a legitimate marriage from a specifically Christian perspective.[7] Lamenting "the absence of anything like a legal or other inquiry," as well as "the absence of sifted and recorded evidence," he nonetheless asserts that Lewes's "condonation of [his wife's] first offence worked a forfeiture of his right of divorce for the second" (8). Yet, he qualifies his own claim in a footnote: "This statement is discredited by an American lawyer." Ames's acknowledgment that the condonation theory is dubious in the absence of "legal inquiry" has disappeared from modern biographies.

Ames's moral defense of Eliot's "marriage" to Lewes might be seen as a refutation of Eliza Lynn Linton's attack on that union's moral superiority in her anonymous 1885 article in *Temple Bar*. Linton is angry at attempts to sanctify a union that only Eliot's fame as an author made socially palatable.[8] The *Temple Bar* article is not the source of the condoning adultery claims, but Linton's *Autobiography of Christopher Kirkland* (also published in 1885) may be.[9] The observations of Linton's fictional narrator have provided a source of information about the Eliot–Lewes–Hunt triangle, which has worked its way into biographies up to the present:

> It must never be forgotten too that he who afterwards posed as the fond husband betrayed by the trusted friend, was, in the days when I first knew them all, the most pronounced Free-lover of the group, and openly took for himself the liberty he expressly sanctioned in his wife. As little as he could go into the Divorce Court for his personal relief, because of that condonation and his own unclean hands, so little did he deserve the sympathy of society for the transfer which afterwards he put forward as his own justification and that friend's condemnation. (280)

Although biographers have mined her fictionalized memories for clues to the Hunt–Lewes circle, they note her animus against Lewes and Eliot. The condoning theory has persisted, but few since Linton have sought to defend Hunt at Lewes's expense.

No biography offers evidence to prove that registering Edmund's birth consti-tuted "condonation" of adultery and thereby precluded Lewes's seeking divorce, especially when the alleged infidelity continued for years after Edmund's birth. Most biographies entertain the idea that Hunt and Lewes "shared" Agnes at least for a time, and yet modern biographies never doubt the paternity of Herbert, St Vincent, and Edmund Lewes, as some earlier accounts had. Paternity was impossible to prove, and the "archaic English law" provided for this. There is a legal presumption that under common law a child conceived when his lawfully married parents are cohabiting is legitimate (this means, that his mother's husband must be his father). While this presumption has finally dropped away because of the accuracy of DNA testing, it was still the law in England and the US until recently. This presumption is predicated on the desire to legitimize as many children as possible – for social and inheritance reasons.

This suggests that it would have been legally impossible for Lewes to deny that Edmund was his child. To do so, he would have to adduce evidence demonstrating that he was physically separated from Agnes around the time of conception. He really had no choice but to accept Edmund as his, and he may have had his own doubts about Edmund's paternity. Legally Edmund was his; the name on the birth certificate merely reiterates this. The presumption of legitimacy was a fundamental principle of the common law. In his *Commentaries on the Laws of England* (1765–9), William Blackstone explains that non-access could only be proved "if the husband be out of the kingdom of England. . . for above nine months" (1:431).[10] The primary rationale underlying the common law's severe restrictions on rebutting the presumption of parentage appears to have been an aversion to declaring children illegitimate as well as an interest in promoting the "peace and tranquility of States and families," a goal that obviously impaired suits against spouses asserting that their children are illegitimate (1:315).[11]

Lewes and Marian began living together in 1854. Most biographers recognize that prior to the 1857 Matrimonial Causes Act, divorce would have been impossible for financial reasons. It is from circumstances following the 1857 Act that questions arise. The condonation clause in the 1857 Matrimonial Causes Act (statute 30) was open to debate and interpretation. Lewes was not prohibited from "seeking" a divorce. After 1857, he, like many men, might have petitioned for a divorce on the grounds of his wife's adultery in the past. He might also have sought a legal separation agreement, as Charles Dickens did from his wife in 1858.[12] Had he chosen to petition, he would have been obliged to state that there was no "collusion or connivance" between husband and wife in seeking the divorce. And, he would have been required to name the alleged adulterer (Hunt) as co-respondent. Hunt would have had the option of counter-charging "condonation." In such a case, the adultery itself would have to be proven and then the charge of condonation would also have to be proven. Further, many of the judgments in cases that came before the newly established Divorce Commission disputed just what constituted condonation. Despite what Eliot biographers assert, registering a birth in itself is not an act of condonation, especially given the presumption of paternity. Rather, condonation means forgiveness and reconciliation generally; specifically, it means returning to conjugal cohabitation.

If Lewes knew of Agnes and Hunt's affair and continued living with her as man and wife, that (not the administrative act of registering births) would constitute condonation. But if he did take her back as his wife, resuming sexual relations, then there would be ambiguity about several of the children involved – St Vincent, Edmund, and Rose. If, on the other hand, he was not having sexual relations with Agnes, can he be said to have taken her back as a wife and condoned the adultery?

Either way, he did not condone adultery that occurred after he left their home, and he had the legal right to pursue a divorce suit or legal separation, but the fact that he was living with another woman would have put him at an insurmountable disadvantage in a trial.

In short, to say that condonation precluded him from appealing for divorce is to judge a trial that never occurred. We can be certain that no one (Lewes, Agnes, Hunt, Eliot) wished to be dragged through the courts and into the public limelight, exposing sensitive and ambiguous questions of sexual conduct and paternity that would be embarrassing to all parties and harmful to the many children now involved, not to mention the new author George Eliot, who came into being the same year as the Matrimonial Causes Act of 1857.[13]

Lewes and Marian demanded that the world call them husband and wife. And while they succeeded in promoting the domestic fiction that she was Mrs Lewes, the legal Mrs Lewes lived on. The continued presence of Agnes Lewes as the "real" Mrs Lewes was a constant reminder that Marian's assumption of this identity was fictional. Too little attention has been paid to the influence that Eliot's intimate knowledge of Lewes's marital irregularities may have had on her fiction. Recurring patterns of secrecy, lies, illegitimacy, and triangulation in her work seem to demand an explanation in light of Lewes's marital complexities. Whatever she knew about Charles Bray's affairs, she knew much more about the Hunt–Lewes triangle than we do.[14]

There are no actual divorces in Eliot's fiction, perhaps because, with the exception of *Daniel Deronda*, they are all set prior to the Matrimonial Causes Act of 1857. But her work abounds in bad marriages ("Janet's Repentance," "The Lifted Veil," *Romola, Felix Holt, Middlemarch, Daniel Deronda*), secret wives and mistresses (*Romola, Silas Marner, Felix Holt, Daniel Deronda*), illegitimate children (*Adam Bede, Romola, Felix Holt, Middlemarch, Daniel Deronda*), and thoughts of separation on the part of wives contemplating the failings of their husbands (*Romola, Middlemarch, Daniel Deronda*). By sifting through the myths perpetuated by biographies and looking at the available facts in the context of fictional clues, we may come to a clearer understanding of both Eliot's life and fiction.

Though married only in the fictional sense, Marian soon experienced the benefits of living with an intellectually compatible partner. In 1855, Chapman asked her to edit the *Belles Lettres* section of the ever-struggling *Westminster*, and she gladly accepted, writing reviews on a wide range of topics including the most important contemporary literature of the day by Matthew Arnold, Alfred Tennyson, Robert Browning, and others. She wrote a sharp critique of evangelical hypocrisy in "Evangelical Teaching: Dr. Cumming" (October 1855) and a knowledgeable essay, "German Wit," on the poet Heinrich Heine (January 1856), about whom Lewes had also written while they were in Germany. She wrote several long review essays for the *Westminster*, including most importantly "The Natural History of German Life" (July 1856) and "Silly Novels by Lady Novelists" (October 1856). These essays set out the literary aesthetic that she had been formulating during her years as a literary critic and editor. The subject matter of "Silly Novels by Lady Novelists," a satirical essay written shortly after her return from Weimar, is summed up in its title. It is an interesting follow-up to the piece on Madame de Sablé, in which she had argued that "in France alone woman has had a vital influence on the development of literature. . . in France alone, if the writings of women were swept away, a serious gap would be made in the national history" ("Women" 9). Both pieces seem to be preparing the way for the contribution she sought to make – and would succeed in making – to her own national literature.[15]

While the essay complains about the species that fall within the genus "Silly Novels by Lady Novelists"("the frothy, the prosy, the pious, or the pedantic") (296), to counterbalance her examples of ridiculous and unrealistic writing she praises her more serious female contemporaries Harriet Martineau, Currer Bell (Charlotte Brontë), and Elizabeth Gaskell, observing: "By a peculiar thermometric adjustment, when a woman's talent is at zero, journalistic approbation is at the boiling pitch; when she attains mediocrity, it is already at no more than summer heat; and if ever she reaches excellence, critical enthusiasm drops to the freezing point" (319). The comment is interesting on a variety of fronts. It shows that she did believe some English women writers had attained excellence, that she was skeptical not only about popular opinion but also about journalistic reviews, and also that she was experimenting with metaphors, especially the scientific metaphors that would characterize her fiction.

"The Natural History of German Life," a review of two works by the German social theorist, Wilhelm Heinrich von Riehl (1823–97) argues against false representations of "opera peasants" and other idealized stereotypes, asserting: "But our social novels profess to represent the people as they are, and the unreality of their representations is a grave evil" (263). Emphasizing the moral importance of realistic representation, she writes: "The greatest benefit we owe the artist, whether painter, poet, or novelist, is the extension of our sympathies" (263), a point she would repeat in authorial asides within the narratives of *Scenes of Clerical Life* and *Adam Bede*. In this essay, we can see the influence of art critic John Ruskin, whose *Modern Painters*, Vol. 3 (1856) she had reviewed in the same year (*Westminster*, April 1856). In her praise of Riehl's sociological and anthropological study of German peasants, she makes the case for realism in art. Thus, her reviews in 1856 established the principles of fiction she had come to uphold and that she would put into practice. Soon, with a few minor exceptions, she would stop writing critical reviews for the periodical press, finding fiction both more satisfying and more lucrative.[16]

During a period when she accompanied Lewes on his scientific research trips to various coastal locales in England in 1856–7, including Illfracombe, Tenby, the Scilly Isles, and Jersey, she decided to experiment with writing fiction. With his numerous connections in the publishing world, Lewes proved invaluable to getting her first story published. He contacted John Blackwood, the editor of *Blackwood's Edinburgh*

Magazine, and told him about a friend who was writing fiction that might appeal to the journal's audience (*GEL* 2:269). Lewes submitted the manuscript of "The Sad Fortunes of the Reverend Amos Barton" to Blackwood on November 6, 1856. All contributions to *Blackwood's* appeared anonymously, but it was unusual for the publisher not to know his author's identity. Yet Blackwood, who would become an important presence in George Eliot's future career and a trusted editor with whom she would maintain a sometimes uneasy balance between professional and personal relations, astutely recognized talent in this mysterious new author. Sensing the potential of Lewes's "clerical friend," he continued to be supportive when the previously unnamed friend identified "himself" as "George Eliot" in February 1857 between the publication of "Amos" and the second "scene," "Mr. Gilfil's Love Story" (*GEL* 2:292). George Eliot continued to correspond with Blackwood until "he" finally came out to the publisher in 1859.

Scenes of Clerical Life

In an unusually expansive and intimate journal entry, published as "How I Came to Write Fiction," Marian explains how she had been thinking of a story but procrastinated in beginning it:

> But one morning as I was lying in bed, thinking what should be the subject of my first story, my thoughts merged themselves into a dreamy doze, and I imagined myself writing a story of which the title was – 'The Sad Fortunes of the Reverend Amos Barton.' I was soon wide awake again, and told G. He said, 'O what a capital title!' and from that time I had settled in my mind that this should be my first story. (*GEJ* 289)

The creative state of a dreamy doze (fictionalized in the opening chapter of *The Mill on the Floss*), as well as the intimate bedroom conversation with Lewes, provides insight into the process of her inspiration and her daily domestic life. She was unlikely to repeat such revealing portraits after she had become famous and self-conscious about even her most personal writing. Her journal entry on how she came to write her next book, *Adam Bede*, for example, is more formal in tone than this account of her beginnings as a writer of fiction.

"Amos Barton," and its linked stories set in the Midland locality she knew so well, "Mr. Gilfil's Love Story" and "Janet's Repentance," were serialized anonymously in *Blackwood's* between January and November 1857. *Scenes of Clerical Life* was published as a book in 1858 under the pseudonym George Eliot. It immediately stirred up interest and controversy in London and in Nuneaton, where residents speculated about the identity of the author and about "originals" for characters in the stories. Eliot's brother Isaac had no way of knowing that his sister was transforming their former acquaintances into fictional characters and that she would soon become famous through novels that drew explicitly on family memories. He did not immediately suspect her authorship, but he was suspicious of a letter in which his sister informed him that she now had a husband (*GEL* 2:331–2). He had his solicitor ask for particulars of the marriage and Marian was forced to admit that it was not a legal union (*GEL* 2:346). Just as she was finding success as an author, the break with her family became complete. Isaac cut off communications with her and insisted that Chrissey do the same. Fanny, after misunderstanding the letter in which Marian told her about her "marriage," also cut off communication when the actual state of things was revealed. Shortly before her death on March 15, 1859, Chrissey wrote a last letter to Marian regretting her silence. Isaac did not write until 1880, after his famous sister was legally married to Johnny Cross. But after revealing the facts of her relationship with Lewes to Isaac's solicitor, Marian would never return to her Midlands home or see any of her siblings again.[17] As Bodenheimer notes: "The family excommunication determined a shift of signature from Marian Evans to Marian Lewes – a change that followed close upon the adoption of the pseudonym George Eliot" (*Real Life* 129).

Another revelation offered in "How I Came to Write Fiction" is the habitual presence of Agnes Lewes in Marian's life. Musing with satisfaction on the mystery of her identity, about which literary London was speculating after the publication of "Amos Barton," she writes: "Agnes thought I was the father of a family – was sure I was a man who had seen a great deal of society etc. etc." (*GEJ* 290). Her noting of Agnes's reaction and the secret that she and Lewes were keeping from his wife (as well as everyone else) clearly gave her pleasure at this time. Despite her own and Lewes's avowed commitment to "truth," they show a shared willingness to perpetuate falsehoods both as to the identity of George Eliot and the marital status of Mrs Marian Lewes. They were surprisingly willing to blur fact and fiction, to lie when the lie seemed necessary to their larger purposes.

It is noteworthy that Agnes, as a full-time mother, felt sure from reading "Amos Barton" that the author was a father. The subject matter of "Amos Barton" suggests that, though not a mother herself, Eliot carefully observed the burdens of mothers, including the dangers of childbirth and the endless drudgery of housework. The title suggests that its primary intention is to sympathize with the mediocrity of Amos, but the title is a cover for its exposure of Amos's ill-treatment of his wife Milly.[18] At the center of the plot is a triangle that develops when Amos invites a faux Polish countess to move into his house, further burdening his wife and stirring up damaging gossip in his parish. The suspicion of adultery (to which Amos is oblivious), is secondary to the indictment of his selfishness toward his wife, her suffering and her eventual death as a result of multiple pregnancies.

Milly Barton is elevated to saintliness and martyrdom by her gentle, maternal, uncomplaining nature, but in fact, she is merely a passive vessel, a somewhat bovine, pretty woman who is loved and pitied by her friends but who has little to say and seems content to raise children and soothe a petulant husband. While there was speculation that Amos Barton was based on Reverend John Gwyther, curate of Eliot's childhood parish of Chilvers Coton (1831–41), it seems certain that Milly with her six children – and resulting struggles with poverty – was influenced by Marian's widowed sister Chrissey with her six children. Milly's death in childbirth seems almost a foreboding of Chrissey's death in 1859. It is also possible that there is an element of Agnes in Milly. By 1857, Agnes had borne at least nine children (seven of which survived), and, as far as we know, was thoroughly preoccupied with raising them with the help of Martha Baker Bell (Haight, *Biography* 303), called "Nursie" by the family and whose domestic role may have been similar to that of the outspoken Nannie in "Amos Barton."

While contemporary and later commentators have tended to focus on the moral issue of adultery, and Eliza Lynn Linton defended Thornton Hunt for indulging his passions, Eliot's first fictional work implies that she detected other moral problems related to childbearing that applied to women whether married or not. Perhaps Hunt's true moral culpability came in the form of keeping two women constantly pregnant – not of sleeping with another man's wife or even betraying his own. As mentioned, Marian had met and admired Thornton's wife Kate Hunt (who was pregnant at the time) in 1851. Presumably, Agnes and Kate had some agency when it came to their pregnancies, but Milly is too passive, too conventional, or too ignorant to take whatever steps might be required to prevent pregnancy. "Amos Barton" is the story of a man who fails to realize that he is killing his wife through multiple childbirths and overwork in child care. The "affair" with the Countess is secondary and irrelevant, merely typical of Amos's insensitivity to the consequences of his actions for others. It is a strange plot device, adding the false appearance of an affair to what is otherwise the story of a woman's compliance in her own abuse. Significantly, the other stories in *Scenes* treat related themes. Caterina in "Mr. Gilfil" dies as a result of a pregnancy she was probably never strong enough to withstand. Janet's physically and psychologically abusive marriage is mercifully childless. After Dempster's death, however, Janet adopts an orphaned child.

Agnes's burdensome fertility, together with the treatment of reproduction in Eliot's fiction, suggests that Lewes and Eliot had confirmed views about not producing more children. The reasons that they did not have children together must have included the fact that they were not legally married, that Lewes already had children to worry about, and that children would have interfered with their respective careers. Eliot may also have taken a broader ethical and social position on what childbirth did to women like Milly, Chrissey, Agnes, Kate Hunt, and possibly even Christiana Evans, who became an invalid after bearing a total of five children and losing the last two twin boys. Eliot admired competent mothers like Dolly Winthrop in *Silas Marner*, and the happiness of large families like the Garths in *Middlemarch*. But from Milly Barton onward, her fiction portrays women of all classes whose potential for development beyond motherhood will never be realized because they are harassed by domestic cares. We see these physical, mental, and economic effects of over-producing children to different degrees in Mrs Poyser in *Adam Bede*, Gritty Moss in *The Mill on the Floss*, and Mrs Davilow in *Daniel Deronda*. In contrast, stronger women like the Dodson sisters in *The Mill on the Floss* are able to control their own reproduction more successfully: Aunts Pullet and Glegg have no children; Aunt Dean has only Lucy; and Mrs Tulliver has only Tom and Maggie. Furthermore, it may be that Eliot simply thought it wrong to reproduce in an industrializing age when cities were swelling, the poor were hungry, and urban children were not needed to provide labor as rural children had been traditionally. Adoptions of children by Janet, Silas, and Romola are portrayed as morally admirable. According to Barbara Bodichon, Marian and Lewes practiced birth control, which seems entirely probable though it cannot be substantiated.[19]

Adam Bede

After the conservative John Blackwood objected to the subject matter of "Janet's Repentance" (Janet's alcoholism as a response to abuse from her husband), the now-established George Eliot abandoned her plan to write more "clerical scenes" and decided instead to take a "broader canvas" (*GEL* 2:381). She described the proposed new novel to Blackwood as "a country novel – full of the breath of cows and the scent of hay" (*GEL* 2:387). But, combined with its pastoral quality and scenes of provincial humor, the novel would contain elements equally as dark as those to which Blackwood had objected in "Janet's Repentance," albeit packaged in a form that satisfied her publisher by containing plenty of rural color and folksy humor, and by conforming to a happy-ending marriage plot. Like "Janet's Repentance," *Adam Bede* would portray alcoholism in the character of Adam's father, who drowns in a brook on his way home from the pub, and the even darker subjects of unwed pregnancy and child murder.

Three months after the publication of *Scenes of Clerical Life* in January 1858, Eliot and Lewes left for a five month stay in Munich and Dresden. In the future they would continue a pattern of leaving England following the publication of her books so that Eliot could recover from the strain of composition, escape publicity surrounding critical reviews, and begin to contemplate a new project. Much of *Adam Bede* was written in Germany, where the couple felt so much at home socially and intellectually. The novel is set in the Midlands during the Napoleonic wars, which form a dim background to life in the isolated village of Hayslope. It is a drama of rural peasantry, treated realistically in a manner consistent with the call for such representations in "The Natural History of German Life." Boldly, Eliot breaks the frame of the narrative in order to reassert her realist principles in the chapter titled "In which the story pauses a little," now considered an important statement of Victorian realism. In it, her narrator explains: "So I am content to tell my simple story, without trying to make things seem better than they were; dreading nothing, indeed, but falsity, which in spite of one's best efforts, there is reason to dread. Falsehood is so easy, truth so difficult" (176; ch. 17).

In the journal entry later published as the "History of Adam Bede" (November 30, 1858), Eliot insists: "Adam is not my father any more than Dinah is my aunt. Indeed, there is not a single *portrait* in 'Adam Bede'; only the suggestions of experiences wrought up into new combinations" ("History of Adam Bede" 297). But because this fragment was unpublished, it did nothing to deter readers from speculating about the real-life models for her characters. Other than the Derbyshire setting, the borrowed names like Bartle Massey and the Waggon Overthrown, and the fact that Adam is a hard-working, honest carpenter and estate manager, his superficial similarities to her father do not help in interpreting the novel.

Adam is in love with local farmer Mr Poyser's niece, Hetty, an orphan who has been kindly taken in by her uncle and his wife and is expected to work in the couple's farmhouse on land rented from Squire Donnithorne. Hetty is infatuated with the old Squire's grandson and heir, Arthur (himself an orphan), and she entertains fantasies about marrying him and escaping her life of drudgery and childcare for her cousins. Adam's Methodist brother Seth is in love with Mrs Poyser's niece, the orphaned but austere and independent Dinah Morris, a self-appointed Methodist preacher. As Eliot wrote, Dinah was inspired by – but is not a portrait of – her father's sister-in-law Elizabeth Evans (a Methodist preacher), whose contact with a young woman before her execution for child murder is the acknowledged "germ" of Hetty's plot ("History of Adam Bede," 296–7).[20]

As this brief outline suggests, mimetic desire is at the center of the novel. Eliot wrote that when she began, "the only elements I had determined on, besides the character of Dinah, were the character of Adam, his relation to Arthur Donnithorne and their mutual relation to Hetty" ("History of Adam Bede," 297). The young Squire Arthur, who was a childhood friend of Adam's despite the difference in social standing, seduces the naïve but willing Hetty, leading to a violent encounter between Adam and Arthur – a scene suggested by Lewes – and which came to Eliot while the couple were at the Munich opera listening to Rossini's *William Tell Overture* ("History of Adam Bede," 298). The two friends grapple like male animals fighting over a female mate.

Unknown to all, Hetty is pregnant, and her lonely, misguided journey across the Midlands countryside in search of Arthur, who she believes is in Windsor but who has in fact been deployed to Ireland with the militia, was Eliot's deepest and darkest psychological exploration to date. Hetty gives birth on this journey and abandons the child with some confused notion that it might be found. When it is discovered, however, she is charged with and convicted of murder and condemned to death – an elaboration on the "germ" of the story suggested to Eliot by her aunt's experience. In an implausible last-minute rescue (also suggested by Lewes), Arthur returns and has Hetty's sentence transmuted to transportation to Australia. Adam marries Dinah, the

Figure 16   Elizabeth Tomlinson Evans (Coventry History Centre)

woman loved by his brother Seth, who for his part must accept a secondary role as a bachelor uncle to Adam and Dinah's children. In an epilogue similar to that Eliot was to use in *The Mill*, *Romola*, and *Felix Holt*, we learn that Adam and Dinah have had two children, Adam and Lisbeth, that Seth lives with them, and that they are reconciled with Arthur, who informs them that poor Hetty has died on her way back from Australia. In all of these epilogues, the tension of the sexual triangles that has driven much of the previous plot is diffused with rivals reconciled and troublesome egoists killed off.

Despite the upbeat tone of the ending, the overall portrait of family relations is disturbing. Adam's alcoholic father and cloying mother are anything but an ideal family. Lisbeth Bede's favoritism of Adam and psychologically abusive treatment of the meeker, less masculine Seth suggest a family dynamic that Eliot may have recreated from experience and, as discussed in Chapter Two, Mrs Poyser displays alcoholic characteristics. But Eliot shied away from having Hetty executed (the fate of her historical counterpart) and opted instead for a happy ending. That ending was perhaps a concession to popular taste in a first novel that she would not feel obliged to repeat in her second.

Eliot wrote of that first novel, "I love it very much and am deeply thankful to have written it, whatever the public may say to it – a result that is still in darkness" ("History of Adam Bede" 298). *Adam Bede* – in all its darkness and light – was a critical and commercial success, its first edition selling out in a matter of weeks. In the *Times*, for example, E. S. Dallas wrote: "The whole work, indeed, leaves upon us the impression of something highly finished and well matured, and we close the volumes wondering whether the author is to do better in his next novel, – curious, also, to know who the author really is" (*Critical Heritage* 84). George Eliot's popularity soared, as did curiosity to know "his" identity.

Marian Lewes was frustrated in her success and desire to preserve anonymity by the public claims that someone else was the author of *Scenes*. She first heard the rumor from her half-sister Fanny in June 1857 – their last exchange before Fanny realized that Marian was not really married and stopped writing to her (Haight, *Biography* 267). An unemployed, alcoholic native of Nuneaton then residing in Attleborough, Joseph Liggins, was allowing it to be said that he was the author of *Scenes*. Though she had not yet published under the name George Eliot in 1857, Marian told Fanny that the anonymous author was a Mr Eliot (*GEL* 2:336). These rumors escalated into full-blown scandal that would persist through Marian's taking the pseudonym George Eliot and through the publication of *Adam Bede*, which would make the name of George Eliot known throughout the country and raise the stakes for revealing "his" true identity. The strange episode would leave permanent scars, altering Eliot's attitude to authorship, her relationship to her reading public, and the content of her fiction.[21]

Initially Marian and Lewes were amused when the claim for Liggins's authorship of *Scenes* was published in the *Manx Sun* (July 4, 1857), but the rumors became annoying when a set of supporters took up the Liggins charge, turning it into a liberal campaign for the exploited provincial author who had been cheated out of his rightful earnings by an unscrupulous publishing house. This campaign was started by the Reverend James T. Quirk, the vicar of Attleborough, eager to help one of his parishioners, whom he honestly believed to have been mistreated and who was living in pathetic conditions of poverty and neglect. Kathryn Hughes has discovered that the widowed, long-suffering Chrissey Evans lived "just a few hundred yards from Joseph Liggins": "Tellingly, both she and Liggins had ended up in this unattractive industrial village as a consequence of a steep decline in their personal fortunes" ("But Why Always" 46). Quirk organized a letter-writing campaign directed at Blackwood and the press. Eventually he brought another instigator into the crusade on behalf of Liggins. For his part, Liggins remained silent and failed to deny his authorship of George Eliot's books, perhaps hoping to benefit from the strange case of mistaken identity in which he had become passively involved.

Liberal Warwickshire landowner Charles Holte Bracebridge refused to let the matter drop once he became active in the Liggins campaign, even after Lewes had written a letter to the *Times* denying that Liggins was George Eliot, but not naming the real author (April 16, 1859). Marian, Lewes, and Blackwood wanted to keep her identity anonymous, but the situation created tension between the couple and Blackwood, whom they rightly suspected of preferring that the public not associate their conservative firm with the name of a woman living with a married man. All parties worried that the knowledge would affect the sales of future novels.

Marian was also disappointed in the behavior of her friends. She had confided in Spencer, and she suspected him of telling Chapman, who then spread the (true) rumor that George Eliot was Marian Evans Lewes. As these rumors about her authorship became more frequent, she came under personal attack in various publications including the *Athenaeum* (Haight, *Biography* 282–94). She and Lewes felt they had no choice but to deny again that Liggins had anything to do with George Eliot and to stop denying that Mrs Lewes was George Eliot.

It was perhaps naïve of them to think that they could keep such a secret indefinitely. Marian would use the name George Eliot for the rest of her career. What other name could she use? She took the position that Miss Evans no longer existed and that her name was Mrs Marian Lewes; and yet, this was not her legal name. To use it would only call attention to her adulterous union with Lewes and the fact that the legal Mrs Lewes was still living. This bizarre, embarrassing, and disillusioning encounter with the reading public eventually compelled her to reveal her identity, thereby sparking a new round of gossip about the woman living with Mr Lewes.

But the saga still continued: once he conceded that Mary Ann Evans was George Eliot, Bracebridge made it a personal mission to ferret out relatives of hers – including the daughter of her uncle Samuel and aunt Elizabeth Evans. The effect of all this searching out of originals was to revive the uncomfortable implication that George Eliot's fiction, which struck readers as so fresh and original, was really just a "copy" or "portrait" of living people. Bodenheimer sums up the situation:

> No sooner had she announced her presence on the literary scene as a new kind of realist, than she was accused of retelling actual life stories; the Bracebridge affair was a like a ludicrous nightmare in which the gossiping characters in her books rose up and began to circulate rumors about their creator. (*Real Life* 142)

The need to deny this "plagiarism" from life again, as she had had to do after characters from Nuneaton (whom she had assumed were dead) began to make themselves known as originals for characters in *Scenes*, had an impact on her future fiction. It was not simply that she was more careful about her use of the past and real people, or even only, as Bodenheimer notes, that she was beginning to view her "marketplace of readers" as divided between those who understood and appreciated her and the "ignorant gossiping public" that did not (*Real Life* 143).

The very problem of originality came to complicate the way she treated the relationship of reality and fiction. It appears as a theme in her fiction, giving her writing an allusive self-consciousness that eventually turned into a meta-historical form of game-playing and challenge to the audience that at first thought they could catch her in an act of copying from life. She would deploy her immense learning and reading in all fields and languages and make literary allusions work for her in new ways, conflating fictional characters and real people and inflecting them with aspects of herself in ways that make everything she wrote after *Adam Bede* a little more dense and a little less accessible to that gossiping but paying public. As we will see, characters ranging from Nello in *Romola* to Casaubon in *Middlemarch* and Theophrastus in *Impressions of Theophrastus Such* have originals (or namesakes) in historical figures who were also authors. The reader needs to have knowledge of the originals and their writings in order to appreciate the depth of her conceptions. This sophisticated and learned style is still posing challenges to readers and critics, and it began in her next novel, which has, somewhat ironically and sometimes naïvely, been read as an autobiographical novel and used to construct the elusive story of Mary Ann Evans's childhood. Given all that she had just been through in the Liggins/Bracebridge ordeal, it would be no surprise if Eliot was entirely aware as she wrote *The Mill on the Floss* that it, too, would be mined for its originals, as it was and continues to be.

She paused in the composition of this new novel, which she had thought to call "Sister Maggie" or "The House of Tulliver," to write "The Lifted Veil" (1859), a dark, misanthropic short story that uncharacteristically explored supernatural human perceptions and which may reflect her bitterness over both the public's and her friends' behavior in the Liggins matter, as well as her sensitivity to criticism about her unmarried status.[22] Once again, the story has at its core a triangle. The narrator, Latimer, is infatuated with his brother's fiancée, Bertha, and his brother conveniently dies in an accident. As in *Adam Bede*, a brother marries the beloved of brother. But Latimer suffers for this covetousness. Bertha is the one person who defies his uncanny ability to read minds. He is drawn to her because her mind is unknown, and there is an allegorical implication about both the impossibility and the dangers of not knowing one's spouse, and similar themes that Eliot more realistically and expansively explores in her novels. Bertha is not only sadistic, but murderous. Her desire to kill her hyper-sensitive, effeminate husband is kept secret by a maid with whom she is suspiciously intimate. When Mrs Archer dies, her body is used for an experiment performed by Latimer's old friend Meunier, now a celebrated doctor and scientist. Through a blood transfusion the servant Mrs Archer is brought momentarily back to life and survives just long enough to reveal the truth about Bertha.

It is a Gothic story of triangulated desire with a twist of early science fiction. Its European settings in Geneva and Prague are also a departure from the fictions of rural England Eliot had thus far written. Blackwood, who could not like or appreciate the story, reluctantly agreed to publish it in *Blackwood's Magazine*, probably to keep his successful author happy. The piece did not make much impact, and when Eliot reprinted it in later editions of her work, she tried to mitigate its darkness by adding a hopeful, humanistic epigraph of her own composition:

> Give me no light, great Heaven, but such as turns
> To energy of human fellowship;
> No powers beyond the growing heritage
> That makes completer manhood.

(SM 84)

The epigraph cannot counteract the morbidity of the story in which Latimer, one of her few first-person narrators, writes up until the moment of his own death. The story was relatively neglected critically, but in recent years has received attention on a variety of fronts, including its feminist implications, its association of writing and death, its commentary on sympathy, and its use of science.[23]

The Mill on the Floss

In September 1859, Eliot and Lewes traveled to Gainsborough, finding that the town and the River Trent would serve well as models for the setting she had in mind for the new novel. Despite denying, after the publication of *Scenes*, that her characters had originals, she often felt that she needed to find an original place on which to model the settings of her stories, no matter how much she would then fictionalize those settings. In this case, she turned Gainsborough into St Ogg's, the River Trent into the Floss and the Idle into the Ripple. This drawing from life was a consistent feature of her realism as she combined observation of actual places she had visited, such as Florence for *Romola*, with research to describe as accurately as possible the original places on which she modeled the settings of her novels and some of her poems, such as the *Spanish Gypsy*.

There was initial uncertainty about whether or not Eliot would publish her second novel with Blackwood. She felt some residual awkwardness with him over his handling of the Liggins affair because she and Lewes believed that he did not act quickly enough to deny false claims about the authorship of *Scenes* and *Adam Bede*. Furthermore, and inevitably given the success of *Adam Bede*, she was courted by other publishers, particularly Charles Dickens, who hoped to serialize a novel of hers in his magazine, *Household Words*. Through a series of frank letters, Eliot and Blackwood worked out their differences, and she accepted his terms for publishing the novel. It was Blackwood who proposed the ultimate title, *The Mill on the Floss*, despite its inaccuracy (the mill is actually on the Floss's tributary stream, the Ripple).

After several people from Nuneaton and its environs made claims to be the "originals" of characters in *Scenes* and *Adam Bede* (and wrote to Blackwood to assert those claims), Eliot was obliged to deny any one-to-one relationship between real people and the characters she created in her fiction. But she clearly based aspects of the young Maggie and Tom Tulliver on Mary Ann and Isaac Evans and the Dodson sisters on her own aunts, the Pearson sisters. Robert Evans's diaries show just how important these relations were in Mary Ann's early life with constant visits to and from the aunts and their respective families. While writing *The Mill*, she admitted to Barbara Bodichon that she was dwelling in her "remotest past," where "there are many strata to be worked through before I can begin to use *artistically* any material I may gather in the present" (*GEL* 3:129). The use of textual allusion in her works increased as her concern about being popular decreased. Hughes observes that she was alarmed by the success of *Adam Bede* and wondered whether its appeal to so many meant that she was doing something wrong (Hughes, *Last Victorian* 205; *GEL* 3:12). Rather than think of *The Mill* as an autobiographical novel, we might more profitably think of it as a novel that explores the idea of an autobiographical novel.

Spencer's claim in *An Autobiography* that Eliot lived with "a current of self-criticism being an habitual accompaniment of anything she was saying or doing" (1:396) is substantiated by Eliot's fictional rendering of the young Mary Ann Evans, who was now only a memory, critically dissociated from the present Marian Lewes. When Maggie gazes on the portrait Philip Wakem painted of her as a child, for example "saw her old self leaning on a table, with her black locks hanging down behind her ears" (*Mill* 300; bk. 5, ch. 1). Cross writes that the young Maggie was "the best autobiographical representation we can have of George Eliot's own feelings in her childhood," but that the incidents in the book are "so mixed with fictitious elements and situations that it would be absolutely misleading to trust to it as a true history" (Cross, *Life* 1:23). In his introduction to the original Riverside edition of *The Mill*, Haight remarks that "readers can hardly help feeling that the childhood experiences of Tom and Maggie Tulliver must have been auto-biographical" because so many incidents seem "too convincing to have been invented" (vii). This is an example of the way that Eliot's early tendency to draw from life led to a devaluing of her imaginative power on the part of critics, as if scenes that are not autobiographical are less "convincing" than autobiographical scenes. While acknowledging the biographical dimensions of *The Mill* in partic-ular, it is equally important to recover the ambiguity signaled by Cross when he wrote that the book reflected and recalled her "feelings in her childhood" rather than any particular events.

Between autobiography and pure invention lies one of the most distinctive attributes of Eliot's art – the naturalized allusion to other texts. *The Mill*'s style of realism integrates historical research – on floods, water rights, and the laws governing financial failure – with literary works familiar to many Victorian readers. Her success and financial prosperity was beginning to free her from concerns about popularity. She could now concentrate on developing a style that recalled her youthful letters with their layers of biblical quotation and their inclination to turn to other texts to express her own thoughts. From this point forward, she would more subtly and ingeniously weave allusions into her realist narratives. As a result, her prose would become denser and more complex. Her rivers invoke mythical and real rivers (Styx, Lethe, Nile, Jordan). The river brilliantly combines her realism of everyday life with a symbolism untried in her earlier fiction. It is both a force of nature and a metaphor for the fluidity of time and memory that enabled her to return to her past and remake it in the present. Such simultaneously real and symbolic intertextual rivers would also run through *Romola* (the Arno) and *Daniel Deronda* (the Thames).[24]

As for the biographical context, it seems that the childhood bond between Mary Ann and Isaac may have grown in significance as it was cultivated in memory and represented in fiction. Before the complete break over Lewes, Isaac had been an overbearing enforcer of respectability and of gender roles felt to be oppressive by his gifted sister. Now cut off from her brother, she looked backward and inward for insight into an intense brother–sister tie. The sibling relationship in *The Mill* shows signs of Wordsworth's influence both because it is an intense experience recollected in the tranquility of later years, and a subject at the heart of the work, much as Wordsworth's relationship to his sister Dorothy is central to "Lines Composed a Few Miles above Tintern Abbey" (1798). At the same time, Eliot resisted Wordsworth's vision of childhood in his "Ode: Intimations of Immortality from Recollections of Early Childhood" (1807), focusing on the intensity of the child's suffering rather than the glory and freshness of his vision and his joy.[25] The most painful sequences of the novel involve Maggie's agonies as a result of Tom's narrow sense of justice. There is bitterness in the analysis of Tom's limitations, even amidst a sympathetic elaboration of the pressures exercised upon him by his family and society generally. To the extent that Tom's character is based on Isaac Evans, it must also have been mingled with the pain and sense of injustice she felt as an adult when her brother acted to cut her off not only from himself but from the other members of her family whose personalities she was incorporating into her novel.

An element of plot and psychology that continued to unify virtually all of her fictional works was the sexual triangle. *The Mill* is plotted around several triangulations. First, Maggie is in the odd position of sneaking off behind Tom's back to see Philip and lying about it in ways that make her intuitively uncomfortable, despite her own rationalization that Tom is wrong to oppose her friendship with Philip. Later, Maggie's relationship with Stephen puts her into a love triangle with her unsuspecting cousin Lucy (often assumed by critics to be a portrait of Chrissey Evans). She loves Lucy, but since childhood has felt competitive and envious of her in ways that she could not explain, as when she jealously pushed the lovely blonde child, so unlike herself, into the mud because Tom was paying too much attention to her. Maggie cannot understand her impulsive motives in this scene, and she seems to be impelled by a force comparable to that which leads her to float down the river with Stephen unconscious of time or distance. Her attraction to Stephen, furthermore, also creates a triangle with Philip, to whom she has made an uneasy, secret, and somewhat coerced commitment. Tom's feelings for his cousin Lucy are delicately implied from his early fondness for her to his gift of a dog. But Tom is notably asexual, and in contrast to his supposed model Isaac Evans, makes no effort that we know of toward a respectable marriage to match the respectable career he has built. At the end, Tom is hard and lonely, living only for work. Eliot chose not to give him any strong sexual desire so that the triangles in which he figures involve his sister and Philip, or, if he is in love with Lucy, a rivalry with Stephen that is unknown to anyone. Perhaps this absence of sexual passion in the pursuit of respectability and money aligns him with his Dodson aunts, the childless Gleggs, and the Pullets.

Maggie's profound emotional ambivalence about where her loyalties should lie (with Tom, Philip, or Stephen) is the major cause of the novel's divisions, the apparent severing of its last books from the earlier ones. That ambivalence is marked by the dreamy passivity of Maggie's boat trip with Stephen, which results in her ostracism from the community to which she stubbornly returns, and the seemingly hopeless, miserable position in which she finds herself prior to the climactic flood. Even her actions during the flood, when she rows out into the river to rescue Tom, are not rational or even conscious: "In the first moments Maggie felt nothing, thought of nothing, but that she had suddenly passed away from that life which she had been dreading: it was the transition of death, without its agony – and she was alone in the darkness with God" (*Mill* 471; bk. 7, ch. 5). As Maggie instinctively rows toward her old home with heroic strength and courage, we realize that the dreaded future is being obliterated by a visitation from the past as she literally and metaphorically returns home and to Tom: "She was driven out upon the flood: – the awful visitation of God which her father used to talk of – which had made the nightmare of her childish dreams. And with that thought there rushed in the vision of the old home – and Tom – and her mother – they had all listened together" (*Mill* 471; bk. 7, ch. 5). And so we are taken back to the narrator's opening reverie of the novel – as well as to the origin of myths about Mary Ann Evans's happy childhood beginnings with Cross's invocation in his *Life* of the happy Evans family sitting together at home. Mr Tulliver tells the story of a great flood that lives in the memory of the St Ogg's community and is part of the mythology of Tom and Maggie's lives. Safely located in the past, it nonetheless contributes to an ominous sense of danger that pervades the novel. The flood becomes a source of nightmares for the child Maggie, and in that instant before she actually drowns, we have a sense of that nightmare coming true. Similarly, the prophecy of death by drowning is made by Mrs Tulliver at several points in the novel when she worries that Maggie may drown in the river.

*" 'It is coming, Maggie!' Tom said, in a deep hoarse voice, loosing the oars and clasping her."—*PAGE 485.

Figure 17 Tom and Maggie from *The Mill on the Floss* (William Blackwood and Sons, Stereotyped Edition)

By the time *The Mill* was published in April 1860, Eliot's estrangement from her past had become a settled fact. Chrissey was dead, and Isaac was unbending in his determination not to speak with her – a firmness of character that she portrayed in Tom with both admiration and censure. Her own identity was now that of a voluntary exile who could not go home again. Family connections existed for her only in memory and in fiction. Isaac might as well have been a been a character in a novel for all the role he played in her daily life. She used her memory and imagination to create – as she often said – fresh combinations. She also used the godlike power of the author to kill off characters – from the problematically fertile Milly and Hetty to the impossibly incestuous Tom and Maggie.

The deluge at the end of *The Mill* did more than depart melodramatically from the realism to which Eliot claimed to adhere, even within the pages of the novel. It also did more than resolve the narrative problem of how Maggie could possibly go on living, divided against herself and scorned by both society and her brother. The violent destruction of Tom and Maggie as they cling to each other and are crushed by a rogue mass of floating machinery, then drowned in the river that had been their livelihood – so lovingly described in the novel's opening pages – was a cathartic, even exorcising act for Eliot. It ended her novel about the common problems of ordinary, uneducated provincial people with a dramatically elevating mythic flood unprecedented in English fiction. And it put an end to her relationship with her family and her own provincial past. Artistically, it ended her need to draw directly on past family relations to create her fiction. The ending of *The Mill on the Floss* marked a personal and aesthetic beginning, and her writing took new directions of consequence for her and for the history of the English novel.

Notes

1. *Leader*, August 1, 1855, 750. Reprinted as "Life and Opinions of Milton" in Pinney. In an interesting analysis of Eliot as "Miltonist," Dayton Haskin makes the biographical connection, noting: "The climactic work of the review was to present Milton not as the author of *Paradise Lost*, but as a stand-in for Lewes . . ." (214). His account of Lewes's actual marital situation, however, is vague (211).
2. Haight reveals that Cross also chose to cut what may be a reference to Lewes's desire to divorce from Eliot's 1860 letter to Barbara Bodichon: "By the way, we have consulted a barrister, very accomplished in foreign and English law, about that matter broached by your friend Mrs. Brodie. He pronounces it *impossible*. I am not sorry. I think the boys will not suffer, and for myself I prefer excommunication" (*GEL* 3:366).
3. Kitchel traces these and other claims back to Linton in an appendix called "Mrs. Lynn Linton's views on Lewes's break with his wife." She discredits Linton's account (though not the condonation claim). Redinger cites Kitchel in tracing the condoning theory, as well as the idea that Lewes and Agnes practiced "free love," back to Linton's *The Autobiography of Christopher Kirkland*. Redinger (like Haight) doubts the validity of this claim. (Kitchel 313; Redinger 249).
4. Biographies prior to Haight's suggest uncertainty about the paternity of several of the children, including St Vincent Arthy Lewes, who lived from May 11, 1848, through March 23, 1850, dying two weeks before Edmund's birth. Fremantle raises doubts about the paternity of Thornie and Bertie, whom Lewes fully accepted as his own, as does Blanche Williams (95). The idea of Thornie, Bertie, or St Vincent's illegitimacy is not broached by Haight, but Redinger also entertains it as a possibility (252–3).
5. Haight continued to assert these claims, for example in "The Carlyles and the Leweses," republished in *George Eliot's Originals*, in which the sources are gossipy letters written by the Carlyles.
6. Without citing sources, Karl writes: "Lewes torpedoed any chance of divorce for adultery by accepting Hunt's child by Agnes as his own" (160), and Hughes (*George Eliot: The Last Victorian*) asserts: "As the law stood, by giving Hunt's child his name Lewes was condoning Agnes's adultery and relinquishing the right to sue at any point for divorce. By this one administrative act he would condemn Marian Evans to a life as a sexual and social outcast" (141). Only Harriet F. Adams questions the story, arguing that the idea of Lewes's relation with Marian as the reason divorce was impossible "has been obscured by the insistence by scholars that what prevented Lewes from divorcing Agnes was his

'condoning' that first Hunt baby" (58). She concludes that there is nothing to substantiate claims that "condonation" prevented divorce.

7. In his analysis of obituaries of Eliot in the Victorian religious press, K. K. Collins observes: "Some religious papers . . . called Lewes her husband or said she had married him and left it at that . . . Others did not mention it – but a few did, and to these it was a stumbling-block far more serious than any doctrinal enigmas" (*Identifying the Remains* 67).

8. Linton does not mention condoning adultery here; rather, speaking of Eliot's union with Lewes as a mistake, she writes that people "condoned that mistake and created it into a virtue" ("George Eliot" 523).

9. See *The Autobiography of Christopher Kirkland* (1885), "George Eliot," (1885), and *My Literary Life* (1899).

10. Traditionally, that presumption could be rebutted only by proof that a husband was incapable of procreation or had had no access to his wife during the relevant period. Lewes traveled a great deal in the months prior to Edmund's birth in April 1850, but in July and August of 1849 he was writing letters from 26 Bedford Place, Kensington (*GHLL* 1:175–6), suggesting that he was at home at the time of conception.

11. Sir William Blackstone's *Commentaries on the Laws of England in Four Books* was a standard source on the laws of England and was consulted by Eliot, for example, when writing the complex legal plot of *Felix Holt*.

12. See Nayder, *The Other Dickens*.

13. In 1871, an acquaintance of the Leweses, Moncure Conway, delivered a paper "On Marriage" to the London Dialectical Society (of which Lewes was a vice-president). His comments provide some insight into the real reason that Lewes did not file for a divorce: "At present the only escape from ill-sorted unions was across the ruins of some person's character. Those who were too kind to ruin a partner's character remained without redress" (4). Conway later published a piece about Eliot's marriage to Cross. My thanks to Claudia Martin for discovering this source as well as for clarifying various legal questions for this chapter.

14. Andrew Dowling's 1995 article, "'The Other Side of Silence': Matrimonial Conflict and the Divorce Court in George Eliot's Fiction," examines Eliot's "texts" in the "context" of the "legal discourse of the first English Divorce Court" (322). His New Historicist focus on silence as a "rhetorical device" that intersects with Divorce Court proceedings following the Matrimonial Causes Act of 1857 overlooks the obvious biographical context. He writes that, although Eliot may have had a personal interest in divorce, "the general literary trend toward the subject of matrimonial misery can be best understood, I think, as a response to this wider social desire to know in greater detail the intricacies of a previously invisible topic" (329). His only mention of Eliot's life comes in a footnote in which he cites the cryptic 1860 letter to Barbara Bodichon (*GEL* 3:366). He does not mention Agnes, adultery, or any other biographical details.

15. On the influence of European travel and Eliot's relationship to European literature, see Rignall, *George Eliot, European Novelist*.

16. Exceptions include her Saccharissa essays in the *Pall Mall Gazette* (1865) and a review in the *Fortnightly* (1865), which Lewes was editing at the time.

17. Hughes objects to the erasure of the extended Evans family in biographies of George Eliot after this point. She has uncovered evidence to show, "From the 1850s until Evans' death

in 1880, and even beyond, information circulated freely between the Midlands and London, ensuring that everyone – both those involved directly in the family quarrel of 1857 and those who were merely onlookers – remained acutely aware of, and reactive to, one another" ("But Why Always" 44).

18. Joseph Allen Boone explores the ideological manifestations of the traditional marriage plot in the Anglo-British novel and identifies a counter-tradition, which reacted to the notion of a happy ending by making marital discord part of the very structure of the novel. He includes *Daniel Deronda* as part of this counter-tradition. Certainly aspects of Eliot's critique of marriage are an indictment of gendered Victorian ideologies and power structures, but the form that her indictments take are distinctive to her.

19. The source is dubious. It derives from a description of a destroyed letter from Bodichon to Bessie Parkes given to Haight by Parkes's daughter (Haight, *Biography* 205, fn. 2). But information about birth control was certainly available to Eliot and Lewes, as well as to Hunt and Agnes, though not to Eliot's rural mothers in fictions set in the early decades of the century. On contemporary practices of birth control and the dissemination of birth control education see Jütte 117–54 and McLaren. On "The Sad Fortunes" in relation to Malthus, see Gallagher, *Body Economic*.

20. For all the conjectured biographical parallels between *Adam Bede* and the Evans family, see also Mottram.

21. The most insightful treatment of the ordeal is found in Bodenheimer (*Real Life*, ch. 5). Hughes adds important new facts as to how it unfolded ("But Why Always"). The two have different takes on Marian's reflexive protecting of her secret identity under pressures to reveal it. Bodenheimer refers to her "exuberant pleasure in hiding" (121) while Hughes refers to her "tendency to resort to half-truths" and to "hide behind equivocation" (*Last Victorian* 45). Welsh argues that after the Liggins affair, each novel "treats secrets curiously if not sympathetically, and each novel proves less content with entire knowingness" (131).

22. For a reading of "The Lifted Veil" and "Brother Jacob" in light of the Liggins affair, see Bodenheimer (*Real Life*, ch. 5).

23. See Knoepflmacher, *George Eliot's Early Novels*; Gilbert and Gubar, *Madwoman in the Attic*; Hertz, *George Eliot's Pulse*; Flint, "Blood"; Greiner, "Sympathy Time"; and Willis, "Clairvoyance."

24. In *English Travels* McCormack argues that the representations of the boating on the Floss as well as the flood were influenced by the years that Eliot and Lewes spent living near the Thames in Richmond (1856–9) (88). See also Jules Law.

25. On Wordsworth and *The Mill*, see Homans; on Dorothea and Dorothy, see Knoepflmacher, "Fusing Fact and Myth."

5

Silas Marner and Romola
1860–4

I think Rome will at last chase away Maggie and the Mill from my thoughts . . .
(George Eliot to John Blackwood, *GEL* 3:285)

On March 24, 1860, with *The Mill on the Floss* completed, Eliot and Lewes left their current home, Holly Lodge south of the Thames in Wandsworth, and set off for a tour primarily of Italy but with stops before in Paris and after in Switzerland. The journey is described in Eliot's "Recollections of Italy 1860" (*GEJ* 336–68). During these three months they pursued an energetic regime of sightseeing in Turin, Genoa, Pisa, Rome, Naples, Florence, and Venice. In starting her "Recollections," written after she returned from the trip as a Wordsworthian exercise in recollection, she expressed her typical attitude toward travel, and toward cultural pursuits generally, saying that this trip to Italy was one she "had looked forward to for years, rather with the hope of the new elements it would bring to my culture, than with the hope of immediate pleasure" (*GEJ* 336). This seriousness about pursuing high culture for the sake of self-improvement would characterize her many trips to Europe in later years. She and Lewes found much pleasure in their pursuit of culture and improvement, but often it was at the expense of physical discomfort, and in later years, they often traveled abroad to visit spas for the sake of their health.

The Life of George Eliot: A Critical Biography, First Edition. Nancy Henry.
© 2012 Nancy Henry. Published 2012 by John Wiley & Sons, Ltd.

In her written account of the trip, Eliot minimized her pleasure by justifying it as study, but she could not contain the ultimate joy she found particularly in Roman and Italian art and architecture, if not always in the life of the local, modern Italians. Describing the "double consciousness" that Spencer was to attribute to her in his *Autobiography*, she writes:

> One great deduction to me from the delight of seeing world-famous objects is the frequent double consciousness which tells me that I am not enjoying the actual vision enough, and that when higher enjoyment comes with the reproduction of the scene in my imagination I shall have lost some of the details, which impress me too feebly in the present because the faculties are not wrought up into energetic action. (*GEJ* 336)

This double (or triple) consciousness and interplay between what she anticipated, the reality of the present as she experienced it, and how she remembers or represents that reality, is important to note for the complicated consciousness of the narrative voice she was developing in her fiction. It is also an indication of how she understood her own process of realistic representation.

In this passage, speaking in her own voice, she explains what happens to her in the moment when she is viewing or being impressed by a great work of art; she is troubled with the consciousness that what will happen later "when higher enjoyment comes" is disappointment that she "shall have lost" details because those details are not impressing her thoroughly enough in the moment to allow her to enjoy them later. This failure to be impressed sufficiently enough by details to recall them in the future, strikes her as a failing. It is clear that in her work to date, and in her future work, she strove to receive present experiences more thoroughly in order to better recall and represent them in her writing.[1]

In addition to the implicit concerns about realism that her "Recollections of Italy" reveal, the double consciousness she describes as constituting her own world view provides an insight into the way her narrators hold their knowledge of past, present, and future in balance, often thinking of how a past experience will affect a character in the future. The double consciousness with which she lived constantly was a state of mind explored in the poetry of Wordsworth, who remained one of her favorite poets and most important influences. For example, in his "Lines, Composed a Few Miles above Tintern Abbey", the poet/speaker reflects, "While here I stand, not only with the sense/Of present pleasure, but with pleasing thoughts/That in this moment there is life and food/For future years" (117; ll. 62–5). He confesses that he is not entirely in the present moment but rather thinking about the future, when he will recall this present. Similarly, when he addresses his sister Dorothy at the end of the poem, he anticipates how, in the future, she will remember the present they are experiencing now: "with what healing thoughts/Of tender joy wilt thou remember me,/And these my exhortations!" (119; ll. 144–6). The anticipation of how the present will be remembered in the future becomes part of the moment's pleasure. In Eliot's case, however, the anticipation that she will not remember well enough becomes another opportunity for her characteristic self-criticism.

In her journal entry, Eliot is particularly interested in the images the word "Rome" had conjured in her mind for the many years she had anticipated visiting the city before actually doing so.[2] In her letters and journal she talks about what a disappointment she had upon entering Rome: "My heart sank, as it would if you behaved shabbily to me," she told Maria Congreve, her friend and neighbor in Wandsworth (*GEL* 3:286). She had lived with a vision of Rome, and it disappointed her as a friend might. But gradually she rose from the "depth of disappointment to an intoxication of delight." It is the delight that she mostly describes in the journal, the layers of history and specific places and works of art that thrilled and moved her. Showing that the Romantic poets were often in her mind, she writes: "A spot that touched me deeply was Shelley's grave" (*GEJ* 348). And as if relating personally to Shelley's own experience as a virtual exile in Rome, she writes that his heart, which was buried there, is "for ever at rest from the unloving cavillers of this world, whether or not he may have entered on other purifying struggles, in some world unseen by us" (*GEJ* 349). It is an interesting insight into her views about the poet who had been so important to Lewes.

Their visit to Rome coincided with the Holy Week of Easter, making them impatient with the crowds and the ceremonies. She wrote to Maria Congreve:

> I knelt down to receive the Pope's blessing. . . . But altogether, these ceremonies are a melancholy, hollow business, and we regret bitterly that the Holy Week has taken up our time from better things. I have a cold and headache this morning, and in other ways am not conscious of improvement from the Pope's blessing. (*GEL* 3:288)

Although Eliot and Lewes stayed a month in Rome, and almost immediately overcame the disappointment of their first impressions, recollections of these experiences during Holy Week would influence Dorothea's bewildered and miserable experience of Rome during her honeymoon in *Middlemarch*, when her first, overwhelming encounter with the Roman Catholic spectacles and ceremonies function as externalizations of her mortifying disillusionment with her recent marriage to Casaubon. Eliot even complains that the lovely marble interior of St Peter's was "half covered with hideous red drapery" (*GEJ* 344), an image that she would transform into one of her most famous and chilling similes, which seems to sum up Dorothea's state of mind, "the red drapery which was being hung for Christmas spreading itself everywhere like a disease of the retina" (182; ch. 20). Such powerful negative impressions of Holy Week may also have inspired the recreation of ceremonies in Florence and the performances of the mock priest who performs Tito and Tessa's "marriage" in *Romola*. She and Lewes loved Italy and returned many times, but always with skepticism toward what he called at the time of this visit the "hateful shams" of Holy Week (GHLJ, April 8, 1860; Haight, *Biography* 324).

This journey was also a turning point in her domestic life. After their tour of Italy, they traveled to Switzerland. At the Hofwyl School near Bern, Eliot met Lewes's three sons, Charles, Thornie, and Bertie, for the first time. Lewes had chosen this boarding school because he wanted them to have a more cosmopolitan education outside England, as he had had himself, and also possibly because he wanted to remove them from exposure to any scandal about their parents' separation that might reach them at home. He had made trips to visit them since his union with Eliot six years before, but this was the first time that she was introduced to them, so it was a significant occasion.

The eldest son, Charles, had finished his schooling, so he returned with them to England. On the way they stopped in Geneva, where Eliot renewed her acquaintance with the D'Albert Durades, granting M. D'Albert Durade the rights to translate her books into French. When they arrived home at Holly Lodge on July 1, 1860, they were a family of three, and for the next several years the future careers of the Lewes boys would be a primary focus of their domestic lives. Charles began studying immediately for the Civil Service examination and preparing for the type of secure, respectable middle-class career that his parents envisioned for him and his brothers.

The trip abroad had been important personally, professionally, and artistically for Eliot. During their two weeks in Florence, Lewes suggested that the life of the Dominican monk Girolamo Savonarola (1452–98) and his brief rule over the city (1494–8) might make a good subject for an historical novel. They began preliminary research for the project during their short stay. Once back in England, however, Eliot set aside the Italian project while she wrote "Brother Jacob" (finished in August 1860) and then *Silas Marner* (finished in March 1861), but the idea of the Florentine story stayed with her.

These works of the early 1860s, constituting the midpoint of Eliot's career, should be considered together. They are linked through themes of family and betrayal viewed from various perspectives and have a correlation to events in her life and to her psychological states when she wrote them. It was a period of adaptation from her identity of social pariah to one of celebrity, as well as from financial uncertainty to financial security.[3] Furthermore, it was a time of distancing herself from her identity as daughter and sister and adjusting to a new family in which she was wife and mother, but also at the same time, neither fully wife nor mother. Writing *Romola* was the most difficult creative process she would ever experience. Expressing doubt about her ability to achieve what she had set out to do, she despaired: "Will it ever be finished – ever be worth anything?" (February 26, 1862; *GEJ* 110). The emotional and physical pain she suffered during *Romola*'s composition contributed to the transformation in her art and her aesthetic ambitions, as is evident in the novel and the works that followed.

Figure 18 Charles Lee Lewes, photograph by George Herbert Watkins, 1863 (© National Portrait Gallery, London)

The process of writing *Romola* also furthered the changes in perspective begun after the Liggins affair. Her acute self-consciousness about the textual nature of history and the ways she "used" the past, as well as her interrogation of originality in life and art, are among the differences from previous works that characterize *Romola*. She seemed to be cultivating the "double consciousness" described in "Recollections of Italy." Her intellectual, philosophical, and highly literary approach to writing now showed a disregard for her work's popularity. She explained to Sara Hennell that "the book is addressed to fewer readers than my previous works" and was never intended to be "as 'popular' in the same sense as the others" (*GEL* 4:49). Furthermore, having come to regard the majority of readers as too insensitive and uneducated to understand her work, she altered the nature of her plea for sympathy with ordinary people as she had expressed it in *Scenes* and *Adam Bede*. Her new cautiousness and skepticism about sympathy – even her warning about its dangers, as seen in the preternaturally knowing Latimer in "The Lifted Veil" – accompanied the less accessible, more experimental, textual and aestheticized prose of her late novels.

Silas Marner

She was brooding about her Italian novel in 1860 when an English story "thrust itself" between her and the more ambitious work about Renaissance Florence (November 28, 1860; GEJ 87). *Silas Marner* has its dark elements of betrayal, secrecy, theft, drug addiction, and death, which contextualize it at the beginning of the rise of the sensation novel throughout the 1860s. But its fable-like quality, and its ultimately uplifting moral that human love and community are greater forces than either religion or money, suggest that its writing was a respite for Eliot after she had refashioned painful memories from her past in *The Mill*, entertained varieties of moral skepticism in her two short stories, and contemplated what would be the darkest of all her forays into individual and collective human psychology in the yet unnamed Italian novel.

Silas Marner departs from some of her previous formal practices. It is exceptional among her novels for its relative inattention to the historical details of time and place. The date of its setting is not precise, and the village of Raveloe, though clearly in the Midlands, does not have a specific "original." This vagueness, even despite other aspects of the novel's realism, adds to the novel's universal, archetypal quality. It is short (published in one volume), and it was written without the agonies of self-doubt that attended the writing of her other major works. It seems to have come from an inspiration rather than the labored research of *Romola* or even the less intensive but thorough research she conducted for *The Mill*. Though it is full of literary echoes and allusions – for example to Wordsworth and the Bible – the novel's interpretation does not depend on knowledge of literary allusions or historical originals. It is uncharacteristic of her writing in its simplicity, yet it is comparable to some of the poetry with which she would experiment in the late 1860s. Though both the setting and the characters are realistic, the narrative is accompanied by an almost magical coincidence and symmetry of form that suggest a temporary loosening of a certain self-imposed realistic constriction on her creativity. The much longer *Romola*, in contrast, would balance its hard historical realism with a dreamy mythic quality introduced in the last section of the novel.

Both the pre-history and the main plot of *Silas* continue the pattern of sexual triangles in Eliot's fiction, which has its source in her consciousness of, and place within, the Lewes–Hunt triangles. She could hardly forget the presence of Agnes Lewes, with whom Lewes was in regular communication and who the Lewes boys called "Mamma," even as they began calling Eliot "Mother" or "Mutter." Thornie's letter to his father before meeting his new Mother lays out the dilemma of her identity more fully than his parents ever seem to have done in their own letters. Writing on March 20, 1860, he asks his father's permission to tell a school friend their family secret that George Eliot was the new mother who would be visiting them. Because the schoolmate "has seen Mamma, and knows her, he will of course see that

Mother is not she . . . ." Cutting through the euphemisms of his elders, he demands clarification: "You have told Mamma, that you had told us, didn't you?" (*GEL* 8:259–60). This suggests the awkwardness felt by the Lewes boys, who corresponded with their real mother, as well as their father, at this time. Thornie wants to be sure that Agnes knows he has met his father's new friend and avoid making a *faux pas* in writing to his "Mamma." Although Haight infers that the boys were told something about Thornton Hunt when Lewes confided in them about his separation from Agnes, it seems more likely that they knew only that their parents were estranged and that Lewes was now living with the famous novelist George Eliot, their new "Mother." Even in Thornie's letters, there is no mention of Hunt, and the fiction that Lewes was the father of all the Lewes children was important to maintain for the benefit of the younger siblings still living at home with Agnes.

The plot of *Silas Marner* is set in motion by a sexual triangle and a betrayal. William Dane is already secretly involved with his best friend Silas's fiancée Sarah when he takes advantage of Silas's cataleptic fits to frame him for the crime of stealing money. William eventually has him banished from the dissenting Christian community of Lantern Yard, which up to that point has constituted Silas's entire world. This double betrayal by William and Sarah turns the devout Silas into an atheistic, disenchanted exile, recluse, and miser, who makes a fetish of the guineas he earns from weaving. The figure of the miser reveling in his gold coins, which he keeps hidden and secretly takes out at night to finger and caress as a displacement for all other pleasures (sexual and communal) and beliefs (religious or moral), seems to epitomize the conflicted feeling Eliot had about her own growing wealth.

This is Silas's condition in the isolated village of Raveloe, when, many years after settling on its outskirts without ever becoming integrated into its community, he unwittingly becomes involved in someone else's secret sexual triangle by adopting the daughter of another man living within the same community but in a social sphere far removed from his own. In the separate plot that intersects with that of the disenchanted miser Silas, the eldest son of the local squire, Godfrey Cass, has made an unfortunate marriage to a lower-class woman, Molly. Having borne Godfrey's child, Molly has become addicted to opium and is kept well hidden from the Cass family. In turn, Godfrey has become vulnerable to blackmail by his feckless, alcoholic younger brother Dunstan, the only family member who knows his secret.

On her confused way to confront Godfrey with their child and her poverty at his New Year's Eve party, the drug-addled Molly freezes to death in a snow storm just a few yards from Silas's modest hut. The child of that unlikely marriage wanders away from the body of her fallen mother and into the hut, appearing like a vision to the bitter, lonely, and near-sighted weaver. His stash of gold had mysteriously disappeared not long before. The money was stolen by Godfrey's brother Dunstan, thus robbing Silas of his only pleasure. Having been accused of theft in his distant past, and then made the victim of theft so recently, Silas feels that this motherless child is a restoration and restitution, a gift destined for him from the God in which he has almost ceased to believe. Only Godfrey knows that the child is his and that Molly's death will free him to marry the woman he now loves, Nancy Lammeter. Godfrey fails to tell Nancy about Molly or to acknowledge Molly's child. Like Arthur Donnithorne in *Adam Bede*, Godfrey, the soon-to-be Squire Cass, takes the coward's way out of his moral obligation to his wife and child and keeps the secret that will inevitably be revealed later in the novel, as almost all such secrets are in Eliot's fiction.

In July 1860, Eliot and Lewes coached Charles Lewes for his Civil Service examination. In August, having passed the exam, Charles began his new job as a clerk in the Post Office. The commute from their current home in Wandsworth was not practical, nor was it fair to isolate the young man from the social and cultural opportunities of London. With shades of Robert Evans's move from Griff to Foleshill to increase Marian's marriage prospects, they moved from Wandsworth to central London to facilitate Charles's career and social life. Inevitably, the move was disruptive to Eliot's writing. After an unsuccessful few months renting at Harewood Square, they settled in December 1860 at 16 Blandford Square, happily near Barbara Bodichon's London home. Eliot wrote most of *Silas Marner* at Blandford Square, balancing writing with a domestic life that included activities to entertain her stepson Charles, with whom she would become closest and who would remain a devoted son to the end of her life.

Eliot's letters at this time emphasize her maternal relationship to Charles but do not mention that Charles's biological mother Agnes was living nearby in Kensington, where Charles and his father might easily visit her and the four children living with her. These letters seem to make parenthood a moral value that gave Eliot a recognizable social position as mother of her husband's sons, normalizing her irregular relationship with Lewes and recalling her own mother's role as stepmother to her father's children by his previous marriage.

The redeeming value of parenthood as a form of human relationship, in contrast specifically to the cash-payment nexus that emerges as a central theme in *Silas Marner*, is not surprising, especially when we consider that Eliot was renegotiating her relationship to money and her new status as a wealthy woman. It was important to her to establish the superiority of parenthood to wealth, as well as to show the ways in which being a step-parent integrated her into a larger community of friends and readers who were also parents. The optimistic view of parenthood generally, and adoption in particular, would be overturned in the Italian novel that was never far from her thoughts, even as she absorbed herself in the familiar Midlands landscape of the fictional Raveloe.

Eliot told her publisher John Blackwood that the inspiration for *Silas Marner* was a recollection from childhood of seeing a linen weaver burdened with a pack on his back (*GEL* 3:384). She recreated the image in the opening paragraph of her novel, in which "those scattered linen-weavers – emigrants from the town into the country – were to the last regarded as aliens by their rustic neighbors, and usually contracted the eccentric habits which belong to a state of loneliness" (6; ch. 1). Again blending childhood memories with elements of her present life while writing the novel, she developed themes that she had explored at the end of *The Mill*, and introduced other themes that would become more pressing for her in the Italian novel. Just as Maggie is unfairly judged and exiled from St Ogg's society by the unforgiving gossip of the "World's Wife," so Silas is unjustly expelled from his Christian but rigidly superstitious Lantern Yard community. Maggie's social crime, however, is specific to a woman. By "running away" with Stephen she becomes a "fallen" woman, even to her brother Tom, and is perceived as having betrayed her cousin Lucy. Maggie's ostracism from the community of her birth because of a supposed sexual transgression recasts Marian Evans's experience after "running away" with Lewes to Germany and being shunned by polite society as a woman who broke up the family of a married man. The false accusation of Silas by his best friend William (with the complicit Sarah), on the other hand, is more reminiscent of Lewes's experience of being betrayed by his best friend and "brother" Thornton.

In *Silas Marner*, the narrator's sympathies are more with Godfrey and the upright Nancy Lammeter than the opium-addicted Molly or the drunken brother Dunstan Cass. These sympathies show Eliot's particular identification and sympathy with the man bound in a marriage he could not escape (John Milton, *Jane Eyre*'s Rochester, and Lewes). They also show her to be more tolerant of sexual transgressions than of drug and alcohol addictions, and in fact more forgiving of sexual sins than of other immoral behaviors. She was certainly forgiving of Charles Bray, whom she may have had in mind when drawing the childless couple Godfrey and Nancy Cass. She seems to have sympathized with Shelley, who fled England in part for his sexual transgressions. Throughout their life together, Lewes and Eliot welcomed male friends whom they knew were having affairs (even painful ones to their wives), including Charles Dickens and Edward Burne Jones.

While sexual transgression is a common feature of her fiction from the beginning, it is far from the most grievous of sins. In *Romola*, Tito's affair with Tessa tends to humanize him in the light of his other betrayals – of his father, father-in-law, and Savonarola. Similarly in *Daniel Deronda*, Grandcourt's most blameworthy act is not his affair with Mrs Glasher but his treatment of her after she had borne four of his children, and also his marrying Gwendolen, thus drawing her into an emotional triangle with his vengeful mistress and her carefully hidden offspring. This pattern of undermining a narrow Victorian morality focused on sexual behavior continued throughout Eliot's career (and life). In *Impressions of Theophrastus Such*, she devotes a chapter called "Moral Swindlers" to criticizing the modern tendency of people generally and of historians particularly to call a man "moral" based on his domestic habits ("not keeping mistresses" and "coming home to dine with his wife and children"), no matter how dishonest or unscrupulous he may be in his business dealings on a daily basis (*Impressions* 131; ch. 16).

Ultimately, *Silas Marner* is the story of salvation through the love of a child. Inspired by Wordsworth but departing dramatically from his poem, "Michael" (1800), which provides the novel's epigraph, she shows the gradual thawing of a heart frozen against human contact. The child Eppie is not a developed character. After her naughty escape from Silas's sight and her ineffectual punishment in the "toal-hole," she proves pure and devoted to her father, growing up to fall in love with a local boy and remaining un-tempted by the advantages that her biological father Godfrey offers her if she will only live with him and his wife. Through her, Eliot develops Silas's character, introducing a realistic psychological portrait within a moral fable, a notable mix of the realistic and the fantastic.[4] The novel posits that human love, community, and duty can serve the same functions as religion, exceeding and supplanting it as a model of reverence.

Silas Marner goes even further to metaphorically cut what had seemed to be Eliot's imaginative, emotional tethers to her past. Maggie has the opportunity to leave St Ogg's with a man offering romantic love and wealth, but instead chooses to return to social disgrace and to a family who cannot appreciate her devotion or her sacrifice. The happy ending of *Silas Marner* (Eppie's affirmation of her father and her class) seems a counter-balance to the tragic deaths of Tom and Maggie, which dramatically eclipse the humanistic sympathy shown to the ostracized Maggie by her mother, Aunt Glegg, and Bob Jakin. But in the final scene of *Silas Marner*, Silas makes a pilgrimage to the site of his past love and betrayal, Lantern Yard, only to find the very place obliterated and replaced by a factory: "The old place is all swep' away. . . the old home's gone; I've no home but this now" (179; ch. 21).

Silas is one of the few characters in Eliot's fiction who makes a successful, moral life for himself after leaving his place of origin. More frequently, she associates lack of roots in place with a lack of faithfulness, sympathy, and moral bearings (Hetty, Tito, Gwendolen). But the ending of *Silas* suggests Eliot's own wish to erase the past and cast her lot with her "husband," his children, and those friends who were willing to uncritically accept her situation. In short, it marks a transition between that delving into her past in her first three books and her break with the places and characters of that past in *Romola*.

Romola

Following the publication of *Silas Marner* (April 2, 1861), she and Lewes returned to Italy with focused attention on *Romola*. Leaving Blandford Square on April 19, 1861, and traveling part of the way in a private carriage, they passed through Nice, Genoa, and Pisa, and arrived for a month's stay in Florence on May 4. Eliot read all the primary and secondary sources she could relating to Florence in the time of Savonarola, including his sermons, poems, and political writings. They also spent five days in the Maglibecchian Library. Established in 1714, the library received a copy of every book published in Tuscany.[5] Lewes visited the monastery at San Marco for her again (since women could not enter) and took notes so that she could describe its interior, including Savonarola's cell. They walked the streets, studying the geography and architecture; they visited the museums. At the end of their stay, they met with Thomas Trollope, who would later provide information about Florence and the Italian language as Eliot wrote her novel. He persuaded them to travel to two beautiful, outlying monasteries, Camaldoli and La Verna. Lewes's account of the trip in his journal provides intimate glimpses of their life: he was "sick and faint" when her horse slipped on the edge of a precipice, and he arranged to sleep with her in the "cowhouse" reserved for women (who could not sleep in the monasteries) (GHLJ, June 3–6, 1861; Haight, *Biography* 346–7).

The eventual product of her research and immersion in Italian culture, *Romola*, would move her into a new phase of literary allusiveness, historical recreation, and mythic symbolism. Its setting places it within the trend of English interest in Italian culture during the ongoing struggle for Italian independence and unification (partly achieved and celebrated while the Leweses were in Florence on June 2, 1861). The writings of the Brownings, who lived in Florence, for example, express this interest, as does the less familiar fiction of Tom Trollope. Harriet Beecher Stowe's *Agnes of Sorrento* was also set during Savonarola's reign and, like *Romola*, was serialized in the *Cornhill* (1861–2). *Romola*'s heavily researched, dense allusiveness made it a unique contribution to the sub-genre of historical novel as established by Sir Walter Scott and his imitators, G. P. R. James and Charles Lever, as well as by Edward Bulwer-Lytton. Eliot had always been devoted to Scott and had read James, Lever, and Bulwer-Lytton, but her conception of history was more complex than theirs. Her distinctive double consciousness recognized that people in the past worried about how the future would remember them (something that of course they can never know), yet at the same time emphasized how those in the present do in fact remember the past. Ironic references to this "looking before and after, which is our grand human privilege" (*Impressions* 17; ch. 2) occur throughout her late fiction, as when Theophrastus refers to that elder England (in which many of Eliot's novels were set) with "all its blank ignorance of what we, its posterity, should be thinking of it" (*Impressions* 24; ch. 2)[6]

Her previous novels had all been set back in the England of a past generation, but *Romola* was different in many ways, including its self-consciousness about how great historical changes affect the private lives of individual people. In telling the story of her fictional heroine Romola and villain Tito, she inserted them into a series of actual events, tracing their marriage plot in light of political intrigue and religious reform in the late fifteenth-century Florentine Republic.[7]

That Lewes suggested the subject matter of *Romola* on their previous trip to Florence in 1860 provides interesting connections to their emotional and domestic lives during the period of her critical and financial successes with *Scenes*, *Adam Bede*, *The Mill*, and *Silas Marner* and her subsequent gradual acceptance into larger and more

Figure 19 Triptych of Dante, George Eliot, and Savonarola (Coventry History Centre)

elite social circles. Lewes's views about historical fiction have been distorted in the accounts of some biographers. Haight states that Lewes thought authors need only cram facts to produce historical romances. On the contrary, Lewes criticized inferior imitators of Scott and appreciated the difficulty of writing good historical fiction.

Reviewing Thornton Hunt's first and only published novel, *The Foster Brother* (1845), for example, Lewes expressed his opinions about historical fiction and about Hunt. As Eliot would do ten years later in "Silly Novels by Lady Novelists" (1856), Lewes provides a taxonomy of novel "species": the historical, the domestic, the *intime*, and the satirical. Since "the great mass of novels are historical" ("Historical Romance" 19), he concludes that this species takes the least amount of talent and appeals to the greatest mass of readers. Such "bastard" species based on "false erudition, joined to a false imagination, produces an abortion" (19). Far from thinking historical fiction easy to write, Lewes argued that "few tales are so false as those 'founded upon facts;' the truth we speak of is truth of character and feeling" (20). Even if Scott got some facts wrong, "no grave historian ever succeeded better in painting the character of the epoch" (20).

While admitting that *The Foster Brother* is not a masterpiece, he nonetheless found it excellent and prophesies "a series of masterpieces" from its author (21). Noting with an insider's perspective that the novel was written "during the intervals of incessant literary toil; and during constant ill health," he believes that Hunt has the qualities of a great writer: "sterling good sense, clear, ample and direct; the almost unrivalled power of painting a picture in words; the knowledge of life and character; the graphic narrative power; and above all, that high conception and relish of what is truly heroic in human nature" (21). Hunt would not go on to write masterpieces, but the language Lewes uses to describe his friend foreshadows Eliot's efforts to transform and advance nineteenth-century realist fiction. He finds Hunt wanting in the skills that Eliot would develop, specifically "Shakespearian revelation of the 'inner being,'... a gift few novelists possess. Scott wanted it. Miss Austen had it..." (24). In 1846, Lewes was looking to the friend he loved as a brother to produce an historical novel that rivaled the novelists he most admired at the time (Scott and Austen), but he did not hold back from criticizing his friend for not meeting these standards.

With Lewes's encouragement, Eliot would attain what Hunt and even Scott had failed to achieve. She threw herself into researching fifteenth-century Florence to capture the "character of the epoch," as well as the realistic details of its everyday life. She also probed the "inner being" of her characters, making *Romola* an example of thoroughly researched historical fiction and also psychologically insightful realist fiction. In "Leaves from a Notebook" (published posthumously in 1884), Eliot wrote that the historical novel should show: "How triumphant opinions generally spread – how institutions arose – what were the conditions of great inventions, discoveries, or theoretic conceptions – what circumstances affecting individual lots are attended on the decay of long-established systems" (*Poetry* 2:204). Such a view applied to all her novels. She wrote to R. H. Hutton, who had reviewed *Romola* in the *Spectator*:

> It is the habit of my imagination to strive after as full a vision of the medium in which a character moves as of the character itself. The psychological causes which prompted me to give such details of Florentine life and history as I have given, are precisely the same as those which determined me in giving the details of English village life in 'Silas Marner,' or the "Dodson" life, out of which were developed the destinies of poor Tom and Maggie. (*GEL* 4:97)

She was always consistent in this attempt to recreate the "medium" (a term central to Lewes's scientific studies) so that she could realistically trace the course of her characters' lives. She told Hutton that perhaps she had not fully succeeded in *Romola*, but her statement shows her self-consciousness of historical purpose, and it retro-spectively explains the lengths to which she went to recreate a particular medium of late fifteenth-century Florence.

Romola was a departure aesthetically and also in terms of its publication history. Blackwood had been following the slow development of the novel, which he expected to publish, and which Lewes and Eliot initially also expected him to publish. On a visit to London, he called at Blandford Square several times (December 22 and December 23, 1861; January 2 and January 12, 1862). On December 23, he brought his wife to meet Eliot for the first time. The success of *The Mill* had dispelled some of the tensions over the terms of its publication, but Eliot had recently written querulous letters about payments and advertising that may reflect the physical pain of which she frequently complained at this time, especially since she later apologized (*GEL* 4:7, 15–16, 18–19).

In 1860, the publisher George Smith of Smith, Elder, & Co. had started the *Cornhill Magazine* with W. M. Thackeray as its editor. Smith, Elder was unusual as a publisher in that it was part of a larger company that also traded in a wide range of goods across the empire, particularly in India. Smith had been involved, for example, in the establishment of the overland mail service to India (Glynn 22). Until the Indian Mutiny in 1857, they had supplied East India Company soldiers, and Smith complained in his *Recollections* (1895) that the Mutiny had "cost him a fortune" because "so many of our debtors were killed" (qtd. in Glynn 114). Jenifer Glynn writes that his financial success "encouraged enterprising publishing, and the dual nature of the business continued until the publishing and the foreign agency work were separated in 1868" (19). Smith also had publishing success, especially with the novels of Charlotte Brontë. He had high ambitions for the *Cornhill*. The initial popularity of the magazine seemed to be waning, and he needed a new novel for serialization to the established pattern. He was ready to invest his riches in securing the talents of the now immensely popular George Eliot.

On January 23, 1862, he called at Blandford Square, ostensibly to discuss the book publication of Lewes's *Studies in Animal Life*, a series that had been discontinued prematurely in the *Cornhill* much to Lewes's disgust. During the visit, he asked Lewes about Eliot's possible interest in a "magnificent" offer for her next book. Giving them time to think about it, he returned on February 27 to make the magnificent offer of £10,000 for serialization in the *Cornhill* and subsequent full copyright of *Romola*, which Eliot had only just begun writing after months of agonized preparation, doubts, and false starts. Lewes wrote in his journal that this was the most ever offered for a novel (GHLJ 23 January, 1862; Haight, *Biography* 355). To put this in perspective, Smith paid Trollope £1,000 for *Framley Parsonage*, successfully serialized in the *Cornhill* (January 1860–April 1861) (*Romola* ix; Introduction). The most known to be offered for a novel previously was £5,000 for Wilkie Collins's *Armadale* in 1861 (Ashton, *GE* 256). Eliot's earnings to date with Blackwood amounted to £8,330 (Haight, *Biography* 357). The Leweses would soon buy a house in London for £2,000.

The terms were not immediately agreeable, as Smith wanted the serialization to begin in April or May 1862, far sooner than Eliot could be ready. After much negotiation over the dates, the number and length of the parts, and the copyright, a deal was struck whereby Eliot would publish *Romola* in 12 monthly parts beginning in July and would be paid £7,000, with Smith holding the copyright for only six years.[8]

As soon as she made this agreement, Eliot wrote to Blackwood. Her tone in recent letters about payments and advertising had been coolly professional, but this letter is particularly distant in handling its awkward subject, perhaps betraying her intuitively uneasy feelings about what she had done. She defensively and rather disingenuously implied that Blackwood did not sufficiently value her work, writing that the offer she had received was "hopelessly beyond your usual estimate of the value of my books to you" (*GEL* 4:34–5). The tone of this letter is more reconcilable with the unpleasant narrator of "Brother Jacob" (written in 1860) than the tolerant and sympathetic narrator of *Silas Marner*. Currently, she was struggling to find the right voice for *Romola*. She wrote to Blackwood that she was not willing to "exchange my relations for any new ones without overpowering reasons" (*GEL* 4:35). The language makes clear that she was not addressing what Haight calls "her good friend" Blackwood (*Biography* 357). Rather, she couches the relationship in economic terms suggesting that their primary exchange was one of business and that she did not feel sufficiently valued.

Blackwood's reply, as she noted in her journal, was "gentlemanly." In response to her reference to "exchanging" her relations, he wrote: "I feel fully satisfied of the extreme reluctance with which you would decide upon leaving your old friend" (*GEL* 4:35–6). His cordial tone emphasizing the personal rather than economic basis of the friendship masks his annoyance, which is revealed in letters between him and his London manager, Joseph Langford. Both were understandably offended when Smith, Elder sent an advertisement to be placed in *Blackwood's Magazine* announcing the publication of a new novel in the *Cornhill* by the author of *Adam Bede*. Langford was particularly sharp in his criticism of "this disgusting transaction" (*GEL* 4:38). He makes a sexual sneer by referring to "Miss Evans" – bait which Blackwood, to his credit, did not take.

Nonetheless, Blackwood betrayed his distaste for the "extortionate" views of Eliot and Lewes. He also correctly surmised that Smith's speculation would not pay off as *Romola* was not likely to suit the readers of the *Cornhill*. After he visited the Leweses during the writing of *Romola* on June 17, 1861, Blackwood alluded obliquely to Eliot's "peculiar circumstances" in a letter to his brother in which he also implied that she regretted her decision (*GEL* 4:44). It seems that Eliot's sexually and socially compromised position was never far from the mind of her "friends" at Blackwood's. This visit itself was part of Blackwood's own long-range strategy for keeping their business relations open. For her part, there may have been something liberating about the purely business transaction with Smith, who unsentimentally later turned down her next novel, *Felix Holt*, which Blackwood was happy to accept.

This episode in which Eliot evaluated and accepted a lucrative business proposition that led her to betray her "friend" (as Blackwood referred to himself) and go over to "the enemy" (as he referred to Smith) is interesting on many levels that have implications for aspects of Eliot's fiction. Some biographers have put her act in taking Smith's offer down to what Blackwood called Lewes's "voracity." It was undeniably a monetary decision that Lewes encouraged. It is also true that Eliot's own desire for money had much to do with Lewes's dependents (three sons, Agnes and the other children, his sister-in-law and her son). Upon first hearing of a magnificent offer, Eliot wrote: "This made me think about money – but it is better for me not to be rich" (January 23, 1862; *GEJ* 108). This belief that she should not be rich is at odds with her resentment that Blackwood did not value her work and suggests the conflicted feeling she had about negotiating for money when it came to her art.

Rather than voracious, Lewes was simply practical and sane. It would have been neither practical nor sane to refuse such an offer as Smith had made. Eliot's puritanical belief in the renunciation of wealth never left her, and her guilt is evident in the actions of her heroines in particular. For example, in Dorothea Brooke, she satirized the mentality of "giving up" via the ever-practical Celia, who makes an excellent marriage to Sir James, attaining both wealth and status. Lewes was not burdened with this Calvinist impulse to scourge and renounce. In this sense he was an influence on her to accept a large offer of money, as he would also be in urging her to accept pleasures that her own earnings afforded, such as first class travel, furniture, jewelry, and trips to fashionable spas. His guiltless negotiation of business deals for her writing released her from the painful conflicts she suffered over being rich, even though that guilt is reflected in her fiction.

The complicated negotiations over *Romola* also raise a variety of questions about matters in which friendship, loyalty, business transactions, gender, class, and money generally are intertwined. In undercutting Blackwood by withdrawing a novel she had led him to believe he would publish, Eliot may have acted in an ethically blameworthy manner. But did she really betray a friend? Is it possible for someone with whom she had momentously consequential business dealings (on both sides) to be also a friend to whom she had loyalties? Would Blackwood, always uncomfortable about her marital state from the point of view of the firm's reputation, have brought his wife to call for the first time had he not had a business "interest" in doing so? In making her decision, did she have a duty to Blackwood or to her "husband's" family or to herself?[9]

These questions touch on transformations within the business of publishing and on even larger questions of what Carlyle had called the "cash payment" nexus of his time in his book *Chartism* (1839), which Eliot read carefully shortly after it was published (*GEL* 1:71). An older, conservative model of publishing was giving way to a newer commercial spirit, embodied in Smith, the speculator and innovator. In fact, Smith and Blackwood were of the same generation and had interestingly similar, parallel careers. Blackwood's father, William Blackwood, had established his publishing business in Edinburgh in 1811. His son John was born in 1818 and was apprenticed as a publisher, taking over the family business in 1852. Smith's father Alexander left his native Scotland to establish his publishing partnership in London in 1816. George Smith was born in 1824, was apprenticed and eventually took over Smith, Elder in 1846. The firm of Blackwood was initially innovative but was always Tory in its orientation. John Blackwood kept the firm conservative and profitable through cautious ventures based on personal connections and friendships – the "intangible assets" that Eliot was insultingly willing to forgo for cash (Finkelstein

26–7). Smith, too, cultivated friendships with authors but had a more enterprising, speculative spirit. While Blackwood oversaw the magazine established by his father, Smith was always experimenting with new projects, launching the *Cornhill* in 1860 and the *Pall Mall Gazette* in 1865. Blackwood thought bargaining vulgar. Smith assumed bargaining was part of his business as a publisher, and he blatantly tried to buy George Eliot. Furthermore, Lewes had a long-standing, cordial business relationship with both men. Smith offered him the editorship of the *Cornhill* in 1862 and of the *Pall Mall Gazette* in 1865. In the future, Lewes continued to conduct business with Blackwood on behalf of himself and Eliot, perhaps never knowing (or caring) that Blackwood thought him grasping and vulgar.[10]

The larger problem raised by this episode, and reflected throughout Eliot's fiction, is the inevitable monetary nature of personal relationships and the difficulty, even impossibility, of distinguishing human bonds from monetary interest. As Eliot was learning in her own life, and as her heroines would also see, love and money were often inseparable. She confronted the economic nature of the nuclear family when her only contact with her once-loved brother was reduced to his dispensing her annuity from their father via a solicitor. In turn, her fictional plots repeatedly construct a conflict and choice between love and money. In *Silas Marner*, Eppie gives up money and status out of loyalty to Silas as well as a firm sense of her own class. In future works, Esther (*Felix Holt*), Dorothea (*Middlemarch*), and Gwendolen (*Daniel Deronda*) all voluntarily give up inherited fortunes for higher ideals of love and restitution, though none suffers poverty as a result.

It is also interesting that "Brother Jacob" became entangled in this exchange. Smith initially offered 250 guineas to publish the story about stolen guineas while he was waiting for *Romola*, but it was only after *Romola* failed to bolster sales of the *Cornhill* as he had hoped that Eliot made a "gift" of it to the magazine, where it was published in 1864. Written in the summer of 1860 just before she began *Silas Marner*, the story is a uniquely cynical and sarcastic piece of writing that dwells on the betrayal of family members for money and touches on themes also explored in *Silas Marner* but with a darker (if more comical) and less uplifting conclusion.

In "Brother Jacob," the protagonist David Faux, true to his name, is unscrupulous in his ambition to steal his mother's carefully saved and hidden stash of guineas and escape his small village by traveling to the West Indies, where he imagines he can become a sort of king among the natives. Here again, Eliot explores the notion of a preconception about a place conjured up by the word as she was at this time imagining for herself what she would see in "Rome." As a result of his limited reading, David's "imagination circled round and round the utmost limits of his geographical knowledge": "Having a general idea of America as a country where the population was chiefly black, it appeared to him the most propitious destination for an emigrant who, to begin with, had the broad and easily recognizable merit of whiteness" (231; ch. 1). He finally decides to try the West Indies where, he imagines, a princess "would want him to marry her, and make him presents of very large jewels beforehand; after which, he needn't marry her unless he liked" (237; ch. 1).

The story is a complex one and might be read on a number of levels, but clearly Eliot meant to signal the dangers of forming impressions about the world based on reading fictions unless, perhaps, they were the type of realist fictions to which she was committed, or at least had been up until this time. The story also contains a critique of colonial mentalities, especially of young English men, which is somewhat surprising given that at the time the Leweses were considering a colonial career for Charles and would later pursue such a course with Thornie and Bertie.

When David Faux inevitably fails in the West Indies, he returns to England and settles down under a new name – Edward Freely. He then opens up a confection shop that seduces (and corrupts) the local housewives into buying expensive prepared confections (rather than doing their wifely duties). He is on the verge of marrying a local girl when his "idiot" brother Jacob, the only person who knows about the stolen guineas, recognizes and exposes him. It is a comic version of Eliot's consistent theme of the Nemesis returning to punish the misdeeds of the past, a subject she would treat more seriously in *Silas Marner* when the discovery of Dunstan's body and Silas's stolen coins leads Godfrey to tell Nancy about Eppie. She would develop the same theme even more darkly in Baldassarre's pursuit and eventual murder of his adopted son Tito in *Romola*. "Brother Jacob," though short, satirical, and sarcastic, is layered with many of the same themes that characterize her more substantial fiction at this time.[11]

Even before it was written, *Romola* was the object of a landmark business deal that put even more pressure on its author. Its serialization was an experiment and a speculation in multiple ways, and its composition was an excruciating process to Eliot as she strove to apply her own high standards of realistic representation to Renaissance Florence. In later life, she reflected that *Romola* was written with her "best blood" and with the "the most ardent care for veracity" (*GEL* 6:335–6). Furthermore, writing to monthly deadlines for the serial publication in a magazine was stressful; the material was difficult to get right emotionally as well as factually. Writing the deaths of Maggie and Tom Tulliver in *The Mill* had been draining. Writing the deaths of Tito and his father was even more so because it followed a probing of the primal instincts for self-preservation on the one hand (Tito), and self-destruction and vengeance on the other (Baldassarre), that went further and deeper into human psychology than anything she had yet written. The dreamy fable of Romola's floating away to a plague-stricken village and helping an orphaned child also went beyond the fantasy of surrogate parenthood in *Silas Marner*, and it coexisted uneasily with the violent historical realism of Savonarola's execution and the hunting down of Tito by his enemies.

Romola does not allow us to make the obvious biographical connections with Eliot's own life that *The Mill* does, but the penetration of the psychological insights into Tito particularly requires us to ask: what aspects of herself, as well as those around her, did Eliot probe in writing *Romola?* Hutton asked in his *Spectator* review: "where can George Eliot have seen the working of a mind exquisitely refined, and even broad, yet so rotten with cowardly selfishness . . . ?" (qtd. in Martin 140). Where could Eliot have "seen" such a mind? Andrew Brown argues that "in its dramatization of a proud and gifted woman's struggle with male (most often patriarchal) authority," Romola is perhaps also her most "most autobiographical" novel (*Romola* xvii; Introduction). Bonaparte also calls it "essentially autobiographical" (54). Karl believes that she reentered her painful relationship with her father in representing Romola's relationship to the demanding, ungrateful Bardo (359). This autobiographical aspect of the novel can also be mapped in the heroine's stages of development and conversions to Christianity, then away from it to an enlightened humanistic perspective. We might also ask whether Tito's psychology was something Eliot saw in herself.

More visibly, Eliot's fiction demonstrates a structural recreation of the two-sibling family with the son being favored over the devoted daughter. The general pattern goes back to Lisbeth Bede's favoritism of Adam over the womanish Seth in *Adam Bede* (in which the father is absent), and even to the squire's favoritism of Godfrey over the profligate Dunstan in *Silas Marner* (in which the mother is absent). In "The Lifted Veil," the feminine Latimer's brother is favored by the father (the mother is absent). The privileging of Tom over Maggie calls out a sense of injustice not mitigated by the father's sentimental preference for his "little wench." Silas nostalgically recalls his mother and sister (the father is absent). Consciously or not, Eliot recreated in fiction this triad of one parent's relationship to two siblings and did so without regard to gender. It is another example of the fluid triangulations she also created in the relationships among lovers in her works.

Marriage and Betrayal

Of the many contending political, cultural, religious, and moral themes in *Romola*, the most powerful is that of betrayal both within the blood family and within marriage. Eliot may have been drawn to this theme from recollections of her own family but also her most immediate experience in the monetary negotiations over *Romola*. Once we let go of gender-bound notions that Eliot wrote herself only into her female characters such as Maggie and Romola, we might consider that Romola's father, the patriarch Bardo, believes that his son Dino has betrayed him by abandoning the course of carrying on his father's work and instead electing to follow Savonarola in becoming a monk. It was Mary Ann Evans, not Isaac, whom Robert Evans looked upon as a traitor to his own social standing when she refused to attend church and jeopardized her prospects for a respectable marriage. It seems clear in *Romola* that Dino does not betray his father by going into the church, but rather has ideological differences from him that interfered with Bardo's notions about perpetuating the Bardi name. In the case of Robert Evans and Bardo, the anger of the father came down to an egoism Eliot deplored. Romola is put in a position not unlike that of Tom Tulliver when she is asked to carry out her father's wishes of maintaining his library intact. Tom is bound by family pride and loyalty to pay off his father's debts and buy back the mill. And Tom's position is like that of Isaac, who staunchly followed the respectable course of upholding the family name and remaining in Coventry. Unlike Tom or Isaac, however, Romola confronts the peremptory will and authority of a husband who does not share her sense of duty.

The turning point in Romola's marriage to Tito is not his sexual infidelity (of which she is ignorant), but rather his selling of Bardo's library, which he had previously promised to preserve to perpetuate the legacy of his father-in-law's life of scholarly research:

> Tito had even been the means of strengthening the hope in Bardo's mind that he might before his death receive the longed-for security concerning his library: that it should not be merged in another collection; that it should not be transferred to a body of monks, and be called by the name of a monastery; but that it should remain for ever the Bardi Library, for the use of Florentines. (182–3; ch. 19)

Romola and her godfather Bernardo take this wish seriously, knowing that Bardo will not leave sufficient funds to provide for the library. Tito, who asks for no dowry in marrying Romola, seems to take charge by inquiring into "Florentine money matters, the secrets of the *Monti* or public funds, the values of real property, and the profits of banking" (184; ch. 19). His interest in managing money appears to be in the service of fulfilling Bardo's wishes.

Yet Bardo is never able to write the great work he imagined. This makes him bitter and pathetic in ways that foreshadow Edward Casaubon in *Middlemarch*, who also wishes to control posterity from the grave by asking his wife to continue his research and withholding her inheritance if she marries Will Ladislaw. But Tito's disregard for Bardo's legacy is one of his most shocking moral transgressions and is devastating to Romola. On a symbolic level, it suggests Tito's lack of reverence for tradition and his characteristic pursuit of immediate gratification, which is linked in the novel to his rootlessness. On a more personal level, his betrayal – specifically with regard to the selling of books – recalls Eliot's "betrayal" of Blackwood in the publication of *Romola*.

When Eliot signed her contract with Smith and wrote her letter informing Blackwood (May 19, 1862), she had written only up to chapter 8. Bardo's wish that Tito specifically should carry on his legacy is outlined in chapter 19; Tito's selling of the library is revealed in chapter 32. In this chapter, Tito suggests to Romola that they leave Florence, foreshadowing Rosamond's belief that she and Lydgate could solve all their problems by leaving Middlemarch. Romola does not yet imagine the truth that Bardo's books and antiquities have already been sold: "'You have *sold* them?' she asked, as if she distrusted her ears" (272; ch. 32). When she asks why the sale might not be reversed, Tito informs her, "'Simply because the sale has been concluded by written agreement; the purchasers have left Florence, and I hold the bonds for the purchase-money'" (273; ch. 32). Their relationship is instantly reduced to a monetary transaction: "'But if you were paid the money? – we will pay you the money'" (274; ch. 32). By distinguishing between "we" (Romola and her godfather) and "you," Tito, Romola puts distance between herself and her husband, redrawing the lines of her alliance. Tito's response is absolute: "'The library is sold, and you are my wife.'"

Eliot's conflicts about her own financial success as an author inevitably influenced her thinking about such topics from the point of Smith's "marvelous" offer and beyond: "This made me think about money." The interrelation of money and human bonds (whether created by blood or by choice) had already proved central to Eliot's fiction. In *The Mill*, Tom's loyalty takes the form of earning enough money to pay off his father's debts; Eppie renounces money out of loyalty to Silas. Tito, in contrast, betrays a trust for monetary gain. The betrayal of trust for money would recur in *Middlemarch* when Bulstrode betrays his first wife by concealing her daughter's whereabouts so that he may inherit her money, and in *Daniel Deronda* when Lapidoth attempts to sell his daughter Mirah to a wealthy suitor.

Eliot was at this time endeavoring to become a mother to Lewes's sons and not to see them as expensive burdens. Her letters reflect a preoccupation with her motherly role. To D'Albert Durade in particular she stressed the nature of her family life as a parallel to his own; whereas once she had been like a daughter in his family, now she shared the experience of parenthood. On January 2, 1862, just as she was again beginning *Romola*, she imagined how happy he must be about his son's marriage, then wrote:

> Our dear boy Charles is as great a comfort to us as ever in the sweetness of his disposition and conscientious discharge of his duties. And Thornton – our second, you know – is working hard at Edinburgh, trying earnestly, we think, to prepare for the Indian examination next summer. (*GEL* 4:4)

She was now doing her duty as a stepmother as she had done her duty as a daughter, and that included supplying the money needed to prepare Charles, Thornie, and Bertie for independence.

All of the Lewes children were victims of their parents' complicated sexual/marital situation. Lewes agreed to take responsibility for educating, housing, and placing the three eldest sons that he acknowledged as his own. Their position is a familiar one to children of divorce. They were shown and returned a degree of love, and they received financial support, but they were not wanted at home and were expected to become independent in ways for which they were ill prepared. We might view their condition differently today had not their lives taken such a sad and wasted course.

In 1859, Agnes Lewes suggested that Charles try for a cadetship in the Indian Army (*GEL* 8:192). John Blackwood's nephew had recently followed this route, but as we have seen Charles chose a position in the Post Office.[12] Anthony Trollope, who had served in the Post Office since 1834, helped Charles by nominating him for a position, for which he also successfully passed the examination. Thornie, perhaps also at Agnes's suggestion, was destined for India. In 1860, he began a year of preparation in Edinburgh for the Indian Civil Service examination. When Thornie passed the first Indian examination in 1861, Lewes wrote to his friend Wathen Mark Wilks Call that Thornie "goes out next year with a salary of 450£ & by the time he is 25 will have 1200£. . . .*That* isn't to be made by Aristotle or Reviewing!" (*GHLL* 2:41).[13] In 1861, *Blackwood's* published two articles on "The Indian Civil Service: Its Rise and Fall," which argued that the "men who go in for the Indian Civil Service, under the competition system, are men who neither have nor think that they have any brilliant prospects at home." They are "content to earn a competence, isolated and forgotten, in a remote Eastern settlement, rather than to incur the risk of being utterly beaten in the great battle of life at home" (Kaye, "Part II" 273).[14] From this perspective, those who can win in the examination system are deserters from the "great battle of life." If the Civil Service of India "is to be thrown open to the general public, the interlopers to be looked for are the failures of the imperial country" (Kaye, "Part II" 273).[15] In this contemporary light, Thornie was already a failure when he sat for the examination. In *Daniel Deronda*, Eliot recalls the time of helping Thornie prepare for his exam through her description of Warham Gascoigne's "cram" for the Indian Civil Service examination with some irony about its content and relevance, as the narrator remarks that it "might disclose the welfare of our Indian Empire to be somehow connected with a quotable knowledge of Browne's Pastorals" (46; ch. 6).

At the time of *Romola*'s stressful composition, Charles had embarked on his career at the Post Office. Thornie seemed on track preparing for his Indian exams in Edinburgh. Lewes told Blackwood in July 1862 that they "hardly expect – nor do we much wish him to pass this year, he is so very young" (*GEL* 4:50). One has to wonder whether he spoke for Eliot. Bertie, the youngest son, who clearly had some kind of learning disability, remained at Hofwyl, and the real challenges in launching sons on independent careers lay ahead.[16]

Whatever Lewes's sons represented to Eliot as she strove to develop creatively and meet the pressing deadlines in order to earn the money held out by the "marvelous" offer, they represented the failed marriage that had produced them. Like the sexual triangle, the bad marriage is a pattern in Eliot's fiction that is only surprising when we think of her own satisfaction within her marriage, which of course, was not one. We may recall that in "Janet's Repentance", Janet Dempster suffered physical and psychological abuse from her alcoholic husband. Lisbeth Bede suffered the consequences of her husband's alcoholism. In *Silas Marner*, Godfrey's marriage to Molly was a mistake, and Eliot's narrator judges the woman harshly: "Molly knew that the cause of her dingy rags was not her husband's neglect, but the demon Opium to whom she was enslaved, body and soul . . ." (107; ch. 12). These examples show a pattern in which drug and alcohol addiction is a factor in unhappy marriages beginning with "Janet's Repentance" and continuing with *Adam Bede*, and possibly reflecting her own home experience. They also show Eliot's ability to sympathize with both husbands and wives.

Romola took the portrayal of marital unhappiness to new extremes. Yet again, it marked a turning point in that drug abuse disappears from the equation, and the source of discontent becomes fundamental incompatibility compounded by tensions over money and social ambition. Following *Romola*, *Felix Holt*'s plot would turn on the mercenary marriage of Mrs Transome to a husband whom she does not love (and who by the start of the novel has become senile), and her affair with the lawyer Jermyn, which produces an illegitimate child who becomes the source of the unfaithful wife's hope and suffering. *Middlemarch* is structured around two of the worst marriages in Victorian fiction as it parallels Dorothea's misguided marriage to Casaubon and Lydgate's misguided marriage to Rosamond. *Daniel Deronda*'s "English plot" is set in motion by Gwendolen's conflicted, money-driven decision to marry the sadistic Grandcourt, knowing that he has a hidden former mistress and four illegitimate children.

While Eliot's narratives also offer examples of relatively successful marriages, such as those of the Poysers in *Adam Bede* and the Garths in *Middlemarch*, the bad marriages are predominant, and patterns emerge that suggest a preoccupation with triangles of deceit, desire, and blackmail. Godfrey conceals his marriage to Molly, leaving himself open to blackmail by his brother; Mrs Transome bears the burden of the secret affair that irrevocably binds her to her former lover; and Gwendolen keeps her husband's secret, exposing herself to moral blackmail by both him and his mistress.[17] When considered in light of Agnes Lewes's background presence in Eliot's life as the embodiment of a situation fraught with deceptions and psychological pressures, her preoccupation with sexual triangles and strained marriages seems to have a biographical component that may be traced to adult rather than childhood experiences.[18]

Within her chosen, extended familial circle in the early 1860s, everyone was lying. Quite apart from the larger public secret of George Eliot's identity, which had been forced out in 1859, there were other fictions and lies. She and Lewes were not really husband and wife, as they claimed. Although some critics inaccurately refer to them as "common law" husband and wife, if this were true, Lewes would be a bigamist, as there was no law that would recognize a second marriage while the first wife was still living. This meant that no matter how committed they were to each other, technically speaking they were adulterers, and so it was all the more important to insist on the fictional marriage. We can only imagine what went on among Agnes Lewes and Thornton and Kate Hunt. The younger Lewes children were misled about their paternity, believing Lewes to be their father. The older boys were asked to accept two mothers. Eliot's fiction is obsessed with realistically representing the psychology of deception, betrayal, and lying, especially within marriage. The urgency of her need to tell the truth in fiction, which also offered a high moral standard to readers, seems driven in part by a desire to compensate for the need of those around her to tell lies in which she was complicit. So perhaps it is not surprising that she represented at this time the psychology of the pathological liar, Tito.

While the temporal and religious contexts of Romola and Tito's marriage may seem far removed from Victorian England, it is in *Romola* that Eliot meditated on the darkest subjects of secrecy, adultery, and illegitimacy. Tito's secret relationship with the peasant Tessa deepens after he has fallen in love with Romola, who acts as an external moral conscience from which Tessa offers an escape. On a day on which he is expected at Romola's home, he encounters Tessa in the hands of a street conjurer, Vaiano, "who was making laughing attempts to soothe and cajole her, evidently carrying with him the amused sympathy of the spectators" (99; ch. 10). Tito extricates the confused girl from the conjurer's grasp amidst the insinuating sneers of the crowd. In so doing, he intensifies her idealization of him as a beautiful, mysterious guardian angel.

The scene is a preparation for the next chance encounter between the two at the peasants' fair. Vaiano has installed himself at a table in mock priest's attire and is offering marriage services: "'Behold my children. . . neglect not the Holy Sacrament of matrimony when it can be had for the small sum of a white quattrino – the cheapest matrimony ever offered, and dissolved by special bull beforehand at every man's own will and pleasure'" (137; ch. 14). He appeals to the maidens: "'Matrimony to be had – hot, eaten, and done with as easily as *berlingozzi*! [ring shaped cakes]'" (138; ch. 14). The joke, in the highly sexualized street life of Florence, irreverently mimics the granting of papal indulgences and pretends to provide unmarried couples a temporary license to have guilt-free sex. The ironic and sinister figure offers not only the cheapest matrimony but a carnivalesque paradox – a matrimony "dissolved beforehand." Since divorce is impossible within the Catholic Church, the mock priest exposes the magical and mystifying rhetoric used to annul marriages while remaining within the church. It also reflects the ongoing theme of the cash payment nexus, reducing solemn personal relations to money transactions and discount ones at that – "the cheapest matrimony ever offered."

Tessa is awed by the spectacle of the priest dressed in "sham episcopal costume," whom she does not recognize as the conjurer she knows. The language echoes Lewes's disgust at the "sham ceremonies" in Rome in 1860. It is an interesting reversal that Eliot felt nothing after being blessed by the Pope while the ignorant girl is awed by a false priest. Carried away by the moment, Tito permits the mock-priest to perform a "mimic ceremony with a liberal expenditure of *lingua furbesca* or thieves' Latin" (144; ch. 14). Vaiano recognizes the couple and assumes that they have come for retroactive legitimation of sins already committed: "'you are come to be married. I commend your penitence – the blessing of the Holy Church can never come too late'" (144; ch. 14). But the savvy charlatan soon realizes his mistake and reinterprets the ceremony as a ploy on Tito's part to pursue sexual relations with an ignorant girl. Although Tito is initially "far from that understanding" (144; ch. 14), after the ceremony is performed and the conjurer paid, the fact of the sham marriage (which Tito intimidates Tessa into concealing), permits him to do exactly what the conjurer imagined – deceive Tessa into believing he is her husband as he proceeds to keep her as a mistress and father her two children. As the conjurer's knowing smile implies, seduction will be easier for the man if the girl thinks she is married.

This marriage which is not one in *Romola* may be viewed as part of Eliot's dense description of Renaissance Florence, and as an indication of the disrespect for the Catholic Church and its teachings that coexisted with – and perhaps inspired – Savonarola's reform movement. The whole strange episode shows Eliot's desire to represent the open secrets of Florentine sexual life, which, in addition to ideas and politics, contributed to the charged atmosphere of the Florentine streets. Tito's fictional marriage is one of his many moral transgressions and is of a different kind from that of other young couples buying false marriages in the street.

The mockery made of marriage (and the church) at the peasants' fair finds its parallel in the profound explicit and implicit questioning of the marriage vow in the scene of Romola's flight from Tito and her encounter with Savonarola. Having learned of her husband's betrayal, Romola attempts to leave Florence in disguise. But on her way, she meets the Frate, who sends her back to her husband: "'I have a command from God to stop you. You are not permitted to flee'" (338; ch. 40). After an emotional debate, Romola is subdued, accepting her duty to stay with Tito and remain in Florence: "'Father, I will be guided. Teach me! I will go back'" (345; ch. 40). Here yet another heroine attempts to confront a personal crisis by submission and renunciation, but like Maggie Tulliver, Dorothea Casaubon, and Marian Evans, the refuge in renunciation of self cannot be a permanent solution to human problems.

Tessa is a victim of Tito's lie, but a victim who never knows the deceit to which she has been subjected. At the same time, Tito's legal marriage to Romola is a moral lie, emphasizing the irrelevance of legal bonds in human relationships, a position that Eliot held with respect to her own fictional marriage but serious moral commitment to Lewes. In one sense, Tito is more of a husband to Tessa than to Romola. He misleads but does not betray her. She is happy, Romola is miserable, and Tessa, not Romola, bears Tito's children.

Repeatedly, Eliot's fiction deconstructs the opposition between legal and fictional marriages. Eliot's marriage was no more legal than Tessa's, but a fictional marriage might be more "real" than a legal one; this helps explain why her fiction is also constantly destabilizing the opposition between wife and mistress. For example, in *Silas Marner*, Molly is both Godfrey's legal wife and the other woman whose existence he hides from Nancy and everyone else. And in *Daniel Deronda*, Gwendolen, though legally married to Grandcourt, may be said to feel like the other woman relative to the mistress who has produced a family and an heir and who makes her moral entitlement and economic expectations known to the legal wife. The most significant explorations of both these social roles and the terminology used to describe them – wife and mistress or "other woman" – undertaken by a woman who insisted that she was a "wife" though she was not married, appears in *Romola*.

Tessa is the "other woman" in Tito's legal marriage to Romola, but Romola is the "other woman" in his fictional marriage to Tessa. When Romola first learns about Tessa from Baldassarre, she feels she can do nothing until she "learned the full truth about the 'other wife' – learned whether she were the wife to whom Tito was first bound" (432; ch. 55). Even the pronoun in "whether she were the first wife" is ambiguous. At this point Romola does not know whether she or Tessa is Tito's legal wife. The following chapter in which Romola discerns the truth of the fictional marriage to Tessa is called "The Other Wife," and the title is also ambiguous because in it Romola is wishing to learn that Tessa and not she is Tito's real wife. She feels "exultation at the thought that the wife's burthen might be about to slip from her overladen shoulders; that this little ignorant creature might prove to be Tito's lawful wife." The narrator adds: "A strange exultation for a proud and high-born woman to have been brought to!" (439; ch. 56).

Having learned from Tessa that the marriage occurred in the street during the peasant's fair, she "was feeling the chill of disappointment that her difficulties were not to be solved by external law" (440; ch. 56). That Romola should interpret her fate as resting on a legal technicality of marriage reflects another transformed autobiographical dimension of the novel. Romola wishes to be freed by learning – in language that echoes the words of the conjurer, "marriages dissolved beforehand" – that "the vows which had bound her to strive after an impossible union had been made void beforehand" (439; ch. 56). Instead, she remains bound to Tito. George Eliot, in contrast, had bound herself to a man she could not marry. Romola's situation in this scene is something like Lewes's, for while he could leave Agnes physically, as long as he was married he was responsible financially, and he could not marry Eliot.

Eliot's conflicted attitudes about the bond of marriage in an age of divorce reform are evident in her fiction.[19] Although her recorded comments about divorce indicate a theoretical approval, she and Lewes did not pursue this option for reasons that might never be known, but which certainly are more complicated than biographies have led us to believe. Her fiction upholds the supremacy of duty, vows, and promises. She never created a fictional scenario to mirror precisely that of her own life situation, but the secrets, lies, triangulations, and betrayals that characterize the representation of marriage in her fiction seem to be informed by more than Victorian literary conventions, or even the broader ideological critiques that such dramatic devices serve. They seem to show a preoccupation that belies the confidence with which she asserted her position as Lewes's wife. It is interesting that when the subject of obtaining a divorce abroad apparently came up (this is not explicit in the letter but rather inferred by biographers), and a lawyer consulted by Lewes pronounced it impossible, she wrote to Barbara Bodichon using the language of the Catholic Church: "I prefer excommunication" (*GEL* 3:366).

Sexuality in *Romola*

The question of where Eliot might have seen a mind like Tito's reflects the general wonder readers still feel at her psychological insights. Sometimes, however, readers have misread aspects of her fiction by not giving her enough credit for knowing. In his *George Eliot* (1902), Leslie Stephen criticizes the femininity of Tito and what he perceives as Eliot's failure to capture the true spirit of the time. He invokes *The Autobiography of Benvenuto Cellini* (written 1558–62, published 1728) as the epitome of a culture in which "the elementary human passions have been let loose" (132) and "there is the strangest mingling of high aspirations and brutal indulgence" (133). He does not name homosexuality as one of those passions or indulgences, but the reference to Cellini implies it, given the explicit references to homosexuality in the *Autobiography*, which Eliot and Lewes read on their first trip to Florence in May of 1860 (Haight, *Biography* 325). Stephen argues that Eliot fails to capture the Renaissance spirit because she is a middle-class English woman who cannot comprehend the nature of the society she is describing, "and though by dint of conscientious reading George Eliot knew a great deal about the ruffian geniuses of the Renaissance, she could not throw herself into any real sympathy with them" (135).[20] It is certain, however, that by "dint of conscientious reading," Eliot knew more about the passions of Renaissance Florentine men than Stephen was able to imagine.

Eliot knew that sodomy was one of the many unchristian practices of which Savonarola wanted to purge Florence. On December 12, 1492, the reforming monk exhorted the Florentine public to "pass laws against that accursed vice of sodomy, for which you know that Florence is infamous throughout the whole of Italy" (Savonarola 157–8). Eliot did not include Savonarola's direct condemnation of sodomy in the novel, but through indirection, innuendo, and allusion, she conveyed the prevalence of love and sex between men on a spectrum, from the idealized love of the teacher for his pupil, as present in the dialogues of Plato that were being revived by the neo-Platonists, to the sodomy that young unmarried men often practiced with younger, passive boys and for which men were frequently arrested.[21] She kept true to the historical record of the time she studied so extensively to recreate, but did so without saying what she, as a Victorian novelist, could not say directly in her fiction. This highly sophisticated, learned historical coding also reveals just how complex the relationship between real life "originals" and her fictional characters had become in the work that was her greatest experiment in recreating a time and place so remote from her own experience and the experience of her readers.[22]

Romola is Eliot's only novel in which people who really lived (Savonarola, Piero di Cosimo, Machievalli) and who are reproduced with accuracy to the historical record, interact with pure inventions (Romola, Tito, Tessa), which as far as we know have no historical "originals." In her other novels, real people, including living authors, are mentioned. In *The Mill*, Maggie fantasizes about going to see Sir Walter Scott, and in *Middlemarch*, Mr Brooke mentions being at Cambridge with Wordsworth, but people who actually lived are not brought to life as characters as they are in *Romola*.

In *Romola*, two characters have strangely indirect relationships to their originals. Among the other functions these characters serve in the narrative, they also suggest the prevalence of Florentine homosexuality in an intriguingly oblique, self-consciously textual way. The characters are the fictional, unmarried barber Nello and the real-life scholar, poet and teacher Angelo Ambrogini or Poliziano (1454–94), known in English as Politian, whose poetry and letters Eliot read in preparation for writing *Romola*. Nello seems to be based on Domenico di Giovanni or Il Burchiello (1404–49), a barber, poet, and political propagandist in the generation before the setting of the novel. But Burchiello is not just a silent real-life original for the fictional Nello. Nello explicitly claims to be an inheritor of Burchiello's mantle, mentioning both his poetry and his role as a prominent barber in Florence. In her reading of Burchiello's poems, Eliot may have seen what twentieth-century critics have demonstrated, that Burchiello's cryptic, "nonsense" poems are full of coded references to sodomy (Alan Smith). Certainly Nello seems central to Eliot's intention of encoding the homoerotic subculture of Florence into her novel.

Nello's shop is a center of male community within Florence, and many important scenes occur there. After meeting Tito, who has appeared as if from nowhere on the streets of Florence, Nello takes the pretty Greek stranger to his barbershop for a shave. He confesses suggestively: "I am quivering with the inspiration of my art even to the very edge of my razor" (31; ch. 3). Throughout the novel, Nello makes a pet of Tito and flirts with him in a shameless, campy way. In one scene, Tito awakens Nello from a nap in his bedroom behind the shop by playing on the lute. Nello responds:

> "What is it, my Orpheus?" here Nello stretched out his arms to their full length, and then brought them round till his hands grasped Tito's curls, and drew them out playfully. "What is it you want of your well-tamed Nello? For I perceive a coaxing sound in that soft strain of yours. Let me see the very needle's eye of your desire, as the sublime poet says, that I may thread it." (126; ch. 13)

Nello's reference to Tito as "Orpheus" foreshadows Tito's singing verses from Poliziano's *Orfeo* later in the novel, and the scene shows that Nello never conceals his delight in the fact that he has been well tamed by the pretty young man.

As part of his plan for *Romola*, George Smith engaged the rising young artist Frederic Leighton (1830–96) to provide drawings that would then be engraved as illustrations in the *Cornhill* serialization.[23] The inclusion of illustrations was yet another way in which *Romola* is a departure from Eliot's other works. The scene in the barbershop was one of the first Leighton undertook, and the illustration enhances the homoeroticism implied in the text. Tito gazes at himself in the mirror (watched by Nello, razor in hand). When she saw the drawing on which this engraving would be based, Eliot was delighted and wrote to Leighton: "Nello is better than my Nello" (*GEL* 4:41).[24]

In the novel, Nello counsels Tito on the importance of remaining beardless: "if you repent, and let your beard grow after it has acquired stoutness by a struggle with the razor, your mouth will by and by show no longer what Messer Angelo calls the divine prerogative of the lips, but will appear like a dark cavern fringed with horrent brambles" (30; ch. 3). Messer Angelo is Poliziano, who never appears as an actual character in *Romola*, but such references make him a shadowy presence throughout. [25]

"SUPPOSE YOU LET ME LOOK AT MYSELF."

Figure 20 "Suppose you let me look at myself." Illustration by Frederic Leighton for *Romola*, 1862–3 (George Eliot, *Romola*, vol. I. London: Smith, Elder, And Co., 1880)

In the chapter called "A Learned Squabble" (ch. 7), Eliot incorporates quotations from the letters of Poliziano. In this sense the presence of his writing, if not his person, is explicit. But Poliziano's presence is also implicit and subtextual. He died in late September 1494 – within the time frame of the novel's action – and, by many accounts, the learned scholar died in disgrace. This information is revealed as Nello, strumming his lute in a shop full of men, remarks sadly, "'the incomparable Poliziano, not two months since, gone – well, well, let us hope he is not gone to the eminent scholars in the Malebolge'" (247; ch. 29). One source that we know Eliot read, *The Elogia* of Paulus Jovius (1483–1552), gives the following account:

> They say [Poliziano] was made an easy prey to fatal disease by his mad love for a noble youth. For, having seized his lute in the heat and fever of his consuming desire, he burst into song with such overmastering passion that presently in his frenzy his voice and the muscles of his fingers and finally breath itself failed, as a shameful death bore down upon him. (Jovius)

Jovius's account clarifies Nello's remark about the Malebolge.[26] Whether or not the story of Poliziano's death was true, it was gossip that would have been known to Nello. Working the scandal of Poliziano's death into her novel in this covert way, Eliot provided the homosexual context within which she wanted her readers to understand the diversity of Florentine sexuality and to which she had gestured through the conjuror's selling of pre-dissolved marriages to peasant couples.

The culmination of Poliziano's function in the novel as a code for the homosexual context of Florentine society is the banquet scene at the Rucellai Gardens. The overall impression is one of decadence and flirtation. When the Mediccean Giannozzo Pucci asks Tito to "lead the last chorus from Poliziano's *Orfeo*" (331; ch. 39), Tito leans towards Pucci, "singing low to him the phrases of the Maenad-chorus" (331). The choice of Poliziano's verse reinforces the homoerotic, seductive power of Tito's serenade as the text ends with Orpheus's renunciation of women. The Maenad chorus has Tito singing a multiple-voiced female part, and also ironically foreshadowing his own hounding to death by an angry crowd of enemies, which Felicity Bonaparte has argued are explicitly figured as Maenads (158).

The depth and range of the allusions in *Romola*, together with its realistic recreation of the past and astoundingly complex mythological and symbolic structures, explain why it was a turning point personally and aesthetically for Eliot. She viewed *Romola* as a "well-defined transition in her life," claiming: "'I began it a young woman, – I finished it an old woman'" (Cross, *Life* 2:352). It was an experiment in her career – the parts publication for a new publisher, the illustrations – but also within the history of English literature. Formally, it took the historical novel, as Bonaparte argues, into the realm of the epic, but also at the same time further into the realm of psychological realism that Eliot pioneered with her earlier works. It grappled with epic themes of religion and culture by treating the moment when Renaissance humanism and Christianity coexisted and conflicted, and in this sense it reflected the Victorian era as tracked in Eliot's own loss of religious consolation and search for meaning within human community.

After completing *Romola*, Eliot had moved so far beyond her earlier work: what could possibly follow? The next few years would be preparations for her greatest and most mature works, *Middlemarch* and *Daniel Deronda*. She would pass through yet another period of experimentation, particularly with poetry, including a verse epic, *The Spanish Gypsy*. Feeling herself to be an "old woman," she thought ever more personally and universally about death, posterity, and the idea of a humanistic afterlife. Her next novel, *Felix Holt*, explores in Mrs Transome the unsatisfactory nature of pinning expectations on children. That novel exposes the follies of belief in the inheritance of land and money. Her own belief in the idea of cultural inheritance – particularly in the form of written texts – would henceforth take on an almost religious importance. Her works would lead her generation into new territories of thinking about culture, national identity, and what fiction could achieve.

Notes

1. Harris and Johnston argue that this journey marks the division between Eliot's early and late career: "the shift from the working out of childhood memories to more studied work on the past in relation to the present" (*GEJ* 333).
2. Compare her analysis in "The Natural History of German Life" (1856) of the different associations conjured by the "word *railways*" in people with different knowledge of railways (260).
3. Looking to invest the profits from *The Mill*, Lewes visited a stockbroker, "who undertook to purchase 95 shares in the Great Indian Peninsular Railway for Polly. For 1825£ she gets 1900£ worth of stock guaranteed 5%" (GHLJ, October 6, 1860). On other investments Eliot made with her new wealth, see Henry, *George Eliot and the British Empire* (ch. 3) and Coleman, "George Eliot and Money" and "Being Good with Money." See also Henry, "George Eliot and Finance."
4. For an analysis of Silas as the portrait of obsessive-compulsive behavior, see Johnstone (ch. 3).
5. It is now the National Central Library of Florence.
6. While she was not a Positivist, in *Romola* her schema for the movement of history is assumed to be influenced by the stages of history as outlined by Comte (the Theological, Metaphysical, and Positivist).
7. *Romola* is set between April 9, 1492, the day after Lorenzo de' Medici's death created a power vacuum in the city, and May 23, 1498, the day on which Savonarola was publicly executed. An epilogue brings the action up to 1509. On the genre of the historical novel, see Sanders. On the mythic conceptions of history evident in *Romola*, see Bonaparte and Carpenter.
8. It was serialized in the *Cornhill* from July 1862–August 1863 and ended up in 14 rather than 12 parts. For the details on these negotiations and the complexity of chapter numbering and production of parts, see Martin.

9. For an examination of Eliot's professional negotiations about the publication of her books and critique of how these have been handled by critics, see Feltes.

10. The original plan was to publish in *Blackwood's* anonymously because the novel was such a departure for George Eliot and might be prejudged by comparison with her English novels. Martin notes that Smith "sought her precisely for her name" (125), and in fact it was at this time that Eliot acknowledged the value of the name as brand (*GEL* 4:25).

11. For a reading of the story in light of the Liggins affair, see Bodenheimer, *Real Life*. For explorations of its colonial implications, see Rodstein and Henry, *George Eliot and the British Empire*.

12. For Charles Lewes's career, see Ashton, *G. H. Lewes* and Bodenheimer, *Real Life*. Blackwood's nephew Charles died within two years of joining the army. Dickens's son Walter died in India in 1863.

13. Call, an intellectual, poet, and clergyman who had renounced his orders, was the second husband of Eliot's friend Rufa Brabant Hennell. Lewes is also referring to his recent book on Aristotle (1864).

14. Kaye, "The Indian Civil Service: Its Rise and Fall, Parts I–II." *Blackwood's*. Jan. 1861 and March 1861: 115–30, 261–76.

15. See Shuman.

16. For the most detailed, sympathetic, and insightful account of Eliot's role as stepmother, see Bodenheimer, *Real Life* (ch. 7). See also Henry, *George Eliot and the British Empire* (ch. 2).

17. On blackmail in Eliot's fiction, see Welsh.

18. While instances of such mediated desire occur in Eliot's fiction, such as William Dane's desire for Silas's fiancée or Hans Meyrick's desire for Mirah, more frequently, Eliot breaks this pattern with fluid triangulations that defy the literary conventions available to her.

19. Eliot seems to encode an analogy between Victorian divorce "reform" and the actions of Pope Alexander the Sixth, whom Vaiano says "intends to reform and purify the Church and wisely begins by abolishing that priestly abuse which keeps too large a share of this privileged matrimony to the clergy and stints the laity" (137; ch. 14). See Duffy, *Saints and Sinners*.

20. Stephen's conception of the Renaissance would have been influenced by the late-century revival of interest in the period in work such as John Addington Symonds's *The Renaissance in Italy* (1875–86). Symonds also translated *The Life of Benvenuto Cellini* (1888) and co-wrote with Havelock Ellis, *Sexual Inversion* (1897). See Fraser, *Victorians and Renaissance Italy* and Dowling, *Hellenism and Homosexuality*.

21. For details on the history of homosexuality in Renaissance Florence, see Rocke. He writes: "The sexual renown of Florentine males was remarked on by both local and foreign chroniclers, condemned by preachers, deplored by concerned citizens, derided – or occasionally admired – by writers and poets" (3). Of unmarried Florentine men, Rocke writes: "Only a small group of 'habitual' sodomites, mainly older unmarried men, can be identified who pursued relations with boys throughout a considerable part of their adult lives" (15).

22. For an elaboration of this argument, see Henry, "The *Romola* Code."

23. The bachelor Leighton became a friend who attended their Sunday afternoons at the Priory beginning in the late 1860s, part of a group of prominent artists who formed their social set, including the Pre-Raphaelites Edward Burne-Jones, William Morris, and Dante Gabriel Rossetti (Haight, *Biography* 408–9).

24. Two engravers worked on the woodcut engravings for the *Cornhill* illustrations and their styles are different. W. J. Linton was responsible for the illustration of Tito and Nello. Eliot wrote in a letter to George Smith that Leighton was not pleased with the engravings, referring to "poor Mr. Leighton's chagrin at the engraver's rendering of Nello" (*GEL* 4:48). Linton was part of the original *Leader* supporters and was also married to Eliza Lynn since 1858, though the couple later separated.

25. Nello's reference to "the divine prerogative of the lips" may derive from Poliziano's early Greek Epigrams, addressed to various young men: "Content yourself, O Jupiter, with Ganymede, and leave to me the splendid Chiomadoro ['golden-curls'] who is sweeter than honey. O, I am thrice and four times happy! For truly I have kissed, and truly I kiss again your mouth, O delightful youth!" (qtd. in Saslow 30). Saslow calls Poliziano "a clear example of a Florentine Neoplatonist who overtly translated homosexual feelings into erotic expression" (29).

26. Dante's Malebolge is not populated by scholars. There are, however, several scholars in the circle to which the sodomites are condemned. It seems that Nello is aware that Poliziano might belong in the circle of the sodomites, but he carelessly uses the Malebolge or ninth circle (Cantos XVI–XXX) as a synonym for all of Dante's hell, conflating it with the seventh circle condemning violence (described in Cantos XV–XVI) – that of the sodomites.

6

Felix Holt and The Spanish Gypsy
1865–9

Say we fail!/We feed the higher tradition of the world/And leave our spirit in our children's breasts.

(*The Spanish Gypsy*: bk. 1; ll. 3152–4)

Historian Scott A. Sandage begins his book, *Born Losers: A History of Failure in America* (2005), with the death of Henry David Thoreau: "The American dream died young and was laid to rest on a splendid afternoon in May 1862" (1). He describes the ethic of ceaseless work that came to characterize American culture and the emergence of a financial term, "failure," as a more general description of a life, asking, "how did financial circumstances evolve into everyday categories of personal identity?" (10). At the time of his death, Thoreau, whose *Walden* (1854) Eliot reviewed in January 1856 in the *Westminster*, six years after she had met Ralph Waldo Emerson at Rosehill, had already failed in life as measured by his financial circumstances. By 1862, Eliot had become a remarkable success, but sadly, failure was a term that she would use to describe Lewes's two youngest sons, whose futures became a great source of anxiety to her at this time.

Though Sandage writes about the emergence of financial failure as an identity within American culture, the "Protestant Work Ethic," a term and concept coined by Max Weber in the early twentieth century, was an important ingredient of England's industrialization and capitalist spirit. Eliot, as we have seen, was influenced by, and inclined to, a puritanical asceticism even after she stopped observing any form of Christian ritual. She grew up in a home where work was considered a virtue, and

The Life of George Eliot: A Critical Biography, First Edition. Nancy Henry.
© 2012 Nancy Henry. Published 2012 by John Wiley & Sons, Ltd.

in the cases of her father and brother, the reward was a certain elevation in social standing. The son of a carpenter, Robert Evans rose through his own efforts to the superior position of estate manager for aristocratic landowners. Isaac's son Fred took another step "up" by becoming a clergyman in the Church of England. In this family, "failure" was not well tolerated. Isaac, for example, only grudgingly took responsibility for Chrissey when her husband Edward Clarke went bankrupt or "failed" in 1845.

The ceaseless drive to work was a central feature of Eliot's life and personality. It was a trait she shared with Lewes, who had no advantages or family support when he rose within the London literary world by a drive to work so manic that – like Eliot – he was often ill from overwork. These shared values and habits allowed them to create remarkably compatible individual and joint regimens of reading, writing, and pursuing other forms of culture (concerts, theater, museums). They even worked hard at their socializing when they established their regular Sunday salon in the late 1860s. Only physical maladies interrupted their writing, and it is likely that overwork contributed to the headaches, faintness, digestive problems, and other discomforts of which they often complained in letters and journals.

Figure 21   George Henry Lewes, photograph by John and Charles Watkins, 1864 (© National Portrait Gallery, London)

In Eliot's fiction, this work ethic is embodied in characters such as Adam Bede and Caleb Garth from *Middlemarch* (both estate managers often said to be based on her father). Adam, who studies at night with the schoolteacher Bartle Massey, and Mrs Garth, who teaches her children at home, represent the other component of the values of self-help and hard work – education. In contrast, the economic and life failures in her fiction include Amos Barton, Thias Bede, Mr Tulliver, and Lydgate (thought to be inspired by Edward Clarke's failed medical practice in the village of Meriden). The shame of financial failure is registered most painfully in *The Mill*, and Tom's dedication to paying off his father's debts redeems his otherwise harshly judged character.[1]

The high value placed on success through industriousness and merit was reflected in Victorian culture generally. Eliot mentions her father's admiration for the American Benjamin Franklin, whose life provided a model of the work ethic (*GEL* 1:128–30). But the ethos was alive in mid-Victorian England too, as illustrated in Dinah Mulock Craik's popular novel, *John Halifax, Gentleman* (1856). Samuel Smiles's best-selling *Self-Help* (1859) and his biographies of businessmen made the connection between hard work and economic success. Eliot read Smiles's *Life* of the railway engineer George Stephenson when it was published in 1857. In 1862, she told Cara Bray that Stephenson was one of her "great heroes" (*GEL* 4:11). This emphasis on application and self-reliance was emerging along with a wealthy middle class in the mid-nineteenth century and presenting an implicit ideological critique of the English class system – based on inheritance of property within families – that was more threatening to that system than other, more radical or revolutionary visions.

These aspects of Eliot's reading and daily life provide the context for her response to the careers of Lewes's sons in the 1860s and also for her fiction throughout the rest of her career. The first chapter of *Adam Bede* establishes the satisfaction of a job well done (apart from monetary compensation) when Adam chastises his fellow carpenters for wanting to leave their task unfinished just because the workday has ended. This value never disappeared from Eliot's fiction or her life, but it became complicated by her monetary needs in relation to negotiating business contracts and in terms of the financial independence she and Lewes expected from the young men in whose careers they were investing time and money. As she and Lewes grappled emotionally and financially with Thornie and Bertie's failures throughout the late 1860s, her fiction continued to contrast the successful, hard-working characters with the lazy, pleasure-loving ones. This contrast is central to the plot of her next novel in which Felix Holt values honest labor over money and social status, while Harold Transome enjoys the benefits of an expected inheritance and indulges in hookah smoking and a "slave" wife, pleasures that he learned to indulge during his years as a merchant and banker in Smyrna.

Harold does not import this pleasure-seeking mentality from the Ottoman Empire, though he does import a servant, Dominic, to cook for him and to help look after the son of the slave wife. Rather, the narrative implies that he inherits his love of pleasure, along with a tendency to gain weight, from his biological father, the lawyer Matthew Jermyn, who had sought the pleasure of an adulterous affair with Mrs Transome in his youth and thereafter benefited materially from the connection and access he had to the Transome estate (cutting timber for his own use, for example). As a newcomer to the town of Treby Magna, reminiscent of Nuneaton with its nearby coal pits and canals, he had developed a spa resort and hotel in order to exploit the area's salt spring. The speculation failed, and the hotel became a much less romantic tape factory. But Jermyn nonetheless became a successful lawyer and man of standing in the town, maintaining his connections with his former mistress Mrs Transome and coming into conflict with their illegitimate son when he returns from abroad with notions of breaking his family's ties with the man he does not know is his biological father.

Felix Holt was the English novel that came between Eliot and the Spanish drama she had been contemplating since 1864, much as *Silas Marner* had come between the conception and completion of *Romola*. The overly complicated legal plot of *Felix Holt* is intended to expose the injustice of a system of inherited wealth in which the unworthy may be rewarded and the worthy denied. It was a world where "men and women who have the softest beds and the most delicate eating, who have a very large share of that sky and earth which some are born to have no more of than the fraction to be got in a crowded entry," nonetheless make themselves at least as miserable as their poorer neighbors (*FH* 22; ch. 1). Inheritance is a system based on bloodlines and legitimacy, but these lucky few within the nation often squander the good fortune of their birth. They have illegitimate children, and become gamblers and alcoholics. They also go to law against each other and greedily wish for the deaths of others so that they or their children might inherit. Mrs Transome wishes for the death of her first son so that her favorite (illegitimate) son Harold may inherit the estate. Her wish is granted, but it does not bring her the happiness she imagined. This notion of hoping for death in order to secure inheritance would be repeated, for example, in the "Christian Carnivora" in *Middlemarch*, who crowd around old man Featherstone waiting for him to die. In *Daniel Deronda*, Gwendolen and her family casually discuss how many people would have to die for Grandcourt to inherit the baronetcy as well as the Mallinger estates.

Those who stood to inherit wealth were robbed of incentive to improve themselves. As she began to rise economically and socially, Eliot was becoming more interested in the lives of the aristocracy, the landed gentry, and the landed middle class. The Cheverels in "Mr. Gilfil's Love Story" are not developed characters, and the squires Donnithorne in *Adam Bede* and Cass in *Silas Marner* are marginal to the main plot. Her aesthetic stance led her to make humble characters the focus of *Adam Bede*, *The Mill*, and *Silas Marner*, but she now began to integrate domestic dramas surrounding the inheritance of wealth into her stories of common life. It was a world she observed growing up, knowing that because of that lottery of birth the Newdigates would always be Newdigates living in Arbury Hall or one of their other estates, which in turn would be managed by the people of her class and farmed by the people of a lower class. That is, unless lawsuits resulted in the turning out of one branch of the Newdigate family by another or until some crime or secret from the past returned to dislodge them from their social supremacy. From *Felix Holt* to *Daniel Deronda*, the class hierarchy and system of inheritance on which it depends are represented as unstable and subject to disruption by the return of repressed secrets.

Eliot recognized the absurdity of the English class system. Like Jane Austen, she saw the unfairness and disastrous social consequences of excluding women from inheriting property. She was continually rereading Austen and reread *Pride and Prejudice* before writing *Felix Holt*. In *Felix Holt*, she criticized the very fabric of English society and its institutionalization of primogeniture and entail, which rewarded people who need not prove their merit. These themes of the absurd lottery-like system of inheritance are the stuff of comedy, as Dickens demonstrated with Jarndyce vs. Jarndyce in *Bleak House* (1852–3). In *Felix Holt*, the narrator explains the secret of the Transome family, that "Thomas, son of John Justus, proving a prodigal, had, without the knowledge of his father, the tenant in possession, sold his own and his descendants' rights to a lawyer-cousin named Durfey" (239; ch. 29). Meaning, through a set of complicated legalities, that the Durfeys and not the Transomes owned the property. This history of sold inheritance is covered up by the lawyer Jermyn, whose illegitimate son with Mrs Transome, Harold, thereby stands to inherit.[2]

Eliot's future inheritance plots are legally correct but less confusing. In *Middlemarch*, Featherstone leaves his estate to his frog-faced illegitimate son (who doesn't want it) just to spite his other grasping relatives. In *Daniel Deronda*, everyone (including Daniel) thinks he is the illegitimate son of Sir Hugo (though he is not). These secrets and misunderstandings were elements of comedy, which Eliot mixed powerfully with the tragedies of her plots. While writing *Felix Holt*, she had put her own Spanish drama on hold and so was thinking deeply about the nature of both comic and tragic form and had reread Aristotle's *Poetics* in 1865 (*FH* vii; Introduction).[3] The challenge for her was translating classically tragic and comic themes into a realistic novel with modern plots and characters.

At every other level of society during the Victorian period, conditions were changing rapidly, a theme established in the "Introduction" to *Felix Holt*, in which the coach ride of the past is contrasted to the rapid rail travel and pace of life in the present. The Victorian belief in hard work and merit came up against the realities and determinism of birth in England. At the time Eliot was writing *Felix Holt*, the question of birth and inheritance versus merit as measures of one's social value was debated on many fronts, including reactions to the introduction of the Civil Service examinations beginning in 1853, which touched Eliot directly through Charles and Thornie Lewes. In her next three novels, Eliot would focus on the indeterminacies of the family structures upon which the system of inheritance is based, epitomized in

Daniel Deronda asking his tutor why the Popes have so many nephews. She also takes up the additional notion that inheritance or the expectation of inheritance corrupts, so central to Dickens's *Great Expectations* (1861), in the Featherstone–Vincy and the Bulstrode–Ladislaw inheritance plots of *Middlemarch*, as well as in the Mallinger–Deronda–Grandcourt inheritance plots in *Daniel Deronda*. Fred Vincy is disappointed in his expectations of inheritance from his uncle Featherstone. Bulstrode is punished for cheating his wife's grandson, Will Ladislaw, out of an inheritance. Grandcourt's morally corrupt tendencies are only furthered by his expectation of inheriting Sir Hugo's property.

Within this emerging context of merit, the Lewes boys epitomize failure. Thornie and Bertie became colonists in South Africa, working to become financially independent of their parents but failing in just about everything they tried. At the time of Thoreau's death in May of 1862, Eliot was completing *Romola*; Charles was employed at the Post Office; Thornie was about to take his second Indian Civil Service exam; and Bertie was still at Hofwyl. In 1862, the careers of the Lewes boys were being decided with all the weight of their successful father and stepmother's expectations. Thornie's namesake, Thornton Hunt, worked hard as a journalist, but could never succeed financially and was, like his father Leigh Hunt, always on the brink of financial disaster and dependent on others to bail him out. This position as one who does not pay his debts was justified by Hunt as a radical gesture of unconventionality. He felt no need to apologize for his views or stop producing offspring. Despite their own new wealth, which they were beginning to invest in stocks and would soon invest in real estate, Eliot and Lewes were determined that Lewes's sons would be financially independent and not follow the path of Thornton Hunt or indeed their mother Agnes.[4]

By July 1863, all three Lewes boys were temporarily living at Blandford Square. Lewes and Eliot had constant anxiety about the younger two from that time until the end of October. Eliot sadly missed the holiday she and Lewes might otherwise have taken. They had traveled briefly to the Isle of Wight and Dorking in April, but after that, action was required to place the younger sons and prevent their further disruption of the household. Thornie, having decided that he did not like the idea of India, failed the second Indian Civil Service exam he had taken in August 1863.

Thornie, in contrast to the responsible Charles and passive Bertie, was becoming a problem, neither responsible nor passive. In 1859, he wrote to Eliot and Lewes one of many letters that expressed enthusiasm for various international political causes, including the unification of Italy (which was secondary to art in Eliot's "Recollections of Italy" in 1860): "You must know, that Schamyl is my favourite hero" (November 17, 1859, Yale MS). Imam Schamyl, a Chechnyan warrior against the Russian Empire, had been a popular hero to the English since before the Crimean War between England and Russia (1853–6), and the Russians remained national enemies in Thornie's eyes. Emigration was a way of restraining him from pursuing his intention to become a volunteer soldier with the Polish insurgents against Russia in the "January Uprising" of 1863. Lewes and Eliot viewed this as preposterous but Thornie almost left against their will.[5]

Ultimately, Barbara Bodichon, the close friend and neighbor at Blandford Square who divided her time between Algeria and London, helped persuade Thornie to emigrate to Natal by enticing him with images of big game hunting and providing letters of introduction to friends she knew in the British colony. With no settled plan for his employment, there was nonetheless an expectation that he find a class-appropriate career. In contrast to Charles, he had lost an opportunity to enter the respectable Civil Service. Eliot emphasized Thornie's exasperating inability to pass the exam, referring in letters to his "companions in failure" (*GEL* 4:102) and "colleagues in failure" (*GEL* 4:105). There is a disguised tone of disgust in such language that betrays how she felt about his performance and its implications.

Lewes and Eliot faced their own version of a larger social problem, what came to be called in the 1880s the "younger son question" (Dunae, "Education" 196). In the mid-nineteenth century, middle-class parents negotiated the complicated British systems of patronage and merit in order to assure their sons' financial independence. Seeking positions for sons that were consistent with their own middle-class life yet geographically far from it, Lewes and Eliot found the colonies an attractive solution, and the only one they seem to have considered for Thornie and Bertie, who at different times were destined for Australia, Van Couver's Island, and Algeria. The United States was not mentioned as a potential destination, probably because of the Civil War, which began in 1861. It is no wonder that sons and their problems feature in *Felix Holt*, *Middlemarch*, and *Daniel Deronda*. Furthermore, the new system of examinations that determined the fates of both Charles and Thornton Lewes put the young men in the center of another 1860s controversy concerning the power of the state and the efficacy of political reforms, providing yet another link between Eliot's experiences as a step-parent and the topics of politics and reform she would explore in her novels. [6]

In October 1863, the 19-year-old Thornie left with "a large packet of recommendatory letters. . . and with what he cares much more for – a first-rate rifle and revolver – and already with a smattering of Dutch and Zulu" (*GEL* 4:109). Bertie was sent to a farm in Scotland to "learn agriculture" (*GEL* 4:117). A month later on November 13, Eliot and Lewes moved into their new home, the Priory, in St John's Wood near Regent's Park, which was being decorated by Owen Jones at great expense and paid for courtesy of George Smith and *Romola*. The rest of 1863 was spent settling into the house where they would live until Lewes's death in 1878.

Established in her new home, with Thornie and Bertie out of sight, Eliot began to think about her next book. 1864 was a year of reading and traveling rather than writing. She and Lewes considered composing a play with their new friend, the actress Helen Faucit, in mind. In February they went to see her perform in Glasgow, visiting Bertie in Thankerton (Lanarkshire, Scotland, southeast of Glasgow) on their way home. On May 4, 1864, they left for a trip to Italy, accompanied by their artist friend

Figure 22 The drawing-room at the Priory (John Walter Cross, *George Eliot's Life*, 1885)

Frederic Burton (who had recently painted a portrait of Eliot). They spent three weeks in Venice immersed in visual art. Eliot was moved by the sixteenth-century artist Titian's painting "The Annunciation" to think about a woman's calling to a larger cause, and she resolved to combine this theme with her desire to write a drama. It was during this trip that *The Spanish Gypsy* was conceived, though it would be several years before she completed the work, which would be interrupted by the writing of a novel and would take a form different from what she originally planned.

After leaving Venice, they spent three more weeks traveling in Italy and Switzerland with a final stop in Paris. Upon returning to London on June 20, 1864, they were surprised to learn that Charles had become engaged in their absence to Gertrude Hill. She had been raised by her grandfather, the medical reformer Thomas Southwood Smith (1788–1861), who was known to Lewes as an initial supporter of his journal the *Leader*. Her sister was Octavia Hill (1838–1912), in whose social reforms Gertrude and Charles would later become actively involved. Lewes felt somewhat melancholy at the thought of his son's entering into such a serious commitment. On the whole, however, they had reason to be pleased with Charles's independence and success. He was making a respectable middle-class life for himself and marrying a woman of whom they approved. They would come to

Figure 23   Drawing of George Eliot by Sir Frederic William Burton, 1865 (© National Portrait Gallery, London)

lean heavily on his reliable, steady nature in the coming years; his life contrasted markedly with the lives of his younger brothers.

Eliot decided that she needed to research the setting on which she had resolved for her drama, Spain in 1492, a time of struggle between Moors and Spanish Christians with Gypsies and Jews caught in the conflict. It was a period when racial identity was foremost, affecting the daily lives and determining the fates of all the diverse groups. This distinct racial and religious context explains why she wrote: "My reflections brought me nothing that would serve me except that moment in Spanish history when the struggle with the moors was attaining its climax" (*The Spanish Gypsy* 274; Appendix). It was a time of war, the Inquisition, persecution, and also discovery, as Columbus embarked upon his voyage to the "New World," a symbolic venture to which Eliot referred in several of her novels. She took extensive notes on all of these historical elements, which threatened to overwhelm her, as the research for *Romola* (also set in 1492) had done. She agonized over both the form and content of the work and wrote the beginning acts of this drama in verse during the summer and fall of 1864. She suffered depression, skepticism, and self-doubt, as she had during the preparation and composition of previous works. Lewes's health was so poor that he

161

went alone for a time to drink the waters and rest at the popular spa in Malvern, Worcestershire. On the whole, fitful work on what she hoped to be her first drama, together with bouts of depression about the difficulty she was having with it, characterized the end of 1864.

Early 1865 was taken up with assorted projects, and Eliot's frustration with her writing became extreme. She wrote in her journal: "George has taken my drama away from me" (February 19–21, 1865; *GEJ* 123). Patronizing as this may sound, it was a wise strategy based on the agonies she suffered over *Romola* and its deadlines. There was no deadline for the drama, and Eliot could afford to take some time away from the work that was making her so miserable. As for Lewes, George Smith asked him to serve as an advisor (with salary) on his new venture, *The Pall Mall Gazette*. Lewes agreed and contributed pieces to the evening paper. Eliot also contributed four rather uncharacteristic short essays published under the pseudonym Saccharissa, her only explicitly female narrator.[7] In March, Trollope persuaded Lewes to accept the editorship of a new journal with which he was involved, *The Fortnightly Review*, which instituted a policy of publishing only signed articles (Nash). Eliot contributed a review essay of W. E. H. Lecky's *History of the Rise and Influence of the Spirit of Rationalism in Europe* (1865), the last review essay she would write.

On March 20, Charles was married. With Lewes immersed in editorial work, Charles's wedding preparations completed, and her verse drama set aside, Eliot began a new novel, which would become *Felix Holt* (March 29, 1865; *GEJ* 124). Unlike *Silas Marner*, her last English novel, *Felix Holt* required a good deal of research. In preparing the context for its setting, she read assorted histories of England and works of political economy.[8] She needed to get a clear sense of the politics and class conflicts that would form the subject matter and major themes of the work. The new novel was a personal landmark for its inclusion of chapter epigraphs or mottoes. She had originally intended to write mottoes for *Romola*, but abandoned the idea. The chapter epigraphs of *Felix Holt* include quotations from other works, many by Shakespeare and the Greek dramatists, indicating how much dramatic form was on her mind. She composed many other of the mottoes herself, continuing to experiment with verse and no doubt thinking about *The Spanish Gypsy*.[9]

As she was writing *Felix Holt*, she and Lewes received letters from Thornie in South Africa. He started a trading business in the Transvaal, but by June 12, 1865, was "bankrupt" (*GEL* 8:343). With Eliot and Lewes now fully involved in new creative projects, and Charles settled down to married life, these letters from Africa must have been troubling but remote. Thornie was the only of the three Lewes boys who had a flare for writing and telling stories, turning his experiences and mishaps into entertaining, but nonetheless disturbing and eventually heart-breaking narratives of failure.

In July, Thornie volunteered for the Natal Frontier Guard, a Boer cavalry corps that was preparing to do battle with the native Basutos to gain territory for the

Orange Free State. The lapse of time between his writing letters and his parents receiving them was extensive, so that Eliot and Lewes did not learn of his activities until after they had traveled to Normandy and Brittany in August 1865. She continued writing *Felix Holt* throughout the fall, experiencing depression, and worrying especially about the details of the complex legal plot. In contrast to *The Mill*, in which the particulars of the legal suits that "ruin" Mr Tulliver are left vague, *Felix Holt* would depend on readers entering into a labyrinth of inheritance laws. In December they had a letter from Thornie describing a battle and the shooting of "Kaffirs." Eliot wrote to her old friend D'Albert Durade on December 17, 1865: "Thornton has had some calamities to encounter in Natal, owing to a monetary crisis in the colony and a war with the natives" (*GEL* 4:212).[10] Again they were concerned, but the second son's calamities, crises, and wars seemed far removed from their domestic realities and efforts to progress with their own writing.

Progress on *Felix Holt* continued. In January 1866, Eliot met the positivist lawyer and friend of the Congreves, Frederic Harrison. She subsequently engaged in a lengthy correspondence with him over the legal details of her plot. She wrote steadily and finished the second of three volumes by April. On the strength of what she had written, Lewes approached George Smith with the manuscript, offering it to him for £5,000. Smith read and declined it on commercial grounds. Lewes then wrote to Blackwood with the same proposal and Blackwood accepted. He was extremely enthusiastic about Eliot's return to an English setting, as well as what he perceived to be the novel's conservative politics. Knowing the publication was secured, Eliot finished *Felix Holt* on the first of June 1866. On June 7, she and Lewes set off for Germany, revisiting many of the places and people from their trip in 1854–5. This time, however, the trip was overshadowed by the war between the Austrian Empire and Prussia (1866). As they had done before, they managed to be out of England when her book was published, putting some distance between themselves and the reviews of the new novel, which was generally well received.

Felix Holt

Often called her "political novel," *Felix Holt* is set in the Midlands during the months immediately following the passing of the first Reform Bill (September 1832–April 1833). The geography and time frame return to those of *Scenes*, *The Mill on the Floss*, and *Silas Marner*. Her heroine, Esther Lyon, must choose between the uncompromising artisan and self-proclaimed radical, Felix Holt and the Byronic and cynical radical, Harold Transome. England also must choose between a radical solution to its social ills of ignorance and poverty and the false promises implied in extending the franchise. With the first Reform Bill the nation chose the latter, easier option. Felix believes that education and moral reform are the only means by which men can elevate themselves above poverty and escape the mindset that submits to oppression and demoralization, especially through alcohol. His views are radical in their critique of democracy; they question the value of representation for the uneducated majority. The politics of the novel, however, must be evaluated in the context of its complexly interrelated plots, which balance the comic with the tragic elements.

Felix Holt begins with an "Introduction" that meditates on the historical changes that have taken place in the 35 years between the setting and writing of the novel, which include the supplanting of the stagecoach by railways. From the perspective of the stagecoach driver, the narrator provides a lyrical description of the Midlands, observing how the various landscapes reflect the economic, religious, and political lives of the people who live in the villages – local color that could be savored on a coach ride but would be overlooked by the hurrying passengers on a train. The introduction establishes the notion of many people comprising one nation – a prelude to the theme of voting reform – but identifying with their local communities. The knowing gossip of the coachman, Samson, provides a condensed version of the novel's complex plot:

> That? – oh, that was Transome Court, a place there had been a fine sight of lawsuits about. Generations back, the heir of the Transome name had somehow bargained away the estate, and it fell to the Durfeys, very distant connexions, who only called themselves Transomes because they had got the estate. But the Durfeys' claim had been disputed over and over again; and the coachman, if he had been asked, would have said, though he might have to fall down dead the next minute, that property didn't always get into the right hands. (10; Introduction)

The Introduction concludes with an observation about the tragedies of everyday life, "for there is much pain that is quite noiseless; and vibrations that make human agonies are often a mere whisper in the roar of hurrying existence" (11; Introduction). And yet despite this sympathy and desire to represent noiseless pain, the narrator is ironic about the very idea of equality that underlies political reform. The "publics" are patronized along political lines, as the narrator observes: "the company at the Blue Cow was of an inferior kind – equal, of course, in the fundamental attributes of humanity, such as desire for beer, but not equal in ability to pay for it" (107; ch. 11). Voting and drinking (in the form of candidate "treating") are inseparable: "the prospect of Reform had even served the voters instead of drink . . ." (153; ch. 16). Belief in reform is simply another intoxicant.

If *Felix Holt* urges the need to educate the working classes, it also shows the need to educate and reform women. Eliot chose to dramatize this through Esther's choice of a husband. When Eliot faced the death of her father in 1849, she feared losing part of her "moral nature" and of turning "earthly sensual and devilish for want of that purifying restraining influence" (*GEL* 1:284). She dedicated the manuscript of *Felix Holt* to George Henry Lewes in "this thirteenth year of their united life, in which the deepening sense of her own imperfectness has the consolation of their deepening love."[11] The dedication reflects ideas addressed in the novel: Eliot believed that Lewes made her a better person, but she never stopped struggling with what she felt to be her own imperfection. Esther's soul-searching over the course of the novel reflects her desire to be the better person she instinctively feels she can become. If Felix were to love her, "her life would be exalted into something quite new – into a sort of difficult blessedness, such as one may imagine in beings who are conscious of painfully growing into possession of higher powers" (194; ch. 22). Under Felix's influence, she has experienced how "incalculable is the effect of one personality on another" (194; ch. 22).

Esther is also influenced by her observations of Mrs Transome, the wreck of a fine lady who has become a disappointed woman. In her young life, Miss Lingon refused to take moral questions seriously. The narrator observes of Miss Lingon that "the notion that what is true and, in general, good for mankind, is stupid and drug-like, is not a safe theoretic basis in circumstances of temptation and difficulty" (27; ch. 1). Miss Lingon married Mr Transome for social status and money and with him produced a son. Then she had an affair with the charming lawyer Jermyn. Raising Jermyn's illegitimate son Harold as the second legitimate son of Mr Transome meant that deception and secrecy entered into her very being and corrupted her life.

Felix Holt develops and explores familiar themes in Eliot's fiction up to this point, including inheritance, the duties of children to parents, illegitimacy, secrecy, deception, adultery, and sexual triangles. The secrecy and deception relate specifically to paternity. The world was willing to accept that Harold was Mr Transome's son, as was Harold himself. The novel is structured around the Transome–Jermyn triangle, while the Felix Holt plot introduces a new triangle as Esther is courted by both Felix and Harold. Esther is similar to Harold in that she is deceived about her own paternity. Her father, the Reverend Rufus Lyon, has kept his own secret – that she is not his daughter. In this sense Harold and Esther share the experience of having been deceived. The revelation of the truth concerning both their fathers links their lives when it establishes that Esther and not Harold is the heir to Transome court. This uncertain parenthood might have provided an emotional bond between them, and Harold does fall in love with her. Their potential marriage seems to provide the perfect solution to the Transome inheritance plot. But Eliot's moral vision for Esther intervenes. Esther's moral education is at the heart of *Felix Holt*, and her choice of Felix over Harold defies romantic expectations of the typical marriage plot.

When Esther visits Transome Court with the knowledge that she is entitled legally to inherit it, the "dimly suggested tragedy" of Mrs Transome's life afflicts her "even to horror": "It seemed to have come as a last vision to urge her towards the life where the draughts of joy sprang from the unchanging fountains of reverence and devout love" (392; ch. 50). She searches for those fountains by rejecting Harold and accepting Felix. Eliot's representation of the old woman's psychology is unique in her fiction. At this time in letters, she refers often to herself as old, and she views Mrs Transome from a different perspective than she had Lady Cheverel in "Mr. Gilfil's Love Story" and Mrs Irwine in *Adam Bede* – imperious, privileged women who have done nothing particular with their lives. Mrs Transome has sinned and escaped without punishment. Like so many other of Eliot's characters, she awaits her Nemesis, which comes in the form of Harold.

Through Mrs Transome, Eliot also explores the subtleties of a relationship between former lovers forced by circumstances to remain allies because of children in common and a monetary relationship. The situation is not unlike that between George and Agnes Lewes. The narrator describes Jermyn in relation to Mrs Transome as the man "who was to pass with those nearest to her as her indebted servant, but whose brand she secretly bore" (98; ch. 9). He appears to be in her employment, but in reality he takes what he wants, deforesting and devaluating her property to build a home for himself and his family. The true power dynamic of the relationship remains invisible.

The political themes of *Felix Holt* resonate through the novel in both the personal and the national narrative lines. Eliot's own radicalism may be found in her questioning of the class hierarchy, and her exposure of institutions based on blood, land, and inheritance as fundamentally unstable, arbitrary, and false. While she sees it as folly that certain unqualified men should be allowed to exercise new influence through the vote, she also exposes the absurdity – the randomness and chance – of the class hierarchy generally. That power relations are not always what they seem is evident in the master/servant relationships.

Furthermore, the value and knowledge of servants is uncharacteristically central to the plot of *Felix Holt*, suggesting the vaguely threatening power of their knowledge in a manner that resonates with the larger themes of democracy and equality. The servants Dominic, Christian, and Denner are all invaluable to their employers. Robert Evans's first wife had been an intimate servant of Mrs Francis Newdigate, whose story may have informed that of Mrs Transome (Taylor 6). The hint at the power of servants is part of the broader consideration of class and the implications of extending the franchise. The plot suggests that there may be only a legal technicality, an undisclosed secret or lost document, standing between a family's possession of an estate and poverty that would disenfranchise its members. Harold's turning Radical after taking a Greek slave as his wife; the exposure of the fraudulent means by which the Transomes have held on to their land; and the bizarre coincidences by which the blackmailing Christian forces the issue of legal fraud into the light are all part of Eliot's overly complicated plot. But the legalities have a thematic significance. The Burkean notion of inheritance as stability disappears in the chaos of sold rights, "base fees," and "remainder-men," legal terms that nonetheless suggest the monetary (rather than the noble familial) basis of land ownership. A political system in which votes are granted on the basis of land ownership is itself flawed and, in this implicit critique, we see reflected not only mid-century debates about voting reform but also about the establishment of "merit" generally as measured by Civil Service examinations.

Felix Holt was published in three volumes on June 14, 1866. Critics were relieved that George Eliot had returned to a setting in the English past. Sales of the book were respectable but not spectacular. At the time she wrote *Felix Holt* and following, Eliot had many reasons to think about class. The second Reform Bill was imminent and it eventually passed in 1867. She now had a house, a large income, investments, and fame though, as a woman, no vote. She had been meeting the intellectual elite since her days at Rosehill and had counted among her friends and acquaintances the most important thinkers and writers of her day. But now her social circle was widening to include titled aristocrats, wealthy patrons of the arts, Cambridge and Oxford men, and artists. Throughout the late 1860s–1870s this circle grew. Lewes's management of her career took on yet another dimension of social coordinator, and the institutionalization of the Sunday afternoons at the Priory in the late 1860s was to play an important role in her late career and her subsequent reputation. In 1867, she wrote to Sara Hennell that "what is called social distinction seems to be in a shifting condition just now" (*GEL* 4:363).

Spain and *The Spanish Gypsy*

In September 1866, Lewes recorded in his journal that Bertie's departure had been "suddenly resolved on" based on a letter from Thornie announcing that he had received a grant of land (GHLJ, September 10, 1866). Bertie left for South Africa as a second-class passenger on a mail steamer on September 9, 1866. He wrote dutifully about his trip from on board but with an edge of resentment in his account of class divisions: "We second class passengers are not allowed to go near the 1st class. They have a piano in the saloon, but of course we 2nd may not touch it" (September 16, 1866, Yale MS). This was a new experience for the boarding school boy who spent his holidays with George Lewes and George Eliot. Although he had been used to living away from home, he had never been treated as second class.

On November 5, 1866, he wrote to Lewes that Thornie had not been there to meet him at the port, and told how he got himself to Durban, meeting some of the English connections that Thornie had made. Eventually, Thornie arrived in Durban from his current base in Verulum. It turned out that Lewes's letters telling him when Bertie would arrive were all being held at the post office in Durban.[12] Bertie wrote of his brother: "He has not altered very much since I last saw him, he is a little stouter and has a foreign look about him. He was dressed in a black suit, the only one that he had, and a shirt that once had been white but was all sorts of colours" (November 5, 1866, Yale MS). He then offered the disturbing news that his rushed departure had been in vain: "Thornton has not received his farm and it is not very likely that he will get one at all. So we bought a couple of horses and are going to ride to the Transvaal to see if we can buy one." Finally, he added the information:

> The colony is in a very poor state, money seems to be very scarce. Thornton's idea is that we shall be able to buy a farm for 50£ in the Transvaal but I don't think we shall get one worth anything for that money. We asked several people in Maritzburg who had farms to sell and they wanted from 150 to 300 for one farm. (November 5, 1866, Yale MS)

In their respective letters home, the Lewes boys, who had received money from Lewes and Eliot to launch themselves in their colonial careers, felt obliged to account for the money spent, and they were apologetic when they needed to ask for more, as they inevitably did. When he received this letter over a month after it was written, Lewes wrote in his journal: "The prospect of the farm seems to have been imaginary" (GHLJ, December 25, 1866). After some further failed ventures, the boys purchased 3–4,000 acres for £100 in the Wakkerstroom district of the Transvaal and began their lives as colonial farmers.

With *Felix Holt* published and all three Lewes sons embarked on careers, Eliot returned to her previous project, the verse drama eventually called *The Spanish Gypsy*. She continued her pattern of immersing herself in the history of the period – Spain at the end of the fifteenth century. Right after Christmas of 1866, she and Lewes traveled to Biarritz. They were seeking a restoration of health. Overworked from editing the *Fortnightly*, Lewes had been getting "thinner and thinner" (*GEL* 4:330). So when they began to discuss a possible trip to Spain, they had doubts about whether they were up to the physical demands of traveling. The appeal was great enough to overcome their fears, and the couple left for Spain on what would become a physically demanding but ultimately rewarding tour of the country lasting from January 26 to March 16, 1866. Enduring marathon train trips (a railway across Spain had been completed in 1864) they visited Barcelona, Granada, Seville, and Madrid, making what Eliot called a "great loop" all around the east and through the center of Spain (*GEL* 4:349) and returning via Biarritz to Paris and then home.

They were impressed by the Moorish architecture – unlike anything they had seen on previous travels – spent hours in the cathedrals and museums learning about Spanish art, and generally enjoyed the landscape, the weather, and the people they met. In contrast to Italy, France, and Germany, Spain was not a common tourist destination for the English and so they did not move within groups of people they already knew or have local hosts, like Tom Trollope in Florence. They encountered Europeans and Americans, but for the most part enjoyed traveling alone, communicating in the Spanish language they had been studying. They were delighted by watching Gypsy folk dancing in Granada, and such dancing appears in *The Spanish Gypsy*. They also visited the home of the Gypsy "captain," a blacksmith who played the guitar for them (Haight, *Biography* 401).[13]

Titian's "Annunciation" inspired the drama Eliot originally intended to write, and she combines the idea of a woman answering a summons (in the case of the Virgin, by God) to a duty higher than marriage with this particular moment in Spanish history and with her life-long fascination with the Gypsy people. She had portrayed Maggie's fantasy of becoming "Queen" of the Gypsies in *The Mill on the Floss* with irony, but she depicts Fedalma's actual ascension to that role with gravity. The historically remote setting recalls historical novels such as Scott's *Ivanhoe* (1819) and Bulwer Lytton's *Leila, or the Siege of Granada* (1839) – full of dukes, minstrels, and evil priests – in which racial conflict was also important. The shadow of the Inquisition creates an atmosphere of intolerance and persecution that makes the Gypsies' imagined desire for a homeland especially urgent. A stateless minority living as outsiders in a variety of countries and maintaining a cohesive identity over time – from fifteenth-century Spain to nineteenth-century England – attracted her with its dramatic potential. She studied their history and culture, reading among other works George Borrow's *The Zincali; or, an Account of the Gypsies in Spain* (1841).

In the themes of collective identity and the longing for a state, which she would develop more fully when writing about the Jews in *Daniel Deronda*, she both reflected the nationalist movements of her time about which young Thornie was so enthusiastic (Greek, Italian, Hungarian, Polish, Chechnyan, German) and predicted the coming preoccupation with national identities that would characterize Europe before and after her death. She took the sacrifice of self to local, familial bonds – as represented by Maggie – onto a grander stage as Fedalma accepts her father Zarca's demand that she lead the Gypsies out of Spain and to a new home in Africa. Henceforth, Eliot was preoccupied with exploring the impulse to greatness that can be worn down by the realities of everyday life. In *Middlemarch*, Dorothea and Lydgate fail to achieve their high ideals for collective good. Their ideals are diffuse and not driven by an hereditary identity, as those of Fedalma and Daniel Deronda are, and yet Fedalma also fails to achieve the establishment of a Gypsy nation, and Daniel's success in helping to establish a Jewish nation is left undefined. It is a new emphasis on non-monetary, racial/cultural inheritance that points to a revitalizing future. As *Daniel Deronda*, suggests, however, she was uncertain whether the collective identity that functions as a life calling for Daniel can answer the problems faced by Gwendolen and English culture generally.[14]

Fedalma's mission to lead the Gypsies to a homeland in Africa – unlike the expulsion of the Jews and Gypsies from Spain in 1492 – has no basis in historical fact. Had such a Gypsy nation been established in the fifteenth century, Eliot might never have encountered the Gypsies she did as a child in the Midlands, a story she retold after she had written *The Spanish Gypsy* in her "Brother and Sister" sonnets (1869). The idealist element of the fantasy leads us to ask how likely she really thought it was that Daniel Deronda would help to establish a Jewish state. Her own practical support for nationalist causes at this time seems to have been minimal. She refused, for example, to contribute money to Italian patriot Giuseppe Mazzini's cause in 1865 (*GEL* 4:200), and she and Lewes had no sympathy with Thornie's desire to fight the Russians for Polish independence. In the 1870s, however, her belief in nationalisms as desirable bases for identity globally in the future would develop into her final political stance.

With the return from Spain to London in the spring of 1867 came renewed depression and physical ailments. In July, she and Lewes traveled again to Germany where she labored on the poem. They returned to London in October 1867, and she continued work. In November 1867, already expecting to publish the work in progress, Blackwood prevailed upon Eliot to write an essay in the voice of Felix Holt that would elaborate on Felix's political views, and thereby contribute to the current debates about the Second Reform Bill (1867). Somewhat reluctantly, she wrote "Address to the Working Men, by Felix Holt," finishing it on December 4, 1867. It appeared in *Blackwood's Magazine* in January 1868. While it is tempting to interpret *Felix Holt*'s politics retroactively in light of the "Address," the distilled political ideas in the essay are more conservative than the novel when we consider the latter's romance and inheritance plots, which question the stability and viability of traditional English class structures. Though it may seem difficult to find connections between this "Address" – expressing some of Eliot's political views through Felix – and the Spanish poem, one similarity is the critique of an Enlightenment ideology of equality upon which democracy generally and the extension of the franchise in particular were based.

She finished her epic poem at the end of April 1868 when it was finally given the title of *The Spanish Gypsy* (rather than the earlier considered "Fedalma" or "Fidalma"). She told Blackwood she preferred *The Spanish Gypsy* as a title in the fashion of the "elder dramatists" with whom she said she had "perhaps more cousinship than with recent poets" (*GEL* 4:428).[15] It was published on May 25, 1868, by which time she and Lewes were traveling in Germany with a focus on consulting German scientists for Lewes's research on his new project, *Problems of Life and Mind*, the ambitious, multi-volume work that would occupy him for the rest of his life. They were again on a quest to regain physical health and left on July 29, to visit several German spas, including fashionable Baden, as well as other smaller watering places, returning on October 1, 1868 (Haight, *Biography* 404).

In *The Spanish Gypsy*, the verse form allowed her to indulge a romanticized portrait of the Gypsies as they sing, dance, and chant. She was trying in her poetry to capture the sounds of music, as she had earlier tried to represent the sounds of speech, whether the regional accents of Derbyshire in *Adam Bede* or the sound of Renaissance Florentine dialect in *Romola*. The characters in *The Spanish Gypsy* do not speak in dialect but in perfect English. The experiment was instead in versification. The influences of Wordsworth, Tennyson, and the Brownings are evident in her blank verse and the verse novel form, though Lewes rejected the notion of Robert Browning's influence when the reviewer E. S. Dallas mentioned it (*GEL* 4:452–3).

The Spanish Gypsy

The Spanish Gypsy opens with a description of a river and the plain through which it runs, recalling the first chapter of The Mill. It also recalls the Proem in Romola, tracking the course of the sun at dawn as it rises over Spain:

> This deep mountain gorge
> Slopes widening on the olive-plumed plains
> Of fair Granada: one far-stretching arm
> Points to Elvira, one to eastward heights
> Of Alpujarras where the new-bathed Day
> With oriflamme uplifted o'er the peaks
> Saddens the breasts of northward-looking snows ...
>   (bk. 1; ll. 12–18)

The beginning of book III with its mythical, panoramic flight over Spain is not unlike the realistic coach ride through the Midlands in Felix Holt: "Quit now the town, and with a journeying dream/Swift as the wings of sound yet seeming slow/Through multitudinous pulsing of stored sense/And spiritual space, see walls and towers/Lie in the silent whiteness of a trance ..." (bk. 3; ll. 1–5). Her fantasy of time travel here invokes sound and silence as part of her atmosphere.

Throughout, the poem shows its origins as a drama in scenes and dialogue (including stage directions), introducing the characters in a tavern run by the converted Jew or "converso" Lorenzo, whose real name was Ephraim.[16] As in Romola, the cast of characters revolves around a strong woman, Fedalma, "stolen" at age four from the Gypsy camp of her widowed father. Fedalma has been raised by Spaniards and, ignorant of her origins, is in love with the Duke of Bedmár, Don Silva, whose mother raised her. Silva is at war with the Moors (who are aided by the Gypsies) in the service of King Ferdinand and Queen Isabella. He is honor-bound to fight but his nature is inclined to love and tolerance. When the action begins he is deferring his military duties in order to marry Fedalma clandestinely and in defiance of his uncle, a Catholic priest bent on crusade against the infidels and determined to prevent the marriage.

Fedalma makes her first appearance in the streets of Bedmár (an actual town near Granada) to which she is inexplicably drawn and where she is overcome by a desire to dance the folk dance of the Gypsies. The communion she feels but does not understand with the crowd of watchers is sexualized, "stretching her arm beauteous; now the crowd/Exultant shouts, forgetting poverty/In the rich moment of possessing her" (bk. 1; ll. 1421–3). In the midst of her dance, she is seen by the imprisoned Gypsy chieftain Zarca, who catches her eye and stops her dance in a scene reminiscent of the prisoner Baldassarre's grasping his son Tito in the streets of

Florence, or Kalonymos arresting Daniel Deronda in Frankfurt – all examples of recognition through physical appearance and family resemblance. She stands: "With level glance meeting that Gypsy's eyes,/That seem to her the sadness of the world/Rebuking her" (bk. 1; ll. 1464–5). Yet Fedalma cannot understand the power that the Gypsy's gaze has over her.

Silva proposes their hurried marriage, his love for Fedalma and desire to make her his duchess overcoming the revulsion he feels upon learning that she has danced like a commoner in the streets. Meanwhile Zarca escapes his captivity and appears in her chamber, revealing the secret of her birth and demanding that she renounce her Spanish identity and her marriage in favor of following him and assuming her inherited role as his successor. Struggling with her love for Silva, Fedalma resolves to help her father lead the dispersed Gypsies out of Spain to establish a homeland on the shores of Africa.[17]

The Spanish Gypsy retains the traces of Eliot's original plan to write it as a tragic drama. It sets up a painful choice for its heroine between the man she loves and the father who demands her help. The dilemma between love and familial duty is reminiscent of Maggie's choice between love of Stephen and duty to her family; it also reflects Eliot's study of Greek tragedies like *Antigone* and *Iphegenia* in which female characters are confronted with impossible choices. Don Silva struggles to understand how Fedalma could leave him, and is schooled in the preeminence of racial allegiance by the Jewish astronomer Sephardo. In contrast to the "converso" Lorenzo, Sephardo professes loyalty to his people in the face of his obligation to Silva, under whose protection he lives to practice his science and his art: "I am a Jew;/And while the Christian persecutes my race,/I'll turn at need even the Christian's trust/Into a weapon and shield for the Jews" (bk. 2; ll. 689–92). In this notion of racial fidelity among Gypsies and Jews in Spain we can see the seeds of a fuller, more realistic, and nuanced treatment of the topic in *Daniel Deronda*.[18]

The poem, however, does not simply elevate tribalism. It shows why collective identity is a complex choice for more intelligent, self-conscious people who may operate within Romantic traditions and consider love as a higher ideal than duty. Both Fedalma and Silva belong to this category and are mouthpieces for nineteenth-century models of secular identity. Fedalma asks the young Gypsy girl Hinda how she would choose between her lover and her tribe and the girl answers that Gypsies could not live without their tribe. Fedalma reflects: "She knows no struggles, sees no double path:/Her fate is freedom, for her will is one/With her own people's law, the only law/She ever knew" (bk. 3; ll. 759–62). To prove that love is more binding than ethnic identity or upbringing, Silva pledges to join the Gypsies, forsaking his past, wealth, and status. But his choice of love over duty turns him into an outcast.

Originally, Eliot had intended an even bloodier ending, but wrote to assure Blackwood on April 22, 1868: "The poem will be less tragic than I threatened" (*GEL* 4:431). Lewes dissuaded her from killing off Fedalma and Silva, as he had persuaded her to spare Hetty from execution in *Adam Bede*. In both cases, the choice of a happier ending – possibly an attempt to appeal to a broader audience – is questionable. Silva is tortured in his decision to desert his countrymen, and his death seems foreshadowed in a veritable Maenad chorus of Gypsies who surround and taunt him with the Catholicism that his oath of loyalty to the Gypsies cannot erase. In a lurid, savage scene, they chant:

> *Red-cross sword and sword blood-red –*
> *Till it press upon your head,*
> *Till it lie within your brain,*
> *Piercing sharp, a cross of pain,*
> *Til it lie upon your heart,*
> *Burning hot, a cross of fire.*
> (bk. 4; ll. 343–8)

This and many other songs within the poem, including the ballads of the minstrel Juan, the "Orpheus of the Gypsies" (bk. 3; ll. 222), show Eliot experimenting with verse forms within the overarching blank verse narrative. Furthermore, the image of the threatening Maenads recalls Tito's death and foreshadows that of her mythic protagonist in "The Legend of Jubal."

In an era when Jews had been forced to convert, and were then despised for doing so, the Christian Silva finds that he cannot convert and by taking an oath make himself to be something other than he was born and raised to be. He is seized with remorse when his fellow Spaniards are murdered by Zarca. When he sees his once-hated uncle, Father Isidor – symbol of both his blood and his religion – murdered before a crowd of Zarca's supporters, he is driven mad and stabs Zarca. Tragically, Fedalma's love for Silva has thus become the cause of her father's death. The narrative seems to point to the crowd's killing Silva, but before dying, Zarca pardons him and the tension builds lest the crowd "Should tear, bite, crush, in spite of hindering will" (bk. 4; l. 986). Silva flees, "Carrying forever with him what he fled –/Her murdered love – her love, a dear wronged ghost/Facing him, beauteous, 'mid the throngs of hell" (bk. 4; ll. 1003–5). Fedalma then embraces her inherited role as leader and addresses her people:

> Zincali all, who hear!
> Your Chief is dying: I his daughter live
> To do his dying will. He asks you now
> To promise me obedience as your Queen,
> That we may seek the land he won for us,
> And live the better life for which he toiled.
> (bk. 4; ll. 919–24)

Fedalma, however, is not an heroic character in the traditional sense. Drawing on the original inspiration of the "Annunciation," Eliot combines the notion of having a

173

great destiny thrust upon a woman with a psychological analysis of the woman's suffering for what she must sacrifice to that destiny. In the final book, Fedalma sails for Africa with her tribe. But she doubts her ability to achieve her father's dream. Upon their final parting, she tells Silva that "great futures died with him/Never to rise, until the time shall ripe/Some other hero with the will to save/The outcast Zincali" (bk. 5; ll. 262–5). Fedalma is a hero, not in deeds, but in the act of renouncing herself for the sake of her duty.

The one-volume edition of *The Spanish Gypsy* sold relatively well (especially in the US), and the book received positive reviews, encouraging Eliot to embark upon a further period of experimentation in writing poetry from 1869–71. The question remains as to why the ideas with which she grappled in *The Spanish Gypsy* were so appealing to her at this time. A woman's choice about marriage is a constant in her work. The search for a replacement for religion in some form of human community is also an ongoing, personal matter reflected in her writing. As the poem itself and her notes on it indicate, the conflict of races was a powerful attraction in her choice of setting and subject matter.[19]

To a Victorian author – even one whose novels were influential in transforming realist fiction into high art – the most serious form of writing was poetry. Clarifying her grander themes by treating them in verse, she then took those themes back to her domestic English settings in *Middlemarch*, working the high elements of tragedy into her study of provincial life. By freeing herself from the restrictions of realism and conforming to the metrical requirements of poetry, she expressed her beliefs in the need to strive for the high ideals of art in "The Legend of Jubal" (1870) and "Armgart" (1871). She stressed altruism in "Agatha" (1869) and "Armgart"; love in "How Lisa Loved the King" (1869); and corporate identity in *The Spanish Gypsy*. Now, she was not comparing herself to contemporary realist novelists, but rather to Wordsworth, Scott, Goethe, Milton, Shakespeare, and the Greek dramatists.[20]

Shortly before *The Spanish Gypsy*'s publication, William Blackwood told her what she wanted to hear when he sent Lewes the comments of the proof reader. On May 16, 1868, he wrote:

> Of course it is impossible to say how that mysterious reading public, which buys Charles Dickens by the ten thousand for the thousand of Romola or Felix Holt, will take it, but if Fedalma does not, with the better and more thoughtful part of it, place George Eliot as high among poets as she already stands among novelists, my opinion of the reading intellect of the age will go down to zero. (*GEL* 4:441)

The poem did not place her as high among poets as novelists, but it was both more popular and critically praised by contemporary reviewers than its subsequent neglect might suggest. She was striving for literary greatness. Poetry helped her express ideas in universal terms, even as the particular stories of Dorothea and Lydgate were taking shape in her mind. Her journal entry at the end of 1868 stated among her projects for 1869 a novel called *Middlemarch*.

The pattern of Eliot's writing career had always included diversions when she needed to rest her mind from the intensity of creating a new fictional world. "The Lifted Veil" was a break from writing *The Mill on the Floss*. *Silas Marner* thrust itself upon her as she was contemplating *Romola*. *Felix Holt* came between her and the writing of *The Spanish Gypsy*. In retrospect, her poetry seems to be a preparation for *Middlemarch*. As she was contemplating narrative strands that would ultimately combine in her next novel, she wrote her Shakespearean sonnet sequence, "Brother and Sister," reworking material that formed the basis of book I of *The Mill*. In revisiting her own childhood memories, she may also have been thinking of the sibling bonds amongst the Lewes boys, whose lives and failures once again intruded upon her life throughout 1869.

"Our Poor Boy Thornie"

Repeatedly, Eliot's plots validate the choice she did not make: the choice of family, tribe, and corporate identity over the individual benefits of love. But seeing as she left her family before she met Lewes, she may have viewed her higher calling as one of writing. Another inconsistency between what she was writing and her personal experience appears in the letters she and Lewes received from Thornie and Bertie in the late 1860s. Even as she was elevating racial conflicts of the past in an epic poem in which Columbus is discovering the New World and the Gypsies are colonizing Africa, she wrote casually about the "war with the natives" in present-day Africa into which Thornie had joined. Like clashes amongst Spanish Christians, Moors, and Gypsies at the end of the fifteenth century, fighting amongst Boers, English, Basutos, and Zulus would mark the end of the nineteenth century culminating in the First Boer War (1880–1). But though she could see the coming importance of European national identities, she could not see this conflict in Africa as rivaling the significance or dramatic interest of racial conflicts in the past.

Anxieties about the distant, out-of-sight sons continued. The news from Africa – always delayed by months – began to be alarming. One letter in July 1867 recounts a fire which had burned the boys' house to the ground (July 12, 1867, Yale, MS). Worse news was to follow as Thornie wrote in September of what he thought was sciatica: "I lie in agony from sundown till about 3 a.m., when the pain mitigates; & I go to sleep, & worst of all feel so weak in the day that I can't do a stroke of work" (September 16, 1867, Yale MS). In January of 1868, he was diagnosed with a kidney stone and hoped to "get back the use of my loins & legs" (March 9–April 26, 1868, Yale MS). The same letter tells of failed crops. By 1868, Thornie and Bertie were overwhelmed by the difficulties of subsistence farming in an African colony. Having not yet received Thornie's letter, Eliot wrote to

D'Albert Durade in January 1869 that the boys were "very happy in their occupation" (*GEL* 4:419).

There is irony in romanticizing and ennobling the conflict of races in Moorish Spain and the heroism of the warrior Gypsies after denying Thornie's wish to fight for the Poles and minimizing his engagement with the Basutos. Before leaving Hofwyl for Edinburgh, Thornie fantasized that he might run away and join the Italian liberation movement, "so that when in future any one asks, who were the three liberators of Sicily? the answer will be Garibaldi, Türr and Thornton Lewes" (*GEL* 8:271).[21] Thornie's heroes before he left for Africa were anti-imperialist nationalists who represented ideals of freedom and national self-determination. Once in Africa, he romanticized the skirmishes in which he participated. In a letter written on February 24, 1866, he referred to the Basuto War as "an important struggle" in which he was taking part (*GEL* 8:367). His father wrote to Robert Lytton that Thornie was "shooting tigers and Basutos in Natal" (*GEL* 8:366).

Many English men as well as boys were thrilled by the nationalist movements of their time, but it seems that Eliot – like Carlyle, Ruskin, and other contemporaries – found her own age unheroic and unpoetic. In *Middlemarch*, she would make a tragedy out of the impossibility of Dorothea's finding the means to channel her energy and talents. Yet, the Gypsy Fedalma could become a queen and leader of her people, and the sixteenth-century Spanish St Theresa could found a religious order. But living in the nineteenth century, Dorothea would lose herself in the life of her husband and be buried in an unvisited tomb. In the same way, Eliot's "son" Thornie was directed away from heroic pursuits and toward life as a respectable colonial farmer. It was a fate that Dickens and Anthony Trollope wished for their sons as well. Alfred and Plorn Dickens and Fred Trollope also emigrated in the 1860s, but they all faired better in Australia than Thornie and Bertie Lewes did in Africa.

It was not that Thornie and Bertie were drinkers or gamblers or otherwise self-destructive. Their long and painful letters home suggest that they were trying to clear land and plant crops in a remote territory far from Durban and the English settlers to whom they had brought letters of recommendation. In October of 1868, Thornie wrote to his father and asked him "to *lend* us £200 for one year," adding: "I am gradually wasting away" (*GEL* 8:433–4). He requests permission to return to England to consult physicians there. Eliot and Lewes did not receive the letter until January 1869 (*GEL* 5:4). When they did, they sent money for Thornie to return, not expecting to see him for many months. In March, they left for Italy, spending time in Florence and in Rome. It was in Rome that they met an English acquaintance, Mrs Elizabeth Bullock, who was traveling with her widowed mother, Anna Cross, and her brother John Walter. Lewes had met the Cross family when on a walking tour with Spencer in Weybridge in 1867. On April 18, Mrs Cross and her son called on the Leweses. This meeting would result in a flourishing friendship with the entire Cross family back in England, which would be significant to Lewes and Eliot for the rest of their lives.

They returned home on May 5, 1869. On May 7, Lewes wrote to John Blackwood, referring to the Sunday afternoon salons they were about to resume hosting at their home: "You will be up in a few days I suppose and this comes merely to let you know that religious services go on regularly at the Priory" (*GEL* 5:29). On May 8, Lewes wrote in his journal that Thornie had returned from Africa, but he was not yet alarmed by his son's condition: "[James] Mill's Analysis. Went to Mother. Thornie came home. Dreadfully shocked to see him so worn; but his spirits good and he listened with pleasure to music" (*GEL* 5:33). Thornie was so wasted that his brother Charles fainted upon seeing him for the first time. The next day, Sunday, May 9, however, Lewes's tone quickly changed: "A dreadful day – Thornie rolling on the floor in agony. Paget came in the evening and examined him. Up 4 times in the night to give him morphia, etc." (*GEL* 5:33). Sir James Paget was a renowned surgeon who attended Queen Victoria and would serve as one of several doctors that treated and advised Lewes and Eliot until the end of their lives. This was the very Sunday that the American novelist Henry James, who was just a year older than Thornie, called to meet one of his literary heroes, the great George Eliot. In James's *The Middle Years* (1917), he tells the story of dropping in to be introduced at one of the regular Sunday afternoons and instead finding Thornie lying on the floor in pain, Lewes gone for morphia, and a flustered George Eliot. The story is certainly embellished and ends with James offering to go and leave a note for Paget at his home.

James falsely recalled that Thornie had had an accident in the West Indies (Haight, *Biography* 416). But in fact, Paget was not able to give a more precise diagnosis than the doctors in Natal. On June 17, 1869, Eliot told Barbara Bodichon that the "case seems to be rather obscure" (*GEL* 5:45), and wrote again on July 2 to report that the doctors were "as much in the dark as we are" but they "concur in saying that the glandular disorder is more serious than the spinal" (*GEL* 8:457). Haight claims the illness was an hereditary tuberculosis of the spine, but he cites no references for this diagnosis (Haight, *Biography* 417; *GEL* 5:33). Other biographers have followed suit without evidence. While Haight may have had access to information he does not cite, the hereditary tuberculosis theory is problematic because it does not say from whom Thornie inherited the disease, and it also removes any possibility that Thornie contracted whatever he had in Africa and that his illness was a result of his having been sent there.

Whatever guilt Lewes, Eliot, and Agnes might have felt about sending him to Africa, they were devoted to him in his illness. From May until his death in October 1869, the presence of the dying boy would preoccupy Eliot and especially Lewes, who made detailed notes on his physical condition and the steps taken to alleviate his pain (such as the number of drops of morphia). These notes show Lewes's careful attention and habits as a scientist, resembling notes he made when he was conducting scientific experiments – empirical, observant, and objective. Whatever the disease, it was a slow and painful decline. Eliot did her best to nurse, cheer, and distract Thornie. Barbara Bodichon, who had suggested the move to Natal, came regularly to sit with him. His mother Agnes also visited the Priory to see him (Haight, *Biography* 416). They hired a full-time nurse, but Lewes and Eliot also continued to nurse him, even as they continued on with their work. Lewes was making progress on *Problems of Life and Mind* (vol. 1) and Eliot was writing poetry and beginning the story that developed into *Middlemarch*.

On October 19, Thornie died. His death, Eliot reflected, "seems to me the beginning of our own" (*GEJ* 139; *GEL* 5:60). The painful experience of watching Thornie die remained with her as she resumed her story. Writing to Barbara Bodichon in 1862, Eliot reflected that serious illness, "such as seems to bring death near makes one feel the simple human brother and sisterhood." She added: "I suppose if one happened only to hold the hand of a hospital patient when she was dying, her face and all the memories along with it, would seem to lie deeper in our experience than all we knew of many old friends and blood relations" (*GEL* 4:13). In 1863, she had written to Sara Hennell: "Well, our poor boy Thornie parted from us today and set out on his voyage to Natal. I say 'poor' as one does about all beings that are gone away from us for a long while" (*GEL* 4:109). As long as Thornie was far away, she could think of him almost as a character in a novel. But when he returned to die in her home, his suffering entered deeply into her feeling and inevitably influenced what she was writing.

In eulogistic letters, Eliot and Lewes praised Thornie's character in terms that suggest compensation for the fact that they could praise neither his talents nor his accomplishments. Eliot wrote: "Through the six months of his illness, his frank impulsive mind disclosed no trace of evil feeling." (*GEL* 5:60). Lewes wrote to Blackwood that they never discerned "the slightest trace in him of anything mean or unworthy" (*GEL* 5:66). Thornie had lived and died a failure, his father and step-mother able only to praise the absence of evil or meanness in him. Eliot had once hoped that he might turn out to be "something useful and remarkable" (*GEL* 4:117), but his noble impulses struggled amidst imperfect social conditions, and he led a short and wasted life. He was buried in Highgate Cemetery. His only legacy is the sad awareness of mortality that his death cast over the writing of Eliot's masterpiece, *Middlemarch*.

Notes

1. On bankruptcy in the English novel, see Weiss.
2. Thomson writes that if Eliot had eliminated the details of her legal plot, she might have been open to criticism by legal experts, but she would have produced a more straightforward story with "no barrier to the comprehension of her audience" (*FH* viii; Introduction).

3. See her "Notes on the Spanish Gypsy and Tragedy in General" (*Spanish Gypsy* 273; Appendix).

4. Describing Charles Dickens's decision to send as many of his sons as he could to the colonies in the late 1860s after he had separated from his wife, Lillian Nayder, writes: "Arranging to send them to the colonies to establish themselves in life Dickens saw himself providing a necessary antidote to Catherine's influence . . . Becoming financially autonomous, they would no longer be economic burdens like their mother" (Nayder 281). Though there is no such tone in Lewes's letters searching for a colony to which he might send his boys, he did not wish them to follow the examples of Agnes Lewes and Thornton Hunt and become financial burdens to others.

5. In the spring of 1863 there was much talk about Polish nationalism – radical meetings, a rally in London, and calls for England to enter the war against Russia. The politically radical engraver W. J. Linton, who made engravings for *Romola* and married Eliza Lynn, was involved in a London society to support the movement in the 1860s. The summer of 1863 was a crucial time for support of Poland (Smith, *Radical Artisan* 140). It is also worth noting that in *Middlemarch*, Will Ladislaw is the grandson of a Polish patriot.

6. In *Pedagogical Economies* (2000), Cathy Shuman explores the political and economic implications of the mid-Victorian "craze for exams," which owed much "to the huge network of bourgeois campaigns to reform and rationalize British institutions, from Parliament to the Church of England" (10).

7. See Kathleen McCormack, "The Saccharissa Essays: George Eliot's Only Woman Persona."

8. For a reading of *Felix Holt* in light of Eliot's readings in classical political economy, see Coleman, "Being Good with Money," ch. 4.

9. For an analysis of *The Spanish Gypsy*'s form in relation to its history as a drama, see Kurnick.

10. Natal experienced economic depression in the second half of the 1860s. Many banks and companies in the colony failed at this time. See Guest and Sellers, *Enterprise and Exploitation in a Victorian Colony*.

11. "Felix Holt," Rignall, *Oxford Reader's Companion to George Eliot*, 116.

12. Unfortunately, all of Lewes and Eliot's letters to the boys in South Africa seem to have been lost.

13. Bonnie McMullen argues that they viewed the local people in an anthropological, distanced way: "They were spectators, and Spain was the spectacle" (129). She draws out the Orientalist implications of their response to the people and the vast, dry, brown landscape as more a part of the East. As Eliot wrote: "could have fancied myself in Arabia" (*GEL* 4:341).

14. Kurnick writes that *The Spanish Gypsy* "interrogates the ethical defensibility of ethnic nationalism in a global reality where not every ethnic group will enjoy the prerogatives of statehood" (492). He argues against the tradition of seeing *The Spanish Gypsy* as a mere preparation for *Daniel Deronda*'s plot of Jewish ethnic belonging. For an example of this argument, see Semmel.

15. Possibly by this she meant the Restoration dramatists. There is a Jacobean drama called *The Spanish Gypsy* (1623).

16. On the figure of the Jewish convert in nineteenth-century literature, see Ragussis, *Figures of Conversion*.

17. The idea of a national homeland in Africa was her own invention. See Nord.
18. While researching for the drama beginning in 1864, Eliot took extensive notes on the condition of the Jews as well as the Gypsies in Moorish Spain and the persecution of both groups during the Inquisition. Heinrich Heine features a similar theme in his poem, "Donna Clara" (1827), which tells the story of a Spanish princess who unwittingly falls in love with a Jewish knight. Like Sephardo and many of Eliot's other characters, the knight refuses to forsake his people, despite his love for the princess. Rather than continuing to deceive her, he openly proclaims his identity and risks social ostracism.
19. In her Notes on *The Spanish Gypsy*, she outlined her theory about the pre-emptory power of hereditary conditions (*Spanish Gypsy* 273–312).
20. The recent issue of *George Eliot-George Henry Lewes Studies* devoted to Eliot's poetry begins to correct the critical neglect of her poetry. See "The Cultural Place of George Eliot's Poetry."
21. In May of 1860, Garibaldi and his "Red Shirts" embarked on their conquest of Sicily in the name of Italian unification, which was achieved in 1861. Steven Türr (1825–1908) was a Hungarian who fought with Garibaldi against the Austrians.

7

Middlemarch
1870–2

This is life to come, / Which martyred men have made more glorious / For us who strive to follow.

("O May I Join the Choir Invisible," *Poetry* 2:33–5)

After Thornie's funeral, Eliot and Lewes retreated to Limpsfield in the Surrey countryside, not even receiving letters until they had been away for two weeks. Upon emerging from their secluded mourning on November 13, 1869, Eliot wrote to Barbara Bodichon that she felt "a permanently closer companionship with death" (*GEL* 5:70).[1]

Though she had mentioned writing a novel called "Middlemarch" as a goal for 1869, the ordeal of Thornie's illness intervened. During the months of nursing him she had written the "Brother and Sister" sonnets (in July) and worked intermittently on the Vincy–Featherstone plot of *Middlemarch* (August 2, 1869; *GEJ* 137), completing three chapters before giving up in September when she recorded "great depression" (September 24, 1869; *GEJ* 138). On October 5, with Thornie's condition worsening, she began a long poem called "The Legend of Jubal," which she continued writing in Limpsfield and finished on January 13, 1870.

The poem reveals how her thinking about the afterlife had evolved since her first published work, the poem "Farewell" in the *Christian Observer* (January 1840), in which the narrator says goodbye to this world in anticipation of heaven (Haight, *Biography* 25). We do not know what might have been the perspective of a work called "The Idea of a Future Life," which she first contemplated in Coventry, discussed with Sara Hennell, and even allowed to be advertised in the *Leader* as a

The Life of George Eliot: A Critical Biography, First Edition. Nancy Henry.
© 2012 Nancy Henry. Published 2012 by John Wiley & Sons, Ltd.

forthcoming book (June 18, 1853; *GEL* 3:95; Haight, *Biography* 141). The future life for her now took two distinct forms, which she would explore in her last works. One was the living on in others through the influence we have on their lives, as expressed in "O May I Join the Choir Invisible," a poem written in 1867 and published in 1874. In it, she uses music as a metaphor for the good that individuals contribute to a collective "choir." "May I," she asks:

> Be the sweet presence of a good diffused,
> And in diffusion ever more intense,
> So shall I join the choir invisible
> Whose music is the gladness of the world.
>
> (*Poetry* 2:35–43)

While the poem conceives of gladness metaphorically as the art of music, Eliot also thought of art as a form of future life: the artist lives on in her art. As an author, this second form of a future life became increasingly compelling to her, so that the notion of "culture," now being defined by Matthew Arnold in *Culture and Anarchy*, which had been serialized in the *Cornhill* (1867–8), grew in importance to her.[2]

Joining the invisible choir is an idealized form of communal participation. Martha S. Vogeler interprets it as a: "cycle of temporal and transtemporal influence: the noble acts of the living and the dead – those in time and those beyond time – inspire the living, and the living, in their turn, die and inspire their still living counterparts" ("The Choir Invisible" 67).[3] In contrast, contributing books to a storehouse or archive of writing and knowledge that future generations can read is more tangible and lasting. The author does not just transcendentally live on in others, but lives on in the form of her words, written on the page for future generations. Speaking to the future became a chief motive of Eliot's late career, giving a new moral purpose to her artistic drive and aspirations. More than this, however, the question of how the past talks to the present, and the present speaks to the future, became a powerful theme in her late works. Cultural transmission (of Greek culture to Renaissance Italy and of Renaissance Italy to Victorian England) was central to *Romola*. *Felix Holt* explored material inheritance and its absurdities. These twin elements of inheritance would come together to complement and enhance each other in *Middlemarch*.

Eliot viewed the two models of a future life – diffused good and good writing – as important within society generally. But for her personally, intellectual transmission as a mode of passing on literature of the highest artistic and moral quality – the best that has been thought and written – now eclipsed even the value of doing good for others. Her letters and journals had always expressed her concern that she was not doing enough to help other people. On December 31, 1870, for example, she wrote in her journal about the Franco-Prussian War (1870–1), asking: "Am I doing anything that will add the weight of a sandgrain against the persistence of such evil?" (*GEJ* 141). In the same entry, she records that she is happy: "But I am doing little for others" (*GEJ* 142). This typical, private doubt about her own goodness did not prevent her from looking beyond small acts toward a greater contribution to humanity in general and to English national culture in particular.

The shifting of her emphasis in the 1870s from a metaphysical choir to the traditions for transmitting ideas in her considerations of a future life is consistent with her own (and Lewes's) anti-idealism and realism. There is also the matter of what it was realistic to expect from average people as compared to what Eliot might expect from and for authors like herself (and Lewes). Good acts create a legacy that lasts at most a generation; it is the best that ordinary people, such as the "Miss Brooke" of her new story, might achieve. When Eliot began writing fiction and emphasizing the importance of telling stories about common people like Amos Barton and Adam Bede, she was untried and unknown; now, she was famous. With the death of Charles Dickens in 1870, she was recognized as her nation's greatest living novelist. The burden of greatness affected her sense of how she might benefit others. The resistance to biography that she expressed when she wrote that an author's writings are his chief acts, deflects attention from acts done or left undone by her. Despite the agonizing in her journal, she preferred to be judged by what she had written, not how she had acted.

Distinctions between the great and the ordinary began to characterize her writing in *Middlemarch*. Dorothea fails to become a modern St Theresa; Mr Casaubon was not the great man Dorothea imagined him to be; Lydgate's fantasy of doing great work gives way to a mundane reality. For authors, the ideas of inheritance and legacy apply to the transmission of culture, not progeny or property. The great authors of the past had shaped George Eliot, enhancing her life and informing her writing.

"The Legend of Jubal"

While she was trying to begin her novel, she returned to poetry, so that her thoughts alternated between the mythic and the realist registers, and she found poetry more satisfying than writing prose. The mythic subjects and the poetic form in which she chose to treat them allowed her to refine the ideas she would integrate into her fiction and the sense of sound and rhythm that she would achieve in her later prose. The tension between the mythic and the real goes back to the interrogation of the Gospels in the Higher Criticism of Hennell, Strauss, and Feuerbach, the New Testament representing a combination of the mythic and the historical. Her realism had previously achieved this combination, for example in the flood at the end of *The Mill on the Floss*, with its biblical connotations and its naturalized manifestation in the plot. In the immediate aftermath of Thornie's death, and the feeling that it marked the beginning of her own death, she composed her most powerful meditation on how the mortal artist becomes immortal in his works.[4]

"The Legend of Jubal" (published in May 1870 in *Macmillan's Magazine* and the *Atlantic Monthly* in the US), returns to the Old Testament. In this modern Midrash, or elaboration of the biblical narrative, she imagined Jubal, a descendant of Cain, who discovered, or invented, music and therefore was an archetype of the genius who passed on an invaluable gift to future generations. Jubal is mentioned in Genesis as "the father of all such as have the harp and organ" (4:19–20). The biblical source marks a stage in Eliot's relationship to both Christian and Jewish scripture, which spanned from her early evangelical phase, to her translations of Strauss and Feuerbach, to her immersion in Hebrew texts and Jewish history while researching *Daniel Deronda*.

In December 1869, she arranged to start weekly Hebrew lessons with Emanuel Deutsch (1829–73), which would take place at her home (*GEL* 5:73). Since 1855, Deutsch had been a Hebraist, transcriber, and cataloguer at the British Museum. He also published a controversial article on "The Talmud" in the *Quarterly Review* (October 1867), which asserted the importance of the Talmud in Western culture. In 1869, Deutsch had spent three months traveling in the Middle East. In Jerusalem, he helped to identify and decipher transcriptions uncovered by Charles Warren in his excavations of the Temple Mount. He also became a social friend, attending Sundays at the Priory. He was a major influence on her knowledge of Judaism and her thinking about Hebrew mythology at this time. He is considered to be a model for Mordecai in *Daniel Deronda*.[5]

Throughout her work, biblical references and allusions are pervasive, but in "Jubal" she begins with a biblical context and invents her own myth, an allegory for the relationship of the artist to his art. There are many visual and musical artists in Eliot's novels: Philip Wakem, Piero di Cosimo, the minstrel Juan, Armgart, Adolf Naumann, Hans Meyrick, Julius Klesmer, and the Princess Halm-Eberstein. But these figures are bound by the constrictions of a realist narrative. "Jubal" is entirely mythic, and Eliot used it to clarify her thoughts about art and the future life of the artist.

Eliot's legend tells how the exiled Cain tries to keep the knowledge of death from his children, but when one child dies, the tribe's idyllic life ends. With knowledge of death comes civilization: the taming of animals and fire, the invention of tools, the measuring of time in the awareness that it is limited, and the invention of money. The poetic soul, Jubal, is inspired to turn the sounds of nature, human voices, and human labor into a new form of art. Music, which had been metaphoric in "The Choir Invisible," is here literal.

Recalling the work of Romantic poets such as Keats and Shelley, "Jubal" is concerned with inspiration and the relationship of art to nature. It considers the drive

Figure 24   Emanuel Deutsch, drawing by Rudolf Lehmann, 1868 (© The Trustees of the British Museum)

to create permanence – to counter the transience of life and to memorialize the dead – as a foundational element of art. Jubal's brother Tubal-Cain works incessantly as a blacksmith to fashion the tools with which his clan now harnesses nature. His contribution is hard and practical. Jubal is inspired by the sound of his hammer:

> Jubal, too, watched the hammer, till his eyes,
> No longer following its fall or rise,
> Seemed glad with something that they could not see,
> But only listened to – some melody,
> Wherein dumb longings inward speech had found,
> Won from the common store of struggling sound.
> (Poetry 1:247–53)

Jubal's eyes are made glad by sound, a mixing of the visual and aural senses. This paradoxical notion of hearing sight had intrigued Eliot when she chose the motto from Shakespeare's sonnet XXIII for chapter 27 of *Felix Holt*: "to hear with eyes is part of love's rare wit," a misquotation of the line "to hear with eyes belongs to love's fine wit" (l. 14). She quoted the same line again in *Middlemarch* (ch. 27). Perhaps the image reflects her experience of the creative process in which she both saw and heard her characters as she created them.[6]

Having invented music and bequeathed it to his people, Jubal exiles himself. Eventually, he returns to his former home, expecting to be welcomed. Instead, he finds everything changed and foreign to him, not unlike Silas Marner's return to Lantern Yard, or perhaps what Eliot imagined she might have found had she returned to the Midlands as an adult. The ironic, violent scene of Jubal's casting out from his old home for claiming to be the Jubal his tribe now worships represents the ultimate sacrifice of the physical artist who has become a kind of God:

> Two rushed upon him: two, the most devout
> In honour of great Jubal, thrust him out,
> And beat him with their flutes.
>
> (*Poetry* 1:697–9)

The scene invokes the classical figures of the Furies and Maenads that had long captured her imagination: the ritualistic sacrifice of a martyr/victim at the hands of a crowd. This image threatens in *Adam Bede* when Hetty is carted toward her execution with the "waiting watching multitude, cleaving its way towards the hideous symbol of a deliberately inflicted sudden death" (462; ch. 47). But in that scene, the "loud shout, hideous to her ear, like a vast yell of demons ... was not a shout of execration – not a yell of exultant cruelty," but rather (thanks to Lewes's intervention in her plot), the shout announcing Arthur's arrival with a pardon or "hard-won release from death" (462; ch. 47).

The blood-thirsty crowd is more explicitly evident in *Romola*, where the references to the Maenad chorus of Poliziano's *Orfeo* foreshadow Tito's hounding, and his death is paralleled by Savonarola's burning at the stake. The crowd recurs in *The Spanish Gypsy* when Don Silva averts being torn apart by the Gypsy band (again thanks to Lewes) and his uncle is publicly executed by an angry mob. A tamer, more symbolic form of persecution comes in the ostracism of Maggie (foreshadowed through references to the drowning of witches) and in the expulsion of Silas from his community. Maenads, witches, inquisitions and public executions form the darkest elements of Eliot's writing, blending mythic inspiration with historical events. All of these images and themes inevitably return to the crucifixion and the figure of the suffering Christ. That story and image never ceased to move her, even as she was translating Strauss's dissection of the myth and kept her own crucifix in view to remind her of its power.[7]

Jubal's lonely death is a strangely spiritual ending in which a "face" appears to him. Once again, the vision and sound are conflated:

> He knew not if that gaze the music sent,
> Or music that calm gaze: to hear, to see,
> Was but one undivided ecstasy:
> The raptured senses melted into one . . .
> (*Poetry* 1:725–8)

As mythical and fantastic as this poem is, we should take seriously its reflection of Eliot's thinking about art and about herself just as she was on the verge of composing her greatest artistic achievements and thinking seriously about death and how she could contribute in what remained of her life not only to the choir invisible but to the cultural traditions that would survive her. She had thus far suffered physically from the intense demands of writing, yet she was compelled by an inexplicable need to write and create. She had seen Dickens shortly before his death – brought on in part by his drive to keep working – and she had read the first parts of *Edwin Drood*, which he was writing when he died in 1870. She saw daily how Lewes, too, was striving to write what he hoped would be his great contribution to science. Financially speaking, she and Lewes could have retired from writing to concentrate on health, pleasure, and prolonging their lives. But as "Jubal" suggests, Eliot, like others driven to artistic and intellectual achievement, was sacrificing her physical well-being to produce the writings, her chief acts, in which she might attain a kind of immortality. She seems to have been aware that she was sacrificing her life to her art and investing that art with her best self so that "Jubal," mythical as it is, also has its autobiographical elements.

Preparing for *Middlemarch*

After completing "Jubal" in January 1870, she and Lewes left for a trip to Berlin, Prague, Vienna, and Salzburg (March 14–May 6). In Berlin they moved in superior social circles that included diplomats and Prussian royalty. They heard Bismarck speak somewhat dully on "currency," and saw a production of Wagner's *Tannhäuser* (which had premiered 1845), but found it no more to their taste than it had been in 1854 when they had heard it along with *The Flying Dutchman* (premiered 1843) and *Lohengrin* (premiered 1850). The trip was marred for Eliot by a cold resulting in a lacerated throat that kept her away from some of the events to which they were invited. In Berlin, Lewes pursued his research for *Problems of Life and Mind* by visiting laboratories and psychiatric hospitals and consulting with Dr Carl Friedrich Otto Westphal (1833–90) at the Charité (charitable hospital and medical school). Westphal's clinical research into psychiatric diseases and work with the mentally ill produced contributions to the understanding of conditions such as agoraphobia, narcolepsy, and mental states not like unlike that Eliot had represented in Silas Marner's cataleptic fits.

Westphal is cited in histories of sexuality as one of the first scientists to have medicalized the condition of same-sex desire in a paper, published in 1869 shortly before Lewes met him, and titled "Die contrare Sexualempfindung" or the "contrary sexual emotion."[8] Psychiatry was not yet separate from the physical branches of medical science, and Westphal also researched physical diseases (particularly spinal), and hypothesized their relationship to mental states. His work was therefore compatible with Lewes's research. Eliot wrote to Maria Congreve on April 3, 1870, that Lewes had gone for the third time to the Charité,

> to see more varieties of mad people, and hear more about Psychiatrie from Dr Westphal, a quiet, unpretending little man, who seems to have been delighted with George's sympathetic interest in this (to me) hideous branch of practice. I speak with all reverence: the world can't do without hideous studies. (*GEL* 5:86)

It seems clear in this context that Eliot referred to the cases of madness rather than Westphal's interest in "contrary sexual emotion."[9]

Westphal was interested in same-sex attraction between women, and it is interesting that Eliot should write about him to Maria Congreve, one of the women who was in love with her, along with Edith Simcox (whom she first met on December 13, 1872) and Elma Stuart (who first wrote in 1872). These women made no secret of their passion for Eliot. Congreve and Simcox were among those who attended the Sundays at the Priory, which Eliot and Lewes resumed on a regular schedule when they returned from Europe. These gatherings were becoming London social events, less "salons" in the seventeenth-century sense Eliot had written about in her essay on Madame de Sablé (1854) and more of an opportunity of homage from titled aristocrats, famous artists, old friends, and new acolytes like Simcox as well as a number of young Cambridge men (some of them homosexual). In the past, some married women had shunned her because of her adulterous relationship with Lewes. Maria Congreve and Rufa Brabant Hennell (later Mrs Call) were exceptions. Wives were now abundant at her parties, and some of them became Eliot's most devoted followers, confiding in her about their married lives and thereby inviting later critical speculation that they were models for the unhappy wives in *Middlemarch* and *Daniel Deronda*.[10]

Among the many visitors at this time were the Burne-Joneses and Emilia Pattison, the much younger wife of Mark Pattison, the Rector of Lincoln College, Oxford. Lewes records their first visit at the Priory on January 24, 1869, after which they attended frequently, and Mrs Pattison often visited alone. In August of 1868, Lewes went to Oxford for the British Medical Association conference, but Eliot had never been until she accepted an invitation from the Pattisons (May 25–28, 1870). The visit was important in several ways, establishing her intimacy with the Pattisons and introducing her to future friends and Oxford hosts, particularly the classical scholar Benjamin Jowett. While there, she heard lectures by Charles Warren and Emanuel Deutsch on the Moabite Stone. On this visit, she also met Walter Pater, "writer of articles on Leonardo da Vinci, Morris etc." (May 27, 1870; *GEJ* 140).[11]

These travels and new acquaintances influenced the composition of *Middlemarch* in ways that have not always been recognized by biographers, who tend to focus on the experiences of her young life as sources for her fiction. McCormack notes that between 1868 and the publication of *Middlemarch*, the Leweses made more than 20 long and short journeys within England (*English Travels* 110). From June 15 to August 1, they took a holiday on the Yorkshire coast, staying two weeks at Whitby. They encouraged the Burne-Joneses to join them. Georgiana Burne-Jones came with her two small children but without her husband. During this trip, Eliot and Georgiana were together constantly, undoubtedly discussing Edward Burne-Jones's well-known affair with his artist's model, Maria Zambaco. Whatever Eliot's advice may have been to her at this time, Georgiana stayed in her marriage, and the Leweses remained cordial with the couple. Eliot and Lewes demonstrated consistently that neither infidelity nor sexual orientation precluded friendship or invitations to the Priory.

From August 8–29, the Leweses returned to Limpsfield in Surrey. Even in their rural retreat, their attention and sympathy were attracted by accounts of the Franco-Prussian War (1870–1) and the suffering it was causing on both sides. Eliot also worked on her dramatic poem, "Armgart," the last long poem she would write. It tells the story of a singer whose fiancé, Graf, asks her to give up her ambitions to become a wife and mother, the natural role of woman. Passionate about her singing and her professional ambitions, she chooses her career; then, ironically, she loses her voice, after which Graf abandons her and, as Bodenheimer argues, is "unmasked as one of those who participate in nineteenth-century diva worship as a way of cherishing the fantasy that he might increase the value of his own rank by mastering the artist" (*Real Life* 181). The overall scenario reflects Eliot's anxiety that she would, through physical or mental affliction, be unable to repeat her past achievements, or would be otherwise prevented from writing. Critics have noted that it also registers her own conflicted attitude about her ambition and the plight of women who must choose between domestic and professional lives.[12]

When the poem opens, Armgart has just given a brilliant performance as Orpheus in Christoph Willibald Gluck's *Orfeo ed Euridice* (1762), which Eliot and Lewes had seen in Berlin in 1855. With this detail, Eliot returns to the figure of Orpheus she had invoked in "Mr. Gilfil" (when Caterina sings an oratorio from that opera), *Romola* (when Tito sings the Maenad chorus of Poliziano's play), and *The Spanish Gypsy* (in which the minstrel Juan is the "Orpheus of the Gypsies"). That Armgart sings the part of a male character enhances the theme of ambitions and public performances as compromising her womanhood. Furthermore, as her cousin Walpurga explains, Armgart's singing is an outlet without which her soul "must have leaped through all her limbs –/Made her a Maenad – made her snatch a brand/And fire some forest, that her rage might mount/In crashing roaring flames through half the land" (*Poetry* 2:43–6). The ominous, destructive force of the Maenad again appeals to Eliot, this time to embody an internal passion that can only be contained and channeled through creativity and art.[13]

Crucially, Armgart is a performer, like Caterina in "Mr. Gilfil" (who gives up singing for marriage) and Dinah Morris (who gives up preaching for marriage). In *Daniel Deronda*, Mirah Lapidoth gives up singing for marriage and the Princess Halm-Eberstein first sacrifices her family to her art and then sacrifices her art for a second family. Singing is not a form of art that can last; it is jeopardized more than writing by the bodily frailty of the artist. The poem shows Eliot's continued thinking about mortality and art and indicates her wavering between the values of devoting one's life to doing good for others and making a permanent contribution to a wider culture. Armgart's story is a counterpart to that of Jubal, who dies after giving something great to the world. In contrast, Armgart must resign herself to finding satisfaction in the small act of teaching music to others. Lewes described Armgart as a woman who is "obliged to sink into insignificance" (GHLJ, July 13, 1870, qtd. in Ashton, *GE* 309–10), a telling interpretation that suggests the tragedy of her fate and provides a clue to the comparable fate of Dorothea at the end of *Middlemarch*.[14]

Between Thornie's death on October 19, 1869, and her recording of *Middlemarch*'s reception on January 1, 1873, Eliot made few private journal entries, though she filled notebooks with her research. Those journal entries she did make are revealing. On October 27, 1870, she recorded that Bertie Lewes in South Africa was engaged to be married to Eliza Harrison, the daughter of an English colonist. This was happy news, but the intensity with which she followed the lives of the Lewes boys when Thornie was alive had been diffused by geographic, temporal, and emotional distance. The duties of motherhood would never again interfere with writing. She could not know at this time that financial responsibility for Bertie's widow would fall to her as one of the last familial duties of her life.

The journal entry recording Bertie's marriage moves quickly to her composition of "Armgart" and her headache, depression, and "total despair of future work." The comments give us insight into the reason for her keeping the "little old book" in which she erratically recorded both her doings and her unguarded feelings of joy and sadness. Such private writing, which reveals the author freed, at least in part, from the performances of her fiction and her letters, also provided her with a perspective on herself, helping her to maintain her sanity and balance in the midst of recurring depression. She periodically looked back at her journal entries to remind herself that she had experienced and survived similar bouts of depression in the past: "I look into this little book now to assure myself that this is not unprecedented" (October 27, 1870; *GEJ* 141).

She took up writing fiction again in November 1870 with a new story at first unconnected to the interrupted novel *Middlemarch*. On December 2 she was "experimenting in a story" (*GEJ* 141). By December 31, she had written 100 pages of the new story she called "Miss Brooke." It was then she knew that her experiments in verse had served their purpose, writing definitively: "Poetry halts just now" (*GEJ* 142).

The composition of *Middlemarch*, spanning almost four years, broken by poetic experiments and involving the fusion of two distinct stories in a multi-plot, four-volume novel, has received much critical attention. Its innovative publication in eight half-volume parts has also attracted interest.[15] We can parse the chapters, locate the seeds of inspiration, the logic, crafting, and constructing of a plot unified by metaphors and imagery. The novel has been studied from every imaginable critical, historical, and theoretical perspective. All of this is revealing. Yet none of it explains how the research, labor, and anxiety on the part of the author resulted in the masterpiece of *Middlemarch*. Why this novel seems to succeed at every level, where critics see flaws amidst the brilliance of her other novels, remains a mystery that we can only attribute to unconscious genius. Eliot, despairing that she would ever write anything as good as *Felix Holt*, had hit her artistic peak. After *Middlemarch*, she did not decline so much as venture forth into more experimental works with *Daniel Deronda* and *Impressions*, which do not seem, or perhaps even aspire, to cohere to the same degree.[16]

Like *Romola*, *Felix Holt*, and *The Spanish Gypsy*, *Middlemarch* was an endeavor of historical research. But *Middlemarch* does not wear its book learning as heavily as *Romola* or *Felix Holt*. The headings in the now-published notebooks she kept over the four-year period of research and composition of *Middlemarch* include "biography, mythology, philology, historical fiction, medical history, literary history, social and political (primarily Greek and Roman) history" (Pratt and Neufeldt xxiv).[17] *Middlemarch* is as dense with learning, historical research, and allusions as *Romola*, but these elements are all integrated and naturalized in a way that has exempted the novel from the criticisms that her more explicitly historical novel has attracted.

Middlemarch

We used to play at guessing historical characters . . .
(*Middlemarch* 429; ch. 45)

The essential question of Eliot's life and works is: How should we live? Other central questions follow: What do we inherit from the past? What impact will we have on the future? How does this march of history represent not only teleological progress but also a spreading medium of culture that nurtures and forms us, as all organisms are shaped by the medium in which they live? Can we not also influence that medium or culture through our own works and lives? The scientific model for understanding what she had called in *Felix Holt* "the wider public life" (43; ch. 3) would become ever more prevalent in *Middlemarch*, "A Study of Provincial Life," showing the cross-fertilization of her own and Lewes's work as he continued to research *Problems of Life and Mind*. The very word "study," rather than scene, romance, story, or even history, suggests distance and objectivity as a motivation and goal of examining provincial life. *Middlemarch* takes up historical, philosophical, and psychological questions of how that mixture of inherited traits, free will, and circumstances combine to determine the course of individual lives.

The original core of the novel was the Vincy–Featherstone plot. It tells the story of young Fred Vincy, who has expectations of inheriting his uncle Featherstone's estate, and of his sister Rosamond who aspires to rise socially through marriage to the promising newcomer to Middlemarch, Tertius Lydgate. Both the Vincy–Featherstone plot and the plot recounting the courtship, marriage, and widowhood of Dorothea Brooke are stories in which youth encounters the bitterness of age. The interconnected plots are set in the town of Middlemarch (a composite of Nuneaton and Coventry) from the fall of 1829 to the spring of 1832. The First Reform Bill (1832) defines the political climate, as it had in *Felix Holt*, and reforms in medicine (Lydgate and the fever hospital), farming (represented by Caleb and Fred), housing (Dorothea's plans and Sir James's implementation of them), and transportation (the coming of the railway) contribute to the sense that men and women at every level of society believed in the "march" of progress. The narrator, speaking from and to the early 1870s, has sufficient perspective on this generation to know what the new faith in science, technology, and progress generally has been able to accomplish – and also what it has not. To see whether or not we have progressed, we need to look to the past.

Middlemarch begins with a question that moves from the general to the particular:

> Who that cares much to know the history of man, and how that mysterious mixture behaves under the varying experiments of Time, has not dwelt, at least briefly, on the life of Saint Theresa, has not smiled with some gentleness at the thought of the little girl walking forth one morning hand-in-hand with her still smaller brother, to go and seek martyrdom in the country of the Moors? (3; Prelude)

This famous opening sentence displays interesting similarities to, and differences from, her previous novels. *Adam Bede* begins with the more mystical image of the Egyptian sorcerer's drop of ink, but it does not reach out to grip the reader in quite the same way. By asking "Who that cares to know," this narrator invites the reader into a select circle of educated people who seek to "know the history of man" and who know already about the Catholic saints Eliot had researched in preparation for

Middlemarch. Who indeed? The casual assumption that readers will share her knowledge of this anecdote about the childhood of a sixteenth-century nun is welcoming but potentially off-putting, perhaps more so today than at the time it was written. The introduction to *Felix Holt* calls on readers to recollect the days of stagecoach travel, delimiting them by age and experience rather than knowledge of history and hagiography. Yet Victorian readers would not need to have read Theresa's own autobiographical writings; they might be familiar with her life through more contemporary sources, such as Anna Jameson's *Legends of the Monastic Orders* (1850).[18]

Even if readers should happen to know the legend of St Theresa and her brother, would they have interpreted it scientifically as an example of how the "mysterious mixture," man, "behaves under the varying experiments of Time"? It is unlikely that anyone before Eliot had interpreted the writings of St Theresa with precisely this mix of the religious, the scientific, and the mundane. However Victorian readers took this challenge to their knowledge of Catholic history, the passage shows Eliot striking out and determined to do something new in fiction, even as it refers back to her earlier works, including the childhood of the brother and sister from *The Mill* and the setting of Moorish Spain in *The Spanish Gypsy*. By invoking the notion of experiments in time, the Prelude sets out its author's hypothesis that, given the same character traits, medieval Theresa and modern Theresa behave differently under different conditions. This notion of a character type is analogous to an animal species, as emphasized by the image of the cygnet "reared uneasily among the ducklings in the brown pond" (4; Prelude). It refers simultaneously to an Aesop fable as well as to natural history and is essential to the themes and narrative strategies of *Middlemarch*.

Anticipating *Impressions of Theophrastus Such*, Eliot here began experimenting with names (literary legacies, inheritances) as a parallel model of transmission to that of wills, money, and property that are also central to the plot of *Middlemarch*. The nineteenth-century failed scholar Edward Casaubon shares a name with Isaac Casaubon, the seventeenth-century translator of the ancient Greek philosopher Theophrastus. Recognizing the games Eliot is playing and the subtexts she is creating particularly with respect to literary and intellectual lineages, we can appreciate how important the idea of the author's future life was for her personally. The concept of books speaking across generations appears in Maggie Tulliver's reading of *The Imitation of Christ* and in the themes arising from Bardo's concern about his library in *Romola*. The authors of the past had spoken to Eliot. Would she speak to the future? Would her work transcend its historical medium? In this sense, *Middlemarch* introduces to Eliot's writing new and different forms of intertextuality and self-consciously coded communications. Edward Casaubon's relationship to Isaac Casaubon, for example, is more complex than Adam Bede's relationship to the Venerable Bede. What does it add to our interpretation of the story if we make these connections? What is lost if we do not?

Pratt and Neufeldt call this use of past names "historic wit" (xxx), but they do not fully appreciate the implications. Lydgate has an historical prototype in the poet John Lydgate, whose work Eliot recorded in her notebook and who was then, as now, eclipsed by his contemporary, Chaucer. His poetry fails to transcend the limitations of his time. This seeking out of eclipsed or obscured historical figures may also explain the choice of Casaubon. Eliot recorded in her notebooks: "Curious to turn from Shakespeare to Isaac Casaubon, his contemporary" (Pratt and Neufeldt 85). Critical interest in the unforgettable character of Casaubon revived debates about originals in her work.

Was Casaubon based on Dr Brabant, Mark Pattison, R. W. Mackay, or Herbert Spencer? When Eliot's fellow novelist and transatlantic correspondent Harriet Beecher Stowe wrote asking whether Dorothea's marriage experience had been drawn from her own, Eliot denied any similarity between Lewes and Casaubon that might have been inferred from the fact that Lewes was also writing an ambitious, multi-part scholarly work, *Problems of Life and Mind*. She insisted instead on her own resemblance to the pedant: "I fear that the Casaubon-tints are not quite foreign to my own mental complexion" (*GEL* 5:322). This observation is certainly true, explaining her insight into the insecurities of the scholar and the author. She suffered doubts about her self-worth all her life and about the worth of her writing throughout her career. She almost always wondered whether she would be able to complete the work she was currently writing. In the cases of *Romola* and *The Spanish Gypsy*, she had become both overwhelmed by the amount of material she was trying to master and stalled in her ability to turn the research into art.

In its overall structure as well as plot details, *Middlemarch* asks its readers: What is knowledge? What can we know about the past or the future? Casaubon says of himself: "I live too much with the dead. My mind is something like the ghost of an ancient, wandering about the world and trying mentally to construct it as it used to be, in spite of ruin and confusing changes" (16–17; ch. 2). Here Casaubon sounds both like the resuscitated Florentine in *Romola*'s Proem, and also like the author George Eliot attempting to recreate the past through knowledge handed down in texts, all the while anxious about, and fearful of, failure of the sort illustrated by Casaubon and his misguided project. Naïve Dorothea sees only what is worthy in Casaubon's representation of his work: "To reconstruct a past world, doubtless with a view to the highest purposes of truth – what a work to be in any way present at, to assist in, though only as a lamp-holder!" (17; ch. 2).

While Casaubon, like other characters, may be seen as a conflation of people Eliot knew, as well as historical figures, the idea of finding a model for his character has been ongoing from the publication of the novel. The notion of the Leweses' friend Mark Pattison serving as an "original" for Casaubon is particularly flawed, missing the complexities and the playfulness of the text. The theory is based on two main aspects of Pattison's life: he was married to a woman 28 years younger than himself, Emilia

Francis Strong Pattison (claimed to be a model of Dorothea), and he wrote a biography of Isaac Casaubon, published after *Middlemarch*, in 1875. The idea that Pattison was a model for Casaubon was discussed in the nineteenth century and was revived by his biographer John Sparrow (1967). Haight rejected the idea in his biography (1968), but considered the argument important enough to include an appendix on the subject. Basing a mostly unsympathetic character on a friend would have been antithetical to Eliot's aesthetic and moral sensibilities, but Pattison does have a role in what A. D. Nuttall calls "the eerie link to the name 'Casaubon'" (83). That link is not just an example of historic wit, but of a joke, the encrypting of humor through allusion, as she had done with Burchiello and Poliziano in *Romola*, that would increasingly characterize Eliot's writing and constitute its formal experimentation in self-conscious intertextuality.

Eliot certainly knew of Isaac Casaubon from her stay in Geneva (1849–50), the city where he was born and to which he returned to take up a position as professor of Greek. Haight implies that she knew his edition of Theophrastus's *Characters* at this time but does not supply a source for this claim (Haight, *Biography* 448). Casaubon's role as a translator (like Eliot) – in this case from Greek into Latin – and a transmitter of character "types," in which she had an abiding interest, would have caught her imagination and obviously stayed with her to be resurrected in *Middlemarch* and again in *Impressions*. In 1853, Pattison published an article on Casaubon in the *Quarterly Review* and had been working on his biography for years before he published it.[19] Although Eliot had already begun writing the Vincy-Featherstone plot of *Middlemarch* before she and Lewes visited the Pattisons in Oxford (May 25–28, 1870), she did not begin writing "Miss Brooke," in which Casaubon figures, until November of 1870. The timing suggests that conversations with her relatively new friends at Oxford about Pattison's research on Casaubon influenced her conceptualization of the character.[20] In the first chapter of *Middlemarch*, the narrator remarks of Casaubon: "His very name carried an impressiveness hardly to be measured without a precise chronology of scholarship" (11; ch. 1). Among the ironies in this comment is its uselessness in evaluating or predicting the impressiveness of the Mr Casaubon whom Dorothea has yet to meet. That he happens to share a name with a learned scholar of the past (from whom it is not claimed he is descended) can only reflect Dorothea's hopeful illusions. Dorothea, like Isaac Casaubon and the Lewes boys, had been educated in Switzerland (8; ch. 1). Perhaps she had traveled to Geneva and, like Mary Ann Evans, been introduced to the name of Isaac Casaubon there. But the comment is too cryptic for such conclusions and suggests instead a gesture toward Eliot's own learned joke in naming her English clergyman after the now obscure French Protestant classicist. She was the one who measured his name using a precise chronology of scholarship.[21]

While there is little humor in Pattison's approach to the life of his subject, it is easy to see how Eliot would have found self-ironizing identification with the Casaubon-tints in the real-life scholar (if not in his biographer). In his biography, Pattison

Figure 25 Isaac Casaubon, late sixteenth or early seventeenth century (© National Portrait Gallery, London)

writes: "Casaubon thought every moment lost in which he was not acquiring knowledge" (31), a characteristic that is consistent with Eliot's life. He also writes of the physical suffering Casaubon experienced as a result of his research, referring to "the blood and sweat, the groans and sighs, which enter into the composition of a folio volume of learned research" (123), again resonating with Eliot's experience of research and composition. Furthermore, Pattison quotes Casaubon's own morbid but humorous observation that he was like Theophrastus "dying from a holiday" (486). Isaac Casaubon identified with the subject of his research, Theophrastus, and Pattison identified with his subject, Casaubon. These identifications with intellectual heroes of the past were certainly in Eliot's mind as she created her characters in *Middlemarch*, sympathizing particularly with Mr Casaubon and drawing on her own psychology to color his "tints."[22]

The notion of Mr Edward Casaubon as a type, rather than an original, is ironically appropriate precisely because unoriginality is a flaw that dooms the project to which he devotes his life and which is painfully revealed to Dorothea by Will Ladislaw. Not knowing German, he cannot know that his very quest to find a Key to All

Mythologies has been superseded by German scholarship, particularly comparative philology, at least so the jealous Ladislaw claims. Casaubon's ambitions are laughable but also laudable. They are not out of place in the type of expansive reading on "the history of man" Eliot undertook in preparation for writing the novel. She was reading less to know the history of man than to know the history of how others were trying to know and write it (Pratt and Neufeldt xxvi).[23]

Pattison's scholarship, like that of the Cambridge classicist R. C. Jebb (the translator into English of Theophrastus's *Characters*) and Benjamin Jowett at Oxford (whom Eliot first met at dinner with the Pattisons), was important to her late work. Their friendship was also important for her socially and personally (both visited the Priory more than once). Her encounters with the best scholars of her age, with whom she felt an intellectual affinity but who, ensconced in the institutional respectability of Oxbridge, she would not have met previously, surely aroused mixed emotions. Her references to Oxford and Cambridge in her early works as tending to produce members of the clergy who were neither particularly religious nor particularly intelligent suggests her skepticism about the institutions from which she had been excluded because of her sex, and Lewes because of his class. Amos Barton, for example, is poorly educated despite having attended Cambridge; the Reverend Theodore Sherlock, BA, in *Felix Holt* is a Cambridge graduate; Mr Farebrother remarks on the easiness of the exams (which Fred has failed); Casaubon worries about his colleagues at Brasenose (Oxford); and Daniel Deronda finds little to interest him at Cambridge.

But to be acknowledged by the establishment was an honor Eliot did not reject. She and Lewes would continue accepting social invitations to visit friends at Cambridge and Oxford in the future, and Lewes was invited to consult with scientific men while working on *Problems of Life and Mind*. She gained access to this elite culture by virtue of her novels, but she was able to match these men in learning and converse with them as an intellectual and social equal. Oxford and Cambridge men were frequent visitors on Sundays at the Priory, and some, like F. W. H. Myers, Henry Sidgwick, and Oscar Browning, became devotees who left behind accounts of their friendship with Eliot that have been important for biographers. Eliot helped Sidgwick and Myers through their loss of faith, and she turned to the Cambridge men, Michael Foster and Sidgwick, when establishing a Fellowship in Lewes's name after his death.[24]

The idea of the Pattisons as originals for Dorothea and Edward Casaubon was encouraged by the memoirs of Emilia's second husband, Charles Dilke, whom she married after the death of Mark Pattison in 1884. Dilke suggests that Eliot based Dorothea on his wife and Casaubon on his wife's first husband (Pattison) and that she even put Pattison's words into Casaubon's mouth (Haight, *Biography* 564). Dilke's claims are vague and nonsensical, but Haight refutes them on the superficial grounds of Mr Casaubon's physical unlikeness to Pattison. Nuttall takes the claims seriously and shows the fallacies of Haight's defense.[25]

Another obscure historical scholar in whom Eliot took an interest was Joseph Scaliger (1540–1609). The French-born Scaliger figures in Pattison's biography of Casaubon as an important supporter and correspondent of the younger scholar. In *Romola*, so concerned with scholarly genealogy, Eliot's narrator, referring to Bartolomeo Scala and his learned squabble with Poliziano, comments that the "terrible Joseph Scaliger, who was to pronounce him totally ignorant of Latinity, was at a comfortable distance in the next century" (74; ch. 8). Around this time, Lewes was reading Scaliger's father, the Italian Julius Caesar Scaliger (1484–1588), while preparing his book on Aristotle (1864), the first volume of his own uncompleted history of science.[26] Nuttall notes that Pattison planned a study of his "hero" Joseph Scaliger, which he never completed, contributing to his view of himself as a failure: "The completed *Isaac Casaubon* can never have been in Pattison's mind an adequate substitute for the *Joseph Scaliger* he was never to carry through" (121).[27]

Eliot took a humorous view of the pedant Casaubon and may have shared a joke with Pattison about their respective resurrections of an important but historically neglected scholar. Eliot breathed new life into her fictional scholar Edward Casaubon with ironic self-knowledge, creating a bitter, failed, and egocentric author. Pattison was reviving Isaac Casaubon in the form of biography without the imaginative license or humor, but perhaps with some of the personal identification. Pattison's task was historical – to recreate Casaubon as he was and to animate him with the biographer's self-knowledge so that he would live for nineteenth-century readers. Eliot's inspiration was to imagine a modern Casaubon as a parallel to her modern Saint Theresa, suggesting that a true scholar in the nineteenth century might be as anachronistic as a saint. This too could be a private, shared joke with the Pattisons and Lewes, who playfully referred to his own "Key to All Psychologies" (*GEL* 5:338). Becoming self-conscious of her life-long habit of incorporating the quotations of other writers into her own writing may be what led her to make types, originality, and the related topic of plagiarism a chief theme in *Impressions*.

Impressions benefited from the research Eliot was conducting simultaneously with that for *Middlemarch* (as her notebooks show), for a long poem on the Greek military hero Timoleon (411–337 BCE). This unfinished poem became her own ambitious attempt to reconstruct the classical world and a classical hero of action rather than of intellect. It would have been a project unlike any other she had attempted, resurrecting an historical figure as the subject of an epic. *Romola* (with the exception of Savonarola) and *The Spanish Gypsy* focused on fictional characters. We do not know exactly why Eliot gave up her Timoleon project, except that she became absorbed in *Middlemarch*. But she may have had her inability to complete this work in mind as she developed Mr Casaubon and the theme of making historical fragments into wholes again, whether through art or scholarship. Looking back from our knowledge of her treatment of character types in *Impressions*, we can see even more clearly the importance of such types for *Middlemarch*: St Theresa, Casaubon, and also Lydgate.

Lydgate's project to find the "homogeneous origin of all tissues" (428; ch. 45) is implicitly linked with Casaubon's Key to All Mythologies, and though admirable in intention, it is similarly misguided. The narrator knows that the way he put his question about primitive tissue was "not quite in the way required by the awaiting answer" (139; ch. 15). This is one of her ironic comments about posterity, reminders that the narrator already knows whose efforts will be remembered: Poliziano will die in disgrace, and Lydgate's premise is out of sync with future scientific discoveries. The narrator's knowledge emphasizes that the future (perhaps also together with the past) is what we cannot know. *Middlemarch* is structured by these joint failures: one in trying to know the "history of man" and the other in trying to know the body of man. Lydgate's noble ambitions fail because he does not know himself well enough to avoid marrying Rosamond Vincy. He fails because the "spots of commonness" in his moral complexion interact with the medium of Middlemarch and determine that he will not do what he had once meant to do – great work for Middlemarch and mankind.

Eliot identified with Lydgate's frustrations as she had with Casaubon's. The Lydgate tragedy lies in giving up on ambitions:

> Only those who know the supremacy of the intellectual life – the life which has a seed of ennobling thought and purpose within it – can understand the grief of one who falls from that serene activity into the absorbing soul-wasting struggle with worldly annoyances. (695; ch. 73)

The narrator's phrase late in the novel – "Only those who know" – echoes the exclusivity of the Prelude's first line "who that cares much to know." Those who know comprise a select set, and Eliot's narrator (by virtue of her knowledge of past, present, and future) is clearly, as Dante described Aristotle, "the master of those who know."

We experience the pain and grief of Lydgate's fate through the slow, detailed process of his failure, due partly to the yoke that is marriage. His failure to achieve his scientific aims raises the specter of Lewes, who might have sacrificed his own happiness for that of a woman whom he no longer loved had he remained with Agnes. Lydgate's relationship to his namesake, John Lydgate, is less direct than that of Edward to Isaac Casaubon, but in the idea of the type Eliot invokes not only character types but the scientific language of her day – Darwinian evolution – and the animal species or types that have their own history and reproduce and persist and adapt to changing media over time.[28]

Eliot conducted extensive research into medical history to create the context and the genealogy of her medical reformer Lydgate. The prominence of science in the novel and the application of scientific metaphors to her "study of provincial life" were certainly advanced by Lewes's research for *Problems of Life and Mind*, as well as the past scientific investigations in which she had participated. Lewes, like the subjects of his books, Goethe and Aristotle, was a man of both arts and sciences. Eliot represented several types of amateur naturalists in her works: old Mr Transome collects specimens in *Felix Holt*, as does the Reverend Camden Farebrother in *Middlemarch*. In the "The Lifted Veil," she created her only other medical scientist, Meunier, whose Frankenstein-like experiment of blood transfusion brings a dead woman back to life. A pivotal figure in her consideration of the blurred line between magic or superstition and science is the medieval astronomer and astrologer Sephardo in *The Spanish Gypsy*. When Don Silva begs Sephardo to use his astrological chart to foresee the outcome of Silva's quest for Fedalma, the Jewish mystic and man of science speaks in terms that resemble the language and the realist project of *Middlemarch*, explaining to Silva that "the fortunes of a man/Are made of elements refined and mixed":

> And so, my lord, your horoscope declares
> Nought absolutely of your sequent lot,
> But, by our lore's authentic rules, sets forth
> What gifts, what dispositions, likelihoods,
> The aspects of the heavens conspired to fuse
> With your incorporate soul. *(bk. 2; ll. 810–15)*

Astrology, which Sephardo calls alternately science and lore, is one of the many languages that Eliot employs to talk about the fate and determinism involved in any person's specific lot. Those who have sought to know that "strange mixture" of man, "refined and mixed," have done so through reference to gods, God, planets, and – in ways peculiar to the nineteenth century – science and realist fiction.

Like prophecy, astrology, stock market speculation, and scientific experimentation, gambling is a form that the human desire to anticipate unknown outcomes takes. But gambling adds the dishonorable motivation of personal gain. Eliot uses the metaphor of the lottery in *Felix Holt*, while roulette is prominent in *Daniel Deronda*. In *Middlemarch*, gambling is both metaphoric and literal. Fred Vincy bets when playing billiards, and he speculates on the purchase of a horse, which he hopes to sell for a profit. He also has expectations that his wealthy uncle will leave him enough money to become a gentleman without effort and relieve him of the responsibility of becoming a clergyman, as his father wishes. Fred's speculation on his uncle's money was at the heart of Eliot's conception of *Middlemarch*, and it introduces the theme of inheritance, which has far-reaching literal and metaphoric reverberations in the novel. Casaubon inherits a scholarly tradition; Lydgate receives the scientific legacy of the great men who had come before him. Other characters, such as Featherstone's avaricious relatives and the banker Bulstrode, look to more worldly legacies. Eliot's heroes, including Will Ladislaw and Daniel Deronda, are the disinherited.

In a revealing conversation between Lydgate and Mr Farebrother (who is a kind of oracle, as well as a successful gambler), predictions about the future and posterity are mixed with Lydgate's reflections about the legacy of medical research he has inherited. Responding to Farebrother's tactful attempt to warn him about his future in Middlemarch, Lydgate remarks: "It isn't possible to square one's conduct to silly conclusions which nobody can foresee" (428; ch. 45). He is as yet untroubled about money matters or local politics: "A man conscious of enthusiasm for worthy aims is sustained under petty hostilities by the memory of great workers who had to fight their way not without wounds, and who hover in his mind as patron saints, invisibly helping" (429; ch. 45). This passage links Lydgate to Dorothea (the modern St Theresa who will ultimately become his patron); it also makes a crucial contrast to Casaubon, of whom the narrator observes that "his soul was sensitive without being enthusiastic" (262; ch. 29). Brooding that his pamphlets, "by which he tested his public and deposited small monumental records of his march," were not appreciated or even read, Casaubon,

> was in painful doubt as to what was really thought of them by the leading minds of Brasenose, and bitterly convinced that his old acquaintance Carp had been the writer of that depreciatory recension which was kept locked in a small drawer of Mr. Casaubon's desk, and also in a dark closet of his verbal memory. (263; ch. 29)

While the enthusiastic Lydgate is insufficiently sensitive to the outcomes of petty hostilities and thinks instead of intellectual forebears who overcame obstacles, the unenthusiastic Casaubon is overly sensitive to petty hostilities and cannot be sustained by the memory of his great predecessors, for example Isaac Casaubon.

This chapter also reveals Dorothea's wifely point of view and confusion through an historical analogy to a figure of sixteenth-century intellectual history, Richard Hooker: "How far the judicious Hooker or any other hero of erudition would have been the same at Mr. Casaubon's time of life, she had no means of knowing, so that he could not have the advantage of comparison" (184; ch. 20). Before meeting Mr Casaubon, Dorothea had thought about Hooker in relation to marriage: "She felt sure that she would have accepted the judicious Hooker, if she had been born in time to save him from that wretched mistake he made in matrimony" (10; ch. 1). In thinking of Hooker after her marriage, Dorothea desperately desires a comparison to another "hero of erudition" at Mr Casaubon's "time of life." She would have welcomed talking with her husband about such past heroes. Just as Casaubon's lack of enthusiasm is contrasted to Lydgate's enthusiasm through these parallel scenes, so Dorothea's wish to understand Casaubon is contrasted with Rosamond's refusal to understand her husband even when he offers her the very information Dorothea "had no means of knowing," specifically, what a hero of erudition was like at his "time of life."

The chapter in which Farebrother offers his friendly warning is a turning point for Lydgate. His confidence in his future is high and he has only intimations of troubles to come. The narrator remarks: "There was something very fine in Lydgate's look just then, and any one might have been encouraged to bet on his achievement" (429; ch. 45). He returns home to Rosamond, and ventures to tell her about his ambitions:

> "I am thinking of a great fellow, who was about as old as I am three hundred years ago, and had already begun a new era in anatomy."
> "I can't guess," said Rosamond, shaking her head. "We used to play at guessing historical characters at Mrs. Lemon's, but not anatomists." (429; ch. 45)

Rosamond's naïve reference to the game of "guessing historical characters" betrays the ignorance with which she graduated from Mrs Lemon's finishing school and her foggy notion of historical figures as "characters"; it is also an ironic commentary on the game of guessing at characters that Eliot is playing with her readers throughout the novel.

Lydgate, testing his wife's tolerance for anatomy, explains: "His name was Vesalius. And the only way he could get to know anatomy as he did, was by going to snatch bodies at night, from graveyards and places of execution." Rosamond portentously exclaims, "I am very glad you are not Vesalius," adding, "I hope he is not one of your great heroes" (429; ch. 45). The scene is remarkable for its mixture of the comic and the serious. Rosamond next dares to confess: "Do you know, Tertius, I often wish you had not been a medical man." Lydgate must respond seriously: "That is like saying you wish you had married another man" (430; ch. 45). Rosamond persists that medicine is not a "nice profession, dear," and Lydgate commands: "Don't say that again, dear, it pains me" (430; ch. 45).

The chapter ends with Lydgate's realization that he is out of harmony with a wife who refuses to understand any passion of his that does not include her. Rosamond sums up their conversation with an awful power to reduce what matters most to her husband to a facetious lesson: "I will declare in future that I dote on skeletons, and body-snatchers, and bits of things in phials, and quarrels with everybody, that end in your dying miserably" (430–1; ch. 45). Through Rosamond, Eliot is foreshadowing the fact that Lydgate would not become a modern Vesalius and that he would die rather miserably.

The Catholic Vesalius (1514–64) was a contemporary of the Spanish St Theresa (1515–82), and also a close contemporary of the French Protestant Isaac Casaubon (1559–1614) and the English Protestant Richard Hooker (1554–1600). Eliot meant readers to keep in mind the 300-year span of these heroes and prototypes of her early nineteenth-century characters, as well as the cosmopolitan nature of intellectual history. These "historical characters" represent the legacy inherited by modern European culture. Rosamond, like the rest of her nouveau riche family, thinks only of Lydgate's monetary and social inheritance. In this way, Eliot grinds down noble legacies into coarse, soul-wasting monetary ones. This perspective on modern life, which began to develop while watching the Newdigates contest their inheritance, also had precedents in novels such as Dickens's *Bleak House* and the sensation fiction of Mary Elizabeth Braddon and Wilkie Collins. Both personal experience and literary example may account for the centrality of wills in Eliot's plots beginning with *Felix Holt* and carrying on into *Middlemarch*.[29]

The notion that Dorothea, the modern-day St Theresa, lived in a world uncongenial to the gifts and aspirations of her type, is reinforced by Lydgate, the would-be modern Vesalius, being drawn down into worldly cares. Part of the novel's brilliance is its presentation of the nineteenth century as a time of reform, as well as a time of sordid squabbles over legacies and inheritances that might only be overcome by the denial (in the case of Fred) or renunciation (in the case of Dorothea) of the monetary inheritance. Themes of cultural inheritance, gambling, and vocation were preparing George Eliot for her next novel.

The first of *Middlemarch*'s eight parts was published on December 1, 1871. It coincided with the publication of an unusual work of homage to Eliot: *Wise, Witty and Tender Sayings*, edited by the Scottish admirer Alexander Main. This, along with the publication strategy, comprised the elaborate publicity of *Middlemarch*, which enhanced its visibility and made its publication a literary event. It was simultaneously serialized in the US in *Harper's Weekly*. By May 1872, five parts had been written. The Leweses retreated to a rented house in Redhill, Surrey for three months. There, Eliot was able to write without interruptions. By September 1872, eight books had been completed, and the Leweses left for Germany, where the Finale was written and mailed off on October 2. They returned on October 31. The last part was published in December 1872.

The experimental publication format was new to Eliot and to British fiction. Because Eliot was so well known at this time, and perhaps also because of the novelty of the parts publication, individual parts received reviews in periodicals such as the *Athenaeum, Daily News, Echo, Standard, Examiner*, and *Illustrated London News*. Martin observes that "the number and length of the serial reviews were unprecedented for *Middlemarch* and *Daniel Deronda*," which was later published in the same format (186). Martin argues that these reviews had an impact on how Eliot structured the novel, for example, making sure that there were several chapters on Dorothea included in Book II (which had not been the original plan) because reviewers were so impressed with her story (191). These reviews of individual parts, as well as those of the completed novel, were uniformly laudatory. *Middlemarch* became an example of a novel that was recognized for its brilliance in its own time and continues to receive such recognition.

Eliot revised the Finale of *Middlemarch* twice in attempting to explain just what happened to Dorothea: "Certainly those determining acts of her life were not ideally beautiful. They were the mixed result of young and noble impulse struggling with imperfect conditions" (*Middlemarch* 810). This is how the manuscript reads. She revised it for the first edition to read, "struggling under prosaic conditions," and most famously, she revised again for subsequent editions to read, "struggling amidst the conditions of an imperfect social state" (748; Finale). This uncharacteristic wrestling with the language of a passage that is so central to her overall conception of the novel shows the difficulty that Eliot had deciding just what it is in the social medium that hinders or shapes individual impulses and determines individual fates. Her next novel, *Daniel Deronda*, is the story of a man who finds what Dorothea could not, "a coherent social faith and order which could perform the function of knowledge for the ardently willing soul" (3; Prelude). In Judaism, Daniel Deronda discovers a coherent social faith, but the fellowship he finds is of a national sort that Eliot believed was becoming increasingly important as a means of ordering experience and performing the function of knowledge in the changing world around her.

Notes

1. Hardy notes that Haight mistakenly dates this phrase as a quotation from 1878 (*Critic's Biography* 140).
2. For a comparison of Arnold and Eliot's conception of culture, see Knoepflmacher, *Religious Humanism* and Fleishman, ch. 10.
3. After Eliot's death, the poem was appropriated by Frederic Harrison's branch of positivism, which broke away from Congreve's group. This new positivist congregation made "The Choir Invisible" into one of its sacred texts and published it in a book called *Service to Man* (1890). For the history of the poem's use by positivists, as well as its various settings, to music, see Vogeler ("The Choir Invisible" 77).
4. Bodenheimer argues that Thornie's death transformed what Eliot wrote and how she wrote it (*Real Life* 233).
5. See Deutsch's *Literary Remains* and Peter Brier, "Emanuel Deutsch, The Talmud Man: George Eliot's Rabbi." See also Baker, *George Eliot and Judaism*, and on Deutsch's Talmud article and its influence on Eliot's writing, see Kaufman, ch. 5.
6. See Van den Broek's Introduction to "Jubal" in *Poetry*, Vol. I.
7. See Bonaparte, *Triptych* (ch. 4).
8. *Archiv für Psychiatrie und Nervenkrankheiten* 2.73 (1869): 108. Foucault mentions him in his *History of Sexuality*, Vol. I.
9. Dellamora, in discussing Gwendolen Harleth, takes this reference to be to same-sex desire (*Friendship's Bonds*, ch. 5).
10. On Jane Senior as a possible model for Dorothea, see Hardy, *Critic's Biography*. On Georgiana Burne-Jones as a model, see McCormack, *English Travels*.
11. R. C. Jebb, Cambridge classicist and translator of Theophrastus's *Characters*, described his conversation with Eliot about Walter Pater: "I was saying (*a propos* of Pater's *Renaissance*)

that the 'precious' school seemed to be destroying everything – their finesses and small affectations blinding people's eyes to the great lineaments of the great creative works . . . Her face lit up in a moment, and she said, 'It is such a comfort and a strength to hear you say that'" (*Life and Letters* 155).

12. See Gilbert and Gubar; Bodenheimer, *Real Life* (ch. 6); Kathleen Blake "Armgart."

13. On Maenads in Eliot, see Bonaparte, *Triptych* (ch. 6).

14. Like "Jubal," "Armgart" was published in *Macmillan's Magazine* and the *Atlantic Monthly* (July 1871).

15. The first six parts appeared at two-month intervals starting on December 1, 1871, and the last two parts were published at monthly intervals so that the final volume would appear in time for Christmas 1872. See Martin, ch. 5 and Feltes.

16. For a good sampling of *Middlemarch* criticism, see Adam, *This Particular Web*, and Chase, *Middlemarch in the Twenty-First Century*.

17. As she did for *Romola*, *Felix Holt*, *The Spanish Gypsy*, and *Daniel Deronda*, Eliot kept notebooks dedicated specifically to her research on *Middlemarch* and these have been published in various forms over the years. See Beaty, Pratt and Neufeldt, and Wiesenfarth.

18. Judith Johnston shows the influence of Jameson's account on the Prelude and on the characterization of Dorothea. She also identifies S. J. Le Pedro de Ribadeneyra's *Les Vies des saints et fêtes de toute l'année* as a source for the story of Theresa and her brother (59–60). Hilary Fraser suggests that Eliot may have read a new English translation of Theresa's *Life* (1870). See "St. Theresa, St. Dorothea, and Miss Brooke."

19. Bull argues that Eliot probably read this article since she wrote to Sara Hennell about another article in the same issue (218). For other considerations of the Isaac Casaubon–Edward Casaubon connection, see Knoepflmacher, "Fusing Fact and Myth" and Newton, *Modernising George Eliot* (ch. 5).

20. The reference to Casaubon in the Folger notebook (Pratt and Neufeldt) also seems to post-date the meetings with Pattison since it comes on page 160 of 172 of a journal that she finished in December 1871. Casaubon is not on the 1869 list of names for *Middlemarch*, some of which were later used for *Daniel Deronda*: Cadwallader, Gascoigne, Lodowick, Vandernoodt.

21. Nuttall writes that Casaubon's epitaph in Westminster Abbey concludes with the following lines (which he translates from the Latin): "He who would know Casaubon, / Let him read not tombstones but his pages, / Destined to outlast marble / And to profit generations to come" (167). It is possible that Eliot would have read these lines on a visit to Westminster Abbey. The lines reflect her ultimate position that an author's writings are his chief acts.

22. The Leweses both read the manuscript before its publication in 1875 (*GEL* 6:108).

23. Since Eliot received a copy of Pattison's biography in 1875, she would have known about Casaubon's other translations in addition to Theophrastus – of works by Diogenes Laertius (1593) and Athenaeus (1597), both mentioned or alluded to later in *Impressions*.

24. Their first visit to Cambridge was in February 1868, but she did not meet Jebb until 1873. For an account of the influence of Myers, Sidgwick, and Gurney in particular, and including letters not published in *GEL*, see John Beer, ch. 5.

25. Kali Israel has an interesting take on Dilke's mysterious retrospective claims about Eliot's originals, suggesting that Dilke's "own understanding of his second wife's first

marriage was shaped by *Middlemarch*" (98). Nuttall comes to a similar conclusion about Mrs Pattison: "It is entirely possible that, if George Eliot was not describing Francis in the novel, Francis afterward modeled herself upon the heroine" (78).

26. In *Aristotle* (1864), Lewes is scrupulous about citing his secondary sources and recovering neglected scholars of Aristotle, commenting that many important scholars have been completely forgotten and thereby foreshadowing Eliot's revival of forgotten figures in the names of her *Middlemarch* characters.

27. His plans were made obsolete by the publication of Jacob Bernays's book on Scaliger (1855) (Nuttall 120).

28. On the complex role of science and scientific language in *Middlemarch*, see Beer, *Darwin's Plots*, Shuttleworth, and Levine, *Darwin and the Novelists*.

29. Martin points out that while Eliot was writing *Middlemarch*, the trial of the "Tichborne claimant" was in all the headlines (199–201). Eliot and Lewes attended a day of this ongoing, sensational trial on January 17, 1872 (*GEL* 5:237).

8

Daniel Deronda
1873–6

"A vice I have no mind to ..."
(GE to Mrs. William Cross, *GEL* 5:312)

On September 25, 1872, Eliot wrote to her friend Mrs William Cross from Homburg, the German spa town where she and Lewes had recently arrived. She expressed her revulsion at the sight of roulette in the "Kursaal" or common room of the resort. Her language is unusually strong in describing what she calls "a vice I have no mind to," which attracted "hideous women staring at the board like stupid monomaniacs." She declared hyperbolically: "Burglary is heroic compared with it." As if justifying her own compulsion to linger and watch, she continued: "I get some satisfaction in looking on from the sense that the thing is going to be put down" (*GEL* 5:312). She was referring to the abolition of gambling at German spas that was scheduled to take place at the end of 1872. This prohibition of gambling coincided with the formal unification of Germany in 1871, following the defeat of France by Prussia in the Franco-Prussian War (1870–1), which Eliot had lamented as "evil" in her journal (December 31, 1870; *GEJ* 141). But the casinos had actually been set to close following the Prussian defeat of Austria in the Austro-Prussian War (1866), and as Eliot noted in her letters, Homburg and other German spa towns had been given five years to develop an economic plan to stay solvent before the ban on gambling went into effect. The impending closure of the casinos would have been widely discussed when Eliot and Lewes visited Homburg, and her strong moral reaction to the gambling would have been shared by its German residents.[1]

The Life of George Eliot: A Critical Biography, First Edition. Nancy Henry.
© 2012 Nancy Henry. Published 2012 by John Wiley & Sons, Ltd.

The German casinos and their closing would have an impact on the scenes, themes, and even the historical setting of her next novel, *Daniel Deronda*. The fictional German spa in which the novel's opening scene takes place, Leubronn, is a composite of the numerous spas Eliot and Lewes visited in search of health and relaxation. They had been observing the gambling at Baden Baden, for example, since 1868 (McCormack, "George Eliot: Poetry, Fiction and European Spas" 10–11). Eliot had criticized gambling generally in *Middlemarch*, and in *Felix Holt* Jermyn's failed attempt to develop a spa in Treby Magna occurs before the action of the plot and contributes to lingering suspicion about him in the town. But in addition to the theme of gambling's immorality that may have been inspired by visits to casinos, there was also a specific "germ" for the image of Gwendolen as a gambler in the 1872 visit to Homburg. On September 26, the day after Eliot wrote to Mrs Cross about the women gamblers in general, Lewes records in his journal that they saw a Miss Leigh, Byron's grandniece, gambling and losing at the roulette table (Haight, *Biography* 457).

In a letter to John Blackwood, written on October 4, 1872, immediately after she had completed and sent him the Finale to *Middlemarch* on October 2, Eliot described the scene of Miss Leigh at the roulette table:

> The saddest thing to be witnessed is the play of Miss Leigh, Byron's grand niece, who is only 26 years old, and is completely in the grasp of this mean, money-raking demon. It made me cry to see her young fresh face among the hags and brutally stupid men around her. (*GEL* 5:314)

She again mentions the impending ban on gambling with a word about its economic implications:

> Next year, when the gambling has vanished the place will be delightful – there will be a subvention from the government to keep up the beautiful grounds, and it is likely that there will be increase enough in the number of decent visitors to keep the town tolerably prosperous. (*GEL* 5:314–15)

If some of the gambling visitors were not "decent," they were interesting. Lewes records that they again saw Miss Leigh gambling on October 7, reinforcing their mutual disgust but also suggesting their fascination with the scene of vice.

In October 1872, when she was recovering from the strain of writing *Middlemarch* and felt both attracted and repelled by the spectacle of roulette, Eliot was months away from beginning to write *Daniel Deronda*. In a departure from her previous novels, which are set in the early decades of the nineteenth century, *Daniel Deronda* is carefully set only one decade prior to its composition. The action takes place between October 1864 and October 1866, beginning *in medias res* at the roulette table in Leubronn in September 1865.[2] Like *Middlemarch*, it is set on the eve of a major reform bill in England. The Second Reform Bill was passed in 1867, foreshadowed when Gwendolen's uncle tells her: "The best judges are confident that the Ministry will have to appeal to the country on this question of further Reform" (470; ch. 44). The novel refers directly to events such as the Austro-Prussian War (1866), the American Civil War (1861–5), and the Jamaican black workers' uprising (1865), and it captures the economic distress of this period (due in part to the American Civil War) by fictionalizing and consolidating bank failures, such as that of Overend and Gurney in 1866. In the novel, the bank Grapnell & Co., in which Gwendolen's mother and aunt have invested their inheritance, "fails for a million." Gwendolen's mother, Mrs Davilow, blames the failure on the "wicked" speculations of Mr Lassmann. When she writes to Gwendolen, calling her home from Leubronn, she elaborates: "All the property our poor father saved for us goes to pay the liabilities" (10; ch. 2).[3]

Eliot never explained her reasons for this choice of historical setting, but it allowed her to do several important things. She kept her narrator's knowledge of the outcome of historical events, while also giving the impression that life was changing more rapidly than it had in the past, and that in the future, people in England might see as many changes in a decade as they had seen previously in a generation. It also gave her a chance to examine the lives of a specific generation in which she had an interest. Rather than focus on her father's generation, she now focused on a younger generation. Rex and Warham Gascoigne, Gwendolen, Daniel, and Hans are all in their twenties in the 1860s, as were the Lewes boys in the mid-1860s. With this time frame, Eliot was able to explore the particular historical and social circumstances that affected the opportunities available to this generation of young men and women. Furthermore, in order to have gambling at a German spa play a pivotal role in the plot of her novel, she had to set it prior to 1872, after which such gambling was banned.

That Gwendolen and Daniel cross paths at a European spa/casino in 1865 suggests the malaise and lack of culture in upper middle-class English society. Gwendolen actively searches for excitement through gambling, and Daniel unexpectedly finds it through the passive act of watching her gamble. The subject of cultural and moral degeneracy in mid-nineteenth-century England and Europe was new to Eliot's fiction and reflects her experience of moving in circles that would have been unthinkable to her as a young woman in the Midlands and impossible during the years when her relationship with Lewes made her a social pariah. As a famous novelist, she now received, and was received by, titled aristocrats, diplomats, and wealthy business people, as well as the intellectual and cultural elite of London and Oxbridge. As ever, she wrote from experience, describing and analyzing what she observed. Her emergence into high society both at home and abroad coincided with greater social and cultural changes, which she was uniquely equipped to record. She and Lewes took advantage of expanding railway travel throughout Britain and Europe; they invested her money in a diverse portfolio of stocks, shares, and bonds in national and international companies and governments. She had expressed her views about spreading democracy and the Second Reform Bill in Felix Holt's "Address" in 1868. Her travels had made her more attuned to European conflicts and emerging nationalist movements. Through the emigration of Lewes's sons, and the emigration of her friends' sons, including those of Dickens and Trollope, she knew about the practical as well as the ideological implications of colonialism and imperialism. All of these factors – transportation, finance capitalism, spreading democracy, nationalism, and imperialism – contributed to an increasingly cosmopolitan Europe. *Daniel Deronda* suggests that Eliot was ambivalent about these rapid transformations of her world, which seemed to be breaking down traditional social structures and values, even as they offered new potential for a tolerant, pluralistic society. She looked particularly to high culture and nationalism as antidotes to the moral laxity that she perceived as attending these changes, which uprooted people and made them seek alternatives to religion and local community for their moral foundation.

The gambling casino represented for her an effete and dissipated cross section of European nationalities and classes, what she called in an ironic commentary on Enlightenment ideology and contemporary democracy, a "striking admission of human equality" (3; ch. 1). The itinerants of all classes congregated in salons poisoned by an over-abundance of gas lamps. The herd of gamblers with money to waste was well wadded by plush upholstery and thick curtains against the drumbeats of change throughout the world, including nationalist movements in Italy and Germany and the earliest stirrings of what would become the political and cultural movement later called Zionism. The themes and plots of *Daniel Deronda* seem motivated at least in part by Eliot's desire to call middle-class readers out of their materialistic self-absorption and to show them the nobility of higher callings and duties. The model of religious, racial, and national identities that she held up to her English readers was modern Judaism, with its connections to an ancient past and potential for a national future, a move that surprised many of her non-Jewish contemporaries, especially perhaps because it is not clear exactly how this model might apply to English Christians.

The critical, satiric tone of *Daniel Deronda*'s powerful first chapter is distinct from Eliot's previous, more tolerantly ironic position toward the societies she described. In *The Mill* and *Middlemarch*, for example, she looked back at the narrowness of provincial society a generation before her own. Now, she criticized her closer contemporary readers and acquaintances in a turn similar to that taken by Trollope at the same time in *The Way We Live Now* (1874–5), which Eliot was reading as it appeared. In that novel, as in his next, *The Prime Minister* (1876), Trollope represented finance capitalism and the stock market as glorified forms of gambling and gigantic swindles epitomizing the corruption and materialism of modern English society. For the nouveau riche clientele in Leubronn, "taking their pleasure at a higher strength," "the vice of gambling lay in losing money at it" (1; ch. 1). But for Eliot the vice lay in winning, in the man who "sweeps within his arms the ventures of twenty chapfallen companions" (*Middlemarch* 66; ch. 7). In *Daniel Deronda*'s opening scene, "business," in the form of the London tradesman vacationing at Leubronn, is explicitly compared to gambling when the narrator describes the type of people who win money at gambling "in the intervals of winning money in business" (4; ch. 1). It is notable that she describes business as "winning" rather than earning money. We have to wonder how her characterization of "business" was influenced – and received – by some of her new social acquaintances in the business world, such as Frederick Lehmann (partner in an iron and steel firm) and his wife, or even the banker John Walter Cross.

In the months following the 1872 visit to German spas, Eliot began research on *Daniel Deronda*. Soon, she was deep into reading about Judaism. The German Jewish scholar Emanuel Deutsch, to whom the Lehmanns had first introduced her in 1866, had been an important influence on her, as she studied Hebrew with him and corresponded with and visited him when he was ill and living with his neighbors, the Reverend Reginald and Mary Eliza Haweis.

She seemed to sympathize with both the physical symptoms of the cancer from which he was suffering and also with his depressions, writing on July 7, 1871:

> Remember, it has happened to many to be glad they did not commit suicide, though they once ran for the final leap, or as Mary Wolstonecraft did, wetted their garments well in the rain hoping to sink the better when they plunged . . . She lived to know some real joys, and death came in time to hinder the joys from being spoiled. (*GEL* 5:160–1)

This was an image she would draw on in representing Mirah's attempted suicide, from which Deronda saves her. In 1872 Deutsch set off on a second trip to the Middle East, hoping again to reach Jerusalem. But his illness kept him in Alexandria, where he died on May 12, 1873. At the time of his death Eliot was beginning her intensive reading on Jewish topics that would lead to the development of *Daniel Deronda*.[4]

On November 17, she wrote to Emilia Pattison (whose husband would soon complete his biography of Isaac Casaubon) that in the mornings, her "dwelling is among the tombs, farther back than the times of the Medici" (*GEL* 5:461). This image associates her research for *Romola* (into the Medici family) with the research of Mr Casaubon in *Middlemarch* who "lives too much with the dead" (17; ch. 2). Returning proofs for Volume I of *Daniel Deronda* on December 1, 1875, Lewes remarked to John Blackwood: "You are surprised at her knowledge of the Jews? But only learned Rabbis are so profoundly versed in Jewish history and literature as she is" (*GEL* 6:196).

It was in the early 1870s that Eliot and Lewes's Sundays at the Priory became an institution, regularly maintained during the months they spent in London. With no children to tie them, they could now spend the summers in the country (Surrey and Kent), renting houses while they searched for a country home of their own. In

London and in Oxford and Cambridge, she socialized with new friends who would influence those aspects of *Daniel Deronda*'s plot in which Rex Gascoigne attends Oxford and Daniel and Hans Meyrick attend Cambridge. On May 19, 1873, she spent three days in Cambridge with her young friends Henry Sidgwick, Frederick Myers, and Edmund Gurney, the young man whom Leslie Stephen speculated was an "original" for Daniel Deronda (*George Eliot*, 1902). It was at this time that she met R. C. Jebb, discussing Sophocles and Walter Pater with him. In June 1873, she spent two days with Benjamin Jowett at Oxford. All of these men would also appear at the Priory when they were in London.

As ever, Eliot complemented her book learning by travel and observation. In the summer of 1873, the Leweses again traveled to Germany, visiting synagogues in Frankfurt, Homburg, and Mainz and thereby absorbing an atmosphere she would translate into particular descriptions in *Daniel Deronda*. At this time, they also considered a trip to the Middle East, including Egypt, Palestine, Beirut, and Syria. Eliot never described locations she had not visited, so it is tempting to wonder how *Daniel Deronda* might have been different had they made this trip, which they abandoned for reasons of health (Haight, *Biography* 474). As in the past, they traveled in search of English settings that would enable her to describe accurately the places she had in mind as models for the fictional county that she would call Wessex. Coincidentally, the young Thomas Hardy (1840–1928) would also call his fictionalized Dorset "Wessex" in his novels. In October 1874, for example, they visited Salisbury and Lacock Abbey, which was an inspiration for Topping Abbey, Sir Hugo's seat and Deronda's childhood home. They were now discussing the possibility that *Daniel Deronda* might take the form of a play.[5]

On June 25, 1873, Thornton Hunt died. It turned out that he had a life insurance policy naming Agnes as a beneficiary. When Lewes returned to London from the trip to Germany, he helped Agnes collect on this policy by obtaining a required signature from Hunt's wife Katherine (Haight, *Biography* 467). Hunt had ceased to play any role in Lewes's life, and it is unclear whether he had any part in the lives of Agnes and her children at the time of his death. Agnes and her children were still dependent on Lewes and the money he provided with Eliot's help. In fact Haight writes that in 1874: "The largest item in Lewes's account was for Agnes and her brood" (*Biography* 460). But Eliot's wealth was now such that Agnes could not be a financial burden.[6] She was, however, still a figure in the background of Eliot's daily life as a reminder that she was neither really "Mrs Lewes" nor really the stepmother of his sons.

In *Daniel Deronda*, the semi-hidden, socially marginal figure of Grandcourt's former mistress, Lydia Glasher, represents the ambiguities of Agnes's position and the complexity of Eliot's feelings toward the first wife/former lover of her "husband." Agnes was also the mistress of Thornton Hunt, the "other woman" in Hunt's marriage to Katherine Hunt. Lydia Glasher, on the one hand, is a victim of

Grandcourt's insensitivity and cruelty. On the other hand, she is, with a touch of the Gothic appropriate to the sensation fiction of the 1860s, Gwendolen's tormentor. She is scorned and vengeful, but she is also maternal. Her refusal to disappear and her claims to be acknowledged are awkward for Grandcourt and traumatic for Gwendolen. Her son with Grandcourt is the basis for what she sees as a financial entitlement, so that bound up in her character is a complex of emotional and monetary ties from which Gwendolen cannot be freed, just as Eliot was never to be free from Agnes Lewes. Throughout her life with Lewes, Eliot struggled to be fair to Agnes while negotiating feelings of resentment, jealousy, and guilt, a range of emotions that converge in an exaggerated form in Lydia Glasher.

Eliot and Lewes spent September through October 1873 near Bickley in Kent, where Eliot was deeply involved in reading for *Daniel Deronda*, which was now confirmed as a novel rather than a play. In February 1874, Eliot had her first attack of kidney stones. Other episodes would follow, taking their toll on her health (Haight, *Biography* 477). Her father had died of kidney disease following similar attacks, so the episodes could not but seem to Eliot signs of her own mortality. She would, in fact, ultimately die of a heart attack caused by kidney failure. Not yet fully absorbed in writing her new novel, she now felt an urgency to bring out a volume of her collected poems, some previously published and some not. Blackwood's published *The Legend of Jubal and Other Poems* in May of 1874. It had been an active winter and spring of Sundays at the Priory and other socializing. On June 2, 1874, the Leweses removed to Redhill in Surrey for four months, where she was able to write uninterruptedly.

Communication with Bertie Lewes in South Africa was sporadic in the early 1870s as calamities befell him one after the other. He sold the farm he shared with Thornie because it was so remote. Eliza Harrison's father objected to the marriage because of Bertie's poverty. He had regrets, which seem a passive and probably unintentional rebuke of his parents back in England: "I often wish that I had learned some trade" (*GEL* 9:16). He was married on May 25, 1871 (*GEL* 9:18). He leased a farm and after building a house there found the landlord had no right to the land and so the couple had to leave. The sheep he had invested in died, then his servant of five years left him (*GEL* 9:35). In 1872, Eliza had a daughter, whom they named Marian.

Then Bertie's health began to decline – he was suffering with neuralgia and being treated with "Strychnica and Iron" (*GEL* 9:137). He declined further, traveling alone for treatment and writing home on May 17, 1875: "All my glands are swollen and before I left home I got the Mumps. . . I have a very bad cold I had it now two months" (*GEL* 9:154). In his illness, the grammar that had plagued him all his life broke down. On June 29, 1875, Bertie died alone in Durban, where he had gone to seek medical care for a lingering illness strangely similar to that of his brother Thornie. He would never see his second child, born shortly before his death and named George Herbert Lewes. Eliot and Lewes received a letter announcing the birth of this son in July, but did not receive word of Bertie's death (in a letter from John Sanderson who had known both Thornie and Bertie) until August 1875. This letter gives a pathetic account of his small debts (hotel and doctor). He had £14.1.4 in his pocket (*GEL* 9:160).

Eliot wrote wistfully to Johnny Cross:

> He was a sweet-natured creature – not clever, but diligent and well-judging about the things of daily life, and we felt ten years ago that a colony with a fine climate, like Natal, offered him the only fair prospect within his reach. What can we do more than try to arrive at the best conclusion from the conditions as they are known to us. (*GEL* 6:165)

Looking back on the decision to send Bertie to a "fine climate," Eliot's sadly self-justifying analysis belies a larger social pattern in which the colonies served as the last resort for failures at home. The conditions made known to Eliot by Thornie's letters at the time Bertie emigrated included the lack of economic opportunity and the prevalence of violent conflict, but the fantastical optimism of Thornie's letters encouraged Eliot and Lewes's hopes for the "diligent and well-judging" Bertie who died in utter poverty. His half-brother Edmund, who stayed at home, fared better, and Lewes had recently given him £100 to start his practice as a dentist (which he successfully built during his life).

Since Eliot was writing *Daniel Deronda* when she received this news, it seems possible that the young Deronda's quest for a vocation and ultimate emigration with a purpose may reflect her thinking about the wasted lives of her exiled stepsons. There is certainly a nod to Thornie in Warham Gascoigne's "cram" for the Indian Civil Service exam, which he, unlike his prototype, passes. Warham leaves for India during the course of the novel, his career a shadow of what Thornie's might have been in the 1860s had he passed his exam. It is curious that Rex's rash idea of emigrating to Canada after Gwendolen rejects him is treated humorously, and is sternly put down by his father, with an appeal to his duties to his family at home. But Rex, unlike Thornie, is a student at Oxford with a promising future and fair prospects in England.

The tragedy of wasted lives and the search of young English people for careers, vocations, and purposes are all central to *Daniel Deronda*. Eliot now seemed determined to offer a model of vocation that was a more hopeful alternative to the failures with which *Middlemarch* ends. A vague religion of humanity in which good acts diffuse goodness could not suffice in a world of violence and materialistic greed – the world as Eliot had come to see it in the 1870s. National identity and reverence for one's culture (with tolerance and openness to others) seemed the most satisfying, redeeming values that Eliot could offer her own culture – following naturally from her humanism – to take the place of religion.

214

Daniel Deronda

The history of *Daniel Deronda*'s reception has always been overshadowed by the objection of critics that the novel falls into two insufficiently integrated parts: Gwendolen's story and Daniel's story, the English half and the Jewish half. Such a reading angered Eliot and prompted her to insist that she meant "everything in the book to be related to everything else there" (*GEL* 6:290). In 1948, F. R. Leavis, making the case for Eliot's centrality in his version of "the great tradition," did much to revive interest in her work, which had waned in the decades after her death. He made provocative claims about the superiority of *Daniel Deronda*'s English part compared to the Jewish part. He went so far as to undertake the hopeless task of extricating the Jewish material from a novel he thought to publish under the title of *Gwendolen Harleth*, but failed to carry out this impossible surgical operation.[7]

Middlemarch came about as a melding of two plots not initially conceived as a single novel, and its success may have led Eliot to weave the separate narrative threads of *Daniel Deronda*. Individual lives becoming entwined through coincidence as well as choice, and yet never fully merging, is not just a narrative structure; it is also a theme of the novel, reflected in the title of book III, "Meeting Streams," and in Mordecai's vision of a future in which the Jews and other nations have "separateness with communication." This perhaps explains why Daniel and Gwendolen's lives cannot ultimately merge, and on the horizon at the end of the novel is a further divergence of their paths.

The novel begins with a convergence of Gwendolen and Daniel's lives at Leubronn, only to flashback to the fictional English county of Wessex and trace the events that lead to the intersection of these two main characters' lives at the roulette table. The flashback narrative rejoins the original narrative in chapter 21. The narrator tells us at the end of chapter 20: "This was the history of Deronda, so far as he knew it, up to the time of that visit to Leubronn in which he saw Gwendolen Harleth at the gaming table" (193; ch. 20). This reference to what Daniel does not know echoes the epigraph to the chapter recalling Daniel's childhood: "Men, like planets, have both a visible and invisible history" (139; ch. 16). Daniel's Jewish history is invisible to him, and we are asked to speculate about the life he might have lived had circumstances differed. At the same time, we are kept in suspense by the fragmented chronology of the narrative, and by the narrator's hints at revelations to come.

As in *Middlemarch*, the themes of knowledge and knowing in *Daniel Deronda* function at the level of individual characters' knowledge, larger cultural pursuits of knowledge in scholarship and science, and at the level of narrative; the reader knows only what the narrator chooses to reveal. Furthermore, the novel suggests a more supernatural form of knowing in the concept of "second sight": seeing the future foreshadowed as Gwendolen foresees Grandcourt's death, Mordecai foresees the coming of Daniel and Daniel foresees the revelation of his own Jewishness.

Eliot's observation of Miss Leigh at the roulette table was the inspiration for our seeing Gwendolen at the roulette table through Daniel's eyes. His question, the first lines of the novel, "Was she beautiful or not beautiful?", has its parallel in the repeatedly asked question about Daniel's identity: Is he English? The plot that intersects with Gwendolen's involves the Jewish Mordecai Ezra Cohen. His character is at least in part a memorial to Deutsch fused with Lewes's recollections of the Spinoza scholar named Cohen, whom he used to meet at the Red Lion pub in Holborn during his student days in London. It is in Holborn that Daniel discovers Mordecai lodging in the home of the Cohen family and begins a relationship with him that will prepare him to receive the knowledge that he is not merely English but is also a Jew.

Daniel and Gwendolen are linked by coincidental circumstances arising from her move to the county where he was raised. They are also drawn to each other by sexual attraction and their respective emotional needs (hers for help and his to give it). At another, less obvious level, they represent different aspects of Eliot's own character. Gwendolen is the fatherless neurotic who lacks the restraining influence that Mary Ann Evans believed her father provided for her prior to his death, while Daniel is the reluctant father confessor that Eliot uneasily became for her young admirers. Daniel is weary of always being "leaned on instead of being invited to lean" (402; ch. 37), and is exasperated with his role of Gwendolen's confessor: "He was not a priest" (591; ch. 61). Eliot, for her part, grew tired of the pressure of advising others. In a memoir published in 1906, Georgiana Burne-Jones recalled her as saying, "'I am so tired of being set on a pedestal and expected to vent wisdom – I am only a poor woman,'" adding that this was "the meaning of what she said if not the exact phrase, as I think it was" (Collins, *Interviews* 215).

And so *Daniel Deronda*'s main characters have their origins in a combination of Eliot's personal experience and in real people she had encountered. Mordecai drew on her memories of Deutsch with his connections to Jewish tradition. Gwendolen, in turn, was inspired by Byron's grandniece, Geraldine Amelia Leigh (b. 1845), and suggested to Eliot a connection with the Romantic poets. Miss Leigh was the only daughter of Henry Francis Leigh (b. 1820), who was the youngest child of Augusta Mary Byron Leigh, Byron's half sister (Elwin 240–1). Byron's scandalous affair with Augusta caused him to leave England in 1816. Miss Leigh fascinated and repelled Eliot initially because of her gambling, rather than because of her biological connection to Byron and Augusta, though Eliot and Lewes both mention that Miss Leigh was Byron's grandniece. Apparently they did not meet Miss Leigh but only heard gossip about her at Homburg.

The unpleasant episode of Byron's affair with his half-sister had been somewhat gratuitously revived and sensationalized by Harriet Beecher Stowe, who had befriended Byron's widow on a trip to England and felt moved to defend her against claims made in a memoir by the Countess Guiccioli, Byron's married mistress in Italy after he left his wife in England. Stowe rehearsed the accusations of incest

216

between Byron and Augusta and even attempted to prove them by citing passages from his poetry. "The True Story of Lady Byron's Life" appeared in *Macmillan's Magazine* and the *Atlantic Monthly* in September 1869. Louis Crompton writes: "It caused an international furor by making public for the first time the accusation of incest" (361). Stowe's book, *Lady Byron Vindicated* (1870), incorporated many of the (mostly negative) responses to her article, further publicizing the controversy and the issues involved.

Eliot was by this time an intermittent correspondent of Stowe's. She liked and respected the American author of *Uncle Tom's Cabin* (1852) and *Dred* (1856), which she had reviewed in the *Westminster* in 1857. In letters to Stowe throughout the 1870s, Eliot expressed some of her strongest opinions and feelings, particularly regarding *Daniel Deronda*, and in turn received long letters delving into subjects, such as spiritualism, about which Eliot was skeptical. Eliot read Stowe's Byron article when it appeared. She made no secret of the fact that she found the subject distasteful, mentioning it in several letters to friends and even telling Stowe directly that she wished the matter had been left alone. Furthermore, Eliot may have been annoyed by the invocation of her work in Stowe's article (reprinted in the book): "One of the first of living writers, in the novel of 'Romola', has given, in her masterly sketch of the character of Tito, the whole history of the conflict of a woman like Lady Byron with a nature like that of her husband" (*Lady Byron* 435). Since Tito's affair with Tessa was not an incestuous one, it is tempting to speculate that the "nature" of Tito that Stowe discerned was not only adulterous but also homosexual.[8]

So while Miss Leigh's gambling clearly influenced the scene of Gwendolen at the roulette table, her associations with the history of a notorious case of brother–sister incest may have also influenced a subtext of father–daughter incest in *Daniel Deronda*. This literary/biographical genealogy linking the Romantic poets and their Victorian successors is expanded in the novel, allowing Eliot to encode a suggestion of incest, and the psychological terror it might produce if it involved childhood sexual abuse, through allusions to Romantic poets including Coleridge, DeQuincey, Byron, and Shelley. This method of communicating a sexual taboo that cannot be named recalls her practice in *Romola* of encoding homosexuality through allusions to Renaissance and classical literature.

A few critics have sought the source for Gwendolen's hysteria at the sight of the hidden panel at Offendene (revealing an upturned dead face), as well as the night terrors that lead her to sleep in the same room with her mother, in the shadowy references to her relationship with her stepfather, Captain Davilow.[9] She disliked her dead stepfather and everything associated with him, including his four daughters, her annoying, superfluous half-sisters, one of whom is blamed for exposing the secret of the locked panel and seems to intuit that the otherwise superior Gwendolen will be afraid of it, just as she is afraid to sleep alone.

The morbid, Gothic epigraph to *Daniel Deronda*, written by Eliot and appearing at the beginning of each of the eight books in both the separate parts publication and the book, sets the tone of the novel, seeming to refer primarily to Gwendolen's plot:

> Let thy chief terror be of thine own soul:
> There, 'mid the throng of hurrying desires
> That trample o'er the dead to seize their spoil
> Lurks vengeance, footless, irresistible
> As exhalations laden with slow death,
> And o'er the fairest troop of captured joys
> Breathes pallid pestilence.

The lines resonate throughout the novel, beginning in the first chapter with the references to the oppressive exhalations of the gamblers in the over-heated saloons that provide a "suitable condenser for human breath belonging, in great part, to the highest fashion, and not easily procurable to be breathed in elsewhere in the like proportion, at least by persons of little fashion" (3; ch. 1). The notion of breathing in the condensed, mingled breath of others is a powerful image that conveys the reality of a gambling salon but also provides a unique metaphor for something that is at once physical, ethereal, and intangible. To breathe in the breath of others may be contaminating and also morally corrupting, an effect of mingling with a crowd that one cannot escape.

The epigraph also resonates intertextually with other works, for example, Samuel Taylor Coleridge's "The Pains of Sleep" (1803). The poem vividly describes Coleridge's night terrors, enhanced by his opium addiction:

> Up-starting from the fiendish crowd
> Of shapes and thoughts that tortured me:
> A lurid light, a trampling throng,
> Sense of intolerable wrong,
> And whom I scorned, those only strong!
> Thirst of revenge, the powerless will
> Still baffled, and yet burning still! (*Complete Poems*; ll. 16–22)

He continues:

> And shame and terror over all!
> Deeds to be hid which were not hid,
> Which all confused I could not know,
> Whether I suffered, or I did:
> For all seemed guilt, remorse or woe,
> My own or others still the same
> Life-stifling fear, soul-stifling shame. (ll. 26–33)

While Eliot's motto may have had many influences, the repetition of specific words from Coleridge's poem is significant – "throng," "revenge/vengeance," "terror," "soul" – as is the similarity of images and concepts – crowds, trampling, guilt, and death.

That Eliot had Coleridge in mind is evident in the motto for chapter 56 from "The Rime of the Ancient Mariner" (1798), with its themes of horror, terror, guilt, and nightmares:

> The pang, the curse with which they died,
> Had never passed away;
> I could not draw my eyes from theirs,
> Nor lift them up to pray. (589; ch. 56)

Another echo of the Romantic Gothic may be heard in the scene exposing the panel with the upturned dead face.[10] The dead face foreshadows the death of Gwendolen's husband Grandcourt, but also seems to recall something in Gwendolen's past to make her react as she does. The first startling exposure of the panel elicits only shudders of disgust from Gwendolen, but its second, surprise exposure during her performance in the *tableau vivant* reduces her to hysteria. Both episodes precede Gwendolen's involvement with her future husband and the revelation of his discarded mistress and four illegitimate children. So the moral conflict and guilt she feels about marrying Grandcourt cannot account for her earlier terror of the image in the panel. But the image of the fleeing figure and upturned face returns after Grandcourt's death, when she tells Deronda that she saw the face and saw herself fleeing from it (590; ch. 56).

Eliot's representations of childhood experiences in *The Mill on the Floss* had been, together with Dickens's *David Copperfield* (1850) and *Great Expectations* (1861), important developments in the representation of early childhood trauma and in thinking about the psychological effects of such trauma.[11] Looking to childhood to explain adult behavior (neuroses and psychoses) would become standard in Freudian psychology. The portraits of Eliot's most pathological characters, Tito and Grand-court, do not provide explicit childhood experiences to account for later behavior. Yet, *The Mill* tells the story of Maggie and Tom's childhood more for the sake of explaining the intensity of childhood suffering than for explaining their adult personalities. Both Tom and Maggie are more vivid as children than as young adults, and they die before the consequences of those early years can be fully realized.

The influence of Lewes's research into the emergent scientific, medical field of psychology is particularly evident in *Daniel Deronda*. It is only there that Eliot offers revealing flashbacks to the childhood of characters in order to explain aspects of their adult selves. Daniel's (mistaken) epiphany at age 13 that he is the illegitimate son of his "uncle" Hugo imbues him with sympathy for the helpless and dispossessed. Gwendolen has remorse about past acts such as refusing to get out of bed to reach her mother's medicine and strangling her sister's canary (18; ch. 3).[12] Such memories school her to appear more sympathetic than she actually is when misfortune befalls others, for example when her cousin Rex is injured in a riding accident caused by his attempt to follow Gwendolen in the fox hunt.

Feminist criticism influenced by trauma theory has shed new light on Gwendolen's personality, calling attention to otherwise puzzling silences in the novel.[13] Gwendolen's narcissistic personality surpasses in complexity even those of Tito and Casaubon, which owed much to Eliot's self-knowledge. The repressed sense of injustice lashing out in a murder-that-is-not-one recalls Caterina in "Mr. Gilfil's Love Story." Redinger argues that "autobiographical fragments float through this story in surrealist fashion, but always centered in Caterina Sarti, who is as much an alien in Cheverel Manor as George Eliot had felt herself to be in her own home" (318). Redinger also shows that the love Maynard Gilfil has for the younger Tina when they are children reverses the love that Mary Ann Evans felt for her older brother Isaac (318). In *Romola*, we know little about Tito's past, though his fractured identity suggests (through a modern lens) childhood abuse that may predate his adoption by Baldassarre who found him living on the streets, or may be somehow connected to his relationship with his adopted father, whom he betrays and wishes to escape, though no specific motive for wanting to separate himself from the fierce old man is given.

What biographical reasons Eliot may have had for thinking about childhood sexual abuse cannot be definitively known. One possibility is the case of Charles Bray. His "seduction" by his father's cook led, by his own account, to a kind of sex addiction that he confessed to Combe (Haight, "Bastards"). If Bray told this to Combe, he may also have told it to his intimate friend George Eliot. The seduction of a boy by a woman might be transformed in fiction as the seduction of a boy (Tito) by a man or of a girl (Gwendolen) by a man. Such gender switching in the creation of characters is consistent with Eliot's infusion of herself into characters as diverse as Tito, Romola, Casaubon, Dorothea, Gwendolen, and Deronda.[14]

As a child Mary Ann Evans had occasional fits of hysteria, as well as ongoing night terrors, though the night terrors are only explicitly revealed via confessions she made to Cross and which he included in his *Life* (1:12). Gwendolen's night terrors and fits of hysteria are more mysterious than Tito's compulsive lying and appear unmotivated by experience. Yet there are hints of knowledge of various forms of childhood trauma in Eliot's fiction, the most obvious being Maggie's feeling of unhappiness at not being understood by her family and at not having her love reciprocated by Tom. The epigraph to chapter 22 of *Middlemarch*, written by Eliot, also compares the adult Dorothea to frightened child:

> A child forsaken, waking suddenly,
> Whose gaze afeard on all things round doth rove,
> And seeth only that it cannot see
> The meeting eyes of love. (180; ch. 22)

Redinger connects this epigraph with Eliot's own experience of night terrors:

> The seemingly uncaused sadness and the unending need for love were no doubt the remnants of the more violent night terrors, about which – despite their importance in her life, admitted to Cross – George Eliot was apparently reticent. Except for Cross's Sketch, there is no record of them in reported conversations or in her letters, unless (and this seems likely) they are obliquely alluded to when she wrote to Sara Hennell in 1844 about the deep sorrows of childhood . . . Nor is there any trace of it in her fiction until, as Cross notes, the appearance of Gwendolen Harleth in her last novel. Perhaps the fact of having given expression to this series of terrorizing experiences in the portrayal of Gwendolen freed her to talk about them to Cross. (63)

Redinger assumes that Eliot is drawing on these memories of her own night terrors in her portrait of Gwendolen. The narrator offers rootlessness as a cause for Gwendolen's lack of a moral foundation, perhaps in contrast to Eliot's awareness that her own sense of place supplied the memories that inspired her fiction and made her "root of piety," as she wrote (echoing Wordsworth) in the "Brother and Sister" sonnets. The broken nature of Gwendolen's family is more intriguing and intentional even than her lack of roots in a family home as an explanation for her behavior and character.

Daniel Deronda reworks familiar configurations from Eliot's previous books: second marriages, stepsiblings, absent parents, as well as close sibling relations between Mordecai and Mirah, who share the sadness over the loss of a mother and the burden of a problem father. It introduces new, frightening themes, such as Lapidoth's attempt to sell Mirah in marriage to the Count and Reverend Gascoigne's more genteel attempt to sell Gwendolen in marriage to Grandcourt, despite his knowledge of Grandcourt's mistress and illegitimate family. Reflecting on how she came to marry Grandcourt in ignorance of his past, Gwendolen feels "indignation and loathing that she should have been expected to unite herself with an outworn life, full of backward secrets" (253; ch. 27). She does not mention all the people who had this expectation for her. Later in her marriage Gwendolen refers to:

> the husband to whom she felt that she had sold herself, and had been paid the strict price – nay, paid more than she had dared to ask in the handsome maintenance of her mother: – the husband to whom she had sold her truthfulness and sense of justice, so that he held them throttled into silence, collared and dragged behind him to witness what he would without remonstrance. (573; ch. 54)

Her truthfulness and sense of justice are rendered in the powerful images of capture, torture, and possession.

Gwendolen knows very little about her father, who died when she was in "long clothes," that is, an infant. She knows that her mother's first marriage represented a happier time, even though her father's family was superior to that of her mother. Her mother exhibits nostalgia for this past by showing her daughter miniature portraits of both Mr Harleth and his mother, Lady Molly (17; ch. 3). The money inherited by Gwendolen's mother and her sister (Mrs Gascoigne, née Armyn) came from their father, who made his money from a plantation in Barbados. It may be assumed from Mrs Davilow's apparent need to remarry that Mr Harleth was probably a younger son who had no money to leave her and that his family refused to recognize her. He seems to have left no particular legacy to Gwendolen other than an Etruscan necklace made from a chain of turquoise, which she is willing to pawn after learning that her mother's and aunt's legacy from their West Indian father has been lost through a bank failure. It is this necklace that Daniel redeems for her, symbolizing, in view of later plot developments, the preeminence he places on inheritance, though he could not have known that the necklace was Gwendolen's only material link to the father she does not remember and by whose titled family she was herself disinherited.

The "Family under the Rose"

Mrs Davilow's other four daughters are the product of a second marriage to Captain Davilow, the shadowy figure who for the nine years before his death visited his family only "fitfully," indicating the unhappiness of the marriage that has made Fanny Davilow the object of her sister and brother-in-law's disapproving pity (19; ch. 3). The youngest daughter is nine years old, suggesting that something happened to estrange Captain Davilow from his wife after the birth of their fourth daughter since no further children were born in the last nine years of the marriage. Davilow's unexplained title of "Captain" has resonances with Lewes's stepfather, Captain Willim (a retired officer in the East India Company). Lewes was never fond of "the Captain," as they called him, who mistreated Mrs Willim up until his death in 1864, by which time Eliot had become friendly with her "mother-in-law."

As discussed in Chapter Three, Lewes's mother, who was not fortunate in either of her marriages, had been no more "Mrs Lewes" than Marian Evans was "Mrs Lewes." John Lee Lewes was already married with a family in Liverpool when he started a second family with Elizabeth Ashweek. He abandoned the second family, as he had the first, shortly after the birth of his third son with Elizabeth. This son, George Henry Lewes, never knew his father and may have believed that his father died shortly after his birth. There is no evidence that he ever knew the details of his father's life before taking up with his mother or of his father's subsequent career in Bermuda, where he became a "Registrar of slaves" (Ashton, *GHL* 255). Lewes's silence on the subject suggests that he may have known more than he said, especially given his close relationship with his mother until her death in 1870. Eliot's preoccupation with illegitimacy throughout her fiction and her profound concern with the influence of unknown parentage on the psychology of the son in *Daniel Deronda* also suggests that this was a subject very close to her personal experience.

Lewes's family situation, as Ashton uncovered it and as she notes, is an odd foreshadowing of his own future marital entanglements and of Thornton Hunt's children with Agnes. These children, beginning with Edmund, all bore the name Lewes and seem always to have believed that Lewes was their father. Eliot makes no mention of what legal name the four children of Lydia Glasher by Grandcourt bore, though presumably it was that of Glasher, an Irish officer whom she left along with her son for Grandcourt. In the naming of her illegitimate children, Lydia is even more like Agnes in having four children (both have a boy and three girls) whose name is that of her husband (Glasher/Lewes) rather than the children's father (Grandcourt/Hunt).[15] Glasher, unlike Lewes, however, was not available to sign birth certificates (a conveniently moot detail in fiction) or to play the role of father to them. The question of who exactly these four children believe their father to be is not addressed directly but arises implicitly when the narrator, speaking of Grandcourt, tells us that the children had no "particular liking for this friend of mamma's" (291; ch. 30). Just as the Lewes children seem to have believed that Lewes was their father (and we cannot know what they thought of their mother's friend Mr Hunt), the Glasher/Grandcourt children must have believed themselves to be the children of Mr Glasher, at least until Grandcourt dies and designates his illegitimate son the heir to his property contingent upon his taking the name Henleigh Mallinger Grandcourt (613; ch. 59). The psychological responses of these minor characters to their illegitimacy is not explored in the novel, but it is clear that, in not knowing the identity of their father, their situation is parallel to Deronda's, as well as that of Agnes's children.

It is concerning the Lydia Glasher/Grandcourt affair that Eliot makes one of the few references to divorce in her fiction, though she had written on the subject, for example, in her 1855 essay on Milton. The reason is historical. Divorce would have been impossible in the early nineteenth-century settings of her previous novels and among the provincial classes she described. *Daniel Deronda* is her only work set after the 1857 Divorce Act, which made divorce easier, though still far from easy. Significantly, the pre-history of her characters calls some attention to the date of that momentous act. Grandcourt's visit to Lydia takes place in November 1865 (286; ch. 30; Appendix 726). The oldest child was "barely nine" at this time (290; ch. 30). This suggests that the couple were at the height of their passion in 1857. The narrator tells us that "during the days of their first ardour," Grandcourt "would willingly have paid for the freedom to be won by a divorce; but the husband would not oblige him, not wanting to be married again himself, and not wishing to have his domestic habits printed in evidence" (287; ch. 30). Since even after 1857, adultery itself was not sufficient grounds for a woman to obtain a divorce, the ambiguous reference to Glasher's "domestic habits" in the clearly unhappy marriage may refer to physical abuse. Either way, the notion of domestic habits being "printed in evidence" in the case of a divorce trial resonates with Lewes's decision not to pursue a divorce from Agnes even after 1857 for fear of the publicity it would generate. Filling out the bad marriages that pervade the novel (Mrs Davilow, Mrs Glasher, Gwendolen, Mrs Cohen, and Daniel's mother), we might note that the youngest Davilow daughter, Isobel, like the eldest Glasher/Grandcourt daughter Josephine, is nine years old. Nine years ago is pointed to as a marker for the time when Mrs Davilow's marriage turned bad and Grandcourt was beginning his family with Lydia – both times when divorce might have solved marital problems and historically a time (mid-1850s) when divorce was being debated and the 1857 Act was about to be passed.

We do not know whether Mrs Davilow was physically abused by her husband, but her lack of money must have put divorce out of the question. Gwendolen contemplates leaving Grandcourt and insisting on a separation, but in playing out the fantasy, she soon sees its impracticability:

> What could she say to justify her flight? Her uncle would tell her to go back. Her mother would cry. Her aunt and Anna would look at her with wondering alarm. Her husband would have power to compel her. She had absolutely nothing that she could allege against him in judicious or judicial ears. And to "insist on separation!" (515; ch. 48)

She ultimately rejects the idea of leaving as impossible, but the spectre of "judicial" ears emphasizes that Gwendolen would have no grounds of divorce or separation for an adultery that occurred before she was married and one that she implicitly "condoned" by accepting Grandcourt after she knew about it.

The dizzying circle in Eliot's life and writing of children with ambiguous names and imprecise knowledge of their paternity is the context for Daniel's lack of knowledge, and his wrong guesses, about his parentage. The recovery of that past gives his future a purpose, makes his history continuous with that of the Jews, and gives coherence to his character. His experience of finding a people and a vocation is exceptional, but his experience of secrecy, illegitimacy, and imperfect knowledge stands in for a common real-life situation that Eliot observed in the case of Agnes Lewes's children and even in Lewes's family past. It also repeats the experiences of characters in her earlier fiction, including Eppie, Esther, and the thankless inheritor of Featherstone's property, Joshua Rigg. Illegitimacy also has a literary tradition, which Eliot notes by comparing Deronda to the Shakespearean characters Faulconbridge (*King John*) and Edmund of Gloster (*King Lear*) (402; ch. 37). It is a reality Gwendolen confronts directly when rationalizing her acceptance of Grandcourt's proposal, asking her mother whether most men have children before they are married and contemplating the experience of illegitimate children and "illegitimate fathers" (253; ch. 27).

The related idea of a hated stepfather may also be traced to Lewes's experience. Gwendolen's uncle (her mother's sister's husband who assists his sister-in-law and her five girls after the death of Captain Davilow) was himself originally Captain Gaskin (a name again recalling Captain Willim). The narrator sums up Captain

Gaskin as "taking orders and a diphthong" to become Reverend Gascoigne (23; ch. 3). Ostensibly benevolent, the Reverend is vulgarly social climbing and flirtatious with his niece, whom he sees as superior to his own daughter and therefore worthy of financial investment as a marriage prospect. Though she dislikes the displays of affection shown to her by his son Rex, Gwendolen cannot help but use her sexual attractions to impress her uncle and obtain what she wants from him, for example the horse she convinces him to buy so she will look her best when riding about the county.

At first she is less repulsed by Grandcourt's courtship than she would have expected. She thinks she can master him. But after their marriage, his mastery of her seems to be associated with terrors of her childhood, enhanced by the secret of Lydia Glasher and her four children, whom Sir Hugo describes as "the family under the rose" (614; ch. 59). Ironically, Grandcourt thinks of Deronda as his "cousin under the rose" (274; ch. 28). Gwendolen's fear of being alone at night or of finding herself alone in fields (235; ch. 24), her fits of hysteria, and her aversion to being touched or being made love to verbally by men are unexplained traits that may be connected to her hatred of her stepfather. Her resentment about her mother's remarriage and her mother's guilt and desire to compensate the daughter of her first marriage for unspecified hardships attendant upon that remarriage (32; ch. 4; 80; ch. 9) suggest something even worse than the financial conditions that led Captain Davilow to appropriate his wife's jewelry (233; ch. 24). The symbolic loss of Mrs Davilow's jewelry may contribute to Gwendolen's fit of "madness" and hysteria when Lydia Glasher returns the diamonds to her, for Gwendolen's gain of the jewels represents Lydia's loss.

All of these associations are encoded in the text and, as ever, Eliot turns to literary and historical allusion to express what she could not say directly. Gwendolen's troubled emotional, sexual, and moral condition brings together aspects of Eliot's childhood (night terrors and hysteria) with aspects of Lewes's past and the continuation of that past in the figure of Agnes Lewes (living a parallel life to Eliot's as an adulteress with four illegitimate children who were still making claims on Lewes). Gwendolen's story is also deepened by references to a specifically Romantic literary tradition – the literature and the lives of the Romantic poets particularly – in which Eliot found dramas of guilt, terror, and various forms of incest.

Eliot compared her research on Judaism to that on Renaissance Italy (GEL 5:461), and Daniel Deronda casts occasional glances at Romola, as when the narrator says of Rex when describing his love of Gwendolen that "his peace was hardly more stable than that of Republican Florence" (608; ch. 58). She had found examples from fifteenth-century Italian literature and biography to encode homosexuality in Romola, and she found an example from sixteenth-century Italian history as mediated through Romantic poetry to provide a subtext for incest and murder in Daniel Deronda. The climactic events of Daniel Deronda – Daniel's meeting with his mother and Grandcourt's death – are set in Genoa, and this part of the novel is heavy with allusions to Italian literature and culture including a motto (ch. 48) which refers to Machiavelli's opinion of Ceasar Borgia, a comparison of Gwendolen to Dante's Madonna Pia in Purgatory who is imprisoned and murdered by her husband (573; ch. 54), and Hans's comparison of Grandcourt to the Duke in Gaetano Donizetti's opera *Lucretia Borgia* (ch. 45). These connections place Gwendolen's unspeakable and unknowable experience within a literary/historical tradition. They broaden and contextualize her isolated individuality and make a modern Victorian tragedy in which no one is really murdered. The drama is internal and relies on the emotional and psychological states of hatred, intent, guilt, and remorse. But the terror and hatred are just as strong in Gwendolen as they are in the Italian counterparts Eliot invokes. Unlike Madonna Pia's Purgatory, Gwendolen's Purgatory begins on this "green earth" (573; ch. 54).

Lewes once planned to write a biography of Shelley, and he wrote several articles on Shelley's poetry that touch on aspects of his life. Research on Shelley was the means by which Lewes became acquainted with Leigh Hunt and through him Thornton Hunt. Biographers have often asserted that Shelley's life and beliefs about love, sex, and marriage influenced Lewes and Thornton Hunt's own sexual behavior. In his 1841 review essay in the *Westminster*, Lewes states unequivocally that the verse drama, *The Cenci* (1819), which Shelley dedicated to Leigh Hunt, is the poet's greatest achievement. Shelley's tragic play is based on the life of Beatrice Cenci, daughter of a sixteenth-century Italian nobleman known for his debauchery, cruelty, and sadism. In reality, the Count perpetrated a series of sexual crimes, including sodomy, but was able to remain free by paying large sums, thus becoming a source of revenue for the Pope. In Shelley's drama, he imprisons his daughter and second wife in an isolated castle. After he rapes Beatrice, she and her stepmother conspire to murder him, and this flawed plan to commit patricide is at the center of *The Cenci*.[16]

Eliot was thoroughly familiar with Shelley's works. There are glances at Shelley in *Daniel Deronda*, as when the narrator contrasts Deronda's genius to the kind that would write a *Queen Mab* at 19, as Shelley did (152; ch. 16), and in Gideon's quoting from *Prometheus Unbound* at the Hand and Banner (445; ch. 42). This may also be a look back at the young Lewes, whose attendance at the Philosopher's Club in Red Lion Square influenced this scene in *Daniel Deronda*. Lewes's interpretation of *The Cenci* is significant for the intertextual role it takes in *Daniel Deronda*. He emphasizes that in Shelley's account, Beatrice is driven to patricide only after her father had committed incest by abusing her sexually:

It is not until that "deed without a name" has been committed that she rises; and then it is not the animal but the intellectual nature which lifts itself up for revenge. She feels that such a monster must no longer blacken earth. . . . she bore all, and would have borne, but there came that which "swallowed up all consequences" – which sundering all human ties, made Cenci's death not a revenge, but a necessity. (Lewes, "Percy Bysshe Shelley" 340)

Lines from Shelley's drama treating the same unspeakable act provide the motto to chapter 54 of *Daniel Deronda*, set in Genoa, in which Gwendolen allows her husband to drown in a sailing accident. It may also have influenced the epigraph to the novel, which makes vengeance a central motif that is cryptic until Gwendolen reveals her secret thoughts to Deronda following her husband's death and links her thoughts on the yacht to those she had as a child, hating for her stepfather to come home (592; ch. 56). Earlier she had told Deronda that she was frightened of herself because of her hatred and anger toward Grandcourt (388; ch. 36). On the yacht, she felt "locked in a prison" just as Beatrice Cenci had been locked literally in her father's home. The motto to chapter 54 reads:

> The unwilling brain
> Feigns often what it would not; and we trust
> Imagination with such phantasies
> As the tongue dares not fashion into words:
> Which have no words, their horror makes them dim
> To the mind's eye. (*DD* 573; *The Cenci* 2.2.82–7)

The lines are spoken by Giacomo, one of Count Cenci's sons, who has been humiliated by his father and is now being asked by the prelate Orsino to murder him. The words refer to his own abusive treatment by that father, but also to his sister Beatrice's humiliation. In the next scene Beatrice reveals that she has been raped by her father.[17]

The quotation refers to the son's thoughts of patricide and resonates in the chapter with Gwendolen's murderous inclination toward her husband, which links back directly to the fleeing figure and upturned dead face in the panel that so terrified Gwendolen before her marriage. Generally, Eliot's mottoes suggest themes rather than referring to direct correspondences in other works, but the unspeakable horror at the center of Shelley's play is incest in the form of the father's violating the daughter, thus intimating that Gwendolen's hatred for her tyrannical (and perhaps sexually brutalizing) husband has a dim association with her hatred for her stepfather. We know that Grandcourt is sadistic and dissolute.[18] The Italian setting further encourages the atmosphere of sexual deviance as do the mottoes referring to Caesar Borgia, *Lucretia Borgia*, and Count Cenci.

On her 1860 visit to Rome, when she visited Shelley's grave, Eliot saw both the portrait of Beatrice Cenci at the Barberini Palace, which had inspired Shelley, and the sculpture by American Harriet Hosmer, whose studio she visited (*GEJ* 345–6).[19] Count Cenci was infamous for acts of both sodomy and incest. Shelley chose to focus on incest, a theme that circulates in his works and those of his wife Mary Shelley (Jack 80). Incest was also central to the Gothic novel (Perry). The Gothic elements of *Daniel Deronda* are one way in which Eliot encodes her incest theme, which may be more important to the novel as a whole than even those critics who have recognized its presence have realized.

Gwendolen was inspired by Byron's grandniece, descended from the half-sister with whom he was in love, and the scandal of whose affair had been recalled to Eliot by Stowe's 1870 book, which compares the unnamed transgressions of Eliot's Tito Melema with those of Byron. The hints of Gwendolen's violation by her stepfather as a cause of her psychic disorders and the vengeful, murderous fantasies directed at her sadistic husband are enhanced by the chapter epigraph from Shelley's *The Cenci*, a tale of incest and murder. These literary and historical antecedents and allusions add up to a dark subtext in the already dark "English part" of her novel in which Gwendolen feels herself existentially imprisoned by her own choices. But how do they relate to the "Jewish part"?

Daniel's story has its share of real and imagined sexual transgression. Mirah's father, the gambling addict Lapidoth, who returns to plague her and her brother Ezra, had once tried to sell her in marriage to a count. She feared imprisonment and escaped, but her shame was part of what prompted the attempted suicide by drowning from which Deronda saves her. She wets her cloak in preparation for drowning, exactly as Mary Wollstonecraft had done in the episode to which Eliot referred when urging her friend Deutsch not to commit suicide. From the age of 13, Daniel believed that he was the illegitimate son of his "uncle" Hugo. This leads him to sympathize with all disinherited people (including Grandcourt's illegitimate children) and also to think of his unknown mother as either an adulterer or a fallen woman and his father as a seducer. Commenting on Daniel's thoughts about Lydia Glasher, the narrator observes: "His own acute experience made him alive to the form of injury which might affect the unavowed children and their mother" (372; ch. 36).

The scene in which Daniel realizes his illegitimacy (or as it turns out falsely assumes his illegitimacy) involves his reading of Jean-Charles Sismondi's *Histoire des républiques italiennes*.[20] This important scene has been read by critics for the multiple implications it contains. He is 13, the age at which he would have had his Bar Mitzvah ceremony had he been raised as a Jew, something the first-time reader cannot know at this point in the story. He is a beautiful boy sitting at the feet of his Scottish tutor. This scene is also part of Daniel's awakening to sexual transgression through reading about the illegitimate children or nephews fathered by Popes, which leads him to imagine that his uncle is his father. It is also possible that he encountered in Sismondi a case of father–daughter incest. Sismondi publicized as a matter of historical record (as opposed to Shelley's imaginative recreation) the case of Beatrice Cenci in his *Histoire des républiques italiennes du moyen âge* (1840) (Jack 173). As in Shelley's play, the Protestant thrust of the account exposes the corruption of the Catholic Church in general and the Italian popes in particular. Eliot was familiar with Sismondi's history (which she had consulted in writing *Romola* and also later in August 1866; *GEJ* 128), and her insertion of it into Daniel's education prepares not only his misconception about his own origins but also his ready, intuitive sympathy with Gwendolen's psychological imprisonment by Grandcourt and the fear she connects with her stepfather – what Deronda calls her "hidden wound." This encoding of the incest theme reinforces links between the sexual secrets of Daniel, Gwendolen, and Mirah.

In *Daniel Deronda*, Gothic horrors mediated through Romantic tradition are domesticated and naturalized as realistic family drama. Similarly, the Greek and Shakespearean tragedies that Eliot read steadily and repeatedly throughout her life are present in the text and in the narrator's comment invoking *Macbeth* that "a moment is room wide enough for the loyal and the mean desire, for the outlash of a murderous thought and the sharp backward stroke of repentance" (33; ch. 4). It is significant that all the murders in Eliot's work are ambiguous, accidental, or uncompleted. They focus on murderous thoughts rather than actions: Tina and Wybrow, Hetty and her baby, Bertha and Latimer, Bulstrode and Raffles, Gwendolen and Grandcourt. The murders in her fiction are thus distinguished from classical and Shakespearean tragedies and from Victorian sensation fiction. But the thoughts are dark, terrifying, and real, and the language of the motto is echoed throughout the next, "Let thy chief terror be of thine own soul."

I have dwelt on the coded presence of sexual abuse because it is the secret that parallels the secret of Daniel's identity, not merely his circumcision, as argued by Herzog, but his identity more generally. His character is shaped by a secret he cannot know; Gwendolen's character is shaped by a secret only she knows. Similarly, the inability to speak about their secrets with the lone parental figures in their respective lives connects their experiences and is one of the similarities that accounts for the unusual, unspoken bond they feel for each other beyond the instant if unrecognized sexual attraction they experience upon first seeing each other. Sir Hugo knows who Daniel's parents are but never tells him, allowing for the child's and the man's misconceptions about his birth until his mother makes herself known to him. When Alcharisi is mentioned in Daniel's presence at a party, Sir Hugo turns away (375; ch. 36). Gwendolen's expression of regret that her mother remarried instantly shuts down communication between them about both her stepfather and her father. The child's isolation in not being told – and in not being able to tell – reflects Eliot's empathy with childhood suffering and recalls the young Maggie Tulliver. As the plot unfolds, Gwendolen discovers her husband's sexual secret in the form of Lydia Glasher and her children, a secret her uncle should have revealed but rather concealed from her. The pressure of keeping that secret – which she can convey only to Deronda in half-articulated confessional bursts that emphasize her guilt over taking another woman's husband and gaining from the loss of another – drives her to murderous thoughts and the borderline of "madness" (Tromp). The power of Lydia's existence and the terrible promise she exacts from Gwendolen, and which Gwendolen breaks, is intensified by childhood memories that have become part of her being: her night terrors, her hatred and murderous thoughts, which bring instant self-reproach. Daniel encourages her remorse and guilt, urging her to use them to be and do better for others.

Throughout her work, Eliot shows an awareness of the potential victimization of children and women. In Gwendolen, the dangers to the child at the hands of adults and the dangers to women even in marriage converge. Whatever happened to Gwendolen is not something represented in the novel but rather something remembered, dimly and silently. It is her unhappy lot to be abused by both a parental figure and a husband. Vulnerability to sexual use and abuse with the consequence of physically, emotionally, and economically demanding pregnancies, appears in the characters of Milly Barton, Hetty Sorrel, Gritty Moss, Molly Cass, Fanny Davilow, and Lydia Glasher. The overall picture is mixed. Some women, like Tessa and Celia Brooke, are fulfilled by bearing children. Even those who suffer from unwanted or multiple pregnancies exert an element of choice and complicity in their condition, which makes their biological vulnerability something other than victimization. But there is no doubt that Eliot is preoccupied with the biological potential and social expectation that women would bear children, and this reflects her knowledge and experience of her mother (who bore five children and lost two), her sister (who bore nine children and lost three), and Agnes Lewes, who bore nine children that we know of, two of whom died. The experience of women who do not have children, like herself and her closest female friends Cara Bray, Sara Hennell, and Barbara Bodichon, is also registered in her fiction. Janet Dempster adopts a daughter after her husband's death; Nancy Cass feels inadequate for not being able to have children and belatedly wishes to adopt her husband's daughter by another woman; Romola adopts her husband's two illegitimate children after his death; Dorothea's first marriage is childless; Gwendolen's marriage is also childless, and she is terrified that she might have children, specifically an heir to supplant Lydia's son (ch. 28). All of this adds up to the complicated feelings Eliot had about not bearing children herself and to her role as stepmother to sons who were acknowledged by Lewes as his own (whether or not they were). The situations in her fiction also reflect the shadowy presence of Agnes Lewes's other four children, who, like herself, bore the name of Lewes. Lewes pretended to be their father and in fact was their father in law, as he pretended to be Eliot's husband, which he was not in law.

It was acceptable to represent pregnancy as a condition of a woman's sexual experience in Victorian fiction. Death in childbirth and even child murder might be treated in ways that did not preclude a work's publication or popularity. More difficult topics such as homosexuality and incest needed to be encoded through literary allusions. Through such allusions, Eliot signaled her awareness of childhood sexual abuse. Tito moved in Renaissance Florentine circles where the sodomizing of young boys was prevalent. It is conceivable that he experienced this as a boy at the hands of his adopted Italian father (or others) during his childhood in Greece. Gwendolen's implied experience of childhood sexual abuse by her stepfather may have led to a character as fragmented and morally compromised as that of Tito, but one more suppressed by her Victorian, English upbringing and her gender. As always, Eliot attempted to show how the individual character developed within a specific cultural medium.

Daniel Deronda penetrates into the darkest human instincts and emotions, violations, and transgressions – sadism, murder, rape, incest, and the traffic in women – that
lie just beneath the veneer of civilization. Eliot's novels had all asked: How should one
live? But the view in *Daniel Deronda* had widened. The novel's scope is global, as befits
a world becoming accessible through technology, commerce, and conquest. It looks
beyond even the global context, with its planetary, solar, astrological references. For
Eliot, this global and universal perspective was devoid of a god, and the pressing
question remained: How should we live collectively?[21] How can a fragmented society
with no roots of piety in a native soil and with kinship structures that are falsely
propped up with lies or simply broken down through violations of trust and duty
(Captain Davilow, Mr Lapidoth, Reverend Gascoigne, the Princess) move forward
into the future? In Judaism, Eliot found a model that combined a religion of the past
with a nationalism of the future, and it was a model she embraced, even though it
could not literally be adopted by everyone.

For Eliot, Judaism represented an ideal of cultural coherence preserved over
centuries, despite persecution. In *Daniel Deronda*, she began to explore its potential as
an example of future national identity. Earlier, she had been fascinated by the Gypsies
for similar reasons, but the fifteenth-century Spanish setting of *The Spanish Gypsy*
was remote and isolated from English life. Furthermore, the culture of the diasporic
Gypsies was limited to a primitive bond of shared music and dance, preserved in a
vague racial/clannish sense of identity. In the poem, kinship is literal and devoid of
textual tradition. The Gypsies could not represent a great monotheistic culture on a
continuum with Christianity. Gypsies did not contribute to English culture in the
same way that Emanuel Deutsch, Anton Rubenstein, Benjamin Disraeli, and other
Jews with whom Eliot was familiar did. And the projected Gypsy nation in Africa was
pure fantasy, while the "return" of the Jews to Jerusalem and Palestine seemed to be a
potential reality. Fedalma is summoned by a living father while Daniel is compelled
by the writings of a long-dead grandfather only after his assimilated mother tried to
sever him from the bonds of family. She tried to liberate him from Jewish traditions
that she, as a woman, found oppressive and to make him a self-fashioned Englishman,
only to fail when his rootless soul encounters Judaism and finds a home there. Unlike
The Spanish Gypsy, *Daniel Deronda* offered Eliot's hope of regenerating a rootless,
secular, and increasingly cosmopolitan English society through the example of a
people in their midst, too often ignorantly denigrated but whose culture was
antecedent to and continuous with English Christianity.

The gambling motif is an overarching one in *Daniel Deronda*. The narrator is
explicit that Gwendolen's marriage had been a speculation and that she learns to "bear
this last great gambling loss" (379; ch. 36). The novel begins with roulette and returns
to roulette in the end – this time with Eliot's only example of an actual gambling
"mania." When he returns to London and re-enters his children's lives, Mirah and
Mordecai's father is thoroughly given over to his appetite for gambling. Lapidoth is
diseased; he is an addict. While he is unscrupulous and dishonest, he is also pitiful, and

his past as described by his daughter allows some room for sympathy both for his individual lot and for his representation of the Jew who tried and failed to assimilate. His exploitation of his daughter and his wanderings in theater and gambling circles in New York and Europe, his adulterous cohabitation with an Italian singer, and his degeneration into a depression incompletely understood by his young daughter, all suggest that he too is a kind of victim. Mirah tells Mrs Meyrick that it was his way to "turn off" feelings with jokes, that he was silent, gloomy, and prone to fits of sobbing (184; ch. 20). We do not know when or why his family left Poland and came to England, but it was possibly due to persecution. His taking that family's Polish name suggests not only a desire for disguise but a nostalgia for a lost past. Lapidoth has his parallels within the novel. He is not unlike Daniel's mother in trying to escape his Jewish past.[22] He may also be like Gwendolen's stepfather in his abandonment of his wife, his illicit activities, and his financial difficulties. His theft of Daniel's ring is the symbolic obverse of Daniel's restitution of Gwendolen's necklace. He represents one of the various fates of European Jews that Eliot records in the novel, epitomizing the personal and cultural dangers of rootlessness and thereby enforcing the implicit argument for a reconstituted, modern Jewish identity based on national aspirations in conjunction with the memory of a cultural past.

In asking English Gentiles to take an interest in a frequently maligned minority within England, Eliot went further than ever in her attempt to generate sympathy. She wrote to Harriet Beecher Stowe: "There is nothing I should care more to do, if it were possible, than to rouse the imagination of men and women to a vision of human claims in those races of their fellow-men who most differ from them in customs and beliefs" (*GEL* 6:301). She echoed this sentiment in writing to Blackwood, explaining that she sought to "widen the English vision" and "let in a little conscience and refinement" (*GEL* 6:304). In fact, in *Daniel Deronda*, she took everything further than she ever had before: the novel represents her most experimental novelistic structure, her most complex sentences, her most esoteric subjects, her most unusual metaphors, her deepest sexual secrets, and her most ambitious moral and political vision. She seemed to be pushing the limits of the realist novel genre she had helped to elevate as the dominant literary form of the Victorian period.

The novel's obsession with time and the way humans measure it in harmony with the natural world of heart beats, pulses, seasons, and the rotations of planets reflects Eliot's awareness of her own waning time on earth and the limited heartbeats left to her. This concept of conveying oneself to the future through words, or through the transmigration of souls, revives the question of posterity that she had explored in *Middlemarch* and addressed symbolically in "The Legend of Jubal," which she felt moved to publish while she was writing *Daniel Deronda*. Mordecai's impending death from consumption lends urgency to his desire to transmit his ideas to Deronda, hence the aptness of the chapter motto from Keats, also dying from consumption and desperate to express himself through his poetry (ch. 43).

Her insistence on the simultaneous naturalness and artificial arbitrariness of how we count time through the make-believe of a beginning constitutes a reflection on her art and her realism, at once as close to the real as possible but also always a representation of it. She never abandoned her belief in the need for realistic representation and her polemic against falsity in art, but the way she thought about the opposition, and the relationship, between realism and romance, as well as between realism and idealism became more nuanced and complicated at the end of her career than it had been at the beginning.

The publication of *Daniel Deronda* in eight monthly parts occurred from February to September 1876. In June, Eliot and Lewes left for a trip to France and Switzerland, returning in September. She was disappointed by the critical responses generally (December 1, 1876; *GEJ* 146), but was gratified by the positive response from the Jewish community. On December 6, she and Lewes finally purchased their own country home, The Heights at Whitley in Surrey. The house had been found for them by Johnny Cross, on whom they were increasingly dependent as a financial advisor and young friend willing to help the ageing and frequently ailing couple in a variety of practical matters. They were to enjoy two summers together at the country retreat and it was here that Eliot would write her last book, *Impressions of Theophrastus Such*.

Notes

1. Carter writes about the connection between the unification of Germany and the closing of the casinos: "The existence of gambling on German soil inspired an abolitionist effort that dovetailed with aspirations toward national unity" (186). Since casinos were often run by the French, "the fact that the final abolition of the casinos coincided so closely with the Prussian defeat of France in 1870–1 led most observers to connect the two events, interpreting the downfall of gambling as a consequence of the eviction of French cultural influences from the southern Rhineland" (189).
2. See Graham Handley's chronology (*DD* 725–7).
3. See Geoffrey Elliott, *The Mystery of Overend, Gurney & Co.*
4. Peter Briar has discovered a complete letter that was only partially published in William Baker's *George Eliot and Judaism*. This letter, now at the Rosenbach Museum and Library in Philadelphia, is of uncertain date but is probably from 1870. Again Eliot identifies with Deutsch's sensitivity and tendency to depression: "This is not to tell you what you don't know already, O Rabbi, but it is simply the discourse of a fellow Houynhym (spelling improved) who is bearing the yoke with you" (Rosenbach Museum and Library). My thanks to Peter Briar for sharing this letter with me.
5. For details about the models for Topping Abbey, see McCormack, *English Travels* (ch. 9).
6. Haight estimates her income in 1873 to be £5,000, half of it from investments managed by John Cross (*Biography* 458).
7. The argument was first published in Leavis's journal *Scrutiny* (1946–7) and again in *The Great Tradition* (1948). See Claudia Johnson, "F. R. Leavis."

8. Redinger argues that Eliot's reaction to Stowe's book reflected her discomfort with the idea of brother–sister incest, recalling feelings about Isaac Evans. But more recent criticism has made the link between the subject of incest generally and Gwendolen (Dellamora 145–6). See Crompton and Elfenbein on what was known of Byron's homosexuality at the time and the conflation of incest and homosexuality.

9. The case has been made by Penner ("Unmapped Country," 2002) and Herzog ("Tale of Two Secrets," 2005). Without citing Penner, Herzog argues: "*Daniel Deronda* develops as the interrelation between two secrets: Gwendolen's traumatic relationship with her stepfather and Daniel's ambiguously remembered circumcision" (37). Reimer goes furthest in showing the importance of this theme, arguing that the idea of incest "runs like a sinister stream through the narrative, gathering force with the author's striking choice of words, potent images, and repeated references" ("The Spoiled Child," 2007).

10. In his *Confessions of an English Opium Eater* (1821), De Quincey describes his opium-induced hallucinations/dreams: "upon the rocking waters of the ocean the human face began to appear. The sea appeared paved with innumerable faces, upturned to the heavens..." (80). Eliot mentions reading De Quincey's "The English Mail-Coach" (1849), which may have influenced the coach ride in *Felix Holt* (in which opium addiction is represented in the character of Christian).

11. It not surprising that Sigmund Freud's favorite Dickens novel was *David Copperfield* or that he admired both *Middlemarch* and *Daniel Deronda* (Jones 174).

12. On sadism in *Daniel Deronda* and *Romola*, see Fragoso.

13. In "Historicizing Trauma" (2008), Matus discusses Gwendolen's trauma after Grandcourt's death in light of her previous susceptibility. She observes that "we see the convergence in George Eliot of the manifold discourses of Lewes's psychology and the Gothic" (71).

14. Reimer argues: "Given Eliot's sharp eye for psychological nuance, especially regarding women, one can assume that she would not shy away from the reality of sexual abuse" (34).

15. Legally speaking, the husband is the father of children born to his wife.

16. Reimer mentions *The Cenci*, as well as Hawthorne's *The Marble Faun*, as potential influences on Gwendolen's story, but she does not develop the connections (35).

17. Further supporting the Romantic influence, Graham Handley notes that the manuscript of *Deronda* has a deleted motto to this chapter in the left margin. It is from Coleridge's "The Rime of the Ancient Mariner": "Alone, alone, all all alone / Alone on a wide wide sea / And never a saint took pity on / My soul in agony" (*DD* 720).

18. On the homoeroticism of Grandcourt's relationship with Lush, see Press.

19. For the story of Hosmer's and Shelley's versions of the Cenci story, see Jack.

20. This multi-volume work was published 1773–1842. Handley notes the volume Daniel happens to be reading was published in 1831.

21. Unlike her Cambridge friends Myers and Sidgwick, she could not believe in an afterlife or spiritualism. See John Beer.

22. See Brown, "Why Does Daniel Deronda's Mother Live in Russia?"

9

Impressions of Theophrastus Such
1877–9

An ancient Greek might not like to be resuscitated for the sake of hearing
Homer read in our universities...

(*Impressions* 159; ch. 18)

By 1877, Marian Evans Lewes was living a life that would have been inconceivable to the shy child Mary Ann Evans or to her pious teenage self. The world around her had changed, and by virtue of her genius and her remarkable work ethic, she had become a critically revered author, an international celebrity, and a wealthy woman with fashionably decorated homes in both London and the Surrey countryside.

She and Lewes had been in the forefront of progressive thinking and had made their own contributions to the transformations in British thought and culture that characterized the mid-Victorian period. They played important roles as transmitters of German culture to England (her translations of Strauss and Feuerbach, his biography of Goethe), and as contributors to, and editors of, journals including the *Leader*, the *Westminster*, the *Cornhill*, the *Pall Mall Gazette*, and the *Fortnightly*. Lewes had helped to popularize natural history before concentrating on his own original scientific project, *Problems of Life and Mind*. Between them, they knew well or had met many of Victorian Britain's most important thinkers and authors, including J. S. Mill, Carlyle, Ruskin, Darwin, Spencer, Huxley, Arnold, Dickens, Charlotte Brontë, Robert Browning, Tennyson, Harriet Martineau, Thackeray, and Trollope. They socialized with leading painters of the day (Leighton, Burne-Jones, Dante Gabriel Rossetti, Burton) and musicians (none of them English, including Liszt, Wagner, Joachim, Rubenstein). By 1877, their network of friends

The Life of George Eliot: A Critical Biography, First Edition. Nancy Henry.
© 2012 Nancy Henry. Published 2012 by John Wiley & Sons, Ltd.

and acquaintances had expanded to encompass dons, diplomats, businessmen, political reformers, and aristocrats.

Most importantly, in her fiction, Eliot had advanced a realist aesthetic that was underpinned by a scientific method – her studies of provincial life – and which professed in various ways at various times to be based on an ethics of sympathy for others and a belief in common humanity that stood in the place of religious belief. She experimented formally and thematically in multiple genres and maintained the popularity she established with *Adam Bede* while taking the novel genre in innovative new directions that are still being recognized and appreciated today. Now established as the greatest living English novelist, she would never write another novel, but she would write a book that reflected her thoughts on contemporary society, as well as the moral and aesthetic positions she now took from a perspective of fame, wealth, and cultural authority.

While Eliot and Lewes cultivated a literary salon in London, they also sought refuge from social demands in the country. With their new country home, they looked forward to spending ever more time away from London, but the awareness of their failing health and the limited time they had remaining now intensified, causing them both to write with an urgent self-consciousness and, in Eliot's case particularly, with an eye to posterity. In fact, it is fair to say that the idea of posterity – her own, Lewes's, England's, as well as that of a western culture that was becoming simultaneously more cosmopolitan and nationalistic – became her greatest preoccupation. Most significantly, she approached the subject from the point of view of a writer who felt a responsibility to the past, present, and future.

The subject of what writers do with their literary inheritance, and what they produce in the present to bequeath to the future, unifies *Impressions of Theophrastus Such*. Fame and success led Eliot to ask a question that had been present implicitly in her work beginning with *Romola* and continuing through *Middlemarch* and *Daniel Deronda*: Is doing and being good, diffusing oneself into a choir invisible, really a sufficient model for influencing the future, or is it imperative to strive for greatness? The question pervades *Impressions*. For example, in "Only Temper," the narrator observes ironically:

> If the bad-tempered man wants to apologise he had need to do it on a large public scale, make some beneficent discovery, produce some stimulating work of genius, invent some powerful process – prove himself such a good to contemporary multitudes and future generations, as to make the discomfort he causes his friends and acquaintances a vanishing quality, a trifle even in their own estimate. (62; ch. 6)

To do and be good and to sublimate self for the sake of others was a goal and motivation of her life, evident from her earliest letters to her late journal entries. Her fame and celebrity gave her unique opportunities to influence others (including those who were not great and famous). But it also made it impossible for her to deny that whatever she did, said, or wrote would become part of her posthumous reputation and her representation of her generation to the future. She put herself in the company of writers who would survive, not just for a generation, but long into the future, and perhaps this is one reason why she identified with an ancient Greek philosopher in her last work.

Eliot's celebrity is an interesting phenomenon. People responded to her personally with an intensity greater than that generated by any of her contemporary authors, including Dickens. The Sundays at the Priory encouraged worshipful homage, but young men and women seemed to feel toward her a combination of moral reverence and sexual attraction.[1] Young men confessed their loss of faith (Henry Sidgwick, F. W. H. Myers) and women confessed their domestic unhappiness (Georgiana Burne-Jones, Emilia Pattison). Priory visitor and author, Lucy Clifford, wrote of Eliot's admirers: "I always felt that there were those among them who, if they had been asked in the firm sweet voice to go and drown themselves in the near-by canal ... would religiously have done it" (Collins, *Interviews* 202). Among the primary worshippers were Johnny Cross and Edith Simcox (both unmarried). The triangulated way in which each of these admirers fits individually into the Lewes "marriage," and the rivalry between them, creating yet another triangle of desire, are carefully analyzed by Bodenheimer ("Autobiography"). Other particularly intense "daughters" included Elma Stuart (a widow) and Maria Congreve and Georgiana Burne-Jones, with whose husbands Eliot also had independent relationships. Only Cross, however, by dint of persistence, practical usefulness, and connections with an extended family that the Leweses valued, was admitted to the true intimacy that followed from his management of their finances.

Eliot had always inspired emotional friendships with women such as Maria Lewis and Sara Hennell (both of whom loved her, neither of whom married). Her earlier intellectual friendships with Chapman, Spencer, and possibly Bray had crossed over to the sexual. After she formed her union with Lewes, she did not allow sexual relationships to develop until she married Cross, but she invited friendships with women who she knew loved her sexually as well as emotionally. The ambiguous nature of the power she had in the lives of others is bound up with her moral positions and is perhaps most fully explored fictionally in *Daniel Deronda* through the incongruity between how the fictional Gwendolen thinks of Daniel and how he thinks of her – the importance that he has for her life and how that grows to feel a burdensome duty.[2]

Her younger friend in Coventry, Mary Sibree (later Mrs Cash), told Cross that in those days servants and friends came to Mary Ann Evans with their troubles to a degree that "oppressed" her (Collins, *Interviews* 18). In later life, Eliot felt sympathy with – and a duty to – the young people who confided in her, but they could never be to her what she was to them, as implied when she told Georgiana Burne-Jones: "'I am so tired of being set on a pedestal and expected to vent wisdom'" (Collins, *Interviews* 215).

237

That she and Lewes permitted devoted admirers to get as close to her as they did shows an intermingling of the public and private personae that Eliot cultivated once she had become a celebrity. She was ambivalent about making her personal opinions directly public and increasingly resistant to the idea of revealing details of her past or present life. Her unusual path to personal happiness and professional success had left a trail of broken family ties. Her sister Chrissey died in 1859 and her half-brother Robert died in 1864. Her celebrity had not caused her brother Isaac to relent in his refusal to communicate with her. She had contact with some of her nieces and nephews, particularly Chrissey's daughter Emily and more superficially with Robert's son, but none of her own family members were part of her intimate circle of friends.

Two of the three stepsons she had once counted as her family were now dead. With Bertie's widow and children still in Africa, Charles Lewes and his family (related neither by blood nor by law) constituted the extent of her familial circle. She cherished her bonds to Charles and Cara Bray and Sara Hennell, whom strained financial circumstances had uprooted from their once comfortable home in Coventry, but they could not enter into her life of fame or the urgent sense of cultural, even national, duty she felt as a great novelist. Or perhaps they knew her too well from the days before she became great. Spencer still visited but, apart from Lewes, Barbara Bodichon was the longest-standing and closest friend who still played a part in her life.

So the young people were vitally important to her. Bodenheimer sees Simcox as representative of her generation and her journal as "an interrogation of the life plots that would be culturally available to an ambitious young mid-century woman" ("Autobiography" 400). Eliot had traced these life plots specifically in *Daniel Deronda*. Simcox was born in 1844, as was Thornie Lewes; Gwendolen is 20 in 1864, making her an exact contemporary. Cross was born in 1840 and Charles Lewes in 1842. Charles and Thornie were her stepsons. She called Cross "Nephew" and Edith and the other young women were her "daughters." This familial language personalized the relationship with the idolizers and created an extended surrogate family with Eliot and Lewes at its head.

Yet the dynamics within the family were complicated by the nature of the young peoples' desires. Many of the conversations Eliot had with young friends in the 1870s turned on romantic relationships, some of them involving same-sex desire. The friendships with those whom Eliot called her spiritual daughters were alternately flattering and burdensome. Simcox's inability to check her ardor and Eliot's inability to reciprocate it, kept her at a distance both before and after Lewes's death. Simcox loved and revered Lewes as a fellow worshipper of Eliot but was instinctively jealous of Cross, about which Eliot and Lewes teased her (4, 21, 34). Haight, reflecting the perspectives of his own generation, angrily instructs his readers: "The Victorians' conception of love between those of the same sex cannot be understood fairly by an age steeped in Freud. Where they saw only pure friendship, the modern reader assumes perversion" (*Biography* 496). Later scholarship takes a different approach but, in fact, the language Simcox uses in her diary to describe herself is similar ("half a man") to that used by men who were just beginning to study sexuality, including Westphal, J. A. Symonds, and Havelock Ellis, who were inventing phrases such as "contrary sexual attraction" and "inversion." Edith lived and worked within a community of women who loved women, looking upon the idea of marriage with horror and struggling with Eliot's habit of urging it on her (*Shirtmaker* 4, 13–14, 34). But in other contexts Eliot could accept same-sex love, as in the case of Barbara Bodichon's sister Nannie Smith and her female partner. There was a pathological aspect to Simcox's obsession, but her explicitly homoerotic love for Eliot as expressed in her memoir makes clear that Eliot understood the nature of this love and expands our sense of her knowledge and tolerance of non-normative sexualities, even if she advised her female and male admirers to marry as a solution to their frustrated desires.[3]

This is the social context of Eliot's final years, when Lewes's at times alarming ill health inevitably made her think of her own death and of how she might survive if he died. Who would she turn to? Lewes worked steadily on *Problems of Life and Mind* as his health permitted.[4] It was becoming impossible to ignore the fact that he was suffering from a serious illness. He remained as bright and intellectually lively as ever, but his health was declining. Eliot also suffered, but her time at Witley seemed to revitalize her. There, they were within reach of the Surrey homes of the Crosses and the Tennysons, and select visitors could easily make the hour-long train ride from London. During her first summer there between June and October 1877, she took long walks and played lawn tennis. She wrote that she felt healthier than she had in years (*GEL* 6:419). Of course she and Lewes also kept up their reading. At some point, she sketched out plans for a novel that returned to the Midlands and to the early nineteenth century. Ultimately, however, she abandoned the novel in favor of the classically themed *Impressions*.[5]

Back in London for the winter, she and Lewes resumed hosting their Sunday afternoon gatherings. They also attended musical evenings and concerts with an ever widening circle of people eager for their company, including titled aristocrats and two of Queen Victoria's daughters. As Haight writes: "Social acceptance could hardly go further" (*Biography* 511).[6] At this time, she also intensified her connections with friends at Oxford and Cambridge through visits in 1877 and 1878. Her contacts included Benjamin Jowett, Mark Pattison (whose biography of Isaac Casaubon appeared in 1875), and R. C. Jebb (whose English translation of Theophrastus's *Characters* appeared in 1870). These and other Oxbridge friends in turn also attended the Sunday afternoons at the Priory.

On June 12, 1877, Frederic Harrison, the positivist and lawyer whom she had consulted about legal details of *Felix Holt* and *Daniel Deronda*, wrote to Eliot asking her to clarify her philosophical position relative to Comte's Religion of Humanity:

That you differ very much from the form which Comte has given it in such sharp lines, I know, or suppose that I know. But where you differ, wherein, how far; when you agree how far – this is what we all want to know, those who accept Comte's ritual in different degrees, and those who reject it but converge to the general idea of Humanity, as the ultimate centre of life and of thought. (qtd. in Haight, *Biography* 506)

Harrison continues in his demanding tone, claiming that all of Eliot's readers are eager to know her position: "Why, I keep asking myself, should you not quickly answer them, not by way of poetry, but by philosophy" (qtd. in Haight, *Biography* 506). He concludes with a challenge: "There are some things that Art cannot do, and one is, to tell us what to believe; and there are many who will never be satisfied till they know what you have to say" (qtd. in Haight, *Biography* 506).

This letter clearly made an impact on Eliot in its appeal to the desires of a wider readership to hear from her what to do and how to live. Her immediate response was to resurrect a poem that she had written and set aside in 1874, based on her experience talking with undergraduates at Trinity College, Cambridge. After Harrison's letter, she revised the philosophical poem, titled "A Symposium," and Lewes placed it, retitled "A College Breakfast Party," in *Macmillan's Magazine* to feed an audience hungry for any writing of George Eliot's. This decision reflects the importance of the time she spent at Cambridge and at Oxford with the Plato scholar Jowett. The form of the Platonic symposium predicts her undertaking another classical form (the character sketch) in *Impressions*. What has not been recognized is that this challenge from Harrison to provide her readers with a philosophical statement on how to live was ultimately answered in the last chapter of *Impressions*, which returned to the themes of corporate identity, Judaism, and nationalism that had become so important for her since the writing of *Daniel Deronda*.[7]

With *Daniel Deronda*, the habit of her career as a novelist to mine the past of long-stored memories was broken, and the failure to develop the new Midlands novel suggests that she had moved on. Her desire to speak out on the contemporary state of English society and culture emerged in *Impressions*, but her approach took a complicated, multiply framed fictional form that suggests her reluctance simply to pronounce her views despite requests from positivists and others. One of the many Jewish readers with whom she corresponded after the publication of *Deronda* was Haim Guedalla, who asked if he might publish one of her letters to him. In denying this permission, she wrote that "any influence I may have as an author would be injured by the presentation of myself in print through any other medium than that of my books" (*GEL* 6:289). It is unclear exactly what she meant by this, but it seems to reinforce her stance that she could not make her personal opinions overtly known but chose to filter them through her fiction. This notion of an opinion being injured if it were known to come from a particular source is echoed in *Impressions*, when Theophrastus asks: "Is it really to the advantage of an opinion that I should be known to hold it?" (7; ch. 1). Despite her increasing celebrity and social status, she clung to the separation of her self from her opinions and to the masks of her fictional narrators and characters.

A few examples of her past writings seem to anticipate the form of *Impressions*. Critics have connected *Impressions* to her first published essays, "Poetry and Prose from the Notebook of an Eccentric," serialized in the *Coventry Herald* from 1846 to 1847 (Stange). But she had traveled so far intellectually, emotionally, and socially from the positions she held when she made this early foray into fiction that it is more profitable to look to other motivations for her last work. "The Lifted Veil" showed her experimenting with a neurotic, male first-person narrator writing his memoirs with a preternatural knowledge of his own death. In her Saccharissa Essays (*Pall Mall Gazette* 1865), she had tried her only first-person female voice in writing about contemporary society. "Felix Holt's Address to the Working Men" (1868) had expressed her political views under cover of a fictional character taken from a novel. These works seem preparations for *Impressions*. Because Theophrastus is a narrator as well as character, he has all the self-consciousness of her novel's narrators, even as he provides sketches of the "characters" he meets. The book's self-referential playfulness took the meta-fictional framing and learned jokes she had initiated in *Romola* and *Middlemarch* even further. In *Middlemarch*, she had resurrected Isaac Casaubon via her character Edward Casaubon. In *Impressions*, she took the most famous subject of Isaac Casaubon's research – the classical philosopher Theophrastus – and made him into a modern Englishman and failed author (like Edward Casaubon).

Feminist critics have criticized Eliot for never representing a successful female author approximating to herself (Zelda Austen). Even her strongest female characters from Dinah Morris to Armgart and Dorothea are subsumed in the lives of others, playing out that other moral ideal of living for others that she had set aside to pursue her art and her vocation. But authorship as a subject reflecting her personal experience made its way into many of her works, most notably in the failures of Bardo and Casaubon but also jokingly in the Finale to *Middlemarch* (in which Mary, Fred, and Lydgate all become authors of modest works) and in minor characters such as Mrs Arrowpoint in *Deronda* with her "literary tendencies" (35; ch. 5).

The subject of authorship, integral to the plots and themes of *Romola* and *Middlemarch*, became the primary motif in *Impressions*. Not only is her narrator a failed author (of a humorous romance translated into Cherokee), but many of the characters he sketches are also minor authors. The moral responsibility of authorship links the chapters, in which she combines the humorous and the serious, using satire and irony as part of her broader critique of what she calls "debasing the moral currency." In chapters such as "How We Encourage Research," "The Too Ready Writer," and "Diseases of Small Authorship," she expressed her opinions via Theophrastus: the fallacious notion that anyone could be an author and thereby pollute the national archive of literature with inferior productions was detrimental to the health of the national culture. Theophrastus himself is reluctant to publish his own "impressions," not wanting to contribute to the undistinguished mass of books and leaving the judgment of whether to publish or burn his writings to an unnamed friend.

Eliot had mixed feelings about contributing anything more to a glutted literary marketplace. Complaining about the overproduction of bad literature was a displacement of her anxiety about public performance (Gallagher, "George Eliot and *Daniel Deronda*"). Throughout the 1870s, the notion that "excessive literary production is a social offense" recurs in her letters and adheres to her own fears of writing too much or repeating things she has already said, thus jeopardizing the reputation she had now achieved (*GEL* 5:18). Bodenheimer argues that she was trying to dissociate herself from her books and invest them with the power of carrying on her thoughts and her art to future generations quite apart from herself. Yet, a complete separation of her ideas and writings from herself was impossible: "when she imagines herself as a moral teacher set apart from commercial and literary worlds, she acknowledges that reputation is connected with persons, not with books" (*Real Life* 176). Her futile attempt to insist upon the separation of author from text grew with her reputation, and her desire to keep the details of her life private is part of her reaction against biographies late in her life. *Impressions* suggests that her views show an aesthetic/intellectual inclination that anticipates aspects of later literary and critical movements, including aestheticism, Modernism, and New Criticism.[8]

Formally and thematically, *Impressions* explores the inseparability of the author's "character" from his writing. Through the topic of authorship and the persona of Theophrastus, Eliot was able to address important questions of plagiarism and originality, but above all, the transmission of culture (and the self of the authors as unwittingly expressed in their pages) from one generation to the next – the moral responsibility of transmitting the present to the future. This serious subject matter is integrated into a form that allows for the play of learned jokes and social satire. The book's cryptic allusiveness and fragmentary form looks forward to the Modernist experiments with fragmenting the Victorian novel, retrospectively imagined to be somehow organically whole, even as it inveighs against Victorian hypocrisies and "moral swindlers" with a vehemence worthy of the Edwardians.[9]

Impressions of Theophrastus Such

But one cannot be an Englishman and gentleman in general: it is in the nature of things that one must have an individuality, though it may be of an often-repeated type. (55; ch. 5)

Eliot was no longer an outsider. She moved from the provinces to London and, through fame as a writer, she overcame the scandal of living with a married man.

She was well-placed within a literary establishment and within an elite circle that encompassed the best writers of her age. In her next work, she thought about the different perspectives on the world experienced by the insiders and outsiders. Though she had once enjoyed "excommunication," she now welcomed worshippers. In the figure of Theophrastus she brings together the personal experience of the outsider's exclusion and extends her analysis, begun in *Daniel Deronda*, of what we would call "marginality" and "Otherness" to a deeply felt consideration of the Jewish collective experience of diaspora and persecution. With Daniel, she created a character who was raised by an English aristocrat and understood English society from the inside, and yet never felt at home because of his suspected illegitimacy and exclusion from an inheritance to which he might otherwise have been entitled. When Daniel embraces his Jewish heritage, marries a Jewish woman, and determines to devote himself to the improvement of an international Jewish community, he does so with the unique perspective of the English insider, which the novel implies will help him to work toward an ideal of separateness with communication.

That her last major character, Theophrastus – a male, English native of the Midlands and voluntary exile to London, surrounded by friends yet feeling unloved – should be her mouthpiece for articulating the parallels and continuities between Jewish and English experience, reveals the synthetic and expansive direction her thought was taking at the end of her life. While Theophrastus is not George Eliot, he does reflect aspects of her place within an English society that was becoming increasingly cosmopolitan and less secure about its own superiority and identity. This character/narrator/author is unique in her fiction and in English literature at this time. His autobiographical chapters suggest similarities with Eliot's life and her tendency to dwell in her writings on her father's generation – the age of Wordsworth and Scott – and are her way of saying that, as an author, she is a child of Romanticism. Like Eliot, the narrator Theophrastus's mother died when he was young; his father mixed with all classes. Like her, he draws on recollections of a rural Midlands childhood to sustain him in his busy London life. He is unlike Eliot in being a man, a bachelor, and a failed author. At the same time, he is meant to be typical and general as an English man of the moment, and he describes middle-class London society and the "characters" he meets in crowded drawing rooms, at house parties, or on visits to provincial towns. Through him, Eliot meditates on the position of the observer from within and without smaller and larger social communities. He asks:

> Is the ugly unready man in the corner, outside the current of conversation, really likely to have a fairer view of things than the agreeable talker, whose success strikes the unsuccessful as a repulsive example of forwardness and conceit? (8; ch. 1)

With this question, Eliot presents the balanced perspective capable of incorporating but not privileging what Amanda Anderson calls the "excluded particular" ("Jewish

Question"). Balance and sanity were needed at a time when Eliot worried about her own sanity and together with Lewes was thinking about the relationship between mind and body. Throughout *Impressions*, she also balances the reverence for the past with optimism about the future in a manner that epitomizes her own views. Theophrastus observes: "Many ancient beautiful things are lost, many ugly modern things have arisen; but invert the proposition and it is equally true" (18; ch. 2).

The unexpected way in which she allows Theophrastus to articulate his contemporary perspective is complicated by the fact that he is a self-conscious reincarnation of an ancient Greek philosopher whose literary genealogy traces the history of the "character sketch," a sub-genre of literature that began with Aristotle, continued through Theophrastus and La Bruyère, and was an essential if not always recognized component of the novel. The connection is explicit though indirect. So her modern Theophrastus imagines that if he had lived in a different age, he would still be himself:

> I might have wandered by the Strymon under Philip and Alexander without throwing any new light on method or organizing the sum of human knowledge; on the other hand, I might have objected to Aristotle as too much of a systematiser, and have preferred the freedom of a little self-contradiction as offering more chances of truth. (16; ch. 2)

The modern Theophrastus is imagining himself as ancient Theophrastus, the student of Aristotle. But having made this identification, he then distances himself from ancient Theophrastus by referring to him, much as Nello in *Romola* refers directly to the real historical figure (Burchiello) who was also his "original" or model: "I gather, too, from the undeniable testimony of his disciple Theophrastus that there were bores, ill-bred persons, and detractors even in Athens, of species remarkably corresponding to the English, and not yet made endurable by being classic..." (16; ch. 2). This notion of learning something about the English by seeing correspondences with different ages and peoples is central to the project of *Impressions*. Through Theophrastus, Eliot encourages her readers to recognize correspondences between the ancient Greeks and the English, as well as between the English of the past and the present.

In "Looking Backward," she adopts an ironic tone toward the notion of "reform" that had preoccupied her in *Felix Holt* and *Middlemarch*:

> Certainly that elder England with its frankly saleable boroughs, so cheap compared with the seats obtained under the reformed method... its prisons with a miscellaneous company of felons and maniacs without any supply of water... and above all, its blank ignorance of what we, its posterity, should be thinking of it, – has great differences from the England of to-day. Yet we discern a strong family likeness. (*Impressions* 24; ch. 2)

This strategy of emphasizing likeness as a means of sympathizing with others and a way to self-knowledge culminates in the analogies Theophrastus draws between the English and the Jews. The book's final essay begins by stressing the need to recognize sameness, observing that "even at this stage of European culture one's attention is continually drawn to the prevalence of that grosser mental sloth which makes people dull to the most ordinary prompting of comparison – the bringing things together because of their likeness" (143; ch. 18). The chapter proceeds to draw out similarities between the Jews and the English (identifying a continuity of religious traditions) and between the diasporic nature of Jewish culture and of English colonial culture. It also urges readers to see Jewish nationalism in the light of other European nationalisms so that the theme of comparison and correspondences helps to unify the book.

Eliot's novels depend on the sketching of characters, at once particular and typical, and it seems a significant intellectual, personal, and aesthetic move that she chose to break free from the demands of narrative and focus on character types in her last work. As a collection of essays focusing on "character" and on pressing social and cultural problems of the moment, *Impressions* is not unified by a carefully constructed plot, but rather by the author/narrator/character (never actually named) whose observations, opinions, and impressions provide the lens through which the character types populating contemporary English society (though given classical, mythological, and literary names) are viewed. He is a mask, an alter ego, and also a character in his own right whose identity emerges though his descriptions of others. Turning her narrator into a character who is aware of his own biases and subjective "impressions" of others – and of the unconscious revelations he may be making about himself in writing at all – distinguishes Eliot's contribution to the character-writing genre from that of her predecessors. Theophrastus is a playful and a serious embodiment of Eliot's belief: "The best history of a writer is contained in his writings – these are his chief actions" (*GEL* 7:230). Reading first the autobiographical confessions and then the irascible and highly judgmental portraits of "the characters he meets," we are implicitly invited to wonder what knowing Theophrastus contributes to our knowledge of George Eliot and Marian Evans Lewes.

In *Impressions*, the subjects of autobiography, authorship, contemporary morality, as well as the Jews and their simultaneous relationship to nationalist movements and to rootless cosmopolitanism, are all connected in subtle ways by the voice of a Greek philosopher reincarnated as an English insider/outsider speaking about, and in some sense for, the Jews. Interestingly, one of the figures that links the ancient and the modern Theophrastus, Isaac Casaubon, had a knowledge of Jewish writings that has only recently been explored by contemporary scholars.[10] The characters Eliot's Theophrastus describes also differ from those of ancient Theophrastus or La Bruyère in that they are authors (failed, minor, or even only potential authors). This notion that everyone is an aspiring author is part of Eliot's complaint that the explosion of print debases the culture and its "moral currency" and cheapens what the present generation passes on to the next.

According to Plato scholar and Oxford don Benjamin Jowett, who recorded a conversation with Eliot in 1879, she felt it was impossible for her to write any more because she could not get over the "babble of tongues" and also that she feared to write more "because so many persons had written too much, e.g. Wordsworth and Goethe" (Collins, *Interviews* 204). It is worth noting that she puts herself in company with Wordsworth and Goethe. The preoccupations of *Impressions* confirm the observations of Lord Acton (who placed Eliot second to Shakespeare) that "she became, in her latter years, anxious about the stability of her fame. It was in her system to look far ahead, to fix her eye on a future generation," because, Acton thought, she believed that genuine merit "escaped reward" (Collins, *Interviews* 193). The notion that quality is exactly what might not be valued in the future is ironically reflected in *Impressions*, for example in "A Man Surprised at His Originality," when Theophrastus at first assumes that Lentulus "held a number of entirely original poems, or at the very least a revolutionary treatise on poetics, in that melancholy manuscript state to which works excelling all that is ever printed are necessarily condemned" (42; ch. 4). At the same time, *Impressions* displays that tension between the ambition to do something great for mankind and the resolution simply to do good for one's neighbors, as in "Only Temper," in which Theophrastus wishes the bad-tempered man Touchwood would "produce the great book which he is generally pronounced capable of writing ... because I should then have steady ground for bearing with his diurnal incalculableness, and could fix my gratitude as by a strong staple to that unvarying monumental service" (60; ch. 6).

Theophrastus suggests the burden that Eliot felt her greatness to be, even as it was the fulfillment of her ambitions. The role of great author was not always one she could play so she took refuge behind the mask of a narrator who is a failed author (modern Theophrastus). But this modern narrator is textually linked with an important though largely forgotten philosopher whose writings were resurrected and translated from Greek into Latin by Isaac Casaubon, an historical figure with an indirect link to her character, Edward Casaubon. The translator of Theophrastus, Isaac Casaubon, was revived in the late nineteenth-century via the biography of her friend, Mark Pattison at Oxford, while Theophrastus's *Characters* were translated into a new modern English edition by another friend, R. C. Jebb of Cambridge. These modern scholars, also part of her social circle, kept Theophrastus alive in "posterity." Again reflecting this central tension, modern Theophrastus reflects that, had he lived in the age of the ancient Theophrastus, he might have been "one of those benignant lovely souls who, without astonishing the public and posterity, make a happy difference in the lives close around them, and in this way lift the average of earthly joy" (16–17; ch. 1).[11]

We know relatively little about the composition of *Impressions* between June and October of 1878, or about why Eliot decided to resurrect the ancient Greek philosopher and produce a modern version of his *Characters*. In contrast to her other major works, there is little correspondence about it and no notebooks specifically documenting the research she did to produce it, though many of the allusions in the book are to works she cites in notebooks for *Middlemarch* and *Daniel Deronda*.[12] *Impressions* must be understood as an experimental departure from, and self-conscious reflection on, her career, written rather quickly during a relatively tranquil and secluded period when she was living at Witley and was not yet so alarmed by Lewes's health as to prevent her from writing. She could not have known that *Impressions* would be her last work, and she contemplated a second volume if the first succeeded (*GEL* 7:126). She also did not consider it to be as serious a work as her novels and there is no evidence that its writing occasioned the kind of doubts and anxieties that her novels had (*GEL* 7:81), though she would later have a different kind of anxiety about its publication. Perhaps for this reason, its tone is ironic and humorous, and yet the writing is no less dense – it is in fact extremely dense with cryptic allusions and learned jokes. The topics and themes provide insight into her aesthetic, political, cultural, and moral positions at the end of her life, and the book stands as her last and most explicit commentary on the problems of authorship generally (originality, plagiarism) and in her experience particularly.

In "Silly Novels by Lady Novelists," the future George Eliot had defined her aesthetic ground at the expense of female contemporaries and their frivolous productions. She had asserted the need for realism in fiction through merciless criticism of formulaic popular novels, which she divided into "species," dissecting their flaws. It was not until *Daniel Deronda* that she introduced a silly lady writer as a character. Mrs Arrowpoint is not a novelist but rather a fanciful biographer whose wealth allows her the leisure to dabble in literature. Specifically, she writes about Tasso: "So many, you know, have written about Tasso; but they are all wrong ... they are all wrong. I differ from everybody" (37; ch. 5). She makes this statement to Gwendolen, who greets it with meaningless banter intended to make an impression on her wealthy neighbor: "I like to differ from everybody. I think it is so stupid to agree" (37; ch. 5). Mrs Arrowpoint responds with seriousness about her work: "Ah, his life is more interesting than his poetry. I have constructed the early part of his life as a sort of romance. When one thinks of his father Bernardo, and so on, there is so much that must be true" (37). The silly babbling reminds us of Mr Brooke (who had pretensions to write). More importantly, that Eliot's only authoress should be a biographer whose beliefs ("his life is more interesting than his poetry") are directly opposed to Eliot's ("the best history of a writer is contained in his writings") and who turns the life into fiction, is a reflection of Eliot's thoughts about frivolous female writing, the democratization of authorship generally, and the casual, distorted approach to biography that made her refer to it as a "disease" of English literature. She would take up all of these themes in *Impressions*.

247

Authorship, Originality, Plagiarism

We know Theophrastus only through his own words and not by what any narrator tells us about him. He reveals himself by telling us about other characters. Most of these characters are themselves minor authors. Collectively, their triviality is debasing the moral currency and the culture. Implicitly in the structure of the work, as well as explicitly throughout, Eliot challenges, even deconstructs, the idea of "originality" both literarily and in terms of personalities. This harkens back to some of the bizarre incidents in her career, such as the claims of living people to be the originals for fictional characters, the Liggins affair in which someone else claimed to have written her books, and Swinburne's accusation that she had plagiarized parts of *The Mill* from Elizabeth Gaskell.[13] "The Wasp Credited with the Honeycomb" in *Impressions* (ch. 11) addresses the folly of wrong guesses about authorship and the subject of plagiarism. It seems to respond directly both to the old Liggins incident and the Swinburne accusations. She could not know that Priory visitor and friend of Charles Lewes, H. Buxton Forman, would become involved in forging her poetry (*Poetry*; GEL 9:37).

She addressed such questions cryptically and philosophically throughout the chapters of *Impressions*, beginning with the very notion that her narrator/character Theophrastus was not wholly "original" but rather was a modern version of a "dead philosopher" (Theophrastus). Now she skipped over Casaubon and resurrected Theophrastus, whose *Characters* Casaubon first proved to be "authentic" (i.e., written by Theophrastus), and with an awareness of La Bruyère, who is also quoted in the text. In "How We Encourage Research," Merman (a hybrid of fish and man) is the unlikely hero of the story and, like *Middlemarch*'s Edward Casuabon, whose rivals have fish names like Carp, Pike, and Tench, goes up against scholars figured as sea creatures such as Grampus, Narwhal, and Sperm N. Whale. Here, as elsewhere, Eliot is making jokes about her past fiction as well as probably about Lewes's natural history researches.[14] In this respect, she took the self-referential game-playing in which she had indulged in *Middlemarch* even further in *Impressions*, which links itself to *Middlemarch* through the Theophrastus–Casaubon connection and to *Daniel Deronda* through the consideration of Jewish nationalism.

Impressions thus contains both a theory of history and a theory of character. The historical idea is that there are character types. These may be or seem consistent from one era or epoch to the next, but they are also at the same time always distinctive in their historical moment. The interplay of the individual and type evokes the language of Darwinian evolution, as had the same interplay in *Middlemarch* (the ideal type of St Theresa, the situated individuality of Dorothea). Like the hypothetical time-traveling Renaissance Florentine citizen who returns to modern Florence in *Romola*, Theophrastus speculates that he would have the same character if he were transported back to ancient Lesbos, the birthplace of Theophrastus. The "Too Deferential Man," an Athenian type transformed into an Alsatian named

Hinze, has his individuality, though of an "often-repeated type" (55; ch. 5). The theory of individual character turns on the double meaning of "character" as a moral identity of individuals and as a fictional invention, hence Theophrastus measures the characters he meets according to a standard of "high character": "it is essential to what is worthy to be called high character, that it may be safely calculated on, and that its qualities shall have taken the form of principles or laws habitually, if not perfectly, obeyed" (61; ch. 6). The notion of repeated national types and a high ideal of national character follows from this individualized concern with moral behavior and types. At the same time, for the novelist, characters are fictions. *Impressions* frees its fictional characters from the confines of a story and also from history, as suggested by all the metaphoric time traveling that occurs in the chapters (to early nineteenth-century England, to ancient Athens and Lesbos). In this way, Eliot can examine the individuality and the typicality of all the characters (including Theophrastus), thereby revisiting questions about originals and characters, reality and fiction, that had been facets of her career, and themes of her art, from the beginning.

In 1858, for example, she responded to Sir Roger Newdegate's claim to have worked out a key for all the characters in "Mr. Gilfil's Love Story" with a denial and a differentiation of story and history, saying to Blackwood that she could not furnish a key herself: "But where there is no exact memory of the past any story with a few remembered points of character or of incident may pass for a history" (*GEL* 2:460). Reponses to her fiction forced her to think about the relationship between the history of her life and the stories she made up. *Impressions* is, among other things, a response to the reactions of readers to her work over the previous 20 years.

The personalized historical connections and identifications between scholars and authors are registered in the project of resurrecting Theophrastus as a modern English author (whose work was originally imagined to be "edited" by George Eliot). While the first 17 chapters of *Impressions* have little to do with the Jews or Jewish history, the last chapter is a tour de force that brings together the correspondences between the English and the Jews (the continuities of their religions, the similarities of their modern diasporas) with the textual genealogies the book has been implicitly tracing through its allusions to literary works from a variety of periods and cultures. The interplay between past and present – the notion of textually stored memories providing a basis for a national character – lies behind the forceful argument for nationalisms generally and Jewish nationalism in particular in "The Modern Hep! Hep! Hep!"[15]

Theophrastus explains in "The Modern Hep! Hep! Hep!" that the English know who they are: "Because there is a national life in our veins. Because there is something specifically English which we feel to be supremely worth striving for, worth dying for, rather than living to renounce it" (147; ch. 18). The Jews too feel their sense of collective identity, and have a right to a national homeland comparable to that of other modern nations. It is a bold argument, which was articulated by Mordecai in *Daniel Deronda*. Even in *Daniel Deronda*, the affinities with other nationalisms are invoked, as when Mirah sings Leopardi's "Ode to Italy" (414; ch. 39), a contrast to Gwendolen's singing of Bellini, which Klesmer pronounces is the expression of a "puerile state of culture" of people "without any breadth of horizon" (39; ch. 5). But the advocacy of Jewish nationalism by Theophrastus in "The Modern Hep! Hep! Hep!" is more direct and contextualized in relation to other nationalisms. Breadth of horizon is what the Jews are seen to have, and Eliot uses the voice of her Englishman to expose that model of breadth and depth to his English readers so that they will see the Jews in themselves and themselves in the Jews.

But the application of the spiritual nature of nation and culture is broader than just the case of the Jews: "The eminence, the nobleness of a people depends on its capability of being stirred by memories, and of striving for what we call spiritual ends – ends which consist not in immediate material possession, but in the satisfaction of a great feeling that animates the collective body as with one soul" (146). The language recalls that of Mordecai, but it also serves as Eliot's answer to the call from positivist Frederic Harrison in 1877 to state her opinions about what to believe, "not by way of poetry, but by philosophy": "There are some things that Art cannot do, and one is, to tell us what to believe; and there are many who will never be satisfied till they know what you have to say" (qtd. in Haight, *Biography* 506). Eliot chose to answer indirectly, via Theophrastus – an individual and a type, a failed author and everyman as well as a Greek philosopher. Here she shifts her focus from the question of how common people should live to the question of how to be "great":

> An individual man, to be harmoniously great, must belong to a nation of this order, if not in actual existence yet existing in the past, in memory, as a departed, invisible, beloved ideal, once a reality, and perhaps to be restored. A common humanity is not yet enough to feed the rich blood of various activity which makes a complete man. (147; ch. 18)

Through Theophrastus, Eliot gives her final answer to the positivists about where she stood on the question of whether a "common humanity" could suffice as a moral foundation for a modern world. It is "not yet enough" and "the time has not come for cosmopolitanism to be highly virtuous" (147; ch. 18). In the Jews, she did not find a model of religion but of a racially and culturally unified "nation" that did not yet have a geographic center. Yet the choice of the Jews should not obscure the fact, prepared for by *The Spanish Gypsy* and *Daniel Deronda*, that it was national identity she saw as providing social energy and feeding the ideal – supplying the modern spiritual needs that remained in the vacuum left by the displacement of religion.

In "The Modern Hep! Hep! Hep!" Theophrastus stresses that national affiliations "humanize" us, thus following up on the radical questioning of humanness in the previous chapter, "Shadows of the Coming Race," and possibly explaining how the original order of the last two chapters came to be reversed. Originally, the futuristic image presented in "Shadows of the Coming Race," of machines developing the capacity to reproduce themselves and evolving to supplant human beings, concluded the book (xxxiv; Introduction). "Shadows of the Coming Race," a parody of both evolution and degeneration theories and part dialogue between Theophrastus and his friend Trost, shows Theophrastus not merely imagining his own death in the future, as he did in the first chapter, "Looking Inward," but imagining the death of the human race, and becoming almost hysterical as a result. He imagines that machines will be superior because they will not be troubled with "screaming consciousnesses which, in our comparatively clumsy race, make an intolerable noise and fuss to each other about every petty ant-like performance" (139; ch. 17). He imagines the degeneration of the human race, particularly the hyper-conscious intellectuals:

> As to the breed of the ingenious and intellectual, their nervous systems will at last have been overwrought in following the molecular revelations of the immensely more powerful unconscious race, and they will naturally, as the less energetic combinations of movement, subside like the flame of a candle in the sunlight. (141; ch. 17)

While Eliot may have herself in mind when she has Theophrastus imagine the fate of the self-conscious intellectuals, it is tempting to think that the image of the flame may allude to Walter Pater's Conclusion to *Studies in the History of the Renaissance* (1873) with its call to burn with a "hard gem like flame." If so, she is gesturing here to the emerging aestheticist movement and its overwrought nervous sensibilities to external impressions, which she had already cryptically condemned in the chapter on "Moral Swindlers." There, Theophrastus remarks that even this generation will agree that there never can exist "such a combination as that of moral stupidity and trivial emphasis of personal indulgence with the large yet finely discriminating vision which marks the intellectual masters of our kind" (136; ch. 16). She had, after all, agreed with the critique of Pater offered by her friend R. C. Jebb on a visit to Cambridge in 1873 when he said, "[*à propos* of Pater's essays on the Renaissance] that the 'precious' school seemed to be destroying everything – their finesses and small affectations blinding people's eyes to the great lineaments of the great creative works" (Jebb 155). Interestingly, Cross paraphrased what he believed to be Eliot's ultimate view about the value of culture in a manner that seems a similar refutation of the emerging doctrine of "art for art's sake": "Culture merely for culture's sake can never be anything but a sapless root, capable of producing at best a shrivelled branch" (*Life* 3:427–9).

The nationalism of "The Modern Hep! Hep! Hep!" is a rejection of positivism's Religion of Humanity and of the early expressions of what would become aestheticism. The essay picks up on the ironic notion of a burdensome consciousness from "Shadows of the Coming Race" as part of its final answer to the question of what makes us human. Writing of the Jews specifically, Theophrastus asks:

Are they destined to complete fusion with the peoples among whom they are dispersed, losing every remnant of a distinctive consciousness as Jews; or, are there in the breadth and intensity with which the feeling of separateness, or what we may call the organized memory of a national consciousness, . . . the conditions present or approaching for the restoration of a Jewish state [?]. (162; ch. 18)

While the emphasis of "The Modern Hep! Hep! Hep!" is on the Jews, taken in the context of the whole of *Impressions*, the Jews become an example of the traits that make humans human, and the essay-like form of the book, even within the complex self-conscious fiction of Theophrastus as a character, seems to answer the challenge laid down by Harrison for Eliot to give her readers a philosophical statement of her views.

Throughout "The Modern Hep! Hep! Hep!," Theophrastus dwells on the human value of national affiliations: "The pride which identifies us with a great historic body is a humanising, elevating habit of mind, inspiring sacrifices of individual comfort, gain, or other selfish ambition, for the sake of that ideal whole; and no man swayed by such a sentiment can become completely abject" (156; ch. 18). Again, Eliot seems to address the positivists' questions of what exactly she thought about the Religion of Humanity and what she thought "we" should do. She does so by suggesting that without the differences and the bonds of national affiliations (national families), the idea of a common humanity becomes meaningless. It is a philosophical position that responds to the threat of "cosmopolitanism," which, like the fusion of races, she nonetheless seems to think would be the ultimate future of humanity.

Further complicating this advocacy of national affiliation, Theophrastus insists that the "idea of nationalities" is a modern idea that can be usefully deployed to retain and protect the integrity of national characters and cultures. Unsurprisingly, given the personal self-reflexive nature of Eliot's narrator/character, he is also self-conscious about how national identities come into being. Nations are imagined communities that incorporate past memories and textual/cultural traditions – tell stories – to make and remake themselves: "The tendency of things is towards the quicker or slower fusion of races. It is impossible to arrest this tendency: all we can do is to moderate its course so as to hinder it from degrading the moral status of societies by a too rapid effacement of those national traditions and customs which are the language of national genius" (160; ch. 18). And, he adds crucially, "it is in this sense that the modern insistence on the idea of Nationalities has value" (160). Nationality is a modern idea, an idea that is right for the historical moment because it represents the attempts by groups of people to control the natural tendencies to the "effacement" of difference and fusion into other groups. Fusion is a kind of cultural extinction that Eliot believes can be slowed down if not prevented. Theophrastus ends the chapter and book with a final assertion of national feeling of separateness presented in contrast to the Religion of Humanity which would erase or blur national distinctions in one common humanity, a "theory" of human well-being, Theophrastus suggests, that robs human beings of some of their most noble qualities of allegiance and self-sacrifice for a higher cause: "Will any one teach the nullification of this feeling and call his doctrine a philosophy? He will teach a blinding superstition – the superstition that a theory of human wellbeing can be constructed in disregard of the influences that have made us human" (165).

The question arises of how exactly Eliot saw her (non-Jewish) friends and readers relating to these ideas and ideals, since few among them were being called to make sacrifices. If they were, it was most likely in a colonial context, whereas "The Modern Hep! Hep! Hep!" is sharply critical of colonialism. The dwelling on the ideals of national sacrifice may explain why the unwritten novel she was contemplating at the same time focused on war, military service, and treason – themes she had not previously explored. In projecting a differentiated nationalist future, she secured her role as the great national writer whose works would be transmitted, preserving distinctive national memories of an earlier England, as they in fact do. It gave her the hope of living on, through her books, in an English national future.

Notes

1. The phenomenon is explored in Kathleen McCormack's *George Eliot in Society: Travels Abroad and Sundays at the Priory* and illustrated in the excerpts collected in Collins, *Interviews*.
2. Bodenheimer sees Daniel's rejection of Gwendolen as a reflection of everything Eliot had "learned and extrapolated from her relationships with worshipers, everything she forebore to indicate in personal writing or conversation, which made its way into the startlingly original depiction of Daniel's mentorship" (*Real Life* 257).
3. The manuscript of *Autobiography of a Shirtmaker* was first mined by K. A. McKenzie (*Edith Simcox and George Eliot*). A complete annotated edition with an introduction that explores the complex nature of the relationship was published by Fulmer and Barfield (*A Monument to the Memory*). For insightful scholarship that takes Simcox and her work seriously, see Gillian Beer, "Knowing a Life," Bodenheimer, "Autobiography," and Rosenman.
4. Vol. I, *The Foundations of a Creed* (1874), Vol. II (1875), Vol. III, *The Physical Basis of Mind* (1877), all published by Trubner.
5. Eliot left ten manuscript pages and notes toward a novel set in the Midlands during the Napoleonic Wars, which have been dated to some time between 1877 and her death in 1880. See Baker, "A New George Eliot Manuscript." She also left notes for this novel (now at Princeton), which show the subject matter to include the intriguingly new topics of war, military life, and espionage.
6. Recent scholarship has fleshed out the names that are recorded in Lewes's detailed (and still unpublished) journals, in which he lists the visitors to the Priory Sundays. See McCormack, *George Eliot in Society*.
7. For a discussion of "A College Breakfast Party" in the context of her Cambridge visits, see Fleishman, ch. 10.
8. On Eliot as proto-Modernist, see K. M. Newton, *Modernising George Eliot*.

9. Bodenheimer intriguingly argues that with the Daniel–Gwendolen relationship Eliot represented the limits of sympathy on which her literary realism and her moral teachings had been predicated: "Once she had deconstructed sympathy, the fictional form she had shaped was as obsolete for her as it would be for the young writers of the next generation" (*Real Life* 265). This is a possible step toward explaining why she turned from a contemplated historical novel to the new fictional form and content of *Impressions*, in which the plea to sympathize with others becomes a more rationalized plea for tolerance.

10. New scholarship by Anthony Grafton and Joanna Weinberg has revealed the extent of Isaac Casaubon's interest in the Jews and Jewish texts, and that "Hebrew studies played a vital role in his life and thought" (30). Eliot may have known about Casaubon's Hebrew scholarship through Pattison, who examined Casaubon's unpublished manuscripts and marginalia (Grafton and Weinberg 14), but more importantly, the interest in Judaism shows a shared sensibility with Isaac Casaubon that went beyond the creation of the character Edward Casaubon (from whom Dorothea hoped to learn Hebrew).

11. For further correspondences between Theophrastus of Eresus and Theophrastus Such, see Paul Millett, *Theophrastus and his World*.

12. Chapter drafts are at the Huntington Library. We do not know how the published version came to differ from the bound manuscript (at the British Library).

13. Lucy Clifford recalls that she became angry and "almost vehement" in defending herself against the gratuitous charge of unacknowledged borrowing from Gaskell that Swinburne made in his *A Note on Charlotte Brontë* (1877) (Collins, *Interviews* 200).

14. On "How We Encourage Research," see Andrew Miller, "Bruising, Laceration, and Lifelong Maiming."

15. On Eliot's "social-conservative politics of tradition" and "politics of national inheritance" throughout her career (143), especially in relation to positivism, see Semmel. On the concept of culture in *Impressions*, see also Fleishman, *George Eliot's Intellectual Life*.

10

The Final Years
1879 to Cross's Life

"[O]ne would have thought she would have selected a philosopher to lean on more than a businessman . . ."

(William Blackwood to Joseph Langford)[1]

When asked about the convenient deaths that occur throughout her fiction, the deaths that seem to resolve the problems of those who die, or of those around them, George Eliot defended the reality of her stories, maintaining that they were true to what she had observed in life. Her words were recalled from a conversation that occurred in 1880, shortly before her death, by Soph'ia V. Kovalevskaia, a young Priory visitor whom she first met in 1869 and who published her recollections of Eliot in 1885:

> I personally cannot refrain from the conviction that death is more logical than is usually thought. When in life the situation becomes strained beyond measure, when there is no exit anywhere, when the most sacred obligations contradict one another, then death appears; and, suddenly, it opens new paths which no one had thought of before; it reconciles what had seemed irreconcilable. Many times it has happened that faith in death has given me the courage to live. (Collins, *Interviews* 224)

Though the exact words are not Eliot's and are paraphrased by Kovalevskaia, the sentiment seems consistent with the story of Eliot's life. We do not know what problems her mother's death may have resolved, but her father's death opened the path that led her to London, George Henry Lewes, and a career as a novelist.

The Life of George Eliot: A Critical Biography, First Edition. Nancy Henry.
© 2012 Nancy Henry. Published 2012 by John Wiley & Sons, Ltd.

Among the many timely deaths in her fiction, Maggie Tulliver's death reconciles an irreconcilable problem of how she would go on living when both her community and her brother had rejected her. In *Silas Marner*, Molly's death allows Silas to find Eppie and Dunstan to marry Nancy. In *Middlemarch*, Casaubon's death releases Dorothea from the promise to complete his Key to All Mythologies and frees her to marry Will Ladislaw. In *Daniel Deronda*, Grandcourt's death liberates Gwendolen from an intolerable marriage in which she felt increasingly imprisoned. The Princess's terminal illness leads her to reveal Daniel's Jewishness to him just when he was ready to receive that information. Mordecai's death, with which *Daniel Deronda* ends, is perhaps the most "logical," since, having found in Daniel the soul in which his own might live on, he dies in peace, leaving his sister Mirah and Daniel free to pursue a new course that promises to be consistent with his greatest hopes. Deaths in many of Eliot's novels may be timely in terms of plot, and in retrospect deaths observed in her own life may have had a kind of logic. In fiction and in life, death marks profound changes for those who survive.

The Leweses arrived at Witley in June 1878, and during that quiet summer while she was writing what would be her last book, she could not fail to see that Lewes's health was deteriorating. While she was writing *Impressions*, Lewes did his best to read and take notes for the final volumes of *Problems of Life and Mind*. He had been suffering from stomach and intestinal cramps for months and, over the summer, his pain was so acute that he could do little other than walk for relief and sleep. On August 6, he wrote to John Blackwood explaining why he and Eliot could not come to Edinburgh as they had planned: "I can't work at all, and can't read for more than an hour" (*GEL* 7:50). Poor health had always interrupted the writing of the industrious couple, but they both seemed to recognize that this disabling illness was different. Visits from friends, musical evenings, and poetry readings provided diversions from the seriousness of his condition, which they would confront upon their return to London on November 11.

Within a week of their return, Lewes was in agony. James Paget diagnosed the problem as "thickening of the mucus membrane" (Ashton, *GHL* 276), but there was little he could do to help the situation. Lewes dosed himself with "blue pills" and castor oil (Ashton, *GHL* 276). The last entry in his journal on November 20 recorded hopefully, "The storm has passed I think!" (Ashton, *GHL* 276). During a brief respite on November 21, he sent the manuscript of *Impressions* to Blackwood with a note informing him that it was Eliot's "work of the last few months, and it is *not* a story" (*GEL* 7:81). But his symptoms returned. Paget consulted another specialist, but they could offer no hope. Charles Lewes stayed with them constantly. Edith Simcox, who was not admitted, lingered outside the Priory gates and spoke with both the servants and the doctors. Her account gives a sense of the dismal, sad week during which Lewes lay dying. On November 28, she records: "All day yesterday the rain fell . . . somehow I did not dare to go and

Figure 26   George Henry Lewes with Pug, photograph by John and Charles Watkins, 1864 (© National Portrait Gallery, London)

ask and came to the house this morning with a deadly fear" (Simcox 50). At the end, John Cross, whose mother was also dying, was called in to consult on financial matters. On November 30, Lewes died.[2] He was buried at Highgate Cemetery on December 4, 1878. A Unitarian minister, Dr Thomas Sadler, performed the service.

Eliot did not attend the funeral, and she did not leave her room for a week. She had long contemplated and feared the moment of being left alone without Lewes. Writing to Barbara Bodichon as early as 1862, when Lewes was ailing, she reflected: "Those only can thoroughly feel the meaning of death who know what is perfect love" (*GEL* 4:14). And she sympathized with Queen Victoria's loss of her husband Prince Albert in 1861 because, "I am a woman of about the same age, and also have my personal happiness bound up in a dear husband whose loss would render my life simply a series of social duties and private memories" (*GEL* 4:417).

Soon she determined that the most immediate task before her was to complete Lewes's unfinished manuscript of *Problems of Life and Mind*, which lay in the fragmented state in which his illness forced him to leave it. Through this act, she could memorialize her "husband" of 24 years by assuring that his research was published. In this work, she could also find strength to go on living through her grief. The endeavor proved daunting and exhausting, lasting over several months, but the simultaneous intellectual focus and feeling that she was inhabiting Lewes's words in order to turn his research into a book that would make a contribution to science, enabled her to survive what might otherwise have been unendurable pain at his death.[3]

She saw only Charles, and did not step outside or begin answering the many letters of condolence until January 1879. She asked Blackwood to set aside the proofs of *Impressions* until she had finished her work on *Problems*. Lewes's manuscript presented numerous challenges, and she suffered physically from the strain of making it cohere. But she felt that, in finishing his book, she was living with him. Not surprisingly, she even felt that she had been visited by his presence (January 23, 1879; *GEJ* 159). She made an editorial decision to break up the existing material into two volumes. The short fourth volume was published as *The Study of Psychology* (1879). Perhaps because this volume is the most coherent, it became the most influential part of Lewes's work in the history of science. The longer fifth volume was published under the title, *Mind as a Function of the Organism* (1879).

With this editorial work well under control, she was able in March 1879 to move on to correct the proofs of *Impressions*, but she was anxious about how the timing of the publication would look to her public. She had deferred the publication because she was unable to read the proofs, and also because she did not want a new book of hers to appear just after Lewes had died. She was concerned that it might appear as if she had been writing this book during Lewes's illness, and so she arranged to have a special publisher's note inserted at the front of the volume: "The Manuscript of this Work was put into our hands towards the close of last year, but the publication has been delayed owing to the domestic affliction of the Author." *Impressions* finally appeared in May 1879, and she received her first copy at the same time as she received *The Study of Psychology*.

Picking up a theme of his biography, Haight writes that during the difficult time following Lewes's death, "She had no one to lean on" (*Biography* 517). In saying this, he looks forward to Eliot's marriage to John Cross, which was an act that confounded many of her contemporaries. It remains the subject of speculation by biographers, and has even captured the imagination of fiction writers.[4] Why Eliot was drawn to Cross is not such a mystery. He had been close to her and Lewes, and they had come to rely on him for the management of their real estate and investments. Following Lewes's death, Eliot needed a reason to live, as well as practical help to meet her financial responsibilities, especially to Lewes's extended family. Writing, other than to finish *Problems*, hardly seemed possible.

Charles was devoted to her but had a family of his own. The vibrant presence of a younger friend, in whose generation she had taken such an interest, led her down a new path, regardless of what society might think. On January 22, 1879, she wrote to Cross:

> Dearest Nephew,
> Some time, if I live, I shall be able to see you – perhaps sooner than any one else. But not yet. Life seems to get harder instead of easier.
> Yours ever
>
> M.E.L. (*GEL* 7:97)

As she emerged from her seclusion she resumed business and personal correspondence. She signed one of her first letters, to Barbara Bodichon on January 7, "Your loving but half dead Marian" (*GEL* 7:93). She saw Cross for the first time on February 23, 1879 (*GEJ* 163). He invited her to stay with his family in Weybridge, Surrey, but she declined (*GEL* 7:107). Thereafter she saw him regularly. His mother had died in December 1878 just ten days after Lewes, yet another death that seemed to open a path to the future. He was free to attend to Eliot's various needs. She consulted with him on complicated financial matters following Lewes's death, including the consolidation of her wealth under her own name, which she legally changed to Marian Evans Lewes.[5] She also needed financial advice in order to establish a trust to endow a studentship at Cambridge in Lewes's name. She appealed to him to help with a series of unexpected monetary requests, including a surprising one from Bessie Parkes (now Mrs Belloc), who asked for the loan of £500 in April. On Cross's advice, she declined the requested loan (Haight, *Biography* 526).

Additionally, Bertie's widow Eliza Lewes, upon learning of George Lewes's death, left South Africa and arrived in London with her two children on April 28, 1879. Initially, Eliza and her children lived with Charles Lewes and his family in Hampstead. Eliot recognized Eliza as a financial responsibility – one she was willing to accept – but she could not allow this previously unknown family to live with her. She was maintaining the regular payments to Agnes Lewes and she now arranged for payments to be made to Eliza, and saw Bertie's children along with Charles's on arranged visits.[6] According to Cross's account, in April he and Eliot began to read through Dante's *Divine Comedy* together in the Italian. Already devoted to her, and a great admirer of her writing, he was now amazed at "the prodigious stimulus of such a teacher": "The divine poet took us into a new world. It was a renovation of life" (*Life* 3:359).

On May 22, she went to Witley for the summer. On July 15, Blackwood wrote to tell her of the "splendid success" of *Impressions* (*GEL* 7:181). Eliot wrote back the next day, mentioning her poor health and the doctors who were attending her (Paget and Dr Andrew Clark, in addition to a local doctor): "Imagine me having champagne 'to my own cheek!' That is what I am ordered to do, and I certainly relish it better than I do the poisonous decoctions" (*GEL* 7:182). At this stage of her life and her sadness, she was able to relax her objections to opiates and to take some pleasure in declining poisonous medications in favor of champagne, which she could well afford. On October 8, she recorded cryptically in her journal: "Joy came" (*GEJ* 183).

On October 16, she wrote a letter to Cross that has puzzled biographers. It is a love letter of sorts beginning, "Best loved and loving one –," but it moves from her pain to the world's pain in general, to her current state, followed by a joke: "Thou seest I am grumbling today – got a chill yesterday and have a headache. All which, as a wise doctor would say, is not of the least consequence, my dear Madam." She then addresses him in archaic language: "Thou dost not know anything of verbs in Hiphil and Hophal" (she was continuing to study Hebrew), then writing, "but thou knowest best things of another sort, such as belong to the manly heart – secrets of lovingness and rectitude." Serious as this sounds, she quickly undermines the sentiment: "O I am flattering." She then moves on to the business side of her relationship with Cross: "I have *not* the second copy of the deed." The letter is signed "Beatrice" (*GEL* 7:211–12). Making this overwrought, scattered letter even stranger is the fact that it was written on the black mourning paper she regularly used following Lewes's death.

We do not have any of the letters Eliot wrote to Lewes, but in the nine volumes of her surviving letters, this one is unusual, comparable perhaps to the abject letter she wrote to Herbert Spencer in 1852. In both cases she was living alone and unusually isolated. It is possible that the letter to Cross was written under the influence of the pint of champagne a day that Paget had prescribed for her health.[7] Haight's only comment when he quotes this bizarre and contradictory letter underscores his theme: "She was not fitted to stand alone" (Haight, *Biography* 530).

She returned to the Priory on November 1. On November 5, she compiled an inventory of the wine remaining at the Heights. On November 25, she recorded "Another turning point." On Christmas Day 1879, she added a gloomy postscript to a letter she had written to Cross and signed, not Beatrice, but "Your obliged ex-shareholder of A and C Gaslight and Coke": "The fog is dense and one thinks of cab accidents" (*GEL* 7:235). If she was falling in love with Cross, she was also still prone to the depression with which she had lived throughout her life, compounded by the devastating loss of Lewes. She could not seem to write a love letter to Cross that did not betray an ironic self-consciousness about their business dealings.

Her journals indicate that it was Cross who pushed the question of marriage, and that she initially resisted. Her entry for April 9, 1880 records a connection between a visit from Paget and her decision to marry. While she and Paget probably discussed whether her health could withstand marriage to a much younger man, she may also have sought his opinion about whether marrying might in fact be essential to keeping her healthy, even keeping her alive. Following Paget's visit, she writes simply: "My marriage decided" (*GEJ* 202).

Eliot and Cross were married on May 6, 1880. Her journal records: "Married this day at 10.15 to John Walter Cross, at St. George's Hanover Square" (*GEJ* 203). The supportive Charles Lewes gave her away in a small ceremony attended by some of Cross's family members. Afterwards, the couple signed their respective wills, and then departed immediately for an extended European honeymoon, leaving behind friends who were shocked to hear the news, imparted to the closest among them by the dutiful Charles.

The departure to the Continent recalls the trip she had made with Lewes in 1854. The honeymoon journey itself retraced paths she and Lewes had traveled. Eliot had been secretive about this decision to marry, telling no one outside the immediate Lewes–Cross circle. Just as there were hurt feelings on the part of friends when she and Lewes had departed for Germany, so many of her friends now were disturbed by the news of her marriage, particularly her passionate admirers Maria Congreve, Elma Stuart, and Edith Simcox. The latter was best placed to have predicted the step Eliot had taken. Charles visited Edith personally. He expected her to be upset, which suggests that Edith's love for Eliot was well known in the family circle. On May 7, Edith wrote about Charles's visit in her journal:

> I said I was not surprised. I could hardly say anywhere but here that the conception had in some dim form or other crossed my mind. I need not explain to myself how it was. Of course she suffered much – Charles said she had twice broken it off as impossible – had thought of all the difficulties – the effect upon her influence and all the rest: then she consulted Sir James Paget, as a friend, her physician and impartial. He said there was no reason why she should not. (Simcox 121)

More generally, the marriage provided material for gossip in London literary and intellectual circles. For many, it seemed a scandal, first that she should marry so soon after Lewes's death, and secondly that she should marry a much younger man. In contrast, her long-estranged brother Isaac Evans found that any legal marriage was more respectable than an extra-legal one and wrote, for the first time since she had told him about her relationship with Lewes, to congratulate her on her marriage. She responded graciously, noting that "our long silence has never broken the affection for you which began when we were little ones" (*GEL* 7:287). One has to wonder whether Eliot assumed that Isaac had read *The Mill on the Floss* and recognized the fictional account of their relationship, or recognized his own behavior in the harsh judgments of Tom Tulliver. But that novel had been published 20 years earlier. Time had softened her resentment, and the reconciliation in her current, relatively happy state was easy to make.

John Blackwood had died on October 29, 1879, and Eliot had written sadly and simply to Charles Lewes that her publisher "has been bound up with what I most cared for in my life for more than twenty years" (*GEL* 7:217). Upon her marriage,

John Blackwood's nephew William Blackwood wrote from Edinburgh to his long-standing London manager Joseph Langford:

> What does it all mean, and after the state of desolation she was in after poor Lewes' death it is to me almost unaccountable. What would my uncle [John Blackwood] have said, and does it not take away all the romance of her connection with Lewes? (qtd. in Kathleen Adams 179)

The following day he wrote: "When one comes to reflect over George Eliot's position, one is not after all so much surprised, but then one would have thought she would have selected a philosopher to lean on more than a businessman as I understand he is . . ." (qtd. in Kathleen Adams 179). His astonishment reflects the general reaction to Eliot's marriage to Cross. Cross's business skills, of course, were an important part of what recommended him to Eliot as a husband.

During the honeymoon she wrote to various friends, mostly expressing happiness, though also frank sadness at visiting some of the places she and Lewes had been together. She naturally shared this sentiment with Charles Lewes. But then she explained why she had decided to marry Cross, speaking of her decision in abstract terms: "To feel daily the loveliness of a nature close to me, and to be grateful to it, is the fountain of tenderness and strength to endure" (*GEL* 7:283). In her letters to Charles, she also asks about Eliza and the children and mentions the cheques that she has sent them. Her practical responsibility for their well being was clearly an anxiety for her.

Her journals track the stages of her travels with Cross through France and Italy. They arrived in Venice on June 3, 1880. Based on their respective letters, the couple felt the honeymoon journey was going well, with Cross continuing to be amazed both by Eliot's cultural knowledge and by her energy and good health. His own health, however, did not correspondingly improve. Eliot had shown some concern in the weeks before the marriage that he had lost weight. The impending marriage itself, as well as the strain of keeping it a secret, as Eliot wished, may have contributed to a decline in Cross's physical strength (Simcox 128–9, 186).

The stay in Venice began with the usual breakneck sightseeing and visits to churches and museums – a routine that would have been quite normal for the Leweses. But uncharacteristically, on June 15 after going to "the Accademia seeing the Bellinis," they did not go out after lunch (*GEJ* 206). The following day Eliot records: "Dr. Ricchetti called" (*GEJ* 206). According to Cross's own account in his *Life*, the hot weather and bad air from the canals, as well as the lack of exercise that resulted from traveling by gondola and visits to museums and churches, resulted in a breakdown of his health (*Life* 3:407–8). He had wanted to exercise by swimming at the Lido, but, perhaps in deference to his fretful wife's wishes, he did not do so.

As far as we can reconstruct the events, Eliot became so concerned about what may have been Cross's symptoms of depression, that she consulted Dr Ricchetti.

While she was speaking with the doctor in their hotel suite, Johnny went to the balcony overlooking the Grand Canal, and jumped in. He was immediately "rescued" by nearby gondoliers, but exposure to the unclean canal water may have contributed to the subsequent disease he contracted. Information on the event is so sketchy that it has never been exactly clear what happened. Brenda Maddox uncovered two Italian newspaper reports, as well as a police report, that document the jump into the canal and confirm that at the time it was assumed to be a suicide attempt (Maddox 215–17).

Cross's actual motivation, however, cannot be inferred from these external reports. What is certain is that everyone was alarmed. Another doctor, Cesare Vigna, was called in. Eliot telegraphed Cross's brother Willie, who came immediately to Venice. Cross seemed to improve. On June 21, Eliot recorded: "Quiet night, without chloral" (*GEJ* 207). On June 23, she and Willie began the journey back, allowing Johnny to rest for several days in Innsbruck. They also stopped at the spas familiar to Eliot from her journeys with Lewes. At Wildbad, Willie left them, and Eliot took Cross on to Baden.[8] They returned to England, arriving at Witley on July 26, a quite unexpected ending to their honeymoon.

Soon thereafter, they resumed a course of socializing and domestic activities, making visits to Cross's various siblings. What seems noteworthy is how often Eliot records in her diary: "J. to town again," that is, how often she was left alone at Witley while he went to see about their new London home in Chelsea, or to conduct other business in London. He was gone so often during the summer that it seems an event when she recorded on November 20: "J. at home." (*GEJ* 213). When he was at home, he was often engaged in some physical, diverting exercise. On November 2, she recorded: "J. cut down trees in the afternoon" (*GEJ* 212). Their life in the country was very different from her former intimacy with Lewes, when the two would work all morning on their respective books, walk together after lunch, and read to each other in the evenings. Eliot seems to observe her young husband from an eager, anxious distance. Try as he might, Cross could never share the intellectual intensity of Eliot's life, as Lewes had. On December 3, they finally moved into their new home at Cheyne Walk and, after this move, Eliot's diary entries cease.

In London, they immediately began a round of cultural events and socializing. After attending a performance of *Agamemnon* (in Greek) performed by Oxford undergraduates at St George's Hall, Eliot felt a sore throat coming on. The next day she was well enough to receive Spencer and Edith Simcox. But afterwards, her sore throat worsened. A doctor named George Mackenzie diagnosed her with laryngitis, but by the time her regular doctor Andrew Clark came, he found that her heart had been affected by kidney failure. She declined rapidly and died on December 22.[9]

George Eliot was buried in Highgate Cemetery. Dr Thomas Sadler, the same Unitarian minister who had performed Lewes's burial ceremony, also performed hers. There had been some discussion about her being buried in Westminster Abbey because of her status as one of the nation's greatest writers. The Dean, whose decision it was, considered various testimonials by important men. In the end, the idea proved too controversial, seeing that George Eliot was not a practicing Christian and had lived for 24 years with a married man. There seems to have been no doubt that she would be buried beside Lewes. The monument on her grave reads: "Here lies the body of 'George Eliot,'" followed by the name "Mary Ann Cross." There is nothing on the stone to connect her to Lewes and his more modest grave with a flat stone marker just beside hers. The most notable monument in the vicinity is that of their old acquaintance from the *Leader* days, G. J. Holyoake, who arranged to be buried next to Lewes and Eliot with a bust of himself looking over their graves. Elma Stuart is also buried there, next to her beloved.

The funeral was attended by a large crowd. The chief mourners were Cross, Charles Lewes, Cross's brother and three brothers-in-law, and, ironically, Isaac Evans and his son Frederick (Haight, *Biography* 549). Edith Simcox attended and wrote a detailed account in her journal. While she was standing under the colonnade of the Highgate chapel, a child asked her: "Was it the late George Eliot's wife was going to be buried?" (Simcox 138). Oscar Browning, who was there, is alone in remembering that there were protests: "The crowd demonstrated at the funeral against the doctors for their apparent negligence" (291).

Figure 27   Highgate Cemetery (Photograph by M. Ousellam)

Cross's *George Eliot's Life*

George Eliot was buried on December 29, 1880. By January 1, 1881, Edith Simcox was in Nuneaton, visiting places related to Eliot's childhood, picking up bits of information to put together for the story of her life, and trying to learn what she could from those who remembered Mary Ann Evans. On January 8, for example, she spoke with Sara Hennell and, among other things, learned about the letters to Maria Lewis – how Mary Ann recalled them in 1846 and "gave the packet to Miss Hennell who had left them unopened til now" (Simcox 145). And so Simcox was the first to conduct interviews and research that would help biographers construct the life of George Eliot; she hoped that she would be the first to write that biography.

The circle of friends – Charles, Johnny and his sisters, Maria Congreve – seemed to stay in close touch. Simcox records her visits to these friends to talk about Eliot. She was happy to learn, for example, that Maria Congreve "loved my darling lover-wise too" (Simcox 146). On January 20, Cross visited Edith Simcox at home:

> He stayed over half an hour telling me that he had made up his mind to write the life himself: the resolve was quickened by the thought that if he did not some one else would and he had this warrant: as they were walking one day at [Witley] she said he ought to do some one work – a contribution to the world's possessions: she was sure he had the power. He said half playfully, he did not know what he could do, unless it were to write her life if he survived her. She smiled and did not answer – did not protest. (Simcox 148)

And so as Cross interpreted it, by not objecting to his suggestion, Eliot gave her approval to the idea of his writing her life. During this visit, Cross and Simcox discussed the Coventry friends and relatives, the surviving letters, and the inevitable need for someone to write a biography. Simcox observes: "Apparently she had told him very much of her life... and he was anxious to gather quickly all that was remembered by friends no longer young" (Simcox 148). And so George Eliot's widower became her implicitly authorized biographer and made the writing of her *Life* his contribution to the world's possessions.

While she was alive, he could not hope for the marriage of true minds she had with Lewes. Commenting ironically on Eliot's death, Henry James wrote of his meeting with Cross: "He poor fellow, is left very much lamenting but my private impression is that if she had not died, she would have killed him" (Collins, *Interviews* 226). But writing the *Life* was something that Cross could do, and that he felt authorized to do. He could take control of that posterity about which she had been so anxious throughout her career. Significantly, he wrote the life, not of Mary Ann Evans, Marian Lewes, or Mary Ann Cross, but of George Eliot, and he wrote what he modestly called her "autobiography," using as much of her own words (heavily edited by him) as possible and all the materials accessible only to him (letters, journals, notebooks). With the delicacy that any biographer would understand, however, he was highly protective of what he believed to be his wife's wishes, as well as the sensibilities of people still living, including Isaac Evans, Herbert Spencer, Charles Bray, Agnes and her children, and the family of Charles Lewes.

Eliot's first fictional explorations of the author's anxieties about posterity appear in *Romola* through Bardo's obsession with his library. "The Legend of Jubal" develops a myth of the artist sacrificed to his legacy of inventing music. In *Middlemarch*, she gave a tragic cast to Casaubon's and Lydgate's respective failures to bequeath an intellectual legacy to the future. *Daniel Deronda* introduces the metaphysical concept of one soul transmitted after death to the body of another. *Impressions* puts the questions of national inheritance and culture self-consciously at the forefront. As she was exploring these themes of transmission, inheritance, and posterity in her fiction, she was thinking about her own legacy and that of Lewes. She took care to finish Lewes's unfinished work, to intervene in whatever was written about him when she could, and to establish a memorial studentship in his name at a university, Cambridge, which he could not attend.

Eliot shared the common experiences of her contemporaries who had known the death of loved ones (her mother, father, sister, stepsons, and husband). But as an author, she thought broadly beyond personal loss to questions of what it means to pass on a legacy of art to future generations. Her fiction represents the varieties of inheritance and transmission that characterize any culture: children (copies of their parents), wills, books (her own children), and reputations that inevitably emerge from a combination of knowledge about an author's writings and his or her personal actions. Eliot knew that her biography would be written, and she knew it would be important to how she would be remembered, no matter how much she wished to be remembered for her writing alone. She trusted in death, and death came just after she married a devoted young man who had managed her finances and would write her biography. In this sense, Cross became the trustee of Eliot's reputation.[10]

This *Life of George Eliot* began by thinking about the problems and questions raised by the genre of literary biography. It concludes by thinking about the traditions of biography in which Cross's *George Eliot's Life* fits. In his *Life of Samuel Johnson*, a book well known to Eliot, James Boswell explains his method:

> I have resolved to adopt and enlarge upon the excellent plan of Mr. Mason, in his Memoirs of Gray. Wherever narrative is necessary to explain, connect, and supply, I furnish it to the best of my abilities; but in the chronological series of Johnson's life . . . I produce, wherever it is in my power, his own minutes, letters or conversation. (21)

He continues to explain the methodology of the classic work that transformed the art of biography, an art form Eliot appreciated but which she felt to have become corrupted by the mid-nineteenth century. Boswell writes:

Indeed I cannot conceive a more perfect mode of writing any man's life, than not only relating all the most important events of it in their order, but interweaving what he privately wrote, and said, and thought... And he will be seen as he really was... in every picture there should be shade as well as light... (21)

Discussing Cross's *Life* in the Introduction to his *George Eliot Letters*, Haight observes that Cross followed a method "first used effectively by William Mason in his *Memoirs of the Life of Gray* more than a century before" (*GEL* 1:xiii). Haight does not mention Boswell, but Cross's own intelligent, self-conscious explanation of his method echoes Boswell:

> With the materials in my hands I have endeavoured to form an *autobiography* (if the term may be permitted) of George Eliot... By arranging all the letters and journals so as to form one connected whole, keeping the order of their dates, and with the least possible interruption of comment, I have endeavoured to combine a narrative of day-to-day life with the play of light and shade, which only letters, written in various moods, can give, and without which no portrait can be a good likeness. (1:vi)

Cross claims to be an editor rather than a biographer. Despite his disavowal, "I do not know that the particular method in which I have treated the letters has ever been adopted before" (1:vii), he certainly knew Boswell's *Life of Johnson*. Like all future biographers, he owed a debt to that great biography and echoed its very language in his reference to "the play of light and shade."

Haight thought that Eliot lost her sense of humor during the years that Cross knew her, a notion that is discredited by her fiction, especially *Impressions*, which she originally intended to present as a manuscript edited by George Eliot, thereby revealing her own thinking about the value of an editor of manuscripts to the future reception of an author's work. An example of this sense of humor is Eliot and Lewes's relationship to her admirers and worshippers. It has been assumed by biographers that the Leweses lost perspective on the absurdity of the feet-kissing, gifts of underwear, and semi-religious services at the Priory. But their private sense of humor was very much alive. Of the acolytes, apostles, or worshippers that Eliot attracted in the last phase of her life and career, Alexander Main stands out as a figure who was simultaneously encouraged and ridiculed by the Leweses. He may not have sat at her feet like Edith Simcox, or been buried next to her like Elma Stuart, or married her like Johnny Cross, but he published books that remain today as either testimonials to the devotion she inspired or embarrassments to the flattery she encouraged.

John Blackwood called the Scottish Main, whom Eliot never met, "the Gusher." Eliot's version of the Theophrastan character "The Flatterer" is the "Too Deferential Man" (*Impressions*; ch. 5). She and Lewes must have shared some of that irony when allowing Main to publish *Wise, Witty, and Tender Sayings in Prose and Verse selected from the Work of George Eliot* (1871) and *The George Eliot Birthday Book* (1878).[11] Less recognized, however, is the particular way in which they put him off Eliot and onto other projects, specifically a rewriting of Boswell's *Life of Johnson*. The irony (perhaps cruel if humorous) in their suggesting to him such a project does not obscure the implications of both Main's and Cross's Boswell-like relationship to Eliot and their influence on her posthumous reputation.

Eliot's letters to Main were serious, but we can imagine the conversations she and Lewes must have had comparing the Scot Main to the Scot Boswell in their respective devotions to their English idols, Eliot and Johnson. Lewes suggested to Main that he take on a rewriting of Boswell's *Life*, a project both serious and absurd and destined to failure. Main took on the challenge and published *The Life and Conversations of Samuel Johnson (Founded Chiefly Upon Boswell), With a Preface by George Henry Lewes* (1874). In the book, Main tries to efface himself as much as possible, and though he provides no statement of his methodology or introduction to his own work, he sums up his task in the end, unable to resist introducing his idol, George Eliot:

> And now, at the close of our delightful labour, it hardly appears to us that *we* have told this Story of Johnson's Life; it seems rather that the story has told itself. It was fitting that *he* should be everything, and we nothing – except a kind of living note of admiration, marking the finest incidents in a manly career and the finest features in a manly character... Communion, though but for a short while, with the spirit of this man's life, fellowship with his sufferings, sympathy with his sorrows, the sense of his virtues, and the felt presence of his genius, will surely bring a touch of healing to some wounded heart, or a word of strength to some weary brain. It has been well said, "The first condition of human goodness is, something to love; the second, something to reverence." (441)

The quotation is from Eliot's "Mr. Gilfil's Love Story," and so Main was able to work an extract of Eliot's writing into his rewriting or editing of Boswell's *Life of Johnson*.

In the preface he supplied to Main's *Life of Johnson*, Lewes recounts his own plans, first to abridge and then rewrite Boswell's *Life of Johnson*, which occurred to him in 1855–6, the years following the completion of his own biography of Goethe. He barely mentions Main beyond recommending the book he is introducing. Instead, he praises Boswell's achievement while putting forward a position on biography that is consistent with his own practice of biography and with Eliot's realist fiction. He laments the neglect of Boswell's *Life*, owing partly to its length and partly to the general neglect of classic works of literature by a reading audience more interested in the moment: "This neglect of a work which has delighted generations, and will continue to delight posterity, is partly due to the mental enervation produced by a constantly increasing solicitation of the attention to new works, mostly of the mushroom type, springing up in a night to disappear in a day" (viii). In 1874, when his writing had become exclusively scientific and when Eliot was beginning to contemplate *Daniel Deronda*, Lewes expressed an opinion about contemporary literature similar to that Eliot betrayed in *Impressions*. It is interesting that the book he chose to hold up as a classic work of literature was a biography.

Boswell stood as the standard of biographies. Mark Pattison wrote in his biography of Isaac Casaubon:

> Even if Casaubon had found a Boswell, it may be doubted if his talk could have been effectively reported. We have no account of his style of conversation, but we are sure it had not the pith and epigram, which constitute table-talk such as can be carried away. (479)

George Eliot may have objected to modern literary biographies and feared the gossip-mongering and invasion of privacy that diverted attention away from the art of the writer, but throughout her life she appreciated the art of biography as a genre. And she contributed to modern biographies, whether helping Lewes with his *Life and Works of Goethe* or commenting on the manuscript of Pattison's *Isaac Casaubon*. Eliot also made ironic comments about biographies in her fiction, telling us that Grandcourt's biographer need not know anything about the momentous historical events of the time or exposing Mrs Bulstrode's sad illusion that her husband was someone whose memoirs should be written.

Cross was Eliot's Boswell, and he attempted to establish an accurate, respectable, historically situated biography of her. Like the subsequent biographers who have taken their turn, Cross realized that life and fiction informed each other and also that the author is born into an historical context that shapes the works she writes. Eliot's life is a fascinating story in its own right. Retelling that story in conjunction with readings of the stories she told in her novels helps to illuminate both the novels and her life. Eliot need not have feared the fate of Tasso in the hands of his fictional biographer Mrs Arrowpoint, who ominously yet comically proclaimed: "Ah, his life is more interesting than his poetry" (*DD* 37; ch. 5).

Notes

1. Qtd. in Kathleen Adams 179.
2. Ashton says he died of enteritis, an inflammation of the small intestine usually caused by a bacterial infection (Ashton, *GHL* 277). Maddox writes that Paget diagnosed enteritis but a "post-mortem had revealed the reality of the cancer about which Marian was now told" (199). No reference is given.
3. See Collins, "G. H. Lewes Revised," "George Eliot's Sacred Task," and "Reading George Eliot Reading Lewes's Obituaries"; also Vogeler, "George Eliot as Literary Widow" (1988).
4. White, *Johnnie Cross*; Ozick, *The Puttermesser Papers*.
5. On changing her name by deed, see Harriet Adams.
6. The payments were continued by Charles after Eliot's death. A brief *New York Times* obituary from December 24, 1902 reads: "The death is announced of Mrs. Lewes, widow

of George Henry Lewes, who, in 1854, formed a union with George Eliot, the famous novelist." Agnes was worthy of an obituary for being the widow of the man who had (euphemistically) formed a union with George Eliot.

7. This idea was suggested by David Williams in *Mr. George Eliot*. McCormack dismisses it (*George Eliot and Intoxication* 37).

8. On this last visit of Eliot's to a European spa see McCormack, *George Eliot in Society*.

9. A later article in the *Lancet*, which Haight claims was written by Clark, gives all the details of her illness over the previous years and explains that, though the death seemed sudden, it had in fact been prepared for by the attacks of kidney stone she had experienced throughout the 1870s. It probably had nothing to do with the cold and sore throat ("Annotations," January 1, 1881, 26).

10. On Cross's *Life* as a reaction against late nineteenth-century "celebrity culture," see Wah. For an intriguing account of Eliot's reactions to representations of herself in relation to her fame, see Griffith.

11. On Main's practice of extracting Eliot's words in the context of literary anthologies, see Price.

Bibliography

Adam, Ian, ed. *This Particular Web: Essays on Middlemarch*. Toronto: University of Toronto Press, 1975.

Adams, Harriet. "George Eliot's Deed: Reconciling an Outlaw Marriage." *Yale University Library Gazette 75.1-2* (2000): 52–63.

Adams, Kathleen. *Those of Us Who Loved Her: The Men in George Eliot's Life*. Coventry, UK: George Eliot Fellowship, 1980.

Ames, Charles Gordon. *George Eliot's Two Marriages*. Philadelphia: G. H. Buchanan & Co., 1886.

Anderson, Amanda. "George Eliot and the Jewish Question." *Yale Journal of Criticism* 10.1 (1997): 39–61.

Andrews, Alexander. *The History of British Journalism from the Foundation of the Newspaper Press in England, to the Repeal of the Stamp Act in 1855, with Sketches of Press Celebrities*. 2 vols. London: Richard Bentley, 1859.

"Annotations." *The Lancet* January 1, 1881: 26.

Ashton, Rosemary. *142 Strand: A Radical Address in Victorian London*. London: Chatto & Windus, 2006.

Ashton, Rosemary. *G. H. Lewes: A Life*. Oxford: Clarendon Press, 1991.

Ashton, Rosemary. *George Eliot: A Life*. London: Penguin Books, 1996.

Ashton, Rosemary. "New George Eliot Letters at the Huntington." *The Huntington Library Quarterly* 54, no. 2 (1991): 111–26.

Atkins, Dorothy. *George Eliot and Spinoza* (Salzburg Studies in Romantic Reassessment) Lewiston, NY: The Edwin Mellen Press Ltd, 1978.

Atkinson, Juliette. *Victorian Biography Reconsidered: A Study of Nineteenth-Century "Hidden" Lives*. Oxford: Oxford University Press, 2010.

Austen, Zelda. "Why Feminist Critics Are Angry with George Eliot." *College English* 37.6 (1976): 549–61.

Backscheider, Paula R. *Reflections on Biography*. Oxford: Oxford University Press, 1999.

The Life of George Eliot: A Critical Biography, First Edition. Nancy Henry.
© 2012 Nancy Henry. Published 2012 by John Wiley & Sons, Ltd.

Baker, William. "A New George Eliot Manuscript." In: *George Eliot: Centenary Essays and an Unpublished Fragment*. Ed. Anne Smith. Totowa, NJ: Barnes and Noble, 1980, pp. 9–20.

Baker, William. *George Eliot and Judaism* (Salzburg Studies in Romantic Reassessment) Lewiston, NY: The Edwin Mellen Press Ltd, 1975.

Barthes, Roland. *Image, Music, Text*. Trans. Stephen Heath. New York: Hill and Wang, 1977.

Batchelor, John. *The Art of Literary Biography*. Oxford: Clarendon Press, 1995.

Beaty, Jerome. *Middlemarch from Notebook to Novel: A Study of George Eliot's Creative Method*. Urbana: University of Illinois Press, 1960.

Beer, Gillian. "Knowing a Life: Edith Simcox – *Sat Est Vixisse?*" In: *Knowing the Past: Victorian Literature and Culture*. Ed. Suzy Anger. Ithaca: Cornell University Press, 2001, pp. 252–66.

Beer, Gillian. *Darwin's Plots: Evolutionary Narrative in Darwin, George Eliot and Nineteenth-Century Fiction*. Cambridge, UK: Cambridge University Press, 2000.

Beer, Gillian. *George Eliot*. Brighton: Harvester, 1986.

Beer, John. *Providence and Love: Studies in Wordsworth, Channing, Myers, George Eliot and Ruskin*. Oxford: Clarendon Press, 1998.

Benton, Michael. *Literary Biography: An Introduction*. Malden, MA: Wiley-Blackwell, 2009.

Bieri, James. *Percy Bysshe Shelley: A Biography*. 2 vols. Newark: University of Delaware Press, 2004/2005.

Blackstone, Sir William. *Commentaries on the Laws of England*. 4 vols. 1765-9. Chicago: University of Chicago Press, 1979.

Blake, Kathleen. "Armgart: George Eliot on the Woman Artist." *Victorian Poetry* 18 (1980): 75–80.

Blind, Mathilde. *George Eliot. 1883*. Ware: Wordsworth Editions, 2008.

Bodenheimer, Rosemarie. "Autobiography in Fragments: The Elusive Life of Edith Simcox." *Victorian Studies* 44. 3 (2002): 399–422.

Bodenheimer, Rosemarie. *Knowing Dickens*. Ithaca: Cornell University Press, 2007.

Bodenheimer, Rosemarie. *The Real Life of Mary Ann Evans: George Eliot, Her Letters and Fiction*. Ithaca: Cornell University Press, 1994.

Bonaparte, Felicia. *The Triptych and the Cross: The Central Myths of George Eliot's Poetic Imagination*. New York: New York University Press, 1979.

Boone, Joseph Allen. *Tradition Counter Tradition: Love and the Form of Fiction. Women in Culture and Society*. Chicago: University of Chicago Press, 1987.

Booth, Alison. "Biographical Criticism and The 'Great' Woman of Letters: The Example of George Eliot and Virginia Woolf." In: *Contesting the Subject: Essays in the Postmodern Theory and Practice of Biography and Biographical Criticism*. Ed. William H. Epstein. West Lafayette, IN.: Purdue University Press, 1991, pp. 85–108.

Boswell, James. *The Life of Samuel Johnson*. 1791. Ed. David Womersley. New York: Penguin Books, 2008.

Brady, Kristin. *George Eliot*. New York: Macmillan, 1992.

Bray, Charles. *Phases of Opinion and Experience During a Long Life: An Autobiography*. London: Longmans, Green & Co., 1884.

Brick, Allan. "'The Leader': Organ of Radicalism." Diss. Yale University, 1958.

Brier, Peter. "Emanuel Oscar Deutsch, The Talmud Man: George Eliot's Rabbi." 2011. Unpublished manuscript.

Brisbane, Albert. *Association: Or, a Concise Exposition of the Practical Part of Fourier's Social Science.* Communal Societies in America. New York: AMS Press, 1975.

Brown, Catherine. "Why Does Daniel Deronda's Mother Live in Russia?" *George Eliot-George Henry Lewes Studies* 58-9 (2010): 26–42.

Browning, Oscar. *Life of George Eliot.* London: W. Scott, 1890.

Browning, Oscar. *Memories of Sixty Years at Eton, Cambridge and Elsewhere.* London: John Lane the Bodley Head, 1910.

Bull, Malcolm. "Edward Casaubon and Isaac Casaubon." *Notes and Queries* 45. 2 (1998): 218–19.

Bullett, Gerald William. *George Eliot, Her Life and Books.* New Haven: Yale University Press, 1948.

Carpenter, Mary Wilson. *George Eliot and the Landscape of Time: Narrative Form and Protestant Apocalyptic History.* Chapel Hill: University of North Carolina Press, 1986.

Carroll, David, ed. *George Eliot: The Critical Heritage* (The Critical Heritage Series) New York: Barnes and Noble, 1971.

Carter, E. J. "Breaking the Bank: Gambling Casinos, Finance Capitalism, and German Unification." *Central European History* 39. 2 (2006): 185–213.

Chase, Karen, ed. *Middlemarch in the Twenty-First Century.* Oxford: Oxford University Press, 2006.

Cleare, Eileen. *Avuncularism: Capitalism, Patriarchy, and Nineteenth-Century English Culture.* Stanford: Stanford University Press, 2004.

Coleman, Dermot. "Being Good with Money: Economic Bearings in George Eliot's Ethical and Social Thought." Diss. University of Exeter, 2011.

Coleman, Dermot. "George Eliot and Money." In: *George Eliot in Context.* Ed. Margaret Harris. Cambridge, UK: Cambridge University Press, 2013.

Coleridge, Samuel Taylor. *The Complete Poems.* Ed. William Keach. New York: Penguin Books, 1997.

Collins, K. K. "G. H. Lewes Revised: George Eliot and the Moral Sense." *Victorian Studies* 21.4 (1978): 463–92.

Collins, K. K. "George Eliot's Sacred Task." *George Eliot Fellowship Review* 9 (1978): 21–5.

Collins, K. K. "Reading George Eliot Reading Lewes's Obituaries." *Modern Philology* 85. 2 (1987): 153–69.

Collins, K. K. *Identifying the Remains: George Eliot's Death in the London Religious Press.* English Literary Studies Monograph Series. Victoria, BC: ELS Editions, 2006.

Collins, K. K., ed. *George Eliot: Interviews and Recollections.* New York: Palgrave Macmillan, 2010.

Corbett, Mary Jean. *Family Likeness: Sex, Marriage, and Incest from Jane Austen to Virginia Woolf.* Ithaca: Cornell University Press, 2008.

Crompton, Louis. *Byron and Greek Love: Homophobia in 19th-Century England.* Berkeley: University of California Press, 1985.

Cromwell, Richard S. *David Friedrich Strauss and His Place in Modern Thought.* Fair Lawn, NJ: R.E. Burdick, Inc., 1974.

Cross, John Walter. *George Eliot's Life as Related in Her Letters and Journals. Arranged and Edited by Her Husband, J. W. Cross.* 3 vols. Edinburgh: William Blackwood and Sons, 1885.

"The Cultural Place of George Eliot's, Poetry." Special Issue *of George Eliot-George Henry Lewes Studies*. Nos. 60–1. Ed. Kyriaki Hadjiafxendi. (2011).

Dante [Alighieri]. *Inferno*. Trans. with commentary by Charles S. Singleton. Princeton: Princeton University Press, 1970.

De Quincey, Thomas. *Confessions of an English Opium-Eater and Other Writings*. Ed. Barry Milligan. New York: Penguin Books, 2003.

Dellamora, Richard. *Friendship's Bonds: Democracy and the Novel in Victorian England*. Philadelphia: University of Pennsylvania Press, 2004.

Deutsch, Emanuel. *Literary Remains of the Late Emanuel Deutsch With a Brief Memoir*. London: John Murray, 1874.

Dialectical Society (London, England). Debate on Mr. Moncure D. Conway's paper "On Marriage," April 1871. London Dialectical Society, 1871.

"Divorce Bills." *The Leader*. June 1, 1850: 227.

Dodd, Valerie A. *George Eliot: An Intellectual Life*. London: Macmillan, 1990.

Dodds, Dorothy. *The George Eliot Country*. Nuneaton: Nuneaton Borough Council, 1966.

Dolin, Tim. *George Eliot: Authors in Context*. New York: Oxford University Press, 2005.

Donnell, Alison and Pauline Polkey. *Representing Lives: Women and Auto/Biography*. Basingstoke: Macmillan, 2000.

Dowling, Andrew. "'The Other Side of Silence': Matrimonial Conflict and the Divorce Court in George Eliot's Fiction." *Nineteenth-Century Literature 50*. 3 (1995): 322–36.

Dowling, Linda. *Hellenism and Homosexuality in Victorian Oxford*. Ithaca: Cornell University Press, 1994.

Duffy, Charles Gavan. *Conversations with Carlyle*. New York: Scribner, 1892.

Duffy, Eamon. *Saints and Sinners: A History of the Popes*. New Haven: Yale University Press, 1997.

Dunae, P. A. "Education, Emigration and the Empire: The Colonial College, 1887-1905." In: *"Benefits Bestowed"?: Education and British Imperialism*. Ed. J. A. Mangan. Manchester: Manchester University Press, 1988, pp. 193–210.

Dunae, P. A. *Gentleman Emigrants: From the British Public Schools to the Canadian Frontier*. Manchester: Manchester University Press, 1981.

Edel, Leon. "The Poetics of Biography." In: *Contemporary Approaches to English Studies*. Ed. Hilda Schiff. New York: Barnes & Noble, 1977, pp. 38–58.

Elfenbein, Andrew. *Byron and the Victorians*. Cambridge: Cambridge University Press, 1995.

Eliot, George. *Adam Bede* (1859). Oxford World's Classics. Ed. Valentine Cunningham. Oxford: Oxford University Press, 1996.

Eliot, George. "Brother Jacob" (1864). In: *Silas Marner, The Lifted Veil and Brother Jacob*. Ed. Peter Mudford. London: Everyman, 1996 pp. 305–end.

Eliot, George. *The Complete Shorter Poetry of George Eliot*. Ed. A. G. van den Broek.2 vols. The Pickering Masters. London: Pickering & Chatto, 2005.

Eliot, George. *Daniel Deronda* (1876). Oxford World's Classics. Ed. Graham Handley. Oxford: Oxford University Press, 2009.

Eliot, George. *Essays of George Eliot*. Ed. Thomas Pinney. New York: Columbia University Press, 1963.

Eliot, George. "Essays and Leaves from a Notebook." In: *The Complete Shorter Poetry of George Eliot*. Ed. A. G. van den Broek.Vol. 2. The Pickering Masters. London: Pickering & Chatto, 2005.

Eliot, George. "Evangelical Teaching: Dr. Cumming." *Essays of George Eliot*. Ed. Thomas Pinney. New York: Columbia University Press, 1963. pp. 158–89.

Eliot, George. *Felix Holt, the Radical* (1866). Oxford World's Classics. Ed. Fred C. Thomson. Oxford: Oxford University Press, 1988.

Eliot, George. *George Eliot: A Writer's Notebook, 1854-1879, and Uncollected Writings*. Ed. Joseph Wiesenfarth. Charlottesville: University of Virginia Press, 1981.

Eliot, George. "A George Eliot Holograph Notebook: An Edition (Ms Don. G 8). Held at the Bodleian Library, Oxford." Ed. Andrew Thompson. *George Eliot – G. H. Lewes Studies* 50-1 (2006): 1–109.

Eliot, George. *The George Eliot Letters*. Ed. Gordon S. Haight. 9 vols. New Haven: Yale University Press, 1978.

Eliot, George. *George Eliot: Selected Essays, Poems, and Other Writings*. Ed. A. S. Byatt. New York: Penguin Books, 1990.

Eliot, George. *George Eliot's Daniel Deronda Notebooks*. Ed. Jane Irwin. Cambridge, UK: Cambridge University Press, 1996.

Eliot, George. *George Eliot's Middlemarch Notebooks: A Transcription*. Eds. John Clark Pratt and Victor A. Neufeldt. Berkeley: University of California Press, 1979.

Eliot, George. "German Wit: Heinrich Heine." In: *Selected Critical Writings*. Ed. Rosemary Ashton. Oxford: Oxford University Press, 1992, pp. 193–233.

Eliot, George. "History of Adam Bede." In: *The Journals of George Eliot*. Eds. Margaret Harris and Judith Johnston. Cambridge, UK: Cambridge University Press, 1998, pp. 296–8.

Eliot, George. "How I Came to Write Fiction." In: *The Journals of George Eliot*. Eds. Margaret Harris and Judith Johnston. Cambridge, UK: Cambridge University Press, 1998, pp. 289–91.

Eliot, George. *Impressions of Theophrastus Such* (1879). Ed Nancy Henry. Iowa City: University of Iowa Press, 1994.

Eliot, George. *The Journals of George Eliot*. Eds. Margaret Harris and Judith Johnston. Cambridge, UK: Cambridge University Press, 1998.

Eliot, George. "Life and Opinions of Milton." In: *Essays of George Eliot*. Ed Thomas Pinney. New York: Columbia University Press, 1963, pp. 154–7.

Eliot, George. "The Lifted Veil" (1859). In: *Silas Marner, The Lifted Veil and Brother Jacob*. Ed. Peter Mudford. London: Everyman, 1996, pp. 243–304.

Eliot, George. "Margaret Fuller and Mary Wollstonecraft." In: *Selected Essays, Poems, and Other Writings*. Ed. A. S. Byatt. New York: Penguin Books, 1990. pp. 332–38.

Eliot, George. *Middlemarch* (1871-2) Oxford World's Classics. Ed. David Carroll. Oxford: Oxford University Press, 1997.

Eliot, George. *The Mill on the Floss* (1860). Riverside Editions. Ed. Gordon Sherman Haight. Boston: Houghton Mifflin, 1961.

Eliot, George. *The Mill on the Floss* (1860). Oxford World's Classics. Eds. Gordon Sherman Haight and Dinah Birch. Oxford: Oxford University Press, 1996.

Eliot, George. *The Mill on the Floss: Complete Text with Introduction, Historical Contexts, Critical Essays.* New Riverside Edition. Ed. Nancy Henry. Boston: Houghton Mifflin Co., 2004.

Eliot, George. "The Natural History of German Life." In: *Selected Critical Writings.* Ed. Rosemary Ashton. Oxford: Oxford University Press, 1992, pp. 260–95.

Eliot, George. *Romola* (1863). Oxford World's Classics. Ed. Andrew Brown. Oxford: Oxford University Press, 1994.

Eliot, George. *Scenes of Clerical Life* (1858). Oxford World's Classics. Ed. Thomas A. Noble. Oxford: Oxford University Press, 1988.

Eliot, George. *Selected Critical Writings.* Oxford World's Classics. Ed. Rosemary Ashton. Oxford: Oxford University Press, 1992.

Eliot, George. *Silas Marner: The Weaver of Raveloe* (1861). In *Silas Marner, The Lifted Veil and Brother Jacob.* London: Everyman, 1996.

Eliot, George. "Silly Novels By Lady Novelists." In: *Selected Critical Writings.* Ed. Rosemary Ashton. Oxford: Oxford University Press, 1992, pp. 296–321.

Eliot, George. *The Spanish Gypsy* (1868). Ed A. G. van den Broek.The Pickering Masters. London: Pickering & Chatto, 2008.

Eliot, George. "Thomas Carlyle's Life of John Sterling." In: *George Eliot: Selected Essays, Poems, and Other Writings.* Ed. A. S. Byatt. New York: Penguin Books, 1990, pp. 297–301.

Eliot, George. "Women in France." In: *George Eliot: Selected Essays, Poems, and Other Writings.* Ed. A. S. Byatt. New York: Penguin Books, 1990.

Eliot, George. "Worldliness and Other-Worldliness: The Poet Young." In: *George Eliot: Selected Essays, Poems, and Other Writings.* Ed. A. S. Byatt. New York: Penguin Books, 1990, pp. 164–213.

Eliot, T. S. "Tradition and the Individual Talent." In: *The Sacred Wood and Major Early Essays.* Mineola, NY: Dover Publications, 1998.

Elliott, Geoffrey. *The Mystery of Overend and Gurney: A Financial Scandal in Victorian London.* London: Methuen, 2006.

Ellmann, Richard. *Golden Codgers: Biographical Speculations.* New York: Oxford University Press, 1973.

Elwin, Malcolm. *Lord Byron's Family: Annabella, Ada and Augusta, 1816-1824.* London: J. Murray, 1975.

Epstein, William H., ed. *Contesting the Subject: Essays in the Postmodern Theory and Practice of Biography and Biographical Criticism.* West Lafayette, IN: Purdue University Press, 1991.

Escott, T. S. *Masters of English Journalism; A Study of Personal Forces.* London: T. F. Unwin, 1911.

Evans, C. F. H. and A. C. Wood. "George Eliot's Maternal Ancestry." *Notes and Queries* 19.11 (1972): 409–16.

Evans, Robert. Letter to Colonel Francis Newdigate. April 12, 1835. WRO B 3814. MS. Newdegate Family of Arbury Collection. Warwickshire County Record Office, Warwick, UK.

Evans, Robert. Unpublished diaries. MS. The Nuneaton Public Library and Museum, Warwick, UK.

Feltes, N. N. *Modes of Production of Victorian Novels*. Chicago: University of Chicago Press, 1986.

Feuerbach, Ludwig. *The Essence of Christianity*. Trans. Marian Evans. 1854. 2nd edn. London: Trübner & Co., 1881.

Finkelstein, David. *The House of Blackwood: Author-Publisher Relations in the Victorian Era*. University Park, PA: Penn State University Press, 2002.

Fleishman, Avrom. *George Eliot's Reading: A Chronological List. George Eliot-George Henry Lewes Studies*. Supplement to nos. *54-5* (September 2008).

Fleishman, Avrom. *George Eliot's Intellectual Life*. Cambridge, UK: Cambridge University Press, 2010.

Flint, Kate. "Blood, Bodies, and The Lifted Veil." *Nineteenth-Century Literature 51.4* (1997): 455–73.

Foucault, Michel. *History of Sexuality: Vol I*. Trans. Robert Hurley. New York: Pantheon Books, 1978.

Foucault, Michel. "What Is an Author?" In: *Language, Counter-Memory, Practice: Selected Essays and Interviews*. Ithaca, NY: Cornell University Press, 1977.

Fragoso, Margaux. "Imagination, Morality, and the Spectre of Sade in George Eliot's *Romola* and *Daniel Deronda*." *George Eliot Review* 37 (2006): 25–35.

Francis, Mark. *Herbert Spencer and the Invention of Modern Life*. Ithaca: Cornell University Press, 2007.

Fraser, Hilary. "St. Theresa, St. Dorothea, and Miss Brooke in *Middlemarch*." *Nineteenth-Century Fiction* 40.4 (1986): 400–11.

Fraser, Hilary. *The Victorians and Renaissance Italy*. Oxford: Blackwell, 1992.

Fremantle, Anne. *George Eliot*. London: Duckworth, 1933.

Gallagher, Catherine. "George Eliot and *Daniel Deronda*: The Prostitute and the Jewish Question." In: *Sex, Politics, and Science in the Nineteenth-Century Novel*. Baltimore: Johns Hopkins University Press, 1986, pp. 39–62.

Gallagher, Catherine. *The Body Economic: Life, Death, and Sensation in Political Economy and the Victorian Novel*. Princeton: Princeton University Press, 2005.

Galvan, Jill. "The Narrator as Medium in George Eliot's *The Lifted Veil*." *Victorian Studies* 48. 2 (2006): 240–8.

Ganz, Melissa J. "Binding the Will: George Eliot and the Practice of Promising." *ELH* 75 (2008): 565–602.

Gilbert, Sandra M. and Susan Gubar. *The Madwoman in the Attic: The Woman Writer and the Nineteenth-Century Literary Imagination*. New Haven: Yale University Press, 1979.

Girard, René. *Deceit, Desire, and the Novel; Self and Other in Literary Structure*. 1961. Trans. Yvonne Freccero. Baltimore: Johns Hopkins Press, 1976.

Glynn, Jenifer. *Prince of Publishers: A Biography of George Smith*. London: Allison & Busby, 1986.

Grafton, Anthony and Joanna Weinberg. *"I Have Always Loved the Holy Tongue": Isaac Casaubon, the Jews, and the Forgotten Chapter of Renaissance Scholarship*. Cambridge, MA: Harvard University Press, 2011.

Greiner, Rae. "Sympathy Time: Adam Smith, George Eliot, and the Realist Novel." *Narrative* 17. 3 (2009): 291–311.

Griffith, George. "The Face as Legible Text: Gazing at the Portraits of George Eliot." *Victorian Review* 27.2 (2001): 20–41.

Guest, Bill and John M. Sellers, eds. *Enterprise and Exploitation in a Victorian Colony: Aspects of the Economic and Social History of Colonial Natal*. Pietermaritzburg: University of Natal Press, 1985.

Haight, Gordon S. "George Eliot's Originals." In: *George Eliot's Originals and Contemporaries: Essays in Victorian Literary History and Biography*. Ed. Hugh Witemeyer. Ann Arbor: University of Michigan Press, 1992, pp. 3–21.

Haight, Gordon S. "The Carlyles and the Leweses." In: *George Eliot's Originals and Contemporaries*. Ed. Hugh Witemeyer. Ann Arbor: University of Michigan Press, 1992, pp. 91–116.

Haight, Gordon S. "George Eliot's Bastards." In: *George Eliot's Originals and Contemporaries*. Ed. Hugh Witemeyer. Ann Arbor: University of Michigan Press, 1992, pp. 78–88.

Haight, Gordon S. "Male Chastity in the Nineteenth Century." In: *George Eliot's Originals and Contemporaries*. Ed. Hugh Witemeyer. Ann Arbor: University of Michigan Press, 1992, pp. 210–24.

Haight, Gordon S. *George Eliot and John Chapman, with Chapman's Diaries*. 1940. 2nd edn. Hamden, CN: Archon Books, 1969.

Haight, Gordon S. *George Eliot: A Biography*. London: Clarendon Press, 1968.

Haight, Gordon S. *George Eliot's Originals and Contemporaries*. Ed. Hugh Witemeyer. Ann Arbor: University of Michigan Press, 1992.

Haldane, Elizabeth S. *George Eliot and Her Times*. London: Hodder and Stoughton, 1927.

Handley, Graham. *George Eliot: A Guide Through the Critical Maze*. Bristol: Bristol Classical Press, 1990.

Handley, Graham. *George Eliot's Midlands: Passion in Exile*. London: Allison and Busby, 1991.

Hands, Timothy. *A George Eliot Chronology*. London: Macmillan Press, 1989.

Hanson, Lawrence and Elizabeth Hanson. *Marian Evans and George Eliot: A Biography*. New York: Oxford University Press, 1952.

Hardy, Barbara. *George Eliot: A Critic's Biography*. London: Continuum, 2006.

Hardy, Barbara. *The Novels of George Eliot: A Study in Form*. London: Athlone Press, 1959.

Harris, Margaret, ed. *George Eliot in Context*. Cambridge, UK: Cambridge University Press, 2012.

Haskin, Dayton. "George Eliot as a 'Miltonist': Marriage and Milton in *Middlemarch*." In: *Milton and Gender*. Ed. Catherine Gimelli Martin. Cambridge, UK: Cambridge University Press, 2004, pp. 207–22.

Hennell, Charles Christian. *An Inquiry Concerning the Origin of Christianity*. London: Smallfield and Son, 1838.

Henry, Nancy. *George Eliot and the British Empire*. New York: Cambridge University Press, 2002.

Henry, Nancy. "George Eliot and Finance." In: *The Blackwell Companion to George Eliot*. Eds. Amanda Anderson and Harry Shaw. Oxford: Wiley-Blackwell, 2013.

Henry, Nancy. "The *Romola* Code: 'Men of Appetites' in George Eliot's Historical Novel." *Victorian Literature and Culture* 39.2 (2011): 327–48.

Hertz, Neil. *George Eliot's Pulse*. Stanford: Stanford University Press, 2003.

Herzog, Annabel. "Tale of Two Secrets: A Rereading of *Daniel Deronda*." *differences: A Journal of Feminist Cultural Studies 16.2* (2005): 37–60.

Hodgson, Peter Crafts. *The Mystery Beneath the Real: Theology in the Fiction of George Eliot.* Minneapolis: Fortress Press, 2000.

Homans, Margaret. "Eliot, Wordsworth, and the Scenes of the Sisters' Instruction." In: *Writing and Sexual Difference.* Ed. Elizabeth Abel. Chicago: University of Chicago Press, 1982, pp. 53–71.

Horstman, Allen. *Victorian Divorce.* London: Croom Helm, 1985.

Hughes, Kathryn. "'But Why Always Dorothea?': Marian Evans' Sisters, Cousins and Aunts." *George Eliot-George Henry Lewes Studies* 58-9 (2010): 43–60.

Hughes, Kathryn. "Enter the Aunts." *The George Eliot Review* 42 (2011): 49–62.

Hughes, Kathryn. *George Eliot: The Last Victorian.* London: Fourth Estate, 1998.

Hunt, Thornton Leigh. "Communism, Its Principles." *The Leader.* October 19, 1850: 709–10.

Hunt, Thornton Leigh. "The Discipline of Art." *The Leader.* July 3, 1852: 639–40.

Hunt, Thornton Leigh. Letter to George Jacob Holyoake. September 13 1852. MS. National Co-operative Archive, Manchester, England.

Israel, Kali. *Names and Stories: Emilia Dilke and Victorian Culture.* New York: Oxford University Press, 1999.

Jack, Belinda. *Beatrice's Spell: The Enduring Legend of Beatrice Cenci.* New York: Other, 2005.

Jebb, R. C. *Life and Letters of Sir Richard Claverhouse Jebb, By His Wife Caroline Jebb.* Cambridge, UK: Cambridge University Press, 1907.

Johnson, Claudia L. "F. R. Leavis: The 'Great Tradition' of the English Novel and the Jewish Part." *Nineteenth-Century Literature* 56.2 (2001): 199–227.

Johnston, Judith. *George Eliot and the Discourses of Medievalism.* Turnhout, Belgium: Brepols, 2006.

Johnstone, Peggy Fitzhugh. *The Transformation of Rage: Mourning and Creativity in George Eliot's Fiction.* New York: New York University Press, 1994.

Jones, Ernest. *The Life and Work of Sigmund Freud: Vol. I, The Formative Years and the Great Discoveries, 1856-1900.* New York: Basic Books, 1953.

Jovius, Paulus (Paolo Giorio). *Elogia Virorum litteris illustrious.* 1546. Translated as *An Italian Portrait Gallery.* Boston: Chapman and Grimes. Trans. F. A. Gragg, 1935. www.elfinspell. com. Accessed May 14, 2010.

Jütte, Robert. *Contraception: A History.* Trans. Vicky Russell. Cambridge, MA: Polity, 2008.

Kaminsky, Alice R., ed. *Literary Criticism of George Henry Lewes.* Lincoln: University of Nebraska Press, 1964.

Karl, Frederick R. *George Eliot: Voice of a Century: A Biography.* New York: W.W. Norton, 1995.

Kaufman, Heidi. *English Origins, Jewish Discourse, and the Nineteenth-Century British Novel: Reflections on a Nested Nation.* University Park, PA: Pennsylvania State University Press, 2009.

Kaye, John William. "The Indian Civil Service: Its Rise and Fall, Parts I–II." *Blackwood's* January 1861 and March 1861: 115-30, 261-76.

Kern, Louis J. *An Ordered Love: Sex Roles and Sexuality in Victorian Utopias.* Chapel Hill: University of North Carolina Press, 1981.

Kitchel, Anna Theresa. *George Lewes and George Eliot: A Review of Records.* New York: The John Day Co., 1933.

Knoepflmacher, Ulrich C. "Fusing Fact and Myth: The New Reality of *Middlemarch.*" In: *This Particular Web: Essays on Middlemarch.* Ed. Ian Adam. Toronto: University of Toronto Press, 1975, pp. 43–72.

Knoepflmacher, Ulrich C. *George Eliot's Early Novels: The Limits of Realism.* Berkeley: University of California Press, 1968.

Knoepflmacher, Ulrich C. *Religious Humanism and the Victorian Novel.* Princeton: Princeton University Press, 1965.

Koss, Stephen E. *The Rise and Fall of the Political Press in Britain.* 2 vols. Chapel Hill: University of North Carolina Press, 1981/1984.

Kurnick, David. "Unspeakable George Eliot." *Victorian Literature and Culture* 38.2 (2010): 489–502.

Law, Jules David. *The Social Life of Fluids: Blood, Milk, and Water in the Victorian Novel.* Ithaca: Cornell University Press, 2010.

Levine, George, ed. *The Cambridge Companion to George Eliot.* New York: Cambridge University Press, 2001.

Levine, George. *Darwin and the Novelists: Patterns of Science in Victorian Fiction.* Harvard: Harvard University Press, 1988.

Levine, George. "George Eliot's Hypothesis of Reality." *Nineteenth-Century Fiction* 35.1 (1980): 1–28.

Levine, George. *The Realistic Imagination: English Fiction from Frankenstein to Lady Chatterley.* Chicago: University of Chicago Press, 1981.

Lewes, George Henry and Thornton Leigh Hunt. "Prospectus of *The Leader,* A Weekly Paper." *The Leader.* March 30, 1850:22.

Lewes, George Henry. "Communism as an Ideal." *The Leader.* October 26, 1850:733-4.

Lewes, George Henry. "Percy Bysshe Shelley." *Westminster Review* 35.2 (1841): 303–44.

Lewes, George Henry. "Shelley and the Letters of Poets." *Westminster Review* 57.2 (1852): 502–11.

Lewes, George Henry. "Two Magnetic Seances." *The Leader.* June 15, 1850: 284–5.

Lewes, George Henry. "Historical Romance: The Foster Brother and Whitehall." *Westminster Review* 46.1 (1846): 18–29.

Lewes, George Henry. *Life of Goethe.* 1855. 3rd edn. London: Smith, Elder & Co., 1875.

Lewes, George Henry. *The Apprenticeship of Life. The Leader.* March 30–June 8, 1850: 17-8, 42-3, 67-8, 114-16, 139-40, 163-5, 187-9, 211-13, 236-7, 260-1.

Lewes, George Henry. The Journals of George Henry Lewes. MS. George Eliot Henry Lewes Collection. Beinecke Library, Yale University, New Haven, CT.

Lewes, George Henry. *The Letters of George Henry Lewes.* 3 vols. Ed. William Baker. Victoria, BC: English Literary Studies, University of Victoria, vols. 1 and 2 1995; vol. 3 1999.

Lewes, Herbert. Letter to George Henry Lewes and George Eliot. September 16, 1866. MS. George Eliot Henry Lewes Collection. Beinecke Library, Yale University, New Haven, CT.

Lewes, Herbert. Letter to George Henry Lewes and George Eliot. November 5, 1866. MS. George Eliot Henry Lewes Collection. Beinecke Library, Yale University, New Haven, CT.

Lewes, Thornton. Letter to George Henry Lewes and George Eliot. November 17, 1859. MS. George Eliot Henry Lewes Collection. Beinecke Library, Yale University, New Haven, CT.

Lewes, Thornton. Letter to George Henry Lewes and George Eliot. March 9–April 26, 1867. MS. George Eliot Henry Lewes Collection. Beinecke Library, Yale University, New Haven, CT.

Lewes, Thornton. Letter to George Henry Lewes and George Eliot. July 12, 1867. MS. George Eliot Henry Lewes Collection. Beinecke Library, Yale University, New Haven, CT.

Lewes, Thornton. Letter to George Henry Lewes and George Eliot. September 16, 1867. MS. George Eliot Henry Lewes Collection. Beinecke Library, Yale University, New Haven, CT.

Linton, Eliza Lynn. "George Eliot." *Temple Bar* 73 (1885): 512–24.

Linton, Eliza Lynn. *My Literary Life*. London: Hodder and Stoughton, 1899.

Linton, Eliza Lynn. *The Autobiography of Christopher Kirkland* (1885). New York: Garland Publishing, 1976.

Lovesey, Oliver. *The Clerical Character in George Eliot's Fiction*. Victoria, BC: English Literary Studies, 1991.

MacQueen, John Fraser. "A Practical Treatise on Divorce and Matrimonial Jurisdiction under the Act of 1857 and New Orders. . .". London: W. Maxwell, 1858.

Maddox, Brenda. *George Eliot: Novelist, Lover, Wife*. New York: Palgrave and Macmillan, 2010.

Main, Alexander. *The Life and Conversations of Samuel Johnson (Founded Chiefly Upon Boswell), With a Preface by George Henry Lewes*. London: Chapman and Hall, 1874.

Mangan, James A., ed *Benefits Bestowed?: Education and British Imperialism*. Manchester: Manchester University Press, 1988.

Marcus, Sharon. *Between Women: Friendship, Desire, and Marriage in Victorian England*. Princeton: Princeton University Press, 2007.

Martin, Carol A. *George Eliot's Serial Fiction*. Columbus: Ohio State University Press, 1994.

Matus, Jill L. "Historicizing Trauma: The Genealogy of Psychic Shock in *Daniel Deronda*." *Victorian Literature and Culture* 36.1 (2008): 59–78.

McCormack, Kathleen. *George Eliot's English Travels: Composite Characters and Coded Communications*. New York: Routledge, 2005.

McCormack, Kathleen. *George Eliot and Intoxication: Dangerous Drugs for the Condition of England*. New York: St Martin's Press, 2000.

McCormack, Kathleen. "George Eliot: Poetry, Fiction and European Spas." *Journal of European Studies* 40.9 (2010): 9–22.

McCormack, Kathleen. *George Eliot in Society: Travels Abroad and Sundays at the Priory*. Columbus: Ohio State University Press, forthcoming.

McCormack, Kathleen. "The Saccharissa Essays: George Eliot's Only Woman Persona." *Nineteenth-Century Studies* 4 (1990): 41–59.

McKenzie, K. A. *Edith Simcox and George Eliot*. Oxford: Oxford University Press, 1961.

McKeon, Michael. "Writer As Hero: Novelistic Prefigurations and the Emergence of Literary Biography." In: *Contesting the Subject: Essays in the Postmodern Theory and*

Practice of Biography and Biographical Criticism. Ed. William H. Epstein. West Lafayette, IN: Purdue University Press, 1991, pp. 17–42.

McLaren, Angus. *Birth Control in Nineteenth-Century England.* London: Croom Helm, 1978.

McMullen, Bonnie. "'The Interest of Spanish Sights': From Ronda to Daniel Deronda." In: *George Eliot and Europe.* Ed. John Rignall. Brookfield, VT: Scholar Press, 1997, pp. 123–37.

Miller, Andrew. "Bruising, Laceration, and Lifelong Maiming; Or, How We Encourage Research." *ELH* 70. 1 (2003): 301–18.

Millett, Paul. *Theophrastus and His World.* Cambridge, UK: Cambridge Philological Society, 2007.

Mottram, William. *The True Story of George Eliot in Relation to "Adam Bede": Giving the Real Life History of the More Prominent Characters.* London: F. Griffiths, 1905.

Nadel, Ira Bruce. "George Eliot and Her Biographers." In: *George Eliot: A Centenary Tribute.* Eds. Gordon S. Haight and Rosemary T. VanArsdel. Totowa, NJ: Barnes & Noble, 1982, pp. 107–21.

Nadel, Ira Bruce. *Biography: Fiction, Fact, and Form.* New York: St Martin's Press, 1984.

Nash, Sarah."What's in a Name? Signature, Criticism and Authority in the *Fortnightly Review.*" *Victorian Periodicals Review* 42.1 (Spring 2010): 57-82.

Nayder, Lillian. *The Other Dickens: A Life of Catherine Hogarth.* Ithaca: Cornell University Press, 2011.

Newman, Francis W. "Initiation of Socialism." *The Leader.* May 18, 1850: 179.

Newman, Francis W. "Marriage." *The Leader.* June 29, 1850: 325.

"News of the Week." *The Leader.* May 18, 1850: 173.

"News of the Week." *The Leader.* August 3, 1850: 436.

Newton, K. M. *Modernising George Eliot: The Novelist as Artist, Intellectual, Proto-Modernist, Cultural Critic.* London: Bloomsbury Academic, 2011.

Nietzsche, Friedrich. *The Portable Nietzsche.* Ed. and trans. Walter Kaufmann. New York: Penguin Books, 2008.

Nord, Deborah Epstein. *Gypsies and the British Imagination, 1807-1930.* New York: Columbia University Press, 2006.

Nuttall, A. D. *Dead from the Waist Down: Scholars and Scholarship in Literature and the Popular Imagination.* New Haven: Yale University Press, 2003.

O'Brian, Sharon. "Feminist Theory and Literary Biography." In: *Contesting the Subject: Essays in the Postmodern Theory and Practice of Biography and Biographical Criticism.* Ed. William H. Epstein. West Lafayette, IN.: Purdue University Press, 1991, pp. 123–34.

Orel, Harold. *Victorian Literary Critics: George Henry Lewes, Walter Bagehot, Richard Holt Hutton, Leslie Stephen, Andrew Lang, George Saintsbury, and Edmund Gosse.* London: Macmillan, 1984.

Ozick, Cynthia. *The Puttermesser Papers.* New York: Alfred A. Knopf, 1997.

Paterson, Arthur, ed *George Eliot's Family Life and Letters.* London: Selwyn and Blount Limited, 1928.

Pattison, Mark. *Isaac Casaubon, 1559-1614.* London: Longmans, Green Co., 1875.

Paxton, Nancy L. *George Eliot and Herbert Spencer: Feminism, Evolutionism, and the Reconstruction of Gender.* Princeton: Princeton University Press, 1991.

Penner, Louise. "'Unmapped Country': Uncovering Hidden Wounds in *Daniel Deronda*." *Victorian Literature and Culture* 30.1 (2002): 77–97.

Perry, Ruth. "Incest as the Meaning of the Gothic Novel." *Eighteenth Century: Theory and Interpretation* 39.3 (1998): 261–78.

Pinion, F. B. *George Eliot Companion: Literary Achievement and Modern Significance*. London: Macmillan, 1981.

Press, Jacob. "Same-Sex Unions in Modern Europe: *Daniel Deronda*, Altneuland, and the Homoerotics of Jewish Nationalism." In: *Novel Gazing: Queer Readings in Fiction*. Ed. Eve Kosofsky Sedgwick. Durham, NC: Duke University Press, 1997, pp. 299–329.

Price, Leah. *The Anthology and the Rise of the Novel: From Richardson to George Eliot*. Cambridge: Cambridge University Press, 2003.

Qualls, Barry V. "George Eliot and Religion." In: *The Cambridge Companion to George Eliot*. Ed. George Lewis Levine. New York: Cambridge University Press, 2001, pp. 119–37.

Qualls, Barry V. *The Secular Pilgrims of Victorian Fiction: The Novel as Book of Life*. New York: Cambridge University Press, 1982.

Ragussis, Michael. *Figures of Conversion: "The Jewish Question" and English National Identity*. Durham, NC: Duke University Press, 1995.

Rectenwald, Michael. "George Eliot and Secularism." In: *George Eliot in Context*. Ed. Margaret Harris. Cambridge, UK: Cambridge University Press, 2012.

Redinger, Ruby Virginia. *George Eliot: The Emergent Self*. New York: Alfred A. Knopf, 1975.

Reimer, Margaret Loewen. "The Spoiled Child: What Happened to Gwendolen Harleth?" *The Cambridge Quarterly* 36.1 (2007): 33–50.

Riasanovsky, Nicholas Valentine. *The Teaching of Charles Fourier*. Berkeley: University of California Press, 1969.

Rignall, John. *George Eliot, European Novelist*. Burlington, VT: Ashgate, 2011.

Rignall, John, ed. *Oxford Reader's Companion to George Eliot*. New York: Oxford University Press, 2000.

Rocke, Michael. *Forbidden Friendships: Homosexuality and Male Culture in Renaissance Florence*. New York: Oxford University Press, 1996.

Röder-Bolton, Gerlinde. *George Eliot in Germany, 1854-55: "Cherished Memories."* Burlington, VT: Ashgate, 2006.

Rodstein, Susan De Sola. "Sweetness and Dark: George Eliot's *Brother Jacob*." *Modern Language Quarterly* 52.3 (1991): 295–317.

Rose, Phyllis. "Fact and Fiction in Biography." In: *Nineteenth-Century Lives: Essays Presented to Jerome Hamilton Buckley*. Eds. Jerome Hamilton Buckley, Laurence S. Lockridge, John Maynard, Donald David Stone and David Staines. Cambridge, UK; New York: Cambridge University Press, 1989, pp. 188–202.

Rose, Phyllis. *Parallel Lives: Five Victorian Marriages*. New York: Knopf, 1983.

Rosenman, Ellen Bayuk. "Mother Love: Edith Simcox, Maternity, and Lesbians Erotics." In: *Other Mothers: Beyond the Maternal Ideal*. Eds. Ellen Bayuk Rosenman and Claudia C. Klaver. Columbus: Ohio State University Press, 2008, pp. 313–34.

Sandage, Scott A. *Born Losers: A History of Failure in America*. Cambridge, MA: Harvard University Press, 2005.

Sanders, Andrew. *The Victorian Historical Novel, 1840-1880*. New York: St Martin's Press, 1979.

Saslow, James M. *Ganymede in the Renaissance: Homosexuality in Art and Society*. New Haven: Yale University Press, 1986.

Savonarola, Girolamo. *Selected Writings of Girolamo Savonarola: Religion and Politics, 1490-1498*. Trans. and ed. Anne Borelli and Maria Pastore Passaro. New Haven: Yale University Press, 2006.

Sedgwick, Eve Kosofsky. *Between Men: English Literature and Male Homosocial Desire*. New York: Columbia University Press, 1985.

Semmel, Bernard. *George Eliot and the Politics of National Inheritance*. New York: Oxford University Press, 1994.

Shelley, Percy Bysshe. *The Major Works*. Eds. Zachary Leader and Michael O'Neill. Oxford: Oxford University Press, 2003.

Shuman, Cathy. *Pedagogical Economies: The Examination and the Victorian Literary Man*. Stanford: Stanford University Press, 2000.

Shuttleworth, Sally. *George Eliot and Nineteenth-Century Science: The Make-Believe of a Beginning*. Cambridge, UK: Cambridge University Press, 1986.

Sibley, Gay. "Closet Addiction in Fiction: The Search for Christiana Evans." *Social History of Alcohol and Drugs* 21.2 (2007): 183–202.

Simcox, E. J. *A Monument to the Memory of George Eliot: Edith J. Simcox's Autobiography of a Shirtmaker*. Eds. Constance Marie Fulmer and Margaret E. Barfield. London: Garland, 1998.

Simion, Eugen. *The Return of the Author*. Trans. James W. Newcomb. Evanston, IL: Northwestern University Press, 1996.

Smith, Alan K. "Fraudomy: Reading Sexuality and Politics in Burchiello." In: *Queering the Renaissance*. Ed. Jonathan Goldberg. Durham, NC: Duke University Press, 1994, pp. 84–106.

Smith, F. B. *Radical Artisan: William James Linton, 1812-97*. Manchester: Manchester University Press, 1973.

Spencer, Herbert. "Personal Beauty." *The Leader*. April 15, and May 13, 1854: 356-7, 451-2.

Spencer, Herbert. *An Autobiography*. 2 vols. London: Williams and Norgate, 1904.

St Clair, William. *The Godwins and the Shelleys: The Biography of a Family*. London: Faber and Faber, 1989.

Stange, G. Robert. "The Voices of the Essayist." *Nineteenth-Century Fiction* 35.3 (1980): 312–30.

Stephen, Leslie. *George Eliot*. London: Macmillan, 1902.

Stephens, W. B., ed. "The City of Coventry: The Outlying Parts of Coventry, Foleshill." *A History of the County of Warwick: Vol. 8, The City of Coventry and Borough of Warwick* (1969): 57-70. British History Online. Accessed June 23, 2011.

Strachey, Lytton. *Eminent Victorians*. 1918. Oxford World's Classics. Ed. John Sutherland. Oxford: Oxford University Press, 2009.

Strauss, David Friedrich. *The Life of Jesus, Critically Examined*. 1846. 3 vols. Cambridge, UK: Cambridge University Press, 2010.

Symonds, John Addington. "Poliziano's Italian Poetry." *Fortnightly Review* 14.80 (1873): 163.

Tatchell, Molly. "Thornton Hunt." *The Keats-Shelley Memorial Bulletin* 20 (1969): 13–20.

Taylor, Ina. *A Woman of Contradictions: The Life of George Eliot*. New York: Morrow, 1989.

Thompson, Andrew. *George Eliot and Italy: Literary, Cultural and Political Influences from Dante to Risorgimento*. London: Macmillan, 1998.

Todd, Janet. *Mary Wollstonecraft: A Revolutionary Life.* New York: Columbia University Press, 2000.

Tromp, Marlene. "Gwendolen's Madness." *Victorian Literature and Culture* 28.2 (2000): 451–67.

Uglow, Jennifer. *George Eliot.* London: Virago, 1987.

Vogeler, Martha A. "George Eliot as Literary Widow." *Huntington Library Quarterly* 51.2 (1988): 72–87.

Vogeler, Martha A. "The Choir Invisible: The Poetics of Humanist Piety." In: *George Eliot: A Centenary Tribute.* Eds. Gordon S. Haight and Rosemary T. VanArsdel. Totowa, NJ: Barnes & Noble, 1982, pp. 64–81.

von Westphal, Carl Friedrich. "Die contrare Sexualempfindung." *Archiv für Psychiatrie und Nervenkrankheiten* 2.73 (1869): 108.

Wah, Sarah. "'The Most Churlish of Celebrities': George Eliot, John Cross and the Question of High Status." *Journal of Victorian Culture* 15.3 (2010): 370–87.

Weiss, Barbara. *The Hell of the English: Bankruptcy and the Victorian Novel.* Lewisburg, PA: Bucknell University Press, 1986.

Welsh, Alexander. *George Eliot and Blackmail.* Cambridge, MA: Harvard University Press, 1985.

White, Terrence de Vere. *Johnnie Cross.* New York: St Martin's Press, 1983.

Willey, Basil. *Nineteenth-Century Studies: Coleridge to Matthew Arnold.* 1949. Cambridge, UK: Cambridge University Press, 1980.

Williams, Blanche Colton. *George Eliot: A Biography.* New York: Macmillan, 1936.

Williams, David. *Mr. George Eliot.* London: Hodder & Stoughton, 1983.

Willis, Martin. "Clairvoyance, Economics, and Authorship." *Journal of Victorian Culture* 10.2 (2005): 184–209.

Wimsatt, William K. and Monroe C. Beardsley, eds *The Verbal Icon: Studies in the Meaning of Poetry.* Lexington: University of Kentucky Press, 1954.

Wordsworth, William. "Lines Composed a Few Miles above Tintern Abbey." In: *"Lyrical Ballads" and Other Poems, 1797-1800.* Eds. James Butler and Karen Green. Ithaca: Cornell University Press, 1992, pp. 116–20.

Worsley, Francis. "Marriage and Divorce." *The Leader.* June 15 1850: 278.

Index

Page numbers in *italics* denote an illustration

The Life of George Eliot: A Critical Biography, First Edition. Nancy Henry.
© 2012 Nancy Henry. Published 2012 by John Wiley & Sons, Ltd.

Printed and bound by CPI Group (UK) Ltd, Croydon, CR0 4YY